A BIBLIOGRAPHIC HISTORY OF THE BOOK

THE MAGILL BIBLIOGRAPHIES

The American Presidents, by Norman S. Cohen, 1989
Black American Women Novelists, by Craig Werner, 1989
Classical Greek and Roman Drama, by Robert J. Forman, 1989
Contemporary Latin American Fiction, by Keith H. Brower, 1989
Masters of Mystery and Detective Fiction, by J. Randolph Cox, 1989
Nineteenth Century American Poetry, by Philip K. Jason, 1989
Restoration Drama, by Thomas J. Taylor, 1989
Twentieth Century European Short Story, by Charles E. May, 1989
The Victorian Novel, by Laurence W. Mazzeno, 1989
Women's Issues, by Laura Stempel Mumford, 1989
America in Space, by Russell R. Tobias, 1991
The American Constitution, by Robert J. Janosik, 1991
The Classic Epic, by Thomas J. Sienkewicz, 1991
English Romantic Poetry, by Brian Aubrey, 1991
Ethics, by John K. Roth, 1991
The Immigrant Experience, by Paul D. Mageli, 1991
The Modern American Novel, by Steven G. Kellman, 1991
Native Americans, by Frederick E. Hoxie and Harvey Markowitz, 1991
American Drama: 1918-1960, by R. Baird Shuman, 1992
American Ethnic Literatures, by David R. Peck, 1992
American Theater History, by Thomas J. Taylor, 1992
The Atomic Bomb, by Hans G. Graetzer and Larry M. Browning, 1992
Biography, by Carl Rollyson, 1992
The History of Science, by Gordon L. Miller, 1992
The Origin and Evolution of Life on Earth, by David W. Hollar, Jr., 1992
Pan-Africanism, by Michael W. Williams, 1992
Resources for Writers, by R. Baird Shuman, 1992
Shakespeare, by Joseph Rosenblum, 1992
The Vietnam War in Literature, by Philip K. Jason, 1992
Contemporary Southern Women Fiction Writers, by Rosemary M. Canfield Reisman and Christopher J. Canfield, 1994
Cycles in Humans and Nature, by John T. Burns, 1994
Environmental Studies, by Diane M. Fortner, 1994
Poverty in America, by Steven Pressman, 1994
The Short Story in English: Britain and North America, by Dean Baldwin and Gregory L. Morris, 1994

Victorian Poetry, by Laurence W. Mazzeno, 1995
Human Rights in Theory and Practice, by Gregory J. Walters, 1995
Energy, by Joseph R. Rudolph, Jr., 1995
A Bibliographic History of the Book, by Joseph Rosenblum, 1995

A BIBLIOGRAPHIC HISTORY OF THE BOOK
An Annotated Guide to the Literature

by
JOSEPH ROSENBLUM

Magill Bibliographies

The Scarecrow Press, Inc.
Metuchen, N.J., & London
and
Salem Press
Pasadena, CA & Englewood Cliffs, N.J.
1995

Joseph Rosenblum's *A Bibliographic History of the Book: An Annotated Guide to the Literature* is the third title appearing in Bill Katz's "The History of the Book" series

British Library Cataloguing-in-Publication data available

Library of Congress Cataloging-in-Publication data

Rosenblum, Joseph.
　　A bibliographic history of the book : an annotated guide to the literature /
by Joseph Rosenblum.
　　　　p.　　　cm.—(Magill bibliographies)
　　Includes indexes.
　　ISBN 0-8108-3009-4 (acid-free paper)
　　1. Books—History—Bibliography.　2. Writing—History—Bibliography.　I. Title.　II. Series
　　Z4.R69　　　1995
　　016.002—dc20　　　　　　　　　　　　　　　　　　　95-5327

To My Family

CONTENTS

CONTENTS

ACKNOWLEDGMENTS

I wish to thank my editor, John Wilson, for proposing this project, for offering encouragement throughout, and for his many suggestions that have made this a better book than it otherwise would have been.

I want to thank Gaylor Callahan and Wendy Jackson of the Walter Jackson Library, University of North Carolina at Greensboro, for their tireless efforts to get me needed materials through interlibrary loans.

I also wish to express my appreciation to my family, who have borne with my labors, moodiness, and piles of books and notes.

INTRODUCTION

In Canto 33 of the *Paradiso* Dante wrote,

> Nel suo profondo vidi che s'interna,
> legato con amore in un volume,
> ciò che per l'universo si squanderna.

> In the depths of the Eternal Light I saw brought together
> bound through love in one volume
> the leaves that are dispersed throughout the universe.

The idea of the world as a book is a medieval commonplace. For the historian of the book this equation is reversible: The book serves as a speculum mundi, a mirror that discloses the world, because the book both as physical object and as text partakes of the milieu in which it comes into being. As Richard Brodhead observes in *Culture of Letters: Scenes of Reading and Writing in Nineteenth Century America* (Chicago: University of Chicago Press, 1993), "The literary sphere is the subject of plural and changing cultural organizations, determining what forms of writing are in cultural operation at any time or place, what mechanisms of production support such forms, what publics such forms are brought to and what value they have attached to them" (p. 113). Texts and contexts are inseparable; bound in one volume are the technological, economic, social, religious, political, intellectual, and artistic currents of the age. The book might well adopt as its own the humanist credo of Terence, "Liber sum; homini nihil a me alienum puto"—I am a book; nothing pertaining to humanity is alien to me. (The original substitutes "homo" for "liber.") At the same time that the book is a product of diverse forces it also shapes its environment, being at once creation and creator. An examination of the book in antebellum America and late fourteenth century England from the perspective of the historian of the book will reveal the scope of this approach and its power to illuminate an age.

I

On September 27, 1855, at the New York Crystal Palace, the publisher George Palmer Putnam addressed the Association of New York Publishers. In his speech he noted the recent expansion of the industry. Thus, in the period 1830-1842 American publishers had issued a total of 1,115 titles. Of these, 623 had been written by Americans, and the rest had been reprints of works first published abroad. In 1853 alone, 733 works had come from America's presses; of these, 420 were native products. Editions, too, had grown larger. A popular work in the 1820s might have sold 5,000-6,000 copies. By the 1850s an author could hope to sell as many as 60,000 to 100,000 copies in a year. The number of American novels had climbed from a hundred published in the 1820s to a thousand in the 1840s. In the 1820s the publishing industry was a $2.5 million business. Thirty years later publishing produced five times that sum.

Many factors contributed to this expansion. In 1807 Bryan Donkin perfected the Fourdrinier machine for making paper, previously manufactured by hand; the invention cut the cost of this component of the book. Isaac Adams' steam-driven flatbed press (1830-1836) and Robert Hoe's cylinder press (1847) allowed girls to print books that once had required strong men to operate the hand press. Wages for press operators therefore declined. So did wages for typesetters, though for a different reason: The introduction of stereotyping early in the nineteenth century and electrotyping in the 1840s reduced the demand for compositors. New technology also cut binding costs. Although hand sewing persisted throughout the antebellum period, folding and trimming became mechanized.

Alongside this technological transformation of book production came other developments that fostered the expansion of the publishing industry. The availability of better domestic lighting was one such factor; eyeglasses were another. None, however, was more significant than the railroad.

The transportation revolution of the early 1800s, with its canals, steamboats, stagecoaches, and coastal shipping, fostered local publishing centers. David D. Hall's "The Uses of Literacy in New England, 1600-1850" in *Printing and Society in Early America* (William L. Joyce, David D. Hall, Richard D. Brown, and John B. Hench, eds. Worcester, Mass.: American Antiquarian Society, 1983) notes that in the period 1800-1830 the Bible was published in twenty-four locations in Massachusetts. Similarly, between 1800 and 1810 Boston, Philadelphia, and New York accounted for 50 percent of the fiction published in America. Small cities such as Bangor, Maine, and Albany, New York, were homes to major regional publishers. Even metropolitan publishers depended on small-town newspapers to advertise their wares and so subsidized local and regional presses.

The railroad changed all that. After 1850 the Bible was published in Massachusetts only at Boston and Cambridge. By 1841 Boston, New York, and Philadelphia produced 92 percent of the fiction published in

America. In 1850 these three cities accounted for 75 percent of all American publishing in terms of value. The trains that carried books also distributed magazines, many of them started by publishers to promote their wares (e.g., *Harper's* and *G. P. Putnam's Magazine*), and newspapers, so that publishers in New York or Boston no longer needed to pay for advertisements in small-town newspapers. One sign of the new order was the attempt by newspaper publishers in Portland, Maine, to secure high postal rates to exclude their Boston rivals, but the Portland publishers lost. In 1845 urban publishers also stopped accepting rural imprints as payment on accounts. Robert A. Gross, in a paper presented to the American Studies Association on November 6, 1993, cites Homer Merriam, who attempted unsuccessfully to operate a printing and bookselling business in Greenfield, Massachusetts, between 1838 and 1842. Merriam attributed his failure to what Gross describes as "the economic imperialism of urban publishers," though other factors, such as the ability of metropolitan publishers to advertise their books (and so stimulate demand) and the conservative tastes of many rural printers, who failed to satisfy the wants of potential customers, also contributed to the disappearance of rural printing houses.

Where trains went, so did books. Not only did trains allow metropolitan publishers to reach distant markets; trains also provided a time and place for reading. Dr. Henry J. Clark objected to reading in trains but noted how common the practice had become by 1856: "Observe the passengers in the train, on any of our public routes. A shelf of popular novels is passed before the eyes of every individual; next, a pile of magazines, then, illustrated newspapers, while advertisements, guidebooks, newspapers with long, narrow, closely printed columns are distributed or purchased, until all tastes are suited, and before all eyes, young and old, spectacled or otherwise, there oscillates some kind of printed page" (quoted in Ronald J. Zboray, *A Fictive People: Antebellum Economic Development and the American Reading Public*, New York: Oxford University Press, 1993, p. 73). To capitalize on this market, G. P. Putnam in the 1850s launched a series of "Railway Classics" at prices that middle-class travelers could easily afford. For example, Putnam's railway edition of Washington Irving's *Salmagundi*, issued in 1857, sold for fifty cents, about half the cost of the standard hardback.

The railroads guaranteed a steady supply of books and offered opportunities to read them. Trains promoted literacy in another way as well. As transportation improved, the population became more mobile; one of the major incentives fostering literacy was the desire to communicate with friends and relatives who had moved away. The railway took people away but also linked them through the mail. In 1840 residents of the Northeast wrote 1.61 letters per capita. Twenty years later the per capita figure was 5.15, but in the cities the numbers were much higher—30 for the typical New Yorker, 48.8 for the average Bostonian. Between 1837 and 1857, sixty editions of letter-writing manuals appeared to meet the needs of would-be correspondents.

Ronald J. Zboray's *A Fictive People* argues persuasively that the reading of novels provided another link between people no longer connected by geographic proximity. Antebellum fiction reflects this desire for community. Henry Hiram Riley's *The Puddleford Papers* (1857) talks of letters' joining those who have moved away from their hometowns. Catharine Maria Sedgwick's *Home* (1835) speaks of the pioneer's longing for his father's house. John Townsend Trowbridge's *Martin Merrivale* (1854) tells of a youth from the country who suffers homesickness after coming to Boston; the same theme informs Nathaniel Hawthorne's "My Kinsman, Major Molineux" (1832). The popularity of the epistolary novel in this period derives at least in part from its use of a literary form familiar to many.

The desire for financial advancement also encouraged reading. Zboray cites Charles Verle's 1839 comment in the *Moral Encyclopedia*: "Among the various means of acquiring knowledge, books hold a prominent station; they are our best instructors, and do more perhaps to form our intellectual faculties, and moral habits, than all means together" (Zboray, 129). In an increasingly mobile and technologically complex society, print replaced orality as the primary means of instruction. By 1850 the United States had more than 6,000 academies and more than 1,200 public libraries. Lyceums in the North and West drew 400,000 people each week.

These institutions promoted both literacy and nationalism. Works such as Lyman Cobb's *North American Reader* and Noah Webster's *An American Selection of Lessons in Reading and Speaking* as well as Webster's other textbooks overtly stressed patriotism. As Webster wrote in *An American Selection*, "In choice of pieces, I have been attentive to the political interests of America," and in his *The Little Reader's Assistant* he included a "Federal Catechism." These texts further fostered nationalism through their ubiquity. The homogenization of education favored uniformity and system rather than what Zboray calls "the locally oriented, informal, and unstructured" (p. 104).

The desire for moral improvement, either of oneself or of others, provided another impulse toward literacy and book-buying. The American Sunday-School Union, established in 1824, promoted universal basic literacy. One may see this effort as part of the centuries-old Protestant desire for everyone to read the Bible. By 1830 the Union had published six million books and had made these available at low cost. Complementing these activities were those of the American Bible Society and American Tract Society, both of which distributed inexpensive or free literature. Alongside these religious organizations were other reformers such as the American Temperance Society, founded in 1826, the New York Tract Society, established in 1825, and the Female Benevolent Society, which crusaded against prostitution. All supplied reading material that in turn encouraged reading.

The concerns that stimulated the production of mass literature also surface in the works of more serious writers. David S. Reynolds' *Beneath the American Renaissance: The Subversive Imagination in the Age of Emerson and Melville* (New York: Alfred A. Knopf, 1988) observes that Walt Whitman's *Franklin Evans* (1842), Mary L. Fox's *The Ruined Deacon* (1834), George Allen's *The Only Son* (1835), Edgar Allan Poe's "The Black Cat" (1843) and "The Cask of Amontillado" (1846), and Nathaniel Hawthorne's "A Rill from a Town Pump" (1835) draw on popular writings against alcoholism. *The Scarlet Letter* (1850) may owe a debt to the interests of the Female Benevolent Society. In addition to drawing on mass literature for subject matter, the writers of the American Renaissance may have found a more receptive public because of the reformers' efforts that increased literacy. Even Hawthorne, who repeatedly criticized moral crusaders (e.g., "Earth's Holocaust," 1844; "The Custom House Sketch," 1850; *The Blithedale Romance*, 1852), probably profited from their labors.

The book in antebellum America thus emerges as the product of various transformations and also as an agent of change, particularly in establishing a national rather than a local mentality. Yet the book united America selectively, exacerbating divisions of class, gender, region, and ethnicity.

The average hardcover book in the antebellum period cost between $0.75 and $1.25, about half the prevailing price in the late eighteenth century. Zboray's examination of the inventory of Homer Franklin's New York City bookshop in 1840-1841 found that the average cost of a novel was $0.95, of a play $1.98. A skilled laborer earned a dollar a day, and working women might make only twenty-five cents. Even a paperback at fifty cents would cost half a day's work. Educational books in Franklin's store averaged twenty-five cents, and books of advice forty-four cents, so that even educated workers were not likely to read the same books as a lawyer or middle-class entrepreneur. The dime novel and the story papers filled the desire for recreational reading among the working class. A similar division appears in the profile of the patrons of the private New York Society Library. Of those whose occupations Zboray could identify (110 of 179 male members), 38 were lawyers, and those in the professions constitute 58 of the 110 members. Another 46 were merchants; only 6 were engaged in manufacturing. If reading creates interpretive communities, in the antebellum period it also created divisions among varying readerships and excluded those who could not afford books.

The similar charging patterns for men and women at the New York Society Library calls into question at least some of the assumptions of a woman's sphere in antebellum America. Zboray quotes an 1855 letter from Ellen Emerson in which she observes that both she and her father, Ralph Waldo Emerson, are enjoying the same books. Yet the fiction written by women suggests that books participated in and even encouraged the cult of female domesticity. Writing offered a suitable occupation for women, whose options were otherwise limited to such nurturing activities as teaching or nursing. Because of their limited experiences, women writers turned to the hearth for their subject matter. Even when men and women wrote about similar issues, their approaches differed. Richard Henry Dana, Herman Melville, and Harriet Beecher Stowe addressed the question of discipline, corporal punishment versus what Richard H. Brodhead in *Culture of Letters* calls "disciplinary intimacy." The first two protest flogging in *Two Years Before the Mast* and *White Jacket*, novels set in the masculine world of the ship. Stowe's canvas is the plantation household (*Uncle Tom's Cabin*).

Distinctions based on gender surface in other ways as well. Professor Bhaer in *Little Women* (1868-1869) condemns Jo for writing for the story papers, which in their appeal to the working class rejected gentility. Jo's creator had been writing for these papers, but in 1870 Louisa May Alcott rejected the *New York Weekly*'s request that she write for it at her own price. At the other end of the literary spectrum women also were excluded. This segregation becomes pronounced after the Civil War, but one sees a similar division in the antebellum period. One measure is the absence of women among the figures of the American Renaissance. Even if one adds Emily Dickinson to the traditional male panoply, the exception illustrates the principle because she remained virtually unpublished in her lifetime. Most of the best-sellers of the antebellum period were written by women, but none of these, not even *Uncle Tom's Cabin*, would qualify as high art. Like the fictional Ruth Hall, created by Fanny Fern, women often wrote to be fed, not to be famous, and they frequently were compelled to work amid domestic distractions. Sarah Orne Jewett observed that Stowe's *The Pearl of Orr's Island* would have been a better book had Stowe been able to focus on her writing rather than on household chores. Stowe conceded that in writing *Uncle Tom's Cabin* she was not concerned with "style or literary excellence[,] the teaching of the rhetorician or the elocutionist." Class and gender combined to confine women writers to a middle state, to domesticity in literature as well as in life.

The most striking difference in reading habits in antebellum America existed not between rich and poor or men and women but between the South and the rest of the nation. Mark Twain observed that Sir Walter Scott was responsible for the Civil War; Abraham Lincoln greeted Harriet Beecher Stowe as the little lady who had made the great war. In focusing on books, both reflect the divergent communities that arose, not least because of different reading habits and approaches to literacy. Among the causes of the Civil War, along with tariffs and slavery, one cannot ignore the book.

To begin with the observations of Twain and Lincoln, North and South read different works. *Uncle Tom's Cabin*, which sold more than 300,000 copies in America, found few buyers in the states that would become the Confederacy. Scott's audience was less regionally distinct than Stowe's, but the South's Anglophilia contrasts with the literary nationalism that, while not confined to the North, was a powerful force there. Even William Gilmore Simms's Southern rendition of Sir Walter Scott and James Fenimore Cooper had by the 1850s become more popular in his native South than in the North.

The conjunction of the railroad and the book affected the South as much as it did the rest of the country, but in the opposite way because the South lacked the network of trains that linked the Northeast and the West. Transportation in the South continued to depend largely on rivers and wagon roads, adequate to allow Charleston, South Carolina, or Richmond, Virginia, to emerge as a regional but not a national publishing center. The train also redirected the flow of books from North and South in 1800 to East and West in the antebellum period. In the early nineteenth century book agents circulated the wares of Philadelphia and New York publishers. Among the best known was Mason Locke Weems, agent for Matthew Carey of Philadelphia. Concentrating his efforts in the South, he particularly liked to visit the rich Savannah River Valley in Georgia. By the 1850s Northern publishers no longer concerned themselves with Southern markets. One measure of publisher interest is the amount spent on advertising. In 1856 Harper and Brothers spent more on advertisements in *The New York Times* than in the entire South. Of its non-New York advertisements, 24 percent were placed in Western newspapers, 12 percent in Southern publications, or less than the firm spent in the city of Boston.

Such expenditures reflect not only difficulties in transporting books but also the lack of a large reading public. In 1857 Hinton R. Helper lamented in *The Impending Crisis of the South*, "The people of the South are not a reading people. Many of the adult population never learned to read; still more, do not care to read." Drawing on the 1850 census, Helper

noted that throughout the United States the adult illiteracy rate was 1 in
156. In the South the average was 1 in 16. A dispersed population made
schooling difficult. A longer growing season left less time for education
and recreation. Moreover, the Southern aristocracy opposed the common
schools that dotted the North and West. Thomas Jefferson had proposed
an entire public educational system for Virginia, but only the capstone
university was created. The university would serve only those whose
parents could afford private education. As a result of these geographical
and political factors, in Connecticut in 1850 illiteracy stood at 1 in 568
adults, in Vermont 1 in 473. In North Carolina the figure was 1 in 7, in
Virginia 1 in 12.5. The stable, rural culture of the South did not provide
an incentive for letter writing, either, removing another promoter of
literacy. In 1860 the average Southerner sent fewer than two letters a year.
Although Joel Chandler Harris, writing after the Civil War, created a
romanticized version of the antebellum plantation, his Uncle Remus
stories capture the region's oral culture. Oratory and storytelling were
nurtured by Southern society, but literacy was not. Helper commented that
in the South on the eve of secession "newspapers and books seemed
generally ignored."

Most of the public libraries as well as most of the important private
book collections in the antebellum period were located in the North and
Old Northwest. Richard Beale Davis, in his *Intellectual Life in the
Colonial South, 1585-1763* (Knoxville: University of Tennessee Press,
1978), correctly observes that the South had a number of fine private
libraries, but Madeleine B. Stern, in *Antiquarian Bookselling in the United
States: A History from the Origins to the 1940s* (Westport, Conn.: Greenwood Press, 1985), quotes William Charvat's comment in *The Profession
of Authorship in America, 1800-1870* (Columbus: Ohio State University
Press, 1968), "The rich South was the despair of the book trade. There
was money there for the luxury trade, and it was a happy hunting ground
for peddlers of [Matthew] Carey's expensive Bibles and atlases, and for
richly bound special editions. But as a staple-crop region, it was hit hard
by all depressions, which meant bankrupt booksellers and bad debts."
Stern concludes her chapter on Southern antiquarian booksellers by
noting the paucity of bibliopoles: "Apparently, the collecting of books in
the South was never widespread, never democratized. Rather, it was
confined to the few—to the elite among planters and merchants—who
could afford to travel abroad to fill the lacunae of their shelves with
rarities" (p. 187).

Since most blacks lived in the South during this period, they, too, were
excluded from literacy. Even among freed blacks, the literacy rate was
only 50 percent, about half that of their white counterparts in the North-

east. Among slaves the figure was much lower, about 5 percent, because laws prohibited teaching slaves to read.

The history of the book illuminates the centripetal and centrifugal forces operating in antebellum America. In the North and West reading created a unified middle class, as the community of the book replaced the geographically defined unit. At the same time literacy proved divisive—exacerbating, even creating, gaps between classes, regions, and races.

II

Five hundred years earlier, in Chaucer's England, forces similar to those operating in antebellum America were shaping the form and content of the late medieval manuscript. Although far more restricted in fourteenth century England than in nineteenth century America, literacy was increasing during this period. *Wynnere and Wastoure* (1352) complained that minstrels, representatives of the oral tradition, were yielding to poets, who wrote their works. Biblical concordances and handbooks for preaching appeared as literacy supplanted reliance on memory. In a 1373 suit between William of Wykeham and the master of St. Cross, Winchester, twenty-eight witnesses were examined; nearly 40 percent (11/28) were termed "literati." About 1375 Henry of Kirkestede, a monk at Bury St. Edmunds, compiled a *Catalogus Scriptorum Ecclesiae*, a union list of works by 674 authors arranged alphabetically. Earlier in the century English Franciscans, probably based at the house of the Greyfriars, Oxford, created the *Registrum Anglie de Libris Doctorum et Auctorum Veterum*, listing 1,400 works by ninety-eight authors and indicating their locations in 189 monastic and cathedral libraries in Britain. Such reference works emerged only when written records supplanted memory: when one needed to consult a text, not just memorize it. In 1412 Oxford opened its library to students, who had previously been excluded, again suggesting that reading was supplementing if not supplanting listening to lectures. In *Authentic Witness: Approaches to Medieval Texts and Manuscripts* (Notre Dame, Ind.: University of Notre Dame Press, 1991), Mary A. and Richard H. Rouse note how even the layout of the page changed to facilitate consultation. Headings and glosses became part of the *mise en page* in the thirteenth and fourteenth centuries to make books more accessible to readers. The illustrations in the margins of the Ellesmere manuscript of *The Canterbury Tales* not only served as artistic embellishments but also allowed the reader to locate a particular section. Margaret Rickert, who co-authored the eight-volume *The Text of the Canterbury Tales: Studies on the Basis of All Known Manuscripts* (Chicago: University of Chicago

Press, 1940), observed that in twenty-eight illuminated manuscripts of this work, scribes indicated major and secondary divisions through their artwork. Devices range from the elaborate Ellesmere drawings to modest motifs, reflecting a wide range of purses that sought and perhaps commissioned these Chaucerian manuscripts. Orality had by no means yielded to literacy in 1400, but a shift in attitude toward the written word is evident. *The Canterbury Tales* reflects this divided consciousness when Chaucer warns that some of the stories may tell of "harlotrie," so that "whoso list it nat yheere/Turne over the leef and chese another tale." Listening and reading are compounded in these lines.

Books remained expensive; Chaucer's clerk who craved twenty of them clad in black and red would have had to spend sixty times his annual income to secure such a library. Thomas, Duke of Gloucester, owned eighty-three books. When Guy de Beauchamp, grandson of Earl Guy of Warwick, died in 1360, he left forty-two books to the Cistercian Bordesley Abbey in Worcester. Simon de Burley, tutor to Richard II, owned about twenty books. In the prologue to *The Legend of Good Women*, the god of love says to Chaucer's persona, "Yis, God wot, sixty bokes olde and newe/Hast thou thyself, alle ful of storyes grete," but sixty books may not equal sixty volumes, since a codex might contain several titles. The increasing use of paper lowered prices somewhat, though, making books more affordable. By 1400 twenty-five sheets of paper cost as much as a skin of parchment but offered eight times the writing surface. In the fifteenth century the price dropped still further. Manuscripts on paper are not common before 1450, but the material did make books accessible to the middle class. As books became more common, they influenced domestic and public buildings. Monasteries and colleges started building special rooms to house libraries. Clerestory windows allowed reading in the naves of churches; pews began to be equipped with bookrests. The chained library may be the best architectural testimony to the new importance of the book; the first of these known in England was created about 1320 by Bishop Cobham over the Old Congregation House in St. Mary's, Oxford. No longer was the earlier system of keeping books in locked chests adequate—the chests were too inconvenient and too small. When the Carmelites moved to Beaumont Palace around 1317, they stopped the practice of keeping their books in chests and instead placed them in a library to make them more accessible. Although Margaret Deanesley's study of 7,600 wills concludes that even in the fifteenth century many of the English were bookless ("Vernacular Books in England in the Fourteenth and Fifteenth Centuries," *Modern Language Review* 15, 1920, pp. 349-358), secular stationers were earning a living by the middle of the 1300s, and by 1357 they may already have formed an organization. By the early 1400s booksellers were preparing manuscripts in anticipation of sales, not just on commission.

Again, as in nineteenth-century America but on a smaller scale, literacy was promoted by the establishment of grammar schools and colleges, and these in turn led to a greater demand for books, especially in the vernacular. The grammar taught was Latin, which remained the lingua franca, but English increasingly became the language of instruction. Queen's College, Oxford, founded in 1340, was the last to require its students to speak Latin and French. In the mid-1300s students began commonly to construe Latin into English rather than French. In 1362 the English law courts returned to using English after a nearly three-hundred-year hiatus; the reason given was that "French is unknown in the realm." The following year parliament was opened in English for the first time. Chaucer, John Lydgate, and John of Trevisa busily translated works into the vernacular. The late fourteenth century *Speculum Vitae* avoided Latin and French in favor of English, "For that langage es mast schewewd/ Als were among lered als lewed" (for that language is most common among the learned and the laity). Even the thirteenth century *Manuel des pechiez* noted that the bad French of an English native should be pardoned. The Anglo-Norman text of the early fourteenth century *Holkham Bible Picture Book* suggests that the author was not fluent in that dialect. Chaucer captures the foreign nature of French by 1385 when he writes that the prioress speaks that language "After the scole of Stratford atte Bowe," not in the true Parisian manner. The popularity of English is evident also in the increasing use of the vernacular in scientific and medical books intended for a "lered" (learned) audience as well as in religious works, most notably Wycliffe's translation of the Bible. More complete or partial manuscripts survive of Wycliffe's Bible than of any other medieval work.

Thus, religion inspired literacy. The Lollard movement at the end of the fourteenth century was especially influential. William Smith of Leicester taught himself to read so he would have access to Lollard texts. *De Heretico Comburendo* condemned the Lollards because "they make and write books, they do wickedly instruct and inform people." Conversely, *Jack Upland, Fifty Heresies and Errors of the Friars* (c. 1384), and *Of Clerks Possessioners*, all Lollard works, condemned orthodox religious institutions for hoarding books and restricting learning. The orthodox defense was itself an indication of books' growing importance, claiming that books were needed for consultation and so could not be allowed into lay hands. In 1389 Michael Scrivener and William Parchemener were arrested as Lollards. Their names demonstrate the connection of Lollards with the book trade. Another indication is the professional production of most Lollard manuscripts, which were of course produced outside monastic scriptoria.

Chaucer's *The Canterbury Tales* presents the broad range of the English middle class, not the aristocracy—an indication of the audience Chaucer sought to reach. Granted, the largest and most sumptuous libraries still belonged to the aristocrats. Richard de Bury owned some 1,500 manuscripts; Sir John Paston owned about twenty. Charles V of France (1338-1380) used books to enhance his country's prestige by building a library, and the English copied his example. Early in the fifteenth century, Henry V and his brother Humphrey, Duke of Gloucester, cultivated Italian humanists and sought out their texts. Yet only a small percentage of late fourteenth and early fifteenth century manuscripts are armigerous (bear coats of arms), suggesting that they were commissioned by middle-class readers or produced by scribes to be sold to anyone who wanted the work.

Nicholas Love's *Mirror of the Life of Christ*, approved for publication by the Archbishop of Canterbury in 1410, was addressed to "lewed men and wymmen." Chaucer, though a member of the royal court, dedicated *Troilus and Cryseyde* to John Gower and Ralph Strode, not to a nobleman or monarch. *William of Palene* was written for Humphrey de Bohun, Earl of Hereford (d. 1361) but intended "for hem that knowe no frensche, ne never understron," that is, not the earl but the members of his household. Janet Coleman, in *Medieval Readers and Writers 1350-1400* (New York: Columbia University Press, 1981), attributes the "blossoming of English poetry and prose in the fourteenth century [to] a changing social structure and its changing ideals: a broadening of the middle range of society, its greater participation in government and its increasing demand for a literature read for information, for pleasure and for spiritual edification" (p. 24).

Chaucer's knight and squire recite tales of courtly love that emphasize gentility ("gentillesse"). They represent one strain of readership that enjoyed romances, whether in English or in the original French or Burgundian. "The Monk's Tale," a collection of tragic stories, draws on another tradition, that of the anthology, of which *The Canterbury Tales* is itself an example. In *The Book of the Duchess* Chaucer mocked this kind of writing; the narrator falls asleep reading a collection of fables and histories. Yet this was the form Chaucer chose repeatedly and was prized among the middle class. Chaucer's pilgrims reveal their tastes in their reactions to stories as well as in the kinds of tales they tell. When the Franklin begins to talk of "gentillesse," the Host retorts, "Straw for youre gentillesse."

Chaucer's masterpiece offered entertainment but also sought to instruct. At the end of the Nun's Priest's beast fable the speaker advises,

> But ye that holden this tale a folye,
> As of a fox, or of a cok and hen,
> Taketh the moralite, goode men.
> For Seinte Paul seith that al that writen is,
> To our doctrine is it ywrite, ywis;
> Taketh the fruyt, and lat the chaf be stille.

The fruit of *The Canterbury Tales* includes warnings against unscrupulous churchmen, dishonest millers, and greedy doctors. Middle-class audiences of 1400 were reading works that urged reform of abuses in church and state, works like *Piers Plowman* and *Mum and the Sothsegger*. Just as Hawthorne, Poe, and Melville embodied even as they surpassed the popular literature of antebellum America, Chaucer drew on the mass literature of his day.

Reading patterns in part followed social lines, with the nobility choosing romances favoring the status quo and the middle class preferring works that satirized the established order. Reading also created new lines of allegiance, as people began to think of themselves as literate or not. The Peasants' Revolt had diverse causes—poverty, taxes, and laws regulating labor. Yet to the peasants one symbol of the Establishment was the manuscript. At the New Temple in London, rebels burned lawyers' records; at Lambeth Palace they burned the records of Chancery. In Cambridge a mob burned chests of manuscripts as Margery Starre shouted, "Away with the learning of clerks, away with it."

The middle-class writers who recognized many of the same abuses that prompted the peasants to rebel did not support the uprising. John Gower's *Vox Clamantis* criticized peasants and presented them as potential destroyers of the commonwealth. *Piers Plowman* cautioned, "Consaile nat the comune the kyng to displese." Chaucer mocks a leader of the Peasant's Revolt when he writes in "The Nun's Priest's Tale,"

> Certes, ne Jakke Straw and his meynee
> Ne made nevere showtes half so shrille
> Whan that they wolden any Flemyngs kille,
> As thilke day was maad upon the fox.

The Canterbury Tales and the American Literary Renaissance demonstrate how the book serves as a record of its age. The book is not, however, a passive chronicler, for it helps create the events and the conditions it reflects. Every reader must therefore be in some sense a historian of the book, and the more one understands about its physical composition and intellectual milieu, the better one will comprehend a volume's significance.

This recognition of the book's centrality as a shaper and mirror of culture may be dated from 1958, with the appearance of Lucien Febvre and Henri-Jean Martin's *L'Apparition du livre* (English translation by David Gerard in 1976 as *The Coming of the Book*). This study emerged from the French Annales school, of which Febvre and Marc Bloch were the founders. Instead of looking at politics and diplomacy, Febvre was concerned with the "mentality," or mind-set, of individuals and groups in a particular period. *L'Apparition du livre* sought to explain "how and why the printed book was something more than a triumph of technical ingenuity, but was also one of the most potent agents at the disposal of western civilisation in bringing together the scattered ideas of representative thinkers. . . . The book created new habits of thought not only within the small circle of the learned, but far beyond, in the intellectual life of all who used their minds."

Shortly thereafter, two other important works expressed similar ideas. Marshall McLuhan's epigram "The medium is the message," elaborated in *The Gutenberg Galaxy: The Making of Typographic Man* (1962), supported Febvre's view of the book as an agent of change. Jürgen Habermas looked more particularly at the way print culture, when it fully triumphed in the late seventeenth and eighteenth centuries, created a new political force intermediate between the state and the private realm. His *Struckturwandel der Offentlichkeit* (translated as *The Structural Transformation of the Public Sphere*, 1989) appeared the same year as McLuhan's book. Another landmark in the study of the history of the book was Elizabeth L. Eisenstein's *The Printing Press as an Agent of Change* (1979), which Eisenstein had begun in 1963. When she started her work, she found few scholars pursuing Francis Bacon's observation in *Novum Organum*, Aphorism 129, that the printing press, along with the compass and gunpowder, had changed "the appearance and state of the whole world." By the time she published her account, she found herself in the vanguard of a large movement. In 1970 the *Annual Bibliography of the History of the Printed Book with Libraries* appeared; the 1972 edition contained 2,800 citations drawn from more than a thousand journals. Robert Darnton had written such articles as "The High Enlightenment and the Low Life of Literature" (*Past and Present* 51 [1971]: 81-115) and "Reading, Writing, and Publishing in Eighteenth Century France" (*Daedalus*, 1971, pp. 214-257); the École pratique des hautes études had published the two-volume *Livre et société dans la France du XVIII*ᵉ *siècle* (1965); the United Nations had declared 1972 as International Book Year and had sponsored *The Book Through 5000 Years* (London: Phaidon, 1972). The title of Eisenstein's opening chapter, "The Unacknowledged Revolution," suggesting that the impact of printing had gone largely unacknowledged in scholarly circles, is thus something of an anachronism, appropriate for the early 1960s but no longer accurate by 1979.

Eisenstein's work stimulated increased discussion of the role of the printed book, but the study of the book has not been restricted to the post-Gutenberg era. Barry B. Powell's *Homer and the Origin of the Greek Alphabet* (1991) has suggested that the book gave rise to the Greek alphabet, a not altogether fanciful paradox. Powell argues that the desire to record Homer prompted an eighth century B.C. scribe to adapt the West Semitic notational system to write down the poem. In 1993, the University of Notre Dame Press launched its series on the medieval book with Margaret T. Gibson's *The Bible in the Latin West*, and Cambridge University Press, long a leader in publishing works on the history of the book, in 1994 initiated a new series, Studies in Paleography and Codicology. Eisenstein deserves credit for increased interest in the manuscript book, if only because her claims of a revolution brought about by the printing press stimulated such responses as J. B. Trapp's *Manuscripts in the Fifty Years After the Invention of Printing: Some Papers Read at a Colloquium at the Warburg Institute on 12-13 March 1982* (1983) and Hans Bekker-Nielsen, Marianne Borch, and Bengt Algot Sorensen's *From Script to Book* (1986), containing the proceedings of another 1982 symposium. Whether focusing on the printed or manuscript page, students of the book have come to recognize the importance of all facets of a volume, from its creation by the author to its illustration, printing (or transcribing), binding, publication, shipping, sale, and reading. Nor can these elements be considered in isolation from intellectual, economic, social, and political history.

Although it is new, this approach to the book cannot be divorced from older bibliographic studies. Analytical bibliography, concerned with physical description, remains a significant component of the field, particularly in its ability to expose frauds that might mislead the unwary but also in its explanation of the process of book production, whether in the scriptorium or printing office. Even the apparently esoteric study of bookbinding becomes in the hands of a careful student like Mirjam Foot or Anthony Hobson a means of illuminating an era. Thus, Hobson's *Humanists and Bookbinders* (1989) presents fifteenth century gold-tooled Italian bindings as part of the humanist program and a manifestation of trade with the Islamic Near East. Foot observes that changes in binding style correspond to changes in book production. As production increased, binding methods changed to keep pace with demand. Even enumerative bibliographies (of which this volume is an example) are more than innocent listings. Luigi Balsamo's *Bibliography: History of a Tradition* (1990) records twenty Italian regional bibliographies from 1558 to 1683.

These sought, in Balsamo's words, "to assert the distinctiveness and autonomy of the culture" of each region (p. 77). Conrad Gesner's *Bibliotheca universalis* (1545), which attempted to list all printed books in Latin, Greek, and Hebrew, reflected the humanist interest in the classics, and its assembling a universal library responded to the Turkish threat of biblioclasm that had destroyed the library of King Mathias I Corvinus of Hungary. The proliferation of enumerative bibliographies in the seventeenth century is, according to David McKitterick, of a piece with John Ray's classification of flora and Martin Lister's of shells in the effort to find (or impose) order in the natural world (*The Foundations of Scholarship: Libraries and Collecting, 1650-1750*, Los Angeles: William Andrews Clark Memorial Library, 1992).

Jacques Derrida's pronouncement "Il n'y a pas hors de texte" ("There is nothing outside the text") may be modified to read, "Il n'y a pas hors d'histoire du livre." The history of the book draws on and impinges upon all studies, whether technological, scientific, economic, social, political, philosophical, cultural, or intellectual.

A Note on Using This Bibliography

It is hoped that this annotated bibliography will foster an understanding of this vast field by offering a selection of works on the book, primarily though not exclusively in the West. It seeks to list, describe, and evaluate the most important studies but cannot hope to be comprehensive. Of the making of books there is no end, nor is there a dearth of books about books. Classics have been included here regardless of their age, but the bibliography emphasizes more recent material since it is likely to be more useful, especially to the novice for whom the bibliography is primarily intended, though even the scholar should find the listings and comments helpful. Libraries and individuals may use this volume as a guide to collection development.

The user will often find references to reviews, and where possible the annotations place the title within the context of critical discussion on a subject. To avoid repetition, entries generally appear under one heading only, though some cross-referencing appears. As the introduction has sought to indicate, the history of the book is a broad and lively field. It is the hope of the compiler that this bibliography will generate further interest in the discipline and will contribute in some small measure to its continued growth.

PART I
RESOURCES

Chapter 1
BIBLIOGRAPHIES

Anderson, Frank J. *Private Press Work: A Bibliographic Approach to Printing as an Avocation*. South Brunswick, N.J.: A. S. Barnes, 1977.
In 1965, Anderson set up his own private press. This book lists some 160 works most likely to be helpful to anyone considering imitating Anderson, but these books provide historical information for anyone interested in printing. Bibliographic essays deal with printing, alphabets and letterforms, type and typography, book design and production, illustration, bookplates, binding, private presses, printing history, paper and papermaking, and periodicals. On page 163, Anderson distills his lists into ten titles. Other chapters list sources of supplies and important institutional collections dealing with the history of the book and printing. Entries are briefly annotated, and all items listed are recommended.

Appleton, Tony. *A Typographical Tally: Thirteen Hundred Writings in English on Printing History, Typography, Bookbinding, and Papermaking*. Brighton, England: Dolphin Press, 1973.
Divided into three sections: "Printing History and Typography," "Bookbinding," and "Papermaking," the first being by far the longest. Essentially a checklist, giving author, title, place, and date of publication. Does not include publisher and lacks annotations. The lack of subcategories makes this bibliography less useful than it might be otherwise. For example, the student seeking information on the eighteenth century British typographer and printer John Baskerville must look through the entire first section or know the names of the authors who have written about him (in which case one would not be consulting this bibliography on that subject). The lack of an index is another weakness. A handsomely produced little volume.

Barker, Nicolas J. "Book Production and Distribution." In *The New Cambridge Bibliography of English Literature*, edited by George Watson. Cambridge, England: Cambridge University Press, 1974, 1: 925-1006.
This unit of *The New Cambridge Bibliography* is divided into four sections: "Bibliography," "The Accessory Crafts," "Printing and Bookselling," and "Libraries and Book Collectors." As with all sections of this work, arrangement is chronological, with the most recent

studies listed last. Focus is on Britain, but Barker includes many
general studies. Selective; not annotated.

Besterman, Theodore. *Printing, Book Collecting, and Illustrated Books:
A Bibliography of Bibliographies.* 2 vols. Totowa, N.J.: Rowman &
Littlefield, 1971.
A reprinting from Besterman's *A World Bibliography of Bibliographies*
(Lausanne, Switzerland: Societas Bibliographica, 1965-1966) of the
sections dealing with printing, book collecting, illustrated books,
broadsides and pamphlets, book production, paper, publishing, and
bookselling. Generally unannotated, though some entries include short
comments. Besterman always notes the number of entries and sometimes indicates the contents of an item listed. International in scope
though necessarily selective.

Bigmore, Edward C., and Charles W. H. Wyman. *A Bibliography of
Printing with Notes and Illustrations.* 2d ed. 3 vols. London: Quaritch,
1880-1886.
A pioneering effort and still very useful for students of printing through
the nineteenth century. Entries are arranged in a single alphabet and
include material from the fifteenth century onward. Annotations accompany most items and often include biographical sketches of the
authors. Also contains attractive and informative illustrations, such as
portraits and printers' marks. Much information on important printers
such as Caxton and Gutenberg. Still the most comprehensive bibliography on the subject.

*Books About Books: An International Exhibition on the Occasion of the
International Book Year 1972 Proclaimed by UNESCO.* Frankfurt-am-
Main, Germany: Frankfurt Book Fair, 1972.
An annotated, indexed catalog of 1,035 titles then available for purchase. Provides bibliographic information, price, and a brief description for each item. Entries are arranged by subject: author, copyright,
publishing, book production, book distribution, book promotion, the
reader, bibliophily, book and paper history, the book and art, book
statistics, bibliography, documentation, audiovisual, library science,
book trade journals. Contains many attractive illustrations.

Brenni, Vito J. *The Art and History of Book Printing: A Topical Bibliography.* Westport, Conn.: Greenwood Press, 1984.
Contains 1,060 entries arranged by subject, such as "Printing Machinery
and Materials," "History of Book Printing," "Hebrew Printing," and

"Private Presses," with chronological and geographical sub-headings where appropriate. Provides some brief annotations. Selective but useful, especially for the novice.

_____. *Book Printing in Britain and America: A Guide to the Literature and a Directory of Printers*. Westport, Conn.: Greenwood Press, 1983.
A selective guide to 1,021 items organized by country and then by genre or period. Includes a list of 389 printers, typographers, calligraphers, and book designers, with their dates of birth and death and brief descriptions. Michael Patrick Hearn called this "a solid checklist [that] gives much to consider for anyone studying printing in America and Great Britain" (*American Book Collector* 5, March/April, 1984, 62).

Davison, Peter. *The Book Encompassed: Studies in Twentieth-Century Bibliography*. Cambridge, England: Cambridge University Press, 1992.
Commissioned to celebrate the centenary of the Bibliographical Society, the essays in this volume "look back over the past fifty years . . . , consider the present state of work in their subject, and . . . offer some guidance as to the direction of future research." The opening piece examines the scholarly contributions of the Bibliographical Society. Subsequent essays deal with the book as physical object (e.g., John Bidwell's "The Study of Paper as Evidence, Artefact, and Commodity"; Nicolas Barker's "Typographical Studies"), national bibliographies, and such topics as the role of the computer in bibliographic studies. Each contribution surveys the work in the field, and many include a selective bibliography. T. A. Birrell praised the volume as "a compact and comprehensive guide to what modern bibliography is all about" (Times Literary Supplement, April 9, 1993, 28).

Dictionary Catalogue of the History of Printing from the John M. Wing Foundation, the Newberry Library (Chicago). 6 vols. Boston: G. K. Hall, 1962. 1st supplement, 3 vols., 1970.
The Newberry Library houses more than 23,000 volumes of "books and journals descriptive of the graphic arts, national and regional printing histories, works on papermaking, binding, book design, and illustration ancillary to printing." G. K. Hall photographically reproduced the card catalog of this collection, together with the catalog for "finely printed or historically significant books" in the library. Annotations are limited to the subject headings and notes on the cards, which provide complete bibliographic information and access by subject and title as well as author.

Fleck, Robert. *The Alida Roochvarg Collection of Books About Books.* New Castle, Del.: Oak Knoll Books, 1981.

Oak Knoll Books is among the largest dealers in new and old books about books. This work links six catalogs through a comprehensive index. Alida Roochvarg assembled an excellent collection of books about books; these annotated lists include 2,690 items from her library that Oak Knoll offered for sale. Roochvarg wrote the introduction, and the great bookman Lawrence Clark Powell provided a short afterword.

Hart, Horace. *Bibliotheca Typographica In Usum Eorum Qui Libros Amant: A List of Books About Books.* Rochester, N.Y.: Printing House of Leo Hart, 1933.

Based on a reading list that Hart devised for a course he was taking as an undergraduate at Harvard under the legendary George Parker Winship, this handsomely produced, annotated volume with some 250 entries is aimed at a wide audience: "non-academic students, printers who desire to learn something of the history of their craft, collectors who feel they would have a keener appreciation of their acquisitions if they knew more of the technical side of the production of a book, and . . . others who have an amateur's interest in this fascinating subject" (preface). Arranged by subject, such as "Manuscripts and Illumination" or "Printing and Printers." A fine bibliography; short enough to be useful, long enough to cover all the essential points. Indexed.

The History of Printing from Its Beginnings to 1930: The Subject Catalogue of the American Type Founders Company Library in the Columbia University Libraries. 4 vols. Millwood, N.Y.: Kraus International Publications, 1980.

Reproduces some 45,000 cards from the American Type Founders Company Library, which has the largest collection in the United States on the subject. Works are arranged under more than 2,000 subject headings, such as "Bibliography," "Bodoni, Giambattista," and "Greek Printing in France." Henry Lewis Bullen, who founded the American Type Founders Company Library, created his own subject headings. These are listed at the beginning of the catalog but do not suggest cross-references, and items are not cross-listed. Gleason White's *Children's Books and Their Illustrators* appears only under "Illustrated Books—Literature of," while *Children's Illustrated Story Books* is listed only under "Children's Books."

Lehmann-Haupt, Hellmut. *One Hundred Books About Bookmaking: A Guide to the Study and Appreciation of Printing.* 3d ed. New York:

Columbia University Press, 1949.

An annotated list that grew out of earlier editions, *Fifty Books About Bookmaking* (1933) and *Seventy Books About Bookmaking* (1941). Arranged by subject under such headings as "Writing and Lettering," "Illustration," and "Bookbinding and Papermaking." Lehmann-Haupt has provided helpful comments indicating content and audience and explaining the item's importance. A personal selection that includes only a limited number of titles for each section. The chapter on "Printing History and Modern Trends," for instance, lists only thirteen items. Attractively produced. Indexed.

Myers, Robin. *The British Book Trade from Caxton to the Present Day: A Bibliographical Guide Based on the Libraries of the National Book League and St. Bride Institute.* London: Deutsch, 1973.

Myers writes in the preface, "This book consists of a classified and annotated selection of works indicating the way in which the book trade evolved." The scope of the bibliography is actually broader, with chapters devoted to authorship, bookbinding, bookselling, book design and production, book illustration, the book trade, children's books, laws dealing with the trade, the 1899 Net Book Agreement that prohibited discounting book prices, paper and ink, printing, private presses, and publishing. In addition to full bibliographic information, Myers offers brief but useful comments. Excludes almost all periodical articles and foreign language material. David McKitterick called the work "an invaluable introduction" (*The Library* 33, 1978, 179).

National Book League. *Books About Books: Catalogues of the Library of the National Book League.* 5th ed. Cambridge, England: Cambridge University Press for the National Book League, 1955.

A classified library catalog that includes hundreds of books relevant to the history of books and printing, covering such topics as paper and ink, book publishing and bookselling, the care of books, and bibliophily. Indexed but not annotated. Supplements have appeared periodically.

Peddie, R. A. *Catalogue of the Technical Reference Library of Works on Printing and the Allied Arts.* London: St. Bride Foundation Institute, 1919.

A valuable list because the St. Bride Institute houses one of the major collections dealing with the history of books and printing. The Institute has also issued a thirty-five-page *Catalogue of the Periodicals Relating to Printing and Allied Subjects in the Technical Library of St. Bride Institute* (1950). Both remain useful.

Pratt, R. D. *A Thousand Books on Books: A Selection of English Books on
    Book-Making, Book-Selling, and Book-Collecting.* London: Merry-
    thought Press, 1967.
    Like the lists by Horace Hart and Hellmut Lehmann-Haupt noted
    above, this represents a personal choice of English-language works,
    mainly those in Pratt's collection. Arranged alphabetically by author,
    with a subject index that varies in helpfulness. For example, Pratt offers
    a good listing under "Bookbinding" but has no entry in the index for
    bookselling. Under "Private Presses" Pratt does not refer to S. C.
    Cockerell's *A Short History and Description of the Kelmscott Press,*
    even though that title appears in the body of the bibliography. Most
    entries are not annotated.

Schreyer, Alice D. *The History of Books: A Guide to Selected Sources in
    the Library of Congress.* Washington, D.C.: Center for the Book, 1987.
    Schreyer writes in her introduction, "The purpose of this guide is to
    suggest research opportunities at the Library of Congress for those
    interested in the history of books. The guide also serves as an introduc-
    tion to the range of inquiry the history of books encompasses and to
    the diverse types of resources that can support studies in this field."
    Part 1 discusses materials housed in the Manuscript and Rare Book and
    Special Collection Divisions, giving an overview of the various rele-
    vant items such as the papers of the publisher Benjamin Holt Ticknor
    or the splendid library that Lessing Rosenwald donated. Part 2 dis-
    cusses five sections important to historians of the book: Copyright
    Records and Deposits, the Law Library, Geography and Map Division,
    the Music Division, and Prints and Photographs Division. Paul S. Coda
    wrote in *Library and Culture* 23 (1988): 526, "Schreyer is not only a
    first-rate guide; she also has a scholar's understanding of the library's
    potential for book history. Even if one were not able to use the library's
    collection for research, her writings on copyright literature, legal
    literature, and graphic materials (to name only three of several) stand
    alone as required reading for any researcher investigating book history
    in these areas. All persons interested in the history of the book and
    literacy as well as their impact on human life should have *The History
    of Books* in their libraries."

Tanselle, Thomas. *Introduction to Bibliography: Seminar Syllabus.* New
    York: Columbia University Department of English Literature, 1990.
    A reading list of Tanselle's course on bibliography, based on more
    than twenty years of teaching at the University of Wisconsin (1963-
    1975) and Columbia University (1980-   ). Tanselle notes, "The

syllabus is meant to supply a brief list of recommended readings for each topic . . . , supplemented by more extensive unevaluative chronological lists." Under headings such as "Illustration" and "Bindings," Tanselle lists books and articles. Robert and Christine Liska, owners of The Colophon Book Shop, call this 101-page typescript reproduction "the most complete and well-organized presentation of readings in bibliography now available."

_____. "The Periodical Literature of English and American Bibliography." *Studies in Bibliography* 26 (1973): 167-191.
Many important bibliographical discoveries appear first—or only—in periodical articles. Since 1949 *Studies in Bibliography*, published by the Bibliographical Society of the University of Virginia, has included an annual checklist of such work, but even that compilation is selective. Tanselle discusses various other sources that cover the period before 1949 and that also supplement *Studies in Bibliography*. At the end of the article, Tanselle offers a list of important periodicals in the field and notes where these are indexed. Though a number of publications discussed here have ceased operation, have changed their names, or have appeared and disappeared again since 1973, the listing remains valuable, especially for the nineteenth and early twentieth centuries.

Ulrich, Carolyn, and Karl Kup. *Books and Printing: A Select List of Periodicals, 1800-1942.* Woodstock, Vt.: William Edwin Rudge, 1943.
An annotated and indexed international listing of journals dealing with all facets of the history of the book, divided into three units. The first treats the book before printing, printing history, and the history of bookbinding. The second part, "Physical Elements," discusses type, paper, ink and other materials. The final section lists periodicals dealing with authorship, publishing, advertising, the book trade, bibliography, book collecting, and libraries. Appendices list directories, indexes, yearbooks, and organizations concerned with the discipline. Very useful for the period covered, and some of the periodicals listed are still published.

Vervliet, Hendrik D. L., ed. *Annual Bibliography of the History of the Printed Book and Libraries.* Dordrecht, Netherlands: Kluwer Academic Publishers, 1970-   .
Attempts to list "all books and articles of scholarly value which relate to the history of the printed book, to the history of the arts, crafts, techniques, and equipment, and of the economic, social, and cultural environment involved in its production, distribution, conservation, and

description." International in scope; covers the period from around
1450 to the present. Arrangement is by subject, such as printing, book
illustration, or bibliophily. Entries are not annotated, but the listing is
extensive. The 1970 volume contained about 2,500 entries, the 1973
edition had 3,400.

Webber, Winslow L. *Books About Books: A Bio-Bibliography for Collectors.* Boston: Hale, Cushman, and Flint, 1937.
Presents "a few of the books and articles on bibliography and collecting
which should be of most interest and value to the bookman." The first
chapter discusses collecting and books about books. Webber laments
the absence of guides for those interested in these subjects. The second
chapter presents Webber's list and comments, which include discussions of the authors as well as their works. The third and final chapter
cites relevant articles published between 1900 and 1937; these are not
annotated. The book concludes with a brief glossary of bibliographic
terms such as "cancels" (pages cut out of a book by the publisher and
replaced with others), "signatures," and "verso." Oddly, there is no
entry for "recto." Webber's quote from P. B. M. Allen's *The Book
Hunter at Home* (1920) applies to his own book: "To the real collector,
there is no more delightful reading than the literature which deals with
the subject he has made his own; and the more ample and specialized
it be, the greater will be his delight."

Williamson, Derek. *Bibliography: Historical, Analytical, and Descriptive: An Examination Guidebook.* London: Clive Bingley, 1967.
Part 1 provides short bibliographic essays on the history of books,
beginning with "Early Books and Materials." The second chapter deals
with the incunabula period. Chapters 3 and 4 take up the hand-produced
book (1501-1800) and the machine-made book (1800 onward). Subsequent chapters treat writing and typography, illustration, paper and
papermaking, binding, and the book trade. Part 2 deals with analytical
and descriptive bibliography, but this subject receives more cursory
treatment. A readable history and a useful guide to the literature.

Winckler, Paul A. *History of Books and Printing: A Guide to Information
Sources.* Detroit: Gale Research, 1979.
A listing of 769 books, articles, audiovisual materials, associations,
societies, clubs, libraries, special collections, museums, and guides to
dealers concerned with books and printing. Winckler writes in his
introduction, "It is my hope that this work will serve as [a] guide to the
literature of the delightful and fascinating world of the history of the

book. . . . This book has been compiled to fill a gap in the bibliographical literature, and I hope it has accomplished its purpose." Arranged by subject, with helpful author, title, and subject indexes. Annotations describe rather than analyze. The bibliography is of necessity selective, but it ranges widely and will appeal to all interested in the field.

Chapter 2
GENERAL REFERENCES

Allen, Edward M. *Harper's Dictionary of the Graphic Arts*. New York: Harper & Row, 1963.

An alphabetical listing of over 6,500 terms relating to the graphic arts. Allen writes in his foreword, "Words are here defined, production methods and processes are explained, uses and purposes of tools, materials, etc., are stated." Here one can discover what a "kid finish" is on paper ("a smooth finish resembling kid leather"), who Robert Granjon was (a sixteenth century French typefounder), or how quoins function in a hand printing press. Definitions are short but clear.

American Dictionary of Printing and Bookmaking. New York: Howard Lockwood, 1894. Reprint. Detroit: Gale Research, 1967.

In his preface to the 1967 Gale reprint Robert E. Rusner wrote that this work provides "a storehouse of practical, technical, and historical information, and its biographical accounts of printing contemporaries are in many instances the single and only source." Nicely illustrated, with fascinating information about presses and informative accounts of figures important in the development of printing. Still useful despite its age.

Berry, W. Turner, and H. Edmund Poole. *Annals of Printing: A Chronological Encyclopedia from the Earliest Times to 1950*. Toronto: University of Toronto Press, 1966.

Intended for "the student in schools of librarianship, colleges of art and printing and technology, . . . and the non-specialist who is aware of contemporary trends in communication and in the practice of printing and who wishes to look back over its developments." Focuses on innovations, beginning with 105 A.D., the traditional date for the invention of paper. Illustrated and indexed.

Bradley, John William. *A Dictionary of Miniaturists, Illuminators, Calligraphers, and Copyists, with Reference to Their Works, and Notices of Their Patrons, from the Establishment of Christianity to the Eighteenth Century*. 3 vols. London: Bernard Quaritch, 1887-1889.

An extensive list. Sometimes Bradley can say only that a name appeared on a tax list that designated that person as an illuminator, or that a miniaturist worked at Padua in 1541. For other figures he can be more detailed. Thus, for John Carpensis he can offer a list of five manuscripts illuminated by the artist and provide their locations. Includes bibliographical references wherever possible. One wishes for an index that would allow access by manuscript as well as by copyist. One can find under "Eadfrith" that this bishop of Lindisfarne wrote the celebrated Lindisfarne Gospels, but if one did not know the bishop's name, one could not locate information about the work.

Carter, John. *ABC for Book Collectors*. 6th ed., rev. New York: Alfred A. Knopf, 1980.
This authoritative and witty volume has become a standard reference. The fun begins with the dust jacket, which contains a brief description of the book. Below the prose appears "[*Above is a* BLURB]." The endpapers, paste-down and free, are so labeled, as are the head, tail, and fore-edge of the book, the half-title, advertisement leaf, and title page. Though aimed primarily at the collector, who will derive the most chuckles from the barbs aimed at booksellers, there is much information here for anyone concerned with books. How does an "issue" differ from a "state" or an "impression variant" or an "edition"? What is an Edward of Halifax binding? Carter's definitions are clear and accurate.

Clair, Colin. *A Chronology of Printing*. New York: Frederick A. Praeger, 1969.
Like Berry and Poole's *Annals of Printing* (cited in this chapter), this chronology begins with 105 A.D. but continues to 1967. Clair offers "a compendium of information on matters connected with printing, its first introduction into Europe and its spread throughout the world; being an attempt to set in their chronological order those matters most important in the history of the printed book, its manufacture, design, and dissemination." Indexed.

Feather, John. *A Dictionary of Book History*. New York: Oxford University Press, 1986.
Aimed at "scholars, bibliophiles, research students, librarians and booksellers." The dictionary takes a historical approach, avoiding technical explanations. As Feather comments, "The user who wishes to know the history and basic principles of offset lithography should be satisfied, [but] he will not learn how to adjust the blanket cylinder on such a press to obtain the best impression." Focuses on America and Britain. Includes many brief biographical sketches and often provides references for further study. Entries tend to be short but informative.

Glaister, Geoffrey Ashall. *Glaister's Glossary of the Book*. 2d ed.
Berkeley: University of California Press, 1979.
A standard in the field, covering terms "used in papermaking, printing,
bookbinding, and publishing, with notes on illuminated manuscripts
and private presses." Contains 3,932 entries, from ABA (American
Booksellers Association) and the English collector of color-plate books
and fine bindings, John Roland Abbey (1896-1969), to Zip-a-tone ("a
series of *mechanical tints*") and zodiacal signs. Appendix A offers a
selection of type specimens, and Appendix B gives the English equivalent for Latin place-names used in early printed books. Includes a brief
bibliography. Essential.

Greenhood, David, and Helen Gentry. *Chronology of Books and Printing*.
Rev. ed. New York: Macmillan, 1936.
Presents a "broad procession of events in the development of the
Book," beginning in 300 B.C. with the founding of the Alexandrian
library by Ptolemy I. The authors intend "to afford the user of this
manual . . . ready access to a wide variety of facts which, usually, are
obtainable only by consulting several volumes, and those not always
on one shelf or in the same library." Includes an index and brief
bibliography. Most of the book deals with the period since the introduction of printing; the dates get closer together as one approaches the
twentieth century. After 1900 some event is recorded for almost every
year. An attractive and useful book.

Haller, Margaret. *The Book Collector's Fact Book*. New York: Arco, 1976.
Intended for the novice collector but with useful information for
anyone interested in books. "Presents, in one compact volume, many
essential facts about collecting today, including information on books
as physical objects, their construction, the artistry of fine bookmaking,
illustrated and press books, and the history of modern books." Here
one can learn the meaning of "anastic printing" (printing from a zinc
plate), "anopisthographic" (a book with printing on only one side of
its leaves), or "cottage binding." A good complement to John Carter's
ABC for Book Collectors and Geoffrey Ashall Glaister's dictionary,
both discussed above.

Harrod, L. M., and Ray Prytherch. *Harrod's Librarian's Glossary*. 6th ed.
Aldershot, England: Gower, 1987.
Despite its title, this volume is aimed at a wide audience: librarians,
publishers, printers, binders, conservators, computer scientists—
anyone, in short, involved with books. The orientation is British, but

most of the terms included apply to all English-speaking countries. Explains such terms as "stem" in its various contexts, "Perpetua" (a typeface designed by Eric Gill), or "interleaving." A handy guide. Its multiple editions demonstrate its utility.

Hostettler, Rudolf. *Technical Terms of the Printing Industry*. 5th rev. ed. St. Gall, Switzerland: Author, 1969.
This small book offers a wealth of information, much of which is conveyed through pictures as well as text. Among the subjects covered are type families, sizes, and faces; printers' ornaments; parts of a book; readers' marks; and bookbinding. The volume includes a long list of words in English with French, German, Italian, and Dutch equivalents. An index allows access by these other languages.

Kent, Allen, and Harold Lancour, eds. *Encyclopedia of Library and Information Science*. New York: Marcel Dekker, 1968.
Though not devoted exclusively to the history of the book, this multi-volume set contains many entries that will interest and inform the student of that subject. Among the articles are pieces on "Book Exhibits" and "Book Trade," "Calligraphy" and William Caxton, and "Illumination" and Christophe Plantin. Supplements continue to update the work. The 1993 supplement, for example, includes a substantial article on font designs in computer typography.

Lewis, John. *A Handbook of Type and Illustration*. London: Faber & Faber, 1956.
Intended to tell "the artist and designer how a printer . . . deals with the production of illustrated books and the reproduction of oil paintings, water colour drawings, etchings, copper engravings, etc." In the course of the discussion, Lewis examines all facets of the making of the book, with chapters on illustration, typefaces, titling, direct and photographic methods of reproduction, binding, and book jackets. Appendix I presents production data for letterpress and offset printing and for binding. Appendix II offers specimen pages in a range of Old Face and New Face type from Bembo to Gill Sans. The volume is well illustrated and demonstrates through pictures and type the points Lewis wishes to make.

Peters, Jean, ed. *The Bookman's Glossary*. 6th ed., rev. and enl. New York: R. R. Bowker, 1983.
First published in 1925 under John A. Holden's editorship, this work has become a standard reference. The sixth edition includes some 1,800

terms relating to publishing, bookselling, and librarianship. Peters writes in the preface that the work should be "a practical guide to the terminology used in the production and distribution of books new and old, not necessarily the technical languages of the various sectors of the trade, but rather the words in common use in a publisher's office, in a bookstore, or among book collectors." Includes computer terms and brief biographies of figures important in the history of the book. With a four-page bibliography.

Stevenson, George A. *Graphic Arts Encyclopedia*. 2d ed. New York: McGraw-Hill, 1979.
Treats "(1) the products and tools with which an image is formed, (2) the kind of image, and (3) the surface or materials upon which the image is produced." Well illustrated. Explains what a newspaper publisher means by "dinky," how a linecasting machine operates, or how "flong" (damp papier-mâché) is used in printing. With a bibliography, and lists of associations and societies concerned with the graphic arts, trade journals, products, and manufacturers.

Stokes, Roy. *A Bibliographical Companion*. Metuchen, N.J.: Scarecrow, 1989.
Intended for undergraduates and general readers. Stokes offers extended definitions of terms likely to arise in studies of the book. For example, the volume opens with a full-page discussion of "abecedaries" (alphabet books), which date as far back as the fourteenth century B.C. Stokes distinguishes between headbands and headcaps in binding, and explains the difference between uncial and half-uncial letters. Many of the articles also include bibliographical references for further study, and all will instruct the reader.

Wijnekus, F. J. M., and E. F. P. H. Wijnekus. *Elsevier's Dictionary of the Printing and Allied Industries, in Four Languages, English, French, German, Dutch*. 2d ed., rev. and enl. Amsterdam, Netherlands: Elsevier, 1983.
An international dictionary of 14,930 terms used in the printing trade, arranged alphabetically by the English word. In addition to giving foreign-language equivalents, the dictionary also offers definitions and provides technical information about machinery and processes. Here one can find the chemical formula for indigo blue used in printing ink or the first use of the word "incunabula" to describe printing before 1501 (the 1688 *Incunabula Typographicae* by Cornelis a Beughem).

PART II

TECHNICAL ASPECTS

Chapter 3
WRITING SURFACES

Bibliographies

Bidwell, John. "Paper and Papermaking: 100 Sources." *AB Bookman's Yearbook* (1978): 32-43.
In this useful bibliographic essay, Bidwell presents a recommended selection of works. He begins with eleven general histories, then proceeds to books that deal with specific regions—the United States and various European countries. Other categories covered are papermaking manuals, watermarks, reference works, raw materials, machine- and handmade papers, and what Bidwell calls "paper pastimes." At the end of the article, Bidwell presents an alphabetical listing of the titles he discusses.

Hunter, Dard. *The Literature of Papermaking, 1390-1800*. Chillicothe, Ohio: Mountain House Press, 1925.
An annotated bibliography of seventy sources that appeared in Europe and America between 1390 and 1800. Hunter, who not only wrote the text but also designed the book, included facsimile title pages for many of the items, using paper similar to the originals. Nelson Antrim Crawford praised Hunter's commentary for its content and style; Crawford observed that Hunter had turned "bibliography, dullest of subjects, into pageantry" (*The Nation* 121, 1925: 387).

Leif, Irving P. *An International Sourcebook of Paper History*. Hamden, Conn.: Archon Books, 1978.
Contains more than 2,000 entries in a dozen languages. The titles here include general histories, national and regional histories, collections of watermarks, texts on paper history research techniques, and other bibliographies. The entries are not annotated, and the list is better for handmade than machine-made paper. Both *The Book Collector* 27 (1978): 414-417 and *The Library* 1 (1979): 173-174 reviewed the book harshly for its omissions and errors. Still, if used with caution this can be a useful guide.

Studies

Ainsworth, John H. *Paper: The Fifth Wonder*. 2d ed., rev. Kaukauna, Wis.:
Thomas Publishing, 1959.

In the first chapter Ainsworth discusses the many uses of paper. He
then traces the manufacture of wood pulp paper from the forest through
pulping (mechanical and chemical), bleaching, stock preparation, coloring, sizing, and manufacture by machine. Ainsworth goes on to
discuss the printing and binding of books. He includes glossaries of
graphic art and paper terminology and concludes with two chapters on
ink. Intended for the general reader.

Blum, André. *On the Origin of Paper*. Translated by Harry Miller Lydenberg. New York: R. R. Bowker, 1934.

Paper first came to Europe through Arabic Spain, and Spanish Jews
were involved in establishing paper mills from the eleventh to the
fourteenth century. Xativa, Spain, had the earliest European paper mill.
Fabriano, Italy, had the second. France, Germany, and Flanders followed. Papermaking progressed slowly in Europe because the material
was fragile, expensive (costing as much as parchment), and linked in
Christian minds with Moslems and Jews. When linen prices fell and
metal beaters were introduced, paper prices declined and paper's
popularity increased.

Briquet, Charles Moïse. *Briquet's Opuscula: The Complete Works of Dr.
C. M. Briquet Without Les Filigranes*. Hilversum, Netherlands: Paper
Publications Society, 1955.

Twenty-four articles by Briquet, examining the iconography and significance of the watermarks that he reproduced in his classic *Les
Filigranes* (1907). His analysis avoids the fanciful interpretations
sometimes imposed on these symbols. A judicious and learned account
by the master of the subject.

_____. *Les Filigranes: Dictionnaire historique des marques du
papier*. 4 vols. Paris: Picard, 1907.

A standard reference depicting more than 16,000 watermarks beginning in 1282, when the first one appeared, to 1600. Over a period of
twenty-five years, Briquet traveled to more than 200 European libraries
and archives to examine paper, and he went blind in the process. Briquet
arranged the descriptions alphabetically, using the numbers of his
illustrations for references. His notes reveal much about the origins of
papermaking in Europe and often provide fascinating information. For

example, "elephant" sheets derive their name not from their size but from the watermark that appeared on them. Later the term came to be associated with this size of paper, regardless of the watermark. Briquet did not examine paper in Spain, Portugal, Scandinavia, or Great Britain, but for the countries covered this is an indispensable resource.

Britt, Kenneth W., ed. *Handbook of Pulp and Paper Technology.* 2d rev. and enl. ed. New York: Van Nostrand Reinhold, 1970.

A comprehensive textbook and valuable reference dealing with all aspects of the making of paper. Each of the sixty-one chapters is written by a specialist in the particular area being addressed, and each chapter concludes with a bibliography for further study. Filled with diagrams, tables, charts, and photographs.

Butler, Frank O. *The Story of Paper-Making: An Account of Paper-Making from Its Earliest Known Record Down to the Present Time.* Chicago: J. W. Butler Paper Co., 1901.

This account, aimed at the general reader, begins with the earliest writing surfaces: papyrus, parchment, and clay. It then turns to Oriental and Western modes of papermaking by hand and by machine. Although the discussion involves technical processes, the text remains accessible to the general reader. Also provides historical sidelights: during the American Revolution, for example, New York exempted from military service the master and two assistants at each paper mill; in 1801 rags for paper were so scarce that the papermaker Zenas Crane issued an appeal to citizens of Worcester, Massachusetts, to supply him with this needed item.

Churchyard, Thomas. *A Sparke of Friendship and Warme Goodwill.* London: Wynkyn de Worde Society, 1978.

Reprint of Churchyard's 1588 poem on papermaking, the first account of the subject in English. It describes Spillman's Mill at Dartford on the River Darenth; though Churchyard erroneously calls this the first English paper mill, it was the first to endure and the first to receive any detailed mention. Churchyard notes that "the hammers thump, and make as loud a noise,/ A Fuller doth, that beats his woolen cloth." He also observes, "Then it [the pulp] is stamped, and washed as white as snow,/ Then flung on frame, and hanged to dry, I trow." The poem says that the mill was black and white, probably half-timbered in typical Elizabethan fashion. Churchyard's poem is filled with moralizing and nationalism but also serves as an informative account of an industry then in its youth in England.

Clapperton, Robert Henderson. *The Paper-Making Machine: Its Invention, Evolution, and Development.* Oxford, England: Pergamon Press, 1967.
Concentrates on the development of the Fourdrinier papermaking machine during its first century of operation. Clapperton discusses the many contributors to the modern version of this device, beginning with Nicolas Louis Robert in the late eighteenth century. The earliest mechanical means of making paper had a number of defects. Bryan Donkin, John Gamble, and Henry and Sealy Fourdrinier introduced improvements. In 1809 John Dickinson patented a cylinder-mold machine, the ancestor of modern papermaking devices. Clapperton observes that virtually all the pioneers in the field died in poverty. He provides diagrams and illustrations and reprints important contemporary documents. Without ignoring technical issues, Clapperton writes for the general reader. Appendixes provide additional documents, and these are followed by biographies of fourteen people important in the development of mechanical papermaking. Thorough and reliable.

Clapperton, Robert Henderson, and William Henderson. *Modern Paper-Making.* 3d ed. Oxford, England: Basil Blackwell, 1947.
In twenty-two chapters with more than 150 illustrations, the authors take the reader through a papermaking factory. The book opens with a discussion of materials used in the mid-twentieth century, explaining the virtues of each. The authors then follow these materials as they are beaten, sized, dyed, watermarked, cut, sorted, and finished. In the course of the book Clapperton and Henderson explain the operations of the machines involved in modern papermaking. A lucid account.

Day, Frederick T. *An Introduction to Paper: Its Manufacture and Use.* 6th ed. London: Newnes Educational Publishing, 1962.
A brief, accessible overview. The first chapter discusses the history of paper beginning with papyrus and proceeding to the use of wood pulp. Chapter 2 deals with raw materials: rags, grasses, pulps, and straw. Day then explains how paper is made by hand and by machine. Chapter 5 looks at procedures involved in making coated papers; Chapter 6 considers gummed paper. Paper sizes and paper as a raw material for other industries are the subjects of Chapters 7 and 8, and Chapter 9 quickly surveys printing. With a glossary of terms used in the industry.

The Dictionary of Paper, Including Pulps, Boards, Paper Properties, and Related Paper Making Terms. New York: American Paper and Pulp Association, 1978.

An essential reference for students of modern paper. Provides clear definitions of all facets of the subject of machine-made paper and explains the various types and qualities of paper available, together with their uses.

Evans, John C. W., ed. *Trends and Developments in Papermaking*. San Francisco: Miller Freeman, 1985.
A collection of sixteen essays discussing late twentieth century innovations and probable developments in machinery for making paper. Taken together, the essays offer a sound overview of the technology of papermaking. The contributions, aimed at those involved in papermaking, can be overly technical for the general reader. Appendix A discusses alkaline paper, which is more enduring than the conventional acidic variety. In Appendix B various authors examine the applications of new technology, and the volume concludes with details of new products available.

Goerl, Stephen. *A Pictorial History of Paper*. New York: Bulkley, Dunton Pulp, n.d.
A history for the novice, especially suitable for younger readers. The right-hand pages contain black-and-white illustrations with brief captions. The facing pages present somewhat longer explanations. Goerl begins with papyrus and notes important developments in the history of paper, such as its invention in China in 105 A.D., the Arabic discovery of papermaking from Chinese prisoners of war in 751 A.D., and the introduction of the Hollander beater in 1680.

Hardmann, H., and E. J. Cole. *Paper-Making Practice*. Manchester, England: Manchester University Press, 1960.
The authors provide "a concise outline of the most recent ideas on the various topics which had not already appeared in the textbooks and were therefore only to be read in technical publications." A good introduction to the intricacies of the manufacture of paper.

Heller, Jules. *Papermaking*. New York: Watson-Guptill, 1978.
A practical manual on the theory and practice of making paper by hand. After an introductory chapter that discusses different types of paper, Heller offers a photographic essay on papermaking. He then discusses ways of making paper, from simple kitchen methods that use a blender to produce pulp, an old clothes wringer to remove water, and an iron for drying, to more sophisticated and expensive techniques that yield a finer product. Includes a chronology of the history of paper, a

glossary, a list of suppliers, and a bibliography. Well-illustrated. A deluxe edition of this book, entitled *Papermaking: The White Art*, was published by the Scorpio Press, Scottsdale, Arizona, in 1980.

Higham, Robert R. A. *A Handbook of Papermaking*. 2d ed. London: Business Books, 1968.
This study of machine-made paper looks at how raw materials are transformed into the finished product. The approach is technical, with many details that may bewilder the general reader. Those seeking detailed information on the subject of modern paper manufacture will find the book useful.

Hunter, Dard. *Papermaking: The History and Technique of an Ancient Craft*. 2d ed., rev. and enl. New York: Alfred A. Knopf, 1947.
A comprehensive study from the invention of paper in the Orient through its spread to the West; covers both the handmade and machine-made product. Includes a chronology of the history of paper, 317 illustrations, an extensive bibliography, and an index. This standard work is filled with exciting information. Hunter tells how old paper-making mills were villages in themselves, with workers living and eating together. He also describes how difficult and dangerous paper-making was before mechanization in the nineteenth century trans-formed the industry.

_____. *Papermaking in the Classroom*. Peoria, Ill.: Manual Arts Press, 1931.
In his foreword to the 1991 Oak Knoll (New Castle, Del.) reprint, Henry Morris describes this slim book as a manual for the young; it provides "a concise history of papermaking and also tells the student how to make his own paper from rags." It was the first manual written for the amateur papermaker and requires "only simple tools and inexpensive equipment." Hunter suggests, for example, that a meat grinder might serve as a beater (Morris, himself an expert on the making of paper, is skeptical). Hunter also notes that one can buy beaten stock from a paper mill. Good for its historical survey and still useful for the would-be home papermaker.

_____. *Papermaking Through Eighteen Centuries*. New York: William Edwin Rudge, 1930.
An expanded version of Hunter's limited edition 1923 *Old Papermaking*, this work deals "with the early methods of paper fabrication and does not pretend to enter into the history of the numerous writing

substances in use before the advent of paper. . . . It aims to give the bibliophile an insight into the methods used by the old maker of paper, especially after the introduction of printing from movable types, and to interest the etcher, the engraver, and the printer, as well as those engaged in the paper and watermarking trades." In the course of this history Hunter presents a fascinating account on the first attempts to counterfeit British paper currency and the introduction of triple paper with a colored watermark to discourage imitation. With more than 200 illustrations, an excellent history.

Johnson, Malcolm, and A. S. Maney. *The Nature and Making of Papyrus.* Barkston Ash, England: Elmete Press, 1973.
A beautiful book with chapters on the plant itself, the preparation of papyrus rolls and codices, the methods used to write on papyrus, the manufacture of papyrus sheets (including instructions on making papyrus sheets at home), and the future of papyrus. Johnson and Maney suggest that the plant could again serve as an important source of fibers for papermaking. Includes a small sheet of paper made from papyrus as well as nine handmade sheets of rag paper.

Kent, Norman. "A Brief History of Papermaking." *American Artist* 31 (November, 1967): 36-41, 82.
Traces the manufacture of paper from its invention in China in the 2nd century A.D. The Arabs learned the art of papermaking from the Chinese; in 1131, the Moors established a paper mill in Xativa, Spain. In the thirteenth century, Italy began manufacturing fine paper; Germany established a mill in 1320, France by 1348, and England in 1495. In 1690, William Rittenhouse established America's first paper mill in Germantown, Pennsylvania, to supply William Bradford's printing press. In the nineteenth century, wood pulp began to be used to provide fibers for paper. The article includes some instructive illustrations, such as the picture of the paper mill in Nuremberg, taken from the *Nuremberg Chronicle*, and the line engravings from Diderot's *Encyclopédie* demonstrating eighteenth century papermaking technology. A good brief survey of the subject.

Kern, Marna Elyea. *The Complete Book of Handcrafted Paper.* New York: Coward, McCann & Geoghegan, 1980.
The first chapter provides a history of papermaking. Kern then explains how the novice can easily and inexpensively produce paper at home by recycling junk mail, grocery bags, used envelopes, and lint from the clothes dryer. She provides easy-to-follow instructions, with illustra-

tions, on making a mold and deckle, preparing pulp with a blender, couching, drying (which can be done with an iron or in the oven), and sizing. She even includes information on making a watermark. An appendix lists suppliers and schools offering courses in the craft.

Labarre, E. J. *Dictionary and Encyclopedia of Paper and Paper-Making.* 2d ed., rev. and enl. Amsterdam: Swets and Zeitlinger, 1952.
Labarre writes, "This book began as attempt to name and define clearly a number of material things and concepts in the paper field that I had found to be vague, ill-defined or even applied to different objects, processes or ideas." He first presents a selected bibliography of works dealing with various aspects of paper, both historical and technical. Then, in an alphabetical listing, he offers clear explanations of terms and processes. Especially useful is the inclusion of equivalent terms in French, German, Dutch, Italian, Spanish, and Swedish (when available), and each language has a separate index. An indispensable reference. In 1967 E. G. Loeber provided a supplement.

Lavingo, John R. *Pulp and Paper Dictionary.* San Francisco: Miller Freeman, 1986.
An updated complement to the previous title, this work explains more than 5,000 terms used in the pulp and paper industries. Also provides a short history of papermaking. A useful guide for anyone seeking an understanding of the technical terminology of the paper-making industry.

Lewis, Naphtali. *Papyrus in Classical Antiquity.* Oxford, England: Clarendon Press, 1974.
Based on the author's 1934 dissertation but expanded and revised, this study contains three parts. Lewis first discusses the plant itself; she notes that Egypt was the primary source. Papyrus also may have grown in Greece, Sicily, and Babylonia, though she argues that the papyrus referred to in these other areas was not used for making writing material. Lewis observes that papyrus had many uses; it could serve as food and fuel. In the second section, Lewis discusses paper made from papyrus. Pliny the Elder's *Natural History* provides most of the information about the manufacture of writing material from the plant. The concluding part of the book examines what is known of the papyrus industry, which must have been large and well-organized to supply the vast quantities of material needed. Lawrence S. Thompson called Lewis' study "the definitive work on papyrus as a product and an article of commerce" (*Papers of the Bibliographical Society of America* 71, 1977: 408).

Library of Congress. *Papermaking: Art and Craft*. Washington, D.C.: Library of Congress, 1968.

Published in conjunction with an exhibition on the subject, this volume first provides a brief history of paper, noting its Oriental origins and its reaching Europe through Arab intermediaries. A second section deals with the methods of making paper, and the work concludes with a discussion of recent developments in the industry. Includes a brief bibliography and ninety illustrations. Lawrence S. Thompson observed that *Papermaking* can provide "a useful . . . introduction that might well be read by beginning students before approaching" more detailed studies (*Papers of Bibliographical Society of America* 63, 1969: 144).

Long, Paulette, and Robert Levering, eds. *Paper: Art and Technology*. San Francisco: World Print Council, 1979.

Fifteen essays divided into three sections. The first part deals with the history and techniques of papermaking. Leonard B. Schlosser surveys important developments in the history of paper from its invention in China to the introduction of the material into Europe and the invention of the Hollander beater in the seventeenth century. The other three pieces in this unit deal with handmade paper in Japan, Europe, and America. The second section addresses technical considerations. Roy P. Whitney writes on the chemistry of paper. Other essays here discuss paper testing and caring for art on paper. The final section deals with paper as an artistic medium, and the volume concludes with a short glossary.

Maddox, Harry Alfred. *Paper: Its History, Sources, and Manufacture*. 6th ed. London: Sir Isaac Pitman and Sons, 1945.

Intended primarily for those involved in the industry. Maddox describes his work as "a popular handbook which will be sufficiently comprehensive to provide a thoroughly good insight into, and understanding of, paper and its manufacture." Maddox begins by providing a history of the making of paper. He next considers the nature of fibers and the treatment of raw materials. Chapter 7 looks at paper produced by machine, Chapter 8 at handmade paper. Finishes and coatings are discussed in Chapters 9 and 10, and Maddox concludes his short book with a discussion of paper testing. An accessible introduction, useful to anyone interested in the chemical and mechanical aspects of papermaking.

Mason, John. *Paper Making as an Artistic Craft*. Amended ed. Leicester, England: Twelve by Eight, 1963.

Mason began making paper in his kitchen, and he explains how others can do so, too. He also explores more elaborate methods that use a real paper beater, for instance, instead of a food mixer. The slim volume is attractively illustrated, and includes samples of the papers Mason produced. He observes that although linen is the traditional basis of handmade paper, other natural and synthetic materials can serve; however, man-made fibers require special processing.

Narita, Kiyofusa. *Nagashizuki and Tamezuki: Oriental and Western Methods of Papermaking*. Tokyo: Bunseido Press, 1977.
A tiny book of eighteen pages, printed on paper made by Tsuneo Naito; includes eight sample sheets. Narita explains the two traditional ways of making paper by hand. Nagashi-zuki, the more popular method in Japan, involves making an emulsion of mucilage, pulp, and water and then shaking the mixture over a mold. The excess stock is removed when the paper achieves the proper thickness. Tame-zuki, a method adopted from the West, uses no mucilage and places only enough stock on the mold to make the sheet. Nagashi-zuki allows for the manufacture of very thin sheets. Most of this little work deals with the differences between the two methods; it contrasts the two approaches by printing the distinctions on facing pages.

Norris, F. H. *Paper and Paper Making*. London: Oxford University Press, 1952.
Intended for the trade. Discusses "all the . . . aspects of paper manufacture and its ancillary processes in an interesting and easily readable form accessible to all branches of the industry." Norris offers a detailed—and technical—discussion of the processes and machinery involved in modern papermaking, primarily by machine but also by hand. Includes explanations of paper and board qualities and size and a dictionary of trade terms.

Reed, Ronald. *Ancient Skins, Parchments, and Leathers*. London: Seminar Press, 1972.
Although papyrus was the major writing material of the ancient world, leather was being used at least as early as about 2700 B.C. Once the codex triumphed over the roll, parchment replaced papyrus because the latter was not strong enough to resist tearing. Also, the supply of papyrus decreased in the early Christian era. Reed's book explores "the nature of writing and similar materials based on animal skin, their mode of preparation and some of the uses to which they were put." Reed looks first at the anatomy of the animal skin. He then explains

how skins are processed and proceeds to explore the ways that ancient civilizations used these materials. Chapter 5 discusses the nature and manufacture of parchment, and Chapter 6 looks at how archaeologists and curators should treat parchment artifacts, including books. The last three chapters explore the study of such items through the use of ultraviolet light, chemical tests, and physical examination. Each chapter includes helpful illustrations and a brief bibliography.

_____. *The Nature and Making of Parchment*. 2 vols. Leeds, England: Elmete Press, 1975.
Another beautiful production of the Elmete Press. After a short discussion of early writing, Reed explains the anatomy of animal skins. Chapter 3 discusses the ancient manufacture of parchment. The book then examines the use of this material in the classical, early Christian, and medieval periods. Reed notes that parchment permitted the creation of the codex. Though some codices used papyrus, the binding tends to cut that material and so creates loose sheets. With a number of informative illustrations. 425 copies were bound in quarter parchment, twenty-five in full parchment. Volume 2 contains ten parchment specimens.

Spector, Stephen, ed. *Essays in Paper Analysis*. Washington, D.C.: Folger Shakespeare Library, 1987.
A collection of nine essays on paper and the use of evidence of paper analysis in the study of the history of music and literature. Curt F. Buhler begins the book with an examination of the fifteenth century *Catholicon*, probably printed by Gutenberg. The colophon bears the date 1460, but watermarks on the paper suggest that it was printed later. Frederick Hudson reviews the state of scholarship dealing with paper analysis for the study of music and finds many opportunities available for further research. Hilton Kelliher warns that dates included in watermarks can deceive. For example, in 1794 English law began requiring dated watermarks, but some manufacturers kept the 1794 date in their papers until 1800, and a book printed late in 1806 contains paper dated 1807. John Nadas looks at the Reina Codex, an important late medieval music manuscript. Philip Pulsiano provides a bibliography of books and articles that reproduce watermarks, thus supplementing both Charles Moïse Briquet's *Les Filigranes* (1907) and Allan Stevenson's 1976 selective bibliography in *The New Briquet*. Pulsiano's bibliography is arranged alphabetically by author. David Schoonover discusses ways to reproduce watermarks, such as beta-radiography, the Ilkey technique, and the Dylux process. Alan Tyson's contribution deals with the dating of Beethoven's Leonore sketchbook;

William Proctor Williams stresses the importance of paper analysis in the study of seventeenth century English literature. The volume concludes with David Woodward's discussion of the use of paper and ink analysis in examining early maps.

Stevenson, Allan. "Paper as Bibliographical Evidence." *The Library* 17 (1962): 197-212.

Making a case for using paper as bibliographic evidence, Stevenson focuses of the *Missale speciale constantiense*, which, from typographical evidence alone, might be dated as early as 1450. Watermarks show that the book was printed around 1473 in or near Basel (where the book is known to have been bound). Stevenson concludes, "Surely the time has finally come when paper may make a more serious and vital contribution to the unsnarling of bibliographical problems, to the art of the book detective." Stevenson's expanded version of this article, *The Problem of the Missale Speciale* (London: Bibliographical Society, 1967), is one of the landmark studies in the use of paper analysis for bibliographic purposes.

Sutermeister, Edwin. *The Story of Papermaking*. Boston: S. D. Warren, 1954.

An excellent introduction for the novice seeking "a brief, general picture of papermaking operations." The book begins with a history of papermaking to 1900. Sutermeister then devotes three chapters to the materials from which paper is made. Chapters 5-8 examine processes for making pulp, and subsequent chapters take the pulp through bleaching, stock preparation, the actual making of paper by machine, coating, calendaring, and finishing. Well illustrated. Though Sutermeister cannot completely avoid technical terms, he succeeds in keeping his account readable. For a more technical discussion by the same author, see his *Pulp and Paper Making* (New York: John Wiley & Sons, 1920).

Tanselle, G. Thomas. "The Bibliographical Description of Paper." *Studies in Bibliography* 24 (1971): 27-67.

Tanselle begins by complaining that bibliographers often ignore paper in their description of a book, even though paper "gives a book its most obvious physical characteristics." Ignorance and a lack of proper vocabulary have hindered bibliographers from dealing with this matter. Tanselle suggests some key elements to examine and concludes with a few model descriptions that include size, chainlines, watermarks, thickness, color, and finish—details which are useful in analyzing books printed on either handmade or machine-made papers.

Toale, Bernard. *The Art of Papermaking.* Worcester, Mass.: Davis Publications, 1983.

Intended for those interested in making paper by hand or those wanting to learn more about the process. Toale first presents a short history of papermaking and then discusses Oriental techniques. Chapter 3 deals with fibers and their treatment; Chapter 4 looks at traditional and contemporary papermaking by hand in the West. The final chapter considers paper sculpture. With a glossary, list of suppliers of handmade paper and papermaking equipment, and a bibliography. Well-illustrated, with many practical hints for the artist using or considering creating handmade paper.

Turner, Silvie, and Birgit Skiold. *Handmade Paper Today: A Worldwide Survey of Mills, Papers, Techniques, and Uses.* London: Lund Humphries, 1983.

As of the date of this survey, over 115 mills were still producing handmade paper. The authors contacted each to determine how the paper was produced and used. Provides historical information and 250 illustrations, together with a glossary and bibliography. The authors also discuss the care of paper and include a long chapter on the use of handmade paper by such artists as David Hockney, Heinz-Dieter Pietsch, and Joel Fisher. Simon B. Green praised the book for its combination of "clarity, accuracy, and authority" as well as its readability (*Fine Print* 10, 1984: 1).

Van Derveer, Paul D., and Leonard E. Huas, eds. *International Glossary of Technical Terms for the Pulp and Paper Industry.* 5th ed. San Francisco: Miller Freeman, 1989.

Lists over 6,000 terms in English, Swedish, German, French, and Spanish. The compilers claim that "within the covers of this glossary the reader will find an extensive compendium of terms in five languages—all relating to the pulp and paper industry, from the forests to the marketplace." Indexes allow the speaker of one language to find the equivalent term in the other four, but no definitions are provided.

Van Hagen, Victor Wolfgang. *The Aztec and Maya Papermakers.* New York: J. J. Augustin, 1944.

The Aztecs of the fifteenth and sixteenth centuries relied heavily on a kind of paper made from the wild fig tree. Cortés received two books as part of the tribute sent to him at Vera Cruz by Montezuma. Van Hagen describes how the American Indians made their paper from bark and sized it with an extract from corn or manioc; papermaking was widespread in Mesoamerica before the Spanish arrived. This book is another testimony to the highly developed pre-Columbian culture of the Maya and Aztecs and to the importance of paper in their civilizations.

W. J. Barrow Research Laboratory. *Permanence/Durability of the Book.* Vol. 7, *Physical and Chemical Properties of Book Papers, 1507-1949.* Richmond, Va.: Author, 1974.
Why are sixteenth century books often in better condition than their nineteenth and twentieth century counterparts? These studies show that pulp in the sixteenth century was beaten by hand and that alum was not used for sizing; paper was therefore less acidic and more durable. The Hollander beater, which reduced the burden on laborers, and alum created a less resilient product. Papers made before 1610 have a pH of 6.8 (almost neutral). After the introduction of alum around 1610 the pH dropped to 5.4. In the eighteenth century paper quality deteriorated further in response to increased demand for the product. The pH dropped another point, from about 5.3 in 1700 to 4.5 in 1799. Such papers require deacidification if they are to survive. Nineteenth century paper is even worse, proving to be even less durable than that made earlier, as manufacturers sought lower costs and greater productivity. As of 1974, many publishers remained indifferent to this problem of rapidly deteriorating paper, though since the publication of this work many have begun using longer-lasting paper.

Weidenmuller, Ralf. *Papermaking: The Art and Craft of Handmade Paper.* Translated by John Kalish. San Diego: Thorfinn International, 1984.
A translation of the 1980 German text but with corrections and revisions supplied by the author. Chapter 1 surveys the history of papermaking from its origins to the nineteenth century. The next two chapters explain the process of making paper by hand, giving detailed instructions on the materials needed and on making equipment that one may not have, such as a forming frame and a paper press. The final chapter deals with commercial papermaking. The book is well illustrated throughout, and, as Kalish observes in his foreword, "This book can be read simply for general knowledge, . . . or it can serve as a fully detailed instruction book for hand papermaking."

Decorated Papers

Easton, Phoebe Jane. *Marbling: A History and a Bibliography.* Los Angeles: Dawson's Book Shop, 1983.

"The purpose of this book is two-fold: first, to review the history of marbling and to bring it up to date, especially as it developed in the 1970s; and second, to provide reference material for the study of marbled papers, and a guide to the identification of patterns" (preface). The historical account is arranged geographically based on the date of the introduction of marbling. Both the Orient and the West have practiced marbling, though it seems to have begun earlier in the East. The Oriental method uses more delicate colors and clear rather than treated water. Easton includes many beautiful examples of the art from around the world. The bibliography presents 640 items in many languages, including Latin, Turkish, and Japanese. A lovely and informative volume. Richard-Gabriel Rummonds wrote in *American Book Collector* 5 (January, 1984): 33, "The book has been produced with consummate care and skill. . . . This book will be the definitive work on marbling for a long time to come."

Hollander, Annette. *Decorative Papers and Fabrics*. New York: Van Nostrand Reinhold, 1971.
A good introduction for anyone wishing to make or understand the processes involved in producing decorative papers or fabrics. Hollander shows how one can create lovely artifacts without elaborate equipment or a large workshop. Instructions are clear, simple, and concise, and the book is well illustrated. She urges experimentation and spontaneity. Includes a list of American and British suppliers.

Loring, Rosamond Bowditch. *Decorated Book Papers: Being an Account of Their Designs and Fashions*. 3d ed. Cambridge, Mass.: Harvard College Library, Department of Printing and Graphic Arts, 1973.
Originally published in 1942 in an edition limited to 250 copies and containing examples of marbled paper, this third edition includes introductory essays by Walter Muir Whitehill, Dard Hunter, and Veronica Ruzicka dealing with various aspects of Loring's life and work. Loring's text offers a historical survey of marbled papers. Appendices discuss the art of marbling, the preparation of paste papers, and a list of early manufacturers of decorated papers. Contains sixteen plates. Whitehill wrote in his biographical sketch of Loring, "Although the most modest of scholars, she was unsurpassed in her field, and her books . . . are unique sources in regard to the craft that she practiced with such skill."

Nevins, Iris. *Traditional Marbling*. Sussex, N.J.: Author, 1986.
This brief discussion is aimed at the novice. Nevins focuses on the

method of marbling that uses seaweed or carrageenan (watercolor). She lists the necessary tools and discusses setting up a workshop, preparing the paper, carrageenan size and color, making designs, and marbling the sheet. She illustrates and explains fourteen traditional patterns. With a list of British and American suppliers.

Wolfe, Richard J. *Marbled Paper: Its History, Techniques, and Patterns.* Philadelphia: University of Pennsylvania Press, 1989.
A well-illustrated history of the manufacture and use of marbled papers in the West, with over 350 color illustrations and another eighty in black and white. According to Wolfe, Europe encountered marbling in the Islamic Near East in the sixteenth century. In 1646, Athanasius Kircher published the first explanation of the method of marbling. The art declined in the early 1800s with the introduction of mechanical methods of producing similar effects, but Josef Halfer of Budapest did much to revive hand-marbling late in the century. Douglas and Sidney Cockerell also contributed to this effort. After his historical survey, Wolfe provides a detailed explanation of marbling techniques. Bernard Middleton described *Marbled Paper* as "a scholarly and very readable volume which will be the standard work for many years. . . , a major study which will be essential reading for all who have an interest in this compelling and difficult craft" (*The Library* 13, 1991: 81-82).

Geographical Studies

Great Britain

Coleman, D. C. *The British Paper Industry, 1495-1860: A Study in Industrial Growth.* Oxford, England: Clarendon Press, 1958.
According to Coleman, "The present book is essentially not about paper or papermaking but about the paper industry. Its viewpoint is that of economics. It attempts to show the major economic and technical problems with which producers were periodically confronted and the way in which the answers found to these problems shaped the growth and organization of the industry" (preface). The study begins with the first definite date for a paper mill in England, though it may have begun operation several years earlier. In 1860 Parliament repealed the paper excise, and new raw materials began to replace rags in the manufacture of the product. Even in the early 1700s, England imported substantial quantities of paper from the Continent, but the industry had grown significantly during the sixteenth and seventeenth centuries; in the next

hundred years, production quadrupled, and the nineteenth century saw the impact of the Industrial Revolution with the appearance of the Fourdrinier machine. Among the consequences of mechanization was the increase in size and decrease in number of papermaking mills. Coleman looks not only at the organization and finances of the mills but also at working conditions and efforts of laborers to create unions. Arthur J. Taylor calls Coleman's work "an important contribution to industrial history" (*Victorian Studies* 2, 1959: 278).

Hills, Richard L. *Papermaking in Britain, 1488-1988: A Short History.* London: Athlone Press, 1988.
Though written for the general reader, Hills's work presents much original research and many statistics. Hills offers lucid explanations of technical processes and is especially informative on John Tate, England's first known papermaker. The book is less successful in providing historical context for developments in the paper industry, but Hills notes how outside influences could affect manufacturers of the product. The penny post, for example, created greater demand for writing paper. New presses in the nineteenth century led to lower printing costs, and paper consumption rose. This increase in turn led to a search for new raw materials to supplement the inadequate supply of rags. Includes helpful illustrations, a glossary, and bibliographic notes.

Jenkins, Rhys. *Papermaking in England, 1495-1788.* London: Association of Assistant Librarians, 1958.
This brief account first appeared in *The Library Association Record* in 1900-1902. It offers an excellent overview of papermaking in England from the industry's beginnings through the end of the eighteenth century, and is especially sound on technical matters. Includes a section on patented inventions. Still useful despite its age.

Shorter, Alfred Henry. *Paper Making in the British Isles: An Historical and Geographical Study.* Newton Abbot, England: David & Charles, 1971.
In the prefatory notes to this book left unfinished at the time of Shorter's death, the author wrote, "In this volume I have tried to indicate the historical interest of an ancient craft and its modern descendants and representatives; to trace the evolution and development of paper making; and to convey a geographical picture of the diversity and wide distribution, both past and present, of the paper industry in the British Isles." Most of the book concentrates on England, beginning with Sele Mill at the end of the fifteenth century.

Shorter devotes six chapters to England, one chapter each to paper-making in Wales, Scotland, and Ireland (including the Isle of Man and the Channel Islands). Especially good on factors that contributed to the success of certain paper mills and that caused the geographical distribution that prevailed in the industry. For example, the cotton mills of Lancashire provided raw materials, and the availability of water in the area, together with coal and other necessary materials as well as good transportation, stimulated the growth of the industry there in the nineteenth century. Some mills failed even as the demand for paper rose, and Shorter explores the reasons for their lack of success. With an appendix on watermarks and also a bibliography.

_____. *Paper Mills and Paper Makers in England, 1495-1800.* Hilversum, Netherlands: Paper Publications Society, 1957.
Shorter looks at the first three centuries of papermaking in England to identify the mills and determine why they appeared where and when they did. These factors include water supply, proximity to the London market, local demand, and a supply of labor and raw materials. Shorter is less concerned with technical and economic aspects of the subject. The number of mills grew slowly but steadily in the seventeenth century, though French paper remained much in demand. In the eighteenth century, the number of mills increased fourfold, and England became a paper exporter. Technology began to intrude, as steam power was introduced, but most paper was still being produced as it had been in the fifteenth century, by hand in small quantities. Shorter provides maps showing the location of paper mills, a list of mills functioning in England and Wales before 1800, watermarks, and examples of various types of mills, such as those producing white paper and those with more than one vat—most mills as late as 1800 had only one or two.

Thomson, Alistair G. *The Paper Industry in Scotland, 1590-1861.* Edinburgh: Scottish Academic Press, 1974.
This nicely illustrated account traces the history of papermaking in Scotland from its inception late in the sixteenth century to its mechanization in the Victorian era. Thomson is especially helpful in discussing the economic and technical aspects of papermaking. He has examined a wealth of documentary evidence in insurance company files and the Excise Office—the tax on paper had its archival value—and discusses such matters as government policy, which favored the industry, sources of capital, profits, and methods of production. D. C. Coleman described this as "a useful and careful study" (*English Historical Review* 91, 1976: 422).

Japan

Barrett, Timothy. *Japanese Papermaking: Traditions, Tools, and Techniques*. New York: Weatherhill, 1983.
Like Dard Hunter, whose works include *A Papermaking Pilgrimage to Japan, Korea and China* (New York: Pynson Printers, 1936), Barrett went to Japan to learn about Oriental papermaking. In Part 1 he discusses traditional Japanese papermaking and compares it to Western techniques. Part 2 explains in detail how to produce Japanese paper. Barrett offers two approaches. The first, more traditional method yields about 150 sheets in four days. A simpler method will yield 24-49 sheets in two days. Barrett lists suppliers and explains how one can make tools. With ninety-one black-and-white photographs and seventy-five line drawings. Sukey Hughes wrote in *Fine Print* 10 (1984): 53, "*Japanese Papermaking* is papermaking at its most sophisticated, pure, and scientific. It is certainly a boon to present and future papermakers and paper historians as well."

_____. *Nagashizuki: The Japanese Craft of Hand Papermaking*. North Hills, Pa.: Bird and Bull Press, 1979.
Explores the techniques of this craft. Barrett begins with two chapters on producing and processing the fibers. The third chapter explains the actual making of the paper, and the volume concludes with an examination of the tools and equipment and of the past and probable future of handmade paper in Japan. An admirer of the Japanese approach to papermaking, Barrett writes that Japanese paper "is not made but rather becomes. The craftsman only helps the process along. . . . The finished paper is too fine, too possessed of its own glow to be an entirely human product." Includes fourteen paper samples, some of them made by Barrett in Japan, others by noted native artists. Richard Flavin contributed twenty-four illustrations. An expensive volume printed on handmade paper but a useful study.

Goto, Seikichiro, and Iwao Matsuhara, trans. *Japanese Paper and Paper-Making*. 2 vols. Tokyo: Bijutsu Shuppan-sha, 1958-1960.
Goto, a printmaker and printer, became interested in the art of papermaking and has published some excellent works on the subject, such as *Japanese Hand-Made Paper* (Tokyo: Bijutsu Shuppan-sha, 1954), but this is his magnum opus. Volume 1 deals with Northeastern Japan, Volume 2 with the western part of the country. In his introduction Kiyohide Narita writes that Goto visited "nearly all the villages or towns throughout the country where Japanese paper is produced,

recording the characteristic techniques of the art with his talented brush and pen, and collecting genuine specimens of Japanese paper." Goto explains the techniques of papermaking through his illustrations and annotations of the prints he made. The text is in English and Japanese, with 170 black-and-white woodcuts and some in color, together with fifty-nine paper specimens. A beautiful and rare set.

Hughes, Sukey. *Washi: The World of Japanese Paper*. Tokyo: Kodansha, 1978.
Washi is the Japanese word for handmade paper. Hughes observes that paper permeates all aspects of Japanese culture, sacred and secular. Invented in China, paper came to Japan with Buddhism in the seventh century and quickly gained popularity. Hughes discusses the history of Japanese paper, its manufacture, and its many uses. She concludes that despite Japan's focus on industrialization, handmade paper will remain an important part of the culture. This excellent account includes a glossary, bibliography, 236 illustrations, and 102 paper specimens.

Jugaku, Bunsho. *Paper-Making by Hand in Japan*. Tokyo: Meiji-Shobo, 1959.
Written by the dean of historians of Japanese papermaking, this book begins with a historical survey of paper in Japan; here he distinguishes among the different types. The second chapter, also historical, deals with the spread of Japanese paper to the West, beginning with the coming of the Jesuits (who in turn brought the Western printing press to Japan). Chapters 3 and 4 discuss the manufacture of handmade Japanese paper, and the book concludes with bibliographical notes. With many photographs and twenty-four sample sheets.

Narita, Kiyofusa. *Japanese Paper Making*. Tokyo: Hakuseido Press, 1954.
This attractive volume provides a brief history of Japanese handmade paper from its introduction into the country during the reign of Empress Suiku (563-628). During the Samurai period (1192-1603) paper was highly esteemed as a gift because little was available, and the gift implied that the recipient was cultured. The early twentieth century witnessed a decline in handmade papermaking as mechanization increased, but handmade paper has enjoyed a revival. Narita also explains the techniques of papermaking in Japan.

Perkins, P. D. *The Paper Industry and Printing in Japan*. New York: Japan Reference Library, 1940.

Japan's first papermaking factory was opened in 1872. Between 1878 and 1894 wood pulp replaced rags as the basis for machine-made paper. Perkins traces the varying fortunes of the industry, and he discusses the much older method of making paper by hand, in which the Japanese are unsurpassed; the Versailles Treaty of 1919 was written on tori-no-ko paper. Perkins also surveys printing in Japan from its origins to the introduction of the steam-driven press in 1884.

Seki, Yoshishiro. *Kokin Toashihu*. 2 vols. Tokyo: s.n., 1957.
A beautifully produced study of handmade Japanese papers, filled with examples of the art. The first volume discusses Japanese papermaking and includes some specimens. Volume 2 concludes the text and presents more examples of old and new papers. The text is in Japanese.

Tindale, Thomas Keith, and Harriet Ramsay Tindale. *The Handmade Papers of Japan*. 4 vols. Rutland, Ver.: Tuttle, 1952.
Issued in a limited edition of 150 sets, this is a fine study of the subject and a magnificent production. The first volume provides a complete history and discussion of Japanese papermaking. It includes thirty-two full-page photographs of a papermaking village and a hand-colored facsimile, with English translation, of the oldest Japanese illustrated text on papermaking. Volume 2 contains 187 mounted specimens from the paper collection of Yoshikumi Seki, dating as far back as the eighth century; all are described in detail. Volume 3 adds another 139 papers with description, and Volume 4 reproduces twenty watermarks. An envelope includes five specimens of fibers used in Japanese papermaking.

United States

Hunter, Dard. *Papermaking by Hand in America*. Chillicothe, Ohio: Mountain House Press, 1950.
Hunter's magnum opus, designed and printed by Hunter at his private press. Hunter's son made the type for this beautiful oversized volume, appropriately printed on handmade paper. Hunter describes the first paper mill in each of seventeen states from 1690 to 1811, and includes 123 facsimiles of documents and watermarks as well as forty-two reproductions of labels used by early papermakers. A well-written account, exquisitely produced.

_____. *Papermaking in Pioneer America*. Philadelphia: University of Pennsylvania Press, 1952.

In the first chapter, Hunter traces the history of paper from its invention in 105 A.D. to its earliest manufacture in the British colonies of North America in 1690. Hunter then turns to the technology of papermaking, and he carries his account to 1817, when the first papermaking machine was introduced into the United States. Hunter discusses the first paper mill in the eighteen states where paper was made in the colonies and early republic. Hunter also devotes a chapter to Nathan Sellers, whose work in paper was so important that the Continental Congress exempted him from military service. With a checklist of American papers between 1690 and 1817.

Smith, David C. *History of Papermaking in the United States (1691-1969)*. New York: Lockwood, 1970.
The story of papermaking in America differs little from that in other Western countries, though the industry began late here. Smith devotes only about thirty pages of his thick book (nearly 700 pages) to the eighteenth century. He focuses on the machine age, which began with the development of the Fourdrinier machine. The first was produced at Frogmore, England, in 1814. After the Civil War the industry grew rapidly, and it expanded again in the period after World War II, when mergers and consolidations occurred. The text, statistics, and illustrations provide a sound and detailed economic history. Smith has examined many archives as well as secondary sources in writing this well-informed account.

Weeks, Lyman Horace. *A History of Paper-Manufacturing in the United States, 1690-1916*. New York: Lockwood Trade Journal Co., 1916.
Weeks's work was a standard before David C. Smith's book appeared. In one compact narrative, Weeks presents all the facts relating to the industry in America. His focus is on the historical development of paper manufacturing from its beginnings in 1690 in Pennsylvania to the early twentieth century. Still useful for the period it covers.

Chapter 4
INK

Bibliography

Gamble, William Burt. *Chemistry and Manufacture of Writing and Printing Ink: A List of References in the New York Public Library.* New York: New York Public Library, 1926.
An alphabetic listing by author of 728 publications dealing with ink. Includes all languages. For each entry, Gamble provides full bibliographic information, but annotations are limited. Gamble also lists, by country and then alphabetically by inventor, patents held around the world for different kinds of ink. H. M. Lydenberg wrote in the introduction, "Specialist and outsider, connoisseur and casual inquirer, will rejoice that this key to the literature of ink has been so admirably wrought and so conveniently put into his hand." Despite its age, still a valuable resource for the technician and the student of the book.

General Studies

Apps, E. A. *Printing Ink Technology.* London: Leonard Hill, 1958. Reprint. *Ink Technology for Printers and Students.* 2 vols. New York: Chemical Publishing, 1964.
In his preface Apps writes, "It is hoped that this book will help to provide ink technologists with much essential information which can be supplemented by further reading and by day to day experience." This preface also includes a short bibliographic essay. The book's thirty-two chapters make up two parts. The first examines raw materials, while the second considers printing inks and their production. To help ink manufacturers in their task, Apps includes discussions of the various processes, such as lithography or intaglio, that use ink, as well as more specific issues relating to ink, such as drying agents. A useful text and reference.

Bloy, Colin H. *A History of Printing Ink, Balls and Rollers, 1440-1850.* London: Wynkyn De Worde Society, 1967.
Gutenberg inherited the knowledge of oil-based pigments, including Frankfurt black, but he adapted these to his needs. Fust and Schöffer

used a fine red and a less impressive blue in their Mainz Psalter. Bloy presents various early formulas, drawn from contemporary sources, though not until William Savage's *On Printing Ink* (London, 1832) was an entire volume devoted to the subject. Many printers kept their formulas secret. In the early nineteenth century, for example, Charles Whittingham divulged his formulas only to his nephew. Bloy includes a glossary of pigments and varnish components available before 1850 and offers a three-page bibliography. In his foreword to the book, F. W. Stoyle observed that Bloy's is the first to present this historical information "in systematic form." He praises the text as "a fascinating detective story" probing a neglected area of bibliographic study.

Burns, R. *Printing Inks*. 2d ed. London: Sir Isaac Pitman & Sons, 1958.
Intended primarily for the student apprentice, this short book seeks to provide an overview of "the processes involved in manufacturing, blending and application of all types of ink." Chapter 1 offers an introduction and discusses various principles. The text explains that printing inks contain pigments to provide color and stiffness, varnishes to carry the color and aid in drying, and driers and other additives that improve an ink's properties. Each component receives some discussion, as does testing for such qualities as opacity, finish, and strength. Chapter 2 deals with color matching, and Chapter 3 with inks for newsprint, which must dry quickly. Inks for letterpress, lithography, photogravure, and other processes are the subjects of later chapters, and Burns devotes Chapter 7 to additives that will improve the product for a particular purpose.

Carvalho, David N. *Forty Centuries of Ink, or a Chronological Narrative Concerning Ink and Its Backgrounds*. New York: Banks Law Publishing, 1904.
Even the ancients had inks of various colors and used natural substances, such as secretions of shellfish or soot, to provide pigment. In this history, Carvalho reproduces medieval formulas and more recent ones. He discusses modern methods of manufacture (a section useful to the historian, given the age of the book) and court cases that hinged on an analysis of ink to determine a document's authenticity. Later chapters examine writing surfaces and implements. A readable discourse on a technical subject.

Ellis, Carleton. *Printing Inks: Their Chemistry and Technology*. New York: Reinhold, 1940.
In his preface Ellis writes, "The present book attempts . . . to fill the

needs of chemists who are groping for information on printing inks and are unable to find the subject discussed in any comprehensive treatise dealing with it in a modern way." In his introduction, Ellis surveys the three basic modes of printing—relief, intaglio, and planographic. The second chapter provides a history of writing and printing ink. Early printers used a mixture of boiled linseed oil and lampblack. Later slightly more elaborate formulas were developed. The book then addresses the composition of twentieth century inks for various uses, and a final chapter discusses paper for printing. Ellis includes a glossary of terms used among manufacturers of ink. The technical nature of the discussion will limit the audience of the work to those with a serious interest in the subject (and some background in chemistry), but the first two chapters are accessible to all, and others may find it a useful reference for specific topics such as pigments.

Fischer, Earl Knudt. *Printing Ink*. Charlottesville: Bibliographical Society of the University of Virginia, 1947.
This short address provides much information. Fischer first discusses the early formulas of ink, which used lampblack and oil. Early printers made their own inks, and they could produce red, blue, yellow, and green, as well as black. Modern inks still use a vehicle and pigment, and boiled linseed oil remains popular for the former. Pigments and colors have expanded, and different inks are now available for different purposes.

Leach, R. H., et al., eds. *Printing Ink Manual*. 4th ed. London: Van Nostrand Reinhold, 1988.
An authoritative work on the nature of ink, the raw materials used, and methods of production, together with an analysis of the inks needed for different printing processes like letterpress, lithography, and screening. Chapter 14 discusses testing and analysis, and the book concludes with a survey of health, safety, and environmental issues involved in the manufacture of ink. Whether one is a manufacturer or a curious general reader, this work will prove useful and accessible.

Mitchell, Charles Ainsworth. *Inks: Their Composition and Manufacture*. 4th ed. London: C. Griffin, 1937.
The volume begins with an historical survey of ink, noting the transition from a carbon-based product to one using galls and iron in the Middle Ages, and, later, the introduction of aniline dyes and lignone sulphonates. The rest of this nicely illustrated work presents the formulas for a wide range of inks. Those interested in making ink at home

will find some useful recipes. A good reference for chemists, and informative for those curious about the manufacture of the product or the nature of ink's components.

Wiborg, Frank Bestow. *Printing Ink: A History, with a Treatise on Modern Methods of Manufacture and Use.* New York: Harper & Brothers, 1926. Although the Chinese probably did not invent ink, Wiborg's history begins with them because for centuries theirs was a product superior to anything known farther west, and India ink (a misnomer for Chinese ink, Wiborg notes) remains a staple among artists. The account moves generally westward (though Chapter 3 deals with Japan) to central Asia, India, the Levant, and Europe. In Chapter 8, Wiborg turns to technical aspects of modern ink, beginning with a survey of printing methods and the kinds of ink necessary for them. These chapters cover such matters as chemical properties of ink, pigments, and the physical properties of ink needed for different types of printing. With a substantial bibliography and a brief account of the origins of his own ink-making firm.

Chapter 5
THE ALPHABET

Bibliographies

Boyle, Leonard E. *Medieval Latin Paleography: A Bibliographic Intro-duction.* Toronto: University of Toronto Press, 1984.
Intended as "a working bibliography for beginners," but useful for anyone seeking information about the medieval manuscript. Divided into seven sections. "Scholarly Setting" lists reference works and facsimiles. "Cultural Setting" treats writing in general and non-Latin alphabets that influenced Latin script (for example, Greek), as well as studies of the Latin alphabet. "Institutional Setting" looks at the preservation of the medieval legacy. "Physical Setting" considers codicology (materials and instruments of writing and the creation of the book). "Human Setting" deals with the scribes. Transmission of texts appears under "Textual Setting," and "Research Setting" suggests related reference works that can aid paleographers. Each of the 2,207 entries contains full bibliographic information and brief annotations. Includes foreign- language material.

Davis, Jinnie Y., and John V. Richardson. *Calligraphy: A Sourcebook.* Littleton, Colo.: Libraries Unlimited, 1982.
A selective annotated bibliography arranged by script (Latin, Arabic, Chinese, etc.), with some 800 citations of both current and historically significant items. Appendices list fifty-eight films and forty-four major calligraphic societies in America and Europe, though the bibliography does not limit itself to Western scripts. All listings are English-language. The *Journal of Academic Librarianship* 8 (1982): 252 wrote that the book "fills a significant bibliographic void."

Marzoli, Carla C. *Calligraphy, 1535-1885: A Collection of Seventy-two Writing Books and Specimens from the Italian, French, Low Countries and Spanish Schools, Catalogued and Described with Upwards of Two Hundred and Ten Illustrations and an Introduction by Stanley Morison.* Milan: La Bibliofila, 1962.
The bookseller Carla C. Marzoli was already interested in typography when a collection of writing books became available. Marzoli acquired them, and they constitute the majority of the works catalogued here.

In his introduction Morison notes that the collection allows one to trace the decline of the Gothic in favor of the humanistic Italian hand. Morison also discusses some important early bibliographies and studies of the subject. Marzoli's catalog begins with Ugo da Carpi's 1535 *Thesauro de scrittori*, an early writing manual (though not the first, nor even the first edition of this title, which appeared in 1525). It is based on Carpi's work for Ludovico degli Arrighi's *La operina*, c. 1522 (see next entry for a discussion of this date). The bibliography is arranged chronologically by country, beginning with Italy, not only because of the work's origin but also because the first writing manuals appeared there. Includes biographical sketches of the authors and reproductions of various scripts.

Morison, Stanley. *Early Italian Writing Books: Renaissance to Baroque.* Edited by Nicolas Barker. Boston: David R. Godine, 1990.

The opening chapter surveys the teaching of writing from classical Rome to the end of the Middle Ages. Morison then traces the rise of the humanistic hand, promoted by Coluccio Salutati, Niccolò de' Niccoli, and Poggio Bracciolini in the fourteenth and fifteenth centuries. These men drew on late Carolingian script, which they believed was classical. These humanists wrote both italic and roman hands. Morison regards Sigismondo Fanti's *Theorica et pratica . . . de modo scribendi* as the first printed writing manual. From here Morison explores the various publications aimed at teaching penmanship. Central to the development of cursive was Gianfrancesco Cresci, who combined speed with the beautiful lettering of his predecessors and so produced the true chancery script. Barker's epilogue to the first part of the book briefly continues Morison's story to 1700. Part 2 seeks to sort out the chronology of the various Italian writing manuals published between 1524 and 1539. Morison questions the 1522 date on the title page of Ludovico degli Arrighi's *La operina*, recommending a 1524 date instead. He also argues for assigning Arrighi's *Il modo* to some time after February 14, 1526. Morison's careful analysis revises older views about the publication dates of some other items as well, and examines influences of one work on another. Well-printed and well-illustrated.

Manuals

Biegeleisen, Jacob Israel. *The ABC of Lettering.* 4th ed. New York: Harper & Row, 1971.

In his preface Biegeleisen writes, "*The ABC of Lettering* is designed both as an instructional text for students and as a workbook for professionals. It will serve as a handy reference manual for all levels of experience, as it deals with the entire range of lettering techniques, from simple single-stroke free-hand brush lettering to the more finished techniques suitable for reproduction." Biegeleisen lists equipment necessary to the would-be graphic artist, explains basic terminology such as "Gothic," "Roman," "Italic," and "Text," and suggests exercises for the beginner. He then dissects each letter. The alphabets he presents begin with simple characters and move on to more complicated variations. For each alphabet he provides brief descriptions of peculiarities and suggests where these letters will be most effective—for example, on posters, as chapter headings, or in advertisements. Concludes with sample typefaces for comparison.

Child, Heather, ed. *The Calligrapher's Handbook*. 2d ed. New York: Taplinger, 1986.
In her introduction Child writes, "*The Calligrapher's Handbook* is unique in being a collection of articles written by distinguished craftsmen with the aim of making their own methods, experience and workshop practice available to students of calligraphy. . . . While *The Calligrapher's Handbook* is intended to be of practical use to serious students of calligraphy, lettering artists, designers and teachers, amateurs and all enthusiasts of fine writing and lettering should derive both information and pleasure from its contents." This nicely illustrated volume, with its eighteen articles by members of the Society of Scribes and Illuminators, examines writing implements, writing surfaces, calligraphy, illumination, even the binding of manuscripts. Includes a selective bibliography. An updated and expanded version of the 1956 edition prepared by C. M. Lamb. Betsy Tadman regarded the book as "invaluable for anyone engaged in teaching or learning the various techniques" involved in calligraphy and illumination (*Times Educational Supplement*, December 27, 1985, p. 25).

Drogin, Marc. *Medieval Calligraphy: Its History and Technique*. Montclair, N.J.: Abner Schram, 1980.
A calligrapher and illuminator himself, Drogin assembles twelve medieval scripts from the mid-600s to the end of the fifteenth century and explains their development. The focus is on pre-Carolingian forms. Drogin also shows how the modern calligrapher can reproduce these letters. Includes numerous examples drawn from actual manuscripts. With a list of suppliers of calligraphic materials and of facsimiles of medieval manuscripts. More useful for the calligrapher than the paleographer. Richard Rouse observed that book's "merit lies in the preci-

sion with which it focuses our attention on details" (*Library Quarterly* 52, 1982, 79).

Greer, Alan, and Rita Greer. *An Introduction to Lettering*. New York: Viking, 1972.

A textbook for the fledgling graphic artist. The authors first give an overview of the history of the Latin alphabet. They then examine the anatomy of the letter and define basic terms such as "open-face" (letters drawn in outline; not a sandwich) and "swash" (italic letters with flourishes). The book next discusses the equipment necessary for the graphic artist and takes the reader through the processes involved from practice strokes to layout design. Heavily illustrated. Useful for a course or for self-teaching.

Hewitt, Grailey. *Lettering, for Students and Craftsmen*. London: Seeley, Service, 1930.

Hewitt begins with a historical survey of Latin script. He then turns to twentieth-century adaptations and recreations of classical and medieval forms. His audience is primarily the graphic artist, but his analysis, which often draws on earlier writing manuals (such as the *Book of Giovan Battista Palatino* of Venice, 1588), can aid the paleographer as well. Later chapters deal with arrangement of letters on a page and pages in a book, legibility, and materials necessary for calligraphy. Hewitt concludes with a plea for the handmade book: "It will be preferable for its individuality, the personal expression of its creator. It will be more humanly interesting in that it will have eternal variety of nature."

Johnston, Edward. *Writing and Illuminating and Lettering*. 2d ed., rev. New York: Macmillan, 1906.

For sparking a revival of interest in fine handwriting, Johnston has been regarded as the father of twentieth-century calligraphy. His was the first modern instruction manual, describing old techniques and demonstrating their viability; this work remains an important text. Johnston stresses "legibility, beauty, and character," making good letters and arranging them well. He takes the student through the steps necessary to develop a good formal hand, to create a book, to decorate letters, and to illuminate a page. Anyone interested in the handmade book will learn here how classical and medieval scribes created their manuscripts, and the reader will discover how to imitate these practices.

Sassoon, Rosemary. *The Practical Guide to Calligraphy*. New York: Thames and Hudson, 1982.

Sassoon writes that "the aim of this book [is] to give the beginner . . . a grounding in the basic skills of pen and brush lettering and to suggest ways in which these can be developed and used." The first part of the manual teaches the elements of Edward Johnston's "Foundation Hand," based on traditional English scribal practice, though Sassoon also illustrates several variations, and she explores layout as well as individual letters and words. She offers advice for those seeking to reproduce their calligraphy and demonstrates practical uses of the art. Includes a number of historical examples of both script and type.

Studies

Alexander, J. J. G. *The Decorated Letter*. New York: George Braziller, 1978.
Covers the period 400-c.1450. Alexander provides a lengthy introduction, followed by forty illustrative color plates. The first is from the Lindisfarne Gospels (c. 700), the last from Jean Mielot's French translation of the *Speculum Humanae Salvationis*. The manuscript dates from the mid-fifteenth century. Also includes 30 black-and-white illustrations. Alexander observes that decoration arose when literature began to be read rather than just heard and when artists/scribes attained a degree of freedom in creating manuscripts. Hence, the great age of the decorated letter was between 700 and 1300. Once a large book trade emerged, the art tended to become mechanical. *Choice* 16 (1979): 518 recommended this as "a very useful introduction to the subject." David Preiss commented that the book is "lovely to look at and interesting to read" (*American Artist* 42, December, 1978, 12).

Andersch, Martin. *Symbols, Signs, Letters: About Handwriting, Experimenting with Alphabets, and the Interpretation of Texts*. Translated by Ingrid Li. New York: Design Press, 1989.
Andersch, a teacher of penmanship and calligraphy in Germany, argues for more attention to these subjects, and he demonstrates his own instructional methodology. The book is filled with examples of his students' work, as well as numerous historical reproductions. According to Andersch, a knowledge of calligraphy is essential if one is to understand a handwritten text, since writing embodies "pathos [and] gestures" quite as much as speaking. A beautiful book.

Anderson, Donald M. *The Art of Written Forms: The Theory and Practice of Calligraphy*. New York: Holt, Rinehart and Winston, 1969.

Anderson observes in his preface, "It has been my purpose in writing this book to enlarge our generally diminished knowledge of [the alphabet] and to present for professional graphic artists, students, and interested general readers a comprehensive survey of the history, theory, materials and techniques of calligraphy, typography, and constructed letters." Part 1 therefore discusses early writing systems and concludes with Latin inscriptions and cursive letters. Part 2 looks at writing in the medieval West, Part 3 at the scripts and scribes of the Renaissance through the eighteenth century. Part 4 deals with typography, Part 5 with twentieth century lettering. Practical instruction for the calligrapher appears in Part 6, and Part 7 examines non-Latin scripts. With a helpful bibliography. Oversized and richly illustrated.

Atkins, Kathryn A. *Masters of the Italic Letter: Twenty-two Exemplars from the Sixteenth Century.* Boston: David R. Godine, 1988.
In 1514 in Venice Sigismondo Fanti published his *Theoretica et pratica . . . de modo scribendi. No such work had appeared in the fifteenth century in part because printed writing manuals required the skill of a master engraver. Fanti's book included no examples, but Ludovico degli Arrighi's Il modo de temperare le penne* (1523) offered samples of scripts. Italian script spread throughout Europe, and writing manuals followed, including some in manuscript to capture the richness of the letters that engraving somewhat obscured. For each of the writing masters, Atkins provides the title page of their work, sample pages of instruction, and also examples of their handwriting, as well as extended examples of letters that show how these penmen formed both lower- and uppercase letters. Useful for calligraphers, for students of the period, and for collectors of writing manuals. In his foreword to this work, James M. Wells wrote, "Ms. Atkins has provided students of the sixteenth-century italic hand with a highly useful and inspiring tool."

Barbour, Ruth. *Greek Literary Hands* A.D. *400-1600.* Oxford, England: Clarendon Press, 1981. A sequel to C. H. Roberts' *Greek Literary Hands 350 B.C.-A.D. 400* (Oxford, 1955).
Whereas the Latin alphabet evolved into diverse national hands in the Middle Ages because of the fragmentation of the Western Roman Empire, Greek, preserved by the unified Byzantine Empire, remained more uniform. Yet changes did occur. Before the ninth century, uncial was used for biblical and literary texts. In the ninth century, this script became the province of elaborate texts, and minuscule assumed a more prominent role. Despite the large degree of uniformity, Barbour finds

some regional and much individual variation. The majority of the book is devoted to the 110 plates, with Barbour's annotations. The earliest example comes from the early sixth century Vienna Dioscorides, the latest from a 1610 copy of Chrysostom. Each text is reproduced in its original size. Jean Irigoin's review in the *Journal of Hellenic Studies* 103 (1983): 230 concludes that Barbour's book renders a great service to students seeking an introduction to Greek paleography and at the same time offers specialists material for reflection.

Bischoff, Bernhard. *Latin Paleography, Antiquity and the Middle Ages.* Translated by Daibhi O'Croinin and David Ganz. Cambridge, England: Cambridge University Press, 1990.

A thorough discussion of the development of Latin script. Provides a detailed account of the history of the book from antiquity through the Middle Ages and also discusses illumination of manuscripts. Bischoff divides the discussion into three sections. In the first, he treats writing materials and tools, organization of the book, and writing itself. The second part traces the history of Latin script, and the third looks at the cultural aspects of the manuscript. Praising the book in *History: Reviews of New Books* 19 (1991): 131, John Rexine wrote, "*Latin Paleography* is an indispensable resource for every student of Roman antiquity and medieval history and for every librarian, and even for the art historian. For years to come, its authoritativeness and its special value as a guide to the history of writing up to 1500 will remain unchallenged." John J. Contreni was equally enthusiastic in his review in the *Times Literary Supplement* for August 30, 1991 (p. 24): "Every page is punctuated with insights distilled from a lifetime's work, insights supported by over 600 references to manuscripts and to thousands of scholarly articles and books reported in over 1,400 footnotes." A classic.

Blunt, Wilfrid. *Sweet Roman Hand: Five Hundred Years of Italic Cursive Script.* 2d ed. London: James Barrie, 1952.

Taking his title from Shakespeare's *Twelfth Night*, Blunt traces the evolution of italic cursive from the square capitals of classical Rome to the fifteenth century rise of the humanistic hand, probably developed by Niccolò de' Niccoli (1363-1437) and promoted by Popes Eugenius IV and Sextus IV. Blunt concentrates on British use of the italic and presents examples from both writers and writing masters. He credits Robert Bridges and Bridges' wife with reviving handwriting, and Blunt anticipated a renaissance in penmanship that would draw on sixteenth century Italian models for its inspiration.

Brown, Michelle P. *A Guide to Western Historical Scripts from Antiquity to 1600*. Toronto: University of Toronto Press, 1990.

Brown writes in her introduction, "The aim of this work is to provide an aid for a wide variety of readers who wish to trace the evolution of scripts in the West from the world of Antiquity to the early modern period and who desire to read these scripts and to discover more about how they were formed." Covers the Latin alphabet from square capitals in the first century A.D. to the humanistic cursive. For each hand Brown provides a brief introduction, followed by annotated plates. With a short but well-rounded bibliography. *The Book Collector* 39 (1990): 408 regarded this as "a solid and informative paleological study."

Catich, Edward M. *The Origin of the Roman Serif*. Davenport, Iowa: Catfish Press, 1968.

Disagrees with earlier assessments about the source of the serif. Catich argues that the "ordinator," who wrote with a square-cut reed pen, not the chiseler who carved the square capitals, created the serif. Catich attributes the serif to the Romans and says that it moved from the point towards the letter block. The book examines the tools and techniques required to produce the kind of inscription that appears on the Trajan column. Once a sign painter himself, Catich believes that the letters were painted on the stone, chiseled, and then painted again to emphasize light and shadow. Catich's views remain controversial, but the book offers useful information on the tools, techniques, and alphabets of classical Rome.

Chang, Leon Long-Yien, and Peter Miller. *Four Thousand Years of Chinese Calligraphy*. Chicago: University of Chicago Press, 1990.

The volume's opening chapter discusses the long tradition of calligraphy in China. The Emperor Wu (502-549) of the Liang Dynasty collected old examples of calligraphy; even earlier, Ts'ai Yung of the Later Han Dynasty wrote about the theory of the art. The authors also explain the five types of Chinese calligraphy: the formal Chuan, Li, and K'ai, and the Ts'ao and Hsing, which are faster and used for more personal communication. Chapter 2 deals with the "Four Treasures": brush, paper (or silk), ink, and inkstone, the basic tools of the calligrapher. It also briefly treats technique. The rest of the book deals with the history of Chinese calligraphy in reverse chronological order from the 1980s to the Shang-Yin Dynasty, which began in 1766 B.C. The work also highlights outstanding practitioners of the art. The brief text for each chapter complements the extensive illustrative examples. The authors note that while styles change, past practice always remains influential. A lovely and informative book.

Clodd, Edward. *The Story of the Alphabet*. Rev. ed. New York: Appleton-Century, 1938.
Looks at the origins of the Latin alphabet and at other early versions of written communication. Clodd argues that writing proceeds through four stages. At its most primitive it is symbolic, acting as a mnemonic. Then it moves to the pictorial stage, thence to the ideographic, and finally to the phonetic, where a sign represents an entire word, a syllable, or a particular sound. After presenting this theoretical framework, Clodd looks at early forms of writing, beginning with the Indians of the Americas. Then he turns to China and the Near East, discussing cuneiform, hieroglyphics, and Cretan scripts. Clodd is not convinced that the Phoenicians (i.e., Semites) derived their alphabet from the Egyptians, and he hesitates to accept Herodotus' view that the Greeks got their alphabet from the Phoenicians. Clodd suggests that the Greek alphabet may have arisen independently. Clodd's skepticism about the Semitic debt to the Egyptians is still shared by many; no one agrees with his ideas about the independent origin of the Greek alphabet. The text is enriched with some ninety figures and tables. As George H. McKnight wrote in the foreword to the 1938 edition, the "book remains . . . a most convenient compendium of authentic information."

Cohen, Marcel. *La Grande Invention de l' écriture et son évolution*. 3 vols. Paris: Imprimerie Nationale, 1958.
A work in French for the advanced student. Volume 1 provides the text, Volume 2 an annotated bibliography, and Volume 3 the 95 plates showing different forms of writing. Cohen first discusses nonwritten forms of communication, noting that writing is a product of advanced civilizations. Chapters 2-7 look at nonalphabetic graphic systems, including those used by American Indians, Eskimos, Siberians, Africans, residents of Oceania, the Chinese, Egyptians, and inhabitants of Mesopotamia and the eastern Mediterranean. Then Cohen examines alphabetic systems, especially those of the Greeks and Romans. He concludes with a glance at other graphic and visual symbols, such as musical and choreographic notation, and technical innovations like television images and phonodisks. Comprehensive and learned.

Dawson, Giles Edwin, and Laetitia Kennedy-Skipton. *Elizabethan Handwriting, 1500-1650: A Manual*. New York: W. W. Norton, 1966.
Intended to help students read Elizabethan literary manuscripts, which

were executed in the secretary hand, the same script used for correspondence and some forms of records. This form of writing developed
from the "bastard" hand, a combination of the medieval Gothic bookhand and the court handwriting used for legal documents. Whereas the
italic is, as its name indicates, a foreign import into England, the
secretary hand was of native growth. The authors discuss some peculiarities of this writing, including common abbreviations and notations,
and they present fifty plates illustrating the form. These suggest the
wide individual range of the handwriting. Each plate is transcribed and
briefly annotated.

DeFrancis, John. *Visible Speech: The Diverse Oneness of Writing Systems.*
Honolulu: University of Hawaii Press, 1989.
Distinguishing between full and partial systems of communication,
DeFrancis argues that all forms of the latter, whether written, sign, or
touch language, rest on speech. Not all written languages are equally
phonetic, but all rely to some extent on reproducing sounds. All writing
systems also use nonphonetic devices (such as dollar signs and numbers in English). Writing systems may be syllabic, like Japanese and
Chinese, consonantal like Hebrew and Arabic, or alphabetic like Greek
or Korean. DeFrancis further subdivides each category into those that
are "pure" and those that rely on "meaning-plus-sound" systems. Thus,
DeFrancis sees Greek as purely alphabetic, whereas English uses a
meaning-plus-sound alphabetic notation. While certain writing systems use symbols that seem pictographic, they need not be. The Latin
"A" began as a picture of the head of an ox. DeFrancis maintains that
Chinese is particularly misunderstood in this regard. Michael
McCaskey wrote in the *Modern Language Journal* 74 (1990): 250,
"There is no question that this lively and well-written book will be
essential reading from now on for those working in this complex and
fascinating field."

Diringer, David. *The Alphabet: A Key to the History of Mankind.* 3d ed.
2 vols. London: Hutchinson, 1968.
Diringer seeks "to provide an introduction to the fascinating subject of
the history of the alphabet." He begins with the nonalphabetic scripts
of Egypt, Mesopotamia, China, and Central America, then turning to
syllabic systems such as Minoan Linear B and Japanese. In Part 2,
much the larger section, he explores the origins and development of
alphabetic writing, which, he argues, began with the Northern Semites
around 1730-1580 B.C. in the Near East of Israel and Syria. This is the
generally accepted view. A standard work. As the *Times Literary*

Supplement for August 14, 1969, observed, "The two volumes constitute a mine of information from which all who are interested in the history of the alphabet will draw much that is both interesting and important" (p. 901). The first volume contains the text, the second volume the illustrations.

_____. *Writing*. New York: Praeger, 1962.
Part of the *Ancient Peoples and Places* series, this work looks at written forms of communication in the ancient world. Diringer begins with pictures, such as cave paintings and engravings. Some of these are sufficiently stylized to be classified as early forms of writing. He then considers scripts of the Near East, Far East, and pre-Columbian America before treating phonetic scripts and the birth of the Greek and Roman alphabets. A well-written, carefully illustrated introduction by one of the masters of the subject.

Doblhofer, Ernst. *Voices in Stone: The Decipherment of Ancient Scripts and Writings*. Translated by Mervyn Savill. New York: Viking, 1961.
After a brief introduction to the history of writing, Doblhofer examines how various ancient scripts were deciphered and who was responsible for these breakthroughs. Some stories, such as the decoding of Egyptian hieroglyphics by Jean-Francois Champollion, are familiar. Others, like the deciphering of ancient Persian and Mesopotamian cuneiform, are likely to provide revelations to many readers. Though Doblhofer writes for a general audience, he does not oversimplify. A fascinating and informative account that explains many ancient forms of writing.

Driver, Godfrey Rolles. *Semitic Writing: From Pictograph to Alphabet*. 3d ed. Edited by S. A. Hopkins. London: Oxford University Press, 1976.
In this learned disquisition, Driver surveys the bibliography of the origin of the alphabet and offers his own view, according to which the Western (a.k.a. Northern) Semites created three types of writing. One was pictographic-linear, the second cuneiform, and the third linear (the, phonetic alphabet). The first two died out; the last survived and was picked up by the Phoenicians, who then carried it to Greece. With fifty-seven plates and nearly one hundred drawings.

Ege, Otto F. *The Story of the Alphabet*. Baltimore: Norman T. A. Munder, 1921.
This short book offers a pleasant introduction to the origins of the Latin alphabet. Ege focuses on "the desire for speed, and the influence of the

tool, reed, chisel, brush" that led to changes in form. "A," for example, began as a "V" with a bar, representing the head of an ox. The letter became simplified because of the desire for speed. The Greeks, who changed the orientation of many Semitic letters, turned this letter upside down to create their alpha, which became the Latin "A." Ege provides brief descriptions of the evolution of each of the Latin letters and includes a chart depicting the transformations of the letters. Ege calls the Semitic alphabet Phoenician, thus confusing its origin. An attractive book.

Fairbank, Alfred J. *A Book of Scripts*. Harmondsworth, England: Penguin, 1949.
Fairbank's short text begins with a historical sketch of the Latin alphabet. He notes that whereas square and rustic capitals, though influenced by handwriting, derive from inscriptions, the uncial "is truly a penman's letter and owes its form to the quill and to vellum." He follows the changes in medieval book hands and their adaptations by proto-typographers. He also looks at the rise of the writing manual and the teaching of penmanship. Fairbanks then turns to writing implements, then touches on economy and speed, factors sometimes at war with legibility. He devotes a few pages to calligraphy. Here he sets forth his views on what constitutes an attractive script. The text concludes with a bibliography, followed by sixty-four plates illustrating the Latin alphabet, beginning with the Trajan column and concluding with a 1935 sample of Fairbank's own writing.

_____. *The Story of Handwriting: Origins and Development*. New York: Watson-Guptill, 1970.
Primarily for the novice but filled with sound information. Fairbank begins with the Sumerians and traces the history of writing through Egypt, Phoenicia, Greece, Rome, and medieval and Renaissance Europe to the twentieth century. The short text is accompanied by twenty-six figures and forty-two plates, four of them in color. Fairbank supplements his history with discussions of legibility, methods of organizing text, writing materials, and the teaching of penmanship.

Fairbank, Alfred J., and Berthold Wolpe. *Renaissance Handwriting: An Anthology of Italic Scripts*. Cleveland: World, 1960.
The authors maintain that the Italian Renaissance produced "the most agreeable cursive writing" ever developed. Although Niccolò de' Niccoli adapted Carolingian script to create the italic, the form evolved slowly to become both a formal book hand and one used for other

occasions as well. Pope Eugenius IV adopted it for papal briefs in the mid-fifteenth century, and the dissemination of these documents encouraged the use of cursive. Ludovico degli Arrighi's *La Operina* (c. 1522) provided the first instructional manual for this writing. After a brief historical survey of cursive, the authors discuss the techniques involved. With about 100 examples of cursive, all briefly annotated. Includes a two-page bibliography.

Finlay, Michael. *Western Writing Implements in the Age of the Quill Pen.* Carlisle, England: Plain Books, 1990.

As Finlay points out, the quill pen served as "the instrument with which the entire history of western civilization and culture was both developed and recorded over some thirteen hundred years." Even after steel pens began to be mass-produced in the 1820s the quill did not vanish. In 1834, 18,732,000 quills were imported into England. Finlay offers detailed information on the making of a pen from a feather, and he discusses ink, parchment, and paper as well as variations on the quill, such as the quill fountain pen, metallic pens, pencils, porte-crayons, and seals. After the text and bibliographic footnotes, Finlay offers over 300 illustrations depicting the writing implements he discusses. Among these illustrations are a mid-sixth century mosaic showing a quill pen and examples of medieval bronze pens with points shaped like a quill.

Firmage, Richard A. *The Alphabet Abecedarium: Some Notes on Letters.* Boston: David R. Godine, 1993.

The introductory chapter briefly traces the history of the Latin alphabet, noting how the letter forms have changed over history in response to other developments. Thus, the humanists rejected medieval Gothic letters in favor of what they thought were classical (actually Carolingian) forms. In the early twentieth century, designers of the Bauhaus stripped letters of their serifs as part of the effort to remove all extraneous features. The chapters that follow treat each letter in turn, discussing its design and recounting some of the lore associated with it. Two concluding chpaters deal with the alphabet as a whole and with additional signs such as the ampersand. Includes a selective bibliography. This book is at once learned, charming, informative, and attractively produced.

Folsom, Rose. *The Calligraphers' Dictionary.* New York: Thames and Hudson, 1990.

"This book is meant to streamline the study, practice, and appreciation of calligraphy by offering definitions and explanations of words that appear insufficiently explained in other contexts" (preface). A handy reference for the study of manuscripts or calligraphy. Includes examples and concise definitions of terms such as Beneventan or uncial or copperplate script. Lists libraries with important manuscript collections, and names and addresses of calligraphic societies and publications. With a bibliography and list of suppliers of calligraphic books and materials.

Fraenkel, Gerd. *Writing Systems.* Boston: Ginn, 1965.
Deals with "the systematic attempts man has made to develop the best possible means of written communication." The first chapter looks at the nature of writing, which Fraenkel defines as any "acquired arbitrary system of visual marks with which people who know the represented language can communicate." Chapter 2 deals with the alphabet, and Chapter 3 examines deciphering various non-Latin scripts such as Mayan hieroglyphics or Minoan Linear B. Fraenkel concludes by examining attempts to alter writing through a phonetic alphabet that mirrors sound or through other spelling reforms.

Fry, Roger, and Elias Avery Lowe. *English Handwriting, with Thirty-four Facsimile Plates and Artistic and Paleographic Criticisms.* Oxford, England: Clarendon Press, 1926.
Most of the volume is devoted to the facsimiles. The first three date from the fifteenth and sixteenth centuries; the others present examples of what the authors regard as fine cursive penmanship, demonstrating legibility, speed, and beauty. Roger Fry, in his artistic criticism, advocates individual variation rather than conformity to a model, and he adds that for cursive writing combinations of forms, not individual letters, create the aesthetic effect. Lowe's historical survey traces English cursive to the humanistic scripts of the Renaissance, but he finds "an increase in freedom, boldness, and originality" in the late nineteenth- and early twentieth-century examples.

Gaur, Albertine. *A History of Writing.* New York: Scribner's, 1985.
Gaur divides scripts into "thought writing" and "sound writing," that is, ideographic and phonetic. While the former allows more immediate and universal comprehension, it demands a large number of symbols. Because phonetic writing is easier to learn and reproduce, Gaur maintains that it arose where centralized authority and property were important, such as in the Fertile Crescent around 4000-3000 B.C. or Central America about 1000 B.C. In the first two chapters, Gaur

examines the various types of writing, discussing their properties and history. She notes that materials available could influence scripts; thus, cuneiform is well adapted to clay and stylus. Chapter 3 looks at efforts to decode ancient scripts, focusing on the Rosetta Stone and cuneiform. Gaur then considers social attitudes towards writing and notes the importance of the scribe. Hence, "Whenever the ability to write was associated with power and influence, women were, as a rule, excluded." Hindu society, to maintain its exclusivity, eschewed writing, so that Sanskrit never developed its own alphabet. Gaur concludes with a survey of mechanical and electronic means of writing, such as the printing press and computer, and she suggests that technology may someday render obsolete traditional forms of script. Mark Van Stone wrote in *Library Quarterly* 56 (1986): 424, "The articulate and perceptive Gaur has provided us with a thought-provoking, successful reexamination of the concept of writing." Rachel Neaman regarded the book as "a highly readable and informative guide, beautifully produced" (*Times Educational Supplement*, October 18, 1985, 28).

Gelb, Ignace. *A Study of Writing: The Foundations of Grammatology.* Rev. ed. Chicago: University of Chicago Press, 1963.
Gelb "attempts to establish general principles governing the use and evolution of writing on a comparative-typological basis." He looks first at ways of communicating and defines writing as a method that uses "conventional visual marks." Chapter 2 examines precursors of true writing, such as Mayan and Aztec symbols, which Gelb does not regard as true writing systems themselves. The next three chapters look at types of what Gelb does accept as writing: word-syllabic, syllabic, and alphabetic. He attributes the first alphabet to the Greeks because they introduced the regular use of vowels. Chapter 6 traces the movement of writing from pictographic to syllabic and alphabetic systems. Subsequent chapters deal with modern systems of writing that developed among nonliterate cultures through outside pressures; the origin of the major writing systems (Sumerian, Proto-Elamite, Proto-Indic, Chinese, Egyptian, Cretan, and Hittite); the relationship of writing to civilization ("Writing exists only in a civilization and a civilization cannot exist without writing"); and the future of writing. Gelb advocates adopting the International Phonetic Alphabet and combining it with shorthand notation. The book concludes with a glossary and bibliography. Kemp Malone wrote of the first edition, "The book as a whole is a fine piece of work, an investigation that throws much new light on a subject of the first importance" (*American Journal of Philology* 75, 1954, 223).

Gordon, Cyrus H. *Forgotten Scripts: Their Ongoing Discovery and Decipherment.* Rev. and enl. ed. New York: Basic Books, 1982.
The opening chapter discusses decoding. Gordon then looks at the deciphering of hieroglyphics, Old Persian and Sumerian cuneiform, Hittite (which used both cuneiform and hieroglyphics), Ugaritic, and Mycenean (or Minoan) Linear B; and he notes progress on decoding Minoan Linear A. Gordon also devotes a chapter to the discovery of an archival treasury in the ancient town of Ebla, a Sumerian outpost of the third millennium B.C., where Sumerian and Semitic languages met. Chapter 9 presents an anthology of texts revealed through the deciphering of these alphabets. Nicely illustrated. With a three-page bibliography.

Goudy, Frederic William. *The Alphabet and Elements of Lettering.* Rev. and enl. ed. Berkeley: University of California Press, 1942.
Designed "primarily to help the student/craftsman and, by precept and example, return the art of lettering to its original purity of intention—to bring a great craft again to life." Begins with the earliest forms of writing—cuneiform and hieroglyphics. Goudy traces the development of the Latin alphabet and the book hands of the Middle Ages. In Chapter 8, Goudy arrives at printing from movable type, which initially imitated scribal forms. Goudy advocates "pleasing legibility" and notes that "the beauty of a letter depends on the harmonious adaptation of each of its parts to every other in a well-proportioned manner." Goudy cautions against innovation. Well illustrated throughout, the book concludes with twenty-six plates, each showing fifteen versions of a particular letter (ranging from the Trajan column to Goudy's own Kennerley type design), and one giving four forms of the ampersand together with two of Arabic numerals. Lovely and informative.

Gray, Nicolete. *A History of Lettering: Creative Experiment and Letter Identity.* Boston: David R. Godine, 1986.
Gray's book is "about the art of lettering; about letters used as a medium of expression and of design. It is about the means itself—that is, the letter form, the ways in which it can be thought of, and the ways in which it has been altered and reformed; and about the human context of this story, the social factors which have conditioned its changes and development," especially the capital letters of the Latin alphabet (introduction). Gray traces the history of the alphabet from its origins in the sixth or seventh century B.C. to the present. Connects social and political changes with the history of lettering. Thus, the New Cursive emerged in the mid-fourth century A.D. as Rome turned to Christianity

and as the rulers Constantine (306-337) and Theodosius (379-395) reformed the empire. Charlemagne's revival of classical lettering was part of his vision of restoring the Roman world. Gray refines but does not dissent from Stanley Morison's views in *Politics and Script* (cited in this chapter), which stresses the roles of church and state in the formation of letters. Beautifully produced and well illustrated. Joyce Irene Whalley observed in the *Times Literary Supplement* for May 29, 1987, "This [book] is likely to prove not only a basic handbook for many years to come, but also one of those seminal works to which students and practitioners will return again and again" (p. 592).

Havelock, Eric A. *The Literate Revolution in Greece and Its Cultural Consequences*. Princeton, N.J.: Princeton University Press, 1982.
In this collection of Havelock's previously published essays the author argues that "the introduction of the Greek letters into inscription somewhere about 700 B.C. was to alter the character of human culture, placing a gulf between all alphabetic societies and their precursors." Havelock looks at these consequences, which emerged slowly—only in the late fifth century B.C. were letters taught "at the primary level of schooling" and general literacy thus brought about. Even Greek drama of the golden age reflects oral rather than written culture; the latter comes to the fore only in the fourth century B.C. More concerned with the results of the introduction of the alphabet than with the alphabet itself, Havelock offers many insights into Greek culture and the differences between literacy and orality. Havelock agrees with those, like Barry B. Powell and I. J. Gelb, who argue that the Greeks were the first to have a true alphabet, since the Semitic antecedents lacked vowels.

Heal, Ambrose. *The English Writing-Masters and Their Copy-Books, 1570-1800: A Biographical Dictionary and a Bibliography*. Cambridge, England: Cambridge University Press, 1931.
In 1763 William Massey published *The Origin and Progress of Letters*, with biographies of some eighty English writing masters; George Bickham's *Universal Penman* (1733-1741) offered examples of English calligraphy. Until Heal's book, no other work attempted to trace the history of handwriting in Britain (though Peter Jessen's comprehensive *Meister der Schreibkunst aus drei Jahrhunderten*, 1923, includes examples of eleven English calligraphers). In his preface, Heal traces the history of copybooks in England. Part 1 presents biographies and portraits of English writing masters from 1570, when *A Booke Containing Divers Sorts of Hands (based on Jehan de Beauchesne's Le Thresor d'escripture*, 1550) appeared under the name of John Baildon (or

Basildon). The study concludes in 1800. Part 2 contains the bibliography, with reproductions of selected pages from the writing manuals listed. Appendixes list writing schools, known engravers and publishers of copybooks, addenda, and errata. Stanley Morison contributed an essay on the development of handwriting, with an emphasis on England.

Hooker, J. T., ed. *Reading the Past: Ancient Writing from Cuneiform to the Alphabet.* Berkeley: University of California Press, 1990.
Brings together six monographs by experts in their fields dealing with ancient writing systems. C. B. F. Walker treats cuneiform, W. V. Davies discusses Egyptian hieroglyphics, John Chadwick explores Linear B (and, more briefly, Linear A). John F. Healey looks at Semitic alphabets, B. F. Cook examines Greek inscriptions, and Larissa Bonfante writes about Etruscan, which, like the Latin alphabet, is a derivative of Greek. Taken together these works offer an overview of the ways information was recorded in the ancient Mediterranean basin and Middle East. All offer suggestions for further reading, and all are nicely illustrated. David Kaser wrote in *Library Quarterly* 62 (1992): 111-112, "This excellent volume will be of value to many. Its erudition will assure it a place on many library shelves. . . . Its currency and simple style will gain it a large and deserved lay readership."

Hyde, Robert C. *A Dictionary for Calligraphers.* Los Angeles: Martin Press, 1977.
An illustrated dictionary of some 700 terms, briefly defined. Intended for calligraphers and their teachers but useful for anyone seeking information on the subject.

Illich, Ivan, and Barry Sanders. *ABC: The Alphabetization of the Popular Mind.* San Francisco: North Point Press, 1988.
Plato tells the story of King Thammus of Thebes, who rejects the gift of letters, arguing, "This facility will make souls forgetful because they will no longer school themselves to meditate. . . . Things will be recollected from outside by means of alien symbols; they will not remember on their own." The authors consider how the alphabet changed classical ideas about memory and affected medieval society. They also examine how Chaucer, Defoe, and Mark Twain undercut literacy in their works. A thought-provoking monograph on the consequences of literacy.

Irwin, Keith Gordon. *The Romance of Writing from Egyptian Hieroglyphics to Modern Letters, Numbers, and Signs.* New York: Viking, 1956.

This introduction for the general reader tells the story of hieroglyphics, cuneiform, and Semitic, Greek, and Latin alphabets. Although the account draws on earlier histories, Irwin provides sound insights into changes in letterforms. For example, the dot over the "i" developed to distinguish this mark from part of an "n" or "u," and when two i's appeared together the second was elongated into a "j" to avoid similar confusion. U and V, like I and J, were once a single letter but became designated arbitrarily as vowel and consonant. Irwin attributes the modern method of forming contractions to Aldus' adoption of the Greek apostrophe rather than some other designation available to him, such as a line over a letter to denote an omission. An informative, clearly written book with helpful drawings by the author.

Jackson, Donald. *The Story of Writing.* New York: Taplinger, 1981.
Jackson begins with prealphabetic forms of writing, pictures and symbols like cuneiform. Both cuneiform and hieroglyphics moved from pictogram to ideogram to phonogram, but the Egyptians finally developed a true alphabet. The Semitic alphabet served as the basis of Western letters. Jackson traces their development from Greece to Rome to the Middle Ages and beyond. He also considers the development of the fountain pen—Caliph al Mudizz in the tenth century owned the first—and other writing implements. A beautifully illustrated history of the subject.

Jensen, Hans Detlef. *Sign, Symbol, and Script: An Account of Man's Effort to Write.* Translated by George Unwin. 3d ed., rev. and enl. New York: G. P. Putnam's Sons, 1969.
Jensen observes that all writing seeks "to solve the problem of expressing through the simplest possible signs and combinations of signs the greatest possible amount of linguistic material." Generally, alphabetic systems are the most successful, but Chinese, which is not alphabetic, is the oldest form of writing still in use. Jensen surveys numerous scripts: Egyptian, cuneiform, ancient Mediterranean, East Asian, African, Aztec, Mayan, Cherokee, Cree, Alaskan, Chukchee, Semitic, Indian (including Easter Island), Upper Asian, Iranian, Greek, and Germanic-Celtic. All are well-illustrated and clearly described. A comprehensive treatment.

Johnston, Edward. *Formal Penmanship and Other Papers.* Edited by Heather Child. New York: Hastings House, 1971.
Johnston began this work in 1929; he wanted to "make an explicit statement on the art of Formal Penmanship . . . and give a more assured

view than in" his first book, *Writing and Illuminating and Lettering* (cited herein). In Part 1 of this volume, Johnston explores what he regards as the three primary factors of penmanship—the weight of the stroke, the angle of the pen, and the form of the letter. Part 2 looks at the tradition of handwriting, examining medieval scribal practices. Part 3 presents Johnston's philosophy of writing. Among his dicta are: "The scribe's ideal is to give the words perfect presentation"; "This, then, is the scribe's direct purpose—*The making of useful things legibly beautiful.*" Child has included seven articles that Johnston wrote for *The Imprint* in 1913, as well as his 1933 *Addendum to a Paper on the Labelling of Exhibits*, in which he discusses his calligraphic rendering of Shakespeare's Sonnet 116, reproduced as the frontispiece of the book. A classic. Nicolas Barker described it as "a book of major importance to all who are interested in calligraphy, whether historically or as executants" (*The Book Collector* 20, 1971, 536).

Kapr, Albert. *The Art of Lettering: The History, Anatomy, and Aesthetics of the Roman Letter Forms.* Munich: K. G. Saur, 1983.
First published in 1971, *The Art of Lettering* traces the development of the Latin alphabet from cave paintings to photocomposition. Like Stanley Morison's *Politics and Script* (cited in this chapter), Kapr's book relates the development of lettering to social and technical factors. For example, he links the rounding of the Latin cursive to the form of the Byzantine arch. He discusses all the important Latin book hands as well as other letterforms, and all are well-illustrated in the text. The study notes the mutual influences of typography and calligraphy and includes a 120-page collection of type specimens. Jerry Kelly wrote in *The Papers of the Bibliographical Society of America*, "The great variety of epigraphy, calligraphy, lettering, typecutting, and printing displayed here in exceptionally well-chosen illustrations provides an overview of the vast and fruitful field the letter arts have been and continue to be" (79, 1985, 450).

Logan, Robert K. *The Alphabet Effect: The Impact of the Phonetic Alphabet on the Development of Western Civilization.* New York: William Morrow, 1986.
Traces the history of the alphabet from Mesopotamian and Egyptian writing systems through the electronic age. Logan is equally concerned with the consequences of the alphabetic system. He maintains that the very thought processes of the West have been influenced by the phonetic system of writing. For example, Logan argues that "the alphabet creates the environmental conditions under which abstract

theoretical science flourishes." Chinese philosophy, according to Logan, is dialectical, inductive, and analogical because the ideographic writing system fostered such thought patterns, while in the West the alphabet encouraged "abstract notions of codified law, monotheism, abstract science, and deductive logic." Builds on Marshall McLuhan's view that "the medium is the message." Provocative.

Lowe, Elias Avery. *The Beneventan Script: A History of the South Italian Minuscule.* Oxford, England: Clarendon Press, 1914.
The Beneventan script arose in southern Italy in the eighth century A.D. at the Benedictine Monastery of Monte Casino, and its fortunes followed those of the Benedictine order. When the mendicant orders emerged in the thirteenth century, the Beneventan script declined. Lowe presents a detailed history and anatomy of this hand, which endured for some five centuries and which preserved many important manuscripts; an appendix lists 600 extant examples. Lowe treats abbreviations, which increased over time, and punctuation, most of which was imported from the north. Punctuation served not only to mark logical pauses but also to indicate intonation, since even private reading was done aloud. Especially fascinating is the Beneventan use of the question mark, which appears not at the end of the sentence but over the words to be stressed.

_____. *Codices Latini Antiquiores: A Paleographical Guide to Latin Manuscripts Prior to the Ninth Century.* 12 vols. Oxford, England: Oxford University Press, 1934-1971.
Briefly describes "all known Latin literary manuscripts on papyrus, parchment, or vellum, which may be regarded as older than the ninth century." Includes unreduced facsimiles of each manuscript and provides selective bibliographies. Volumes are arranged geographically by location of the manuscripts. Descriptions, reproductions, and bibliography are all excellent. Covers nearly 2,000 manuscripts. Bernard M. Peebles expressed the consensus of the scholarly community when he described the set as "enormously valuable alike to paleographer, codicologist, text-critic, cultural historian, and art historian, as well as for the invariably informative facsimiles and the descriptional details" (*The Classical World* 57, 1964, 362). An indispensable guide to the study of classical and early medieval Latin manuscripts, with much on the creation of each item.

_____. *English Uncial.* Oxford, England: Clarendon Press, 1960.
Uncial, which arose in the second or third century A.D., became the

most popular book hand in the sixth century. When Christian missionaries came to England in 597, the books they carried were almost certainly written in uncial, as were the books that Anglo-Saxon pilgrims such as the Northumbrian Benedict Biscop brought back from Italy. Though imported, uncial acquired peculiarly English characteristics, especially at the scriptorium of Wearmouth-Jarrow in Northumbria. Lowe devotes part of his introduction to refuting the notion that uncial manuscripts in England were executed by Italian scribes. He notes that the Irish never used uncial, and that in England the script was used only for religious works, thus linking the form to English Christianity. Most of the book is devoted to facsimiles, with brief annotations preceding the plates.

_____. *Handwriting: Our Medieval Legacy*. Rome: Edizioni di Storia e Letteratura, 1938.
Lowe observes that scripts changed slowly, suggesting that as an agent of conservation handwriting is itself conservative. This study concentrates on the Latin alphabet. Lowe notes how economic factors encouraged the development of minuscule and of abbreviations. He calls the minuscule the Middle Age's great contribution to writing, and he attributes its origin to seventh century Ireland. Gothic script is the other medieval legacy, though it sprang from Carolingian minuscule. Like Gothic architecture, Gothic script emphasizes the vertical and the pointed rather than the rounded. It also subordinates the part (the letter) to the whole. The Renaissance rejected Gothic lettering, which slowly disappeared from books. Lowe accompanies his discussion with many facsimiles.

_____. *Paleographic Papers, 1907-1965*. 2 vols. Oxford, England: Clarendon Press, 1972.
In his introduction Ludwig Bieler, who edited the volumes, observed, "Dr. Lowe did more to extend our knowledge, to broaden and deepen our understanding of early Western script, than any other scholar of his generation." Between 1934 and 1971, Lowe edited the invaluable twelve-volume *Codices Latini Antiquiores*, the standard work on Latin paleography, and these essays supplement that work. Because the pieces appeared over so long a period, some invariably contain information later superseded, but Lowe's paleographic observations almost invariably remain unchallenged. In the forty-seven essays collected here, Lowe concentrates on Latin manuscripts produced before 800. Includes a bibliography of Lowe's 116 publications, and the 150 plates could in themselves serve as an introduction to Latin paleography.

Mason, William Albert. *A History of the Art of Writing*. New York: Macmillan, 1920.

Mason begins by looking at picture-writing, especially in Mesoamerica. Subsequent chapters treat the hieroglyphics of the South Sea islanders, Chinese ideographic writing, Egyptian hieroglyphics, cuneiform, Hittite, Mediterranean scripts, Phoenician, Greek and Latin alphabets, medieval scripts, and scripts derived from Greek (such as Cyrillic). A brief conclusion deals with printing. Based on wide reading in secondary sources, but Mason's command of ancient languages is shaky, so that the occasional error creeps in. Well illustrated and well written, but caveat lector.

Meyer, Hans, ed. *Die Schriftentwicklung. The Development of Writing. Le Dévelopment de l'écriture*. Zurich: Graphics Press, 1958.

Text in English, German, and French. Extensive illustrations trace the development of writing and typography in the West. Includes a time chart showing the evolution of Latin script, beginning with Greek and Roman inscriptions. Meyer argues that Roman square capitals written on vellum or papyrus sought to imitate inscriptions. The desire to write more quickly led to the creation of Rustic capitals, a modified form of the square capital. Uncial and half-uncial also derived from square capitals. After the fall of Rome, national hands arose. These yielded to Carolingian, and in the twelfth century, Carolingian in turn gave way to Gothic. Gothic Textura (so called because the lines of writing looked like a tapestry) served as the model for the first movable type, and in Germany Fraktur remained the primary book type until the twentieth century. In Italy, Gothic remained rounded, and so was called Rotunda, and it was here that Gothic first yielded to the humanist script based on Carolingian models. These served as the basis for book type, and the spread of humanist learning popularized these letters. Humanistic cursive served as the basis of modern Western handwriting. A short book filled with information.

Moorhouse, A. C. *The Triumph of the Alphabet: A History of Writing*. New York: Henry Schuman, 1953.

An expanded version of Moorhouse's *Writing and the Alphabet* (London: Cobbett Press, 1946). Moorhouse seeks to demonstrate "that the apparently simple art of writing, and especially writing in an alphabetic manner, is one of the world's most original and important intellectual discoveries." Moorhouse divides writing systems into picture-writing, in which an entire scene appears; pictograms, in which each sign represents a separate item; ideograms, using a picture to symbolize an idea; and phonograms, in which signs stand for specific sounds. These signs may represent a word, syllable, or single letter. After a chapter on deciphering lost scripts such as cuneiform, Moorhouse treats pre-alphabetic scripts, the Semitic alphabet, and its offshoots. Part 2 examines the uses of writing, which, according to Moorhouse, made civilization possible.

Morison, Stanley. *Politics and Script: Aspects of Authority and Freedom in the Development of Graeco-Roman Script from the Sixth Century B.C. to the Twentieth Century A.D.* Oxford, England: Clarendon Press, 1972.

Morison argues that letterforms have "been conditioned by movements in religion and politics, friction between Church and State, and schisms between Eastern and Western Christendom." For example, he observes that the Carolingian revival of Augustan Square Capitals was politically inspired to symbolize the break with the immediate past. This decision by Charlemagne accentuated the division between Eastern and Western Christianity because the Eastern Church rejected the Square Capitals as pagan. Morison traces the modern sans serif letter to Greek inscriptions that fascinated the eighteenth century Society of Dilettanti, impressed advertisers with the letters' novelty and adaptability, and fascinated early twentieth century artists with their modern appearance. In the course of this historical survey, Morison discusses the various scripts and the conventions governing them, and he includes nearly 200 facsimiles to demonstrate the various written, engraved, and printed forms he analyzes. In *The British Journal of Aesthetics* 13 (1973): 313-316, F. R. Cowell challenged Morison's thesis that authority influenced scribal practices, but Cowell found the study useful nonetheless, calling it an "immense contribution . . . to the factual study of its subject matter" and an "enduring monument of a great man."

_____. *Selected Essays on the History of Letter-Forms in Manuscript and Print.* 2 vols. Cambridge, England: Cambridge University Press, 1981.

The nineteen essays collected here are arranged under four headings: "The Design of Types," "Letter-forms," "Newspapers," and "The Learned Press." Chronologically they begin with Morison's 1924 "Towards an Ideal Type" and end with "The Learned Press as an Institution" (1963). Included here are two papers that Morison wrote for *The Times* (London) in 1930-1931; they appear here for the first time in published form. Throughout, Morison demonstrates his interest in the transformation of script and type under the influence of social, political, and technological forces. Concludes with a reminiscence of Daniel Berkeley Updike, who influenced Morison. The essays reveal Morison's range of interests, including his concern for calligraphy.

Mote, Frederick W., and Hung-Lam Chu. *Calligraphy and the East Asian Book.* Boston: Shambhala, 1989.
The catalog of a 1989 exhibition held at Princeton that highlighted the holdings of the Gest Oriental Library and Princeton Art Museum. Focus is on the book in China. The 129 illustrations trace the history of writing and printing in China. They show the variety of calligraphic forms and demonstrate how these continued to influence book production well after the introduction of printing. Jason C. Kuo wrote in *The Journal of Asian Studies* 49 (1990): 384, "Based on solid research, this book has opened up new vistas into this new field of scholarly research."

Ogg, Oscar. *The Twenty-Six Letters.* 3d ed., rev. New York: T. Y. Crowell, 1971.
A well-illustrated volume written for the general reader. Ogg traces the history of Latin script. He notes that prehistoric people made marks on bones, and the Inca used knotted cords (quipus) to help them remember. Cave drawings also served as a means of communication. Ogg examines Egyptian hieroglyphics, which he suggests influenced Semitic writing, though he also sees a debt to cuneiform. Ogg follows the alphabet to Greece and Rome, and continues his story through the invention of printing, the decline of good letterforms in the nineteenth century, and the revival of craftsmanship under the influence of William Morris and his followers. The *English Journal* called the book "a valuable resource" (67, December, 1978, 65).

Osley, A. S., ed. *Calligraphy and Paleography: Essays Presented to Alfred Fairbank.* New York: October House, 1965.
The essays here are divided into eight sections: "A Scholar Penman," "Mainly Paleographical," "Arrighi and His Contemporaries," "Some Writing Masters," "Precept and Practice," "The Spread of the Modern Italic," "Pen to Paper," and an anthology of articles that first appeared in the *Bulletin and Journal of the Society for Italic Handwriting*; four of these pieces are by Fairbank. Among the essays are Albinia de la Mare's work on the Florentine scribe Piero Strozzi, Philip Hofer's study of Arrighi's *La operina*, Ray Nash on the American writing master Benjamin Franklin Foster, and Nicolete Gray on "Expressionist Lettering." A diverse collection, touching on many aspects of the letter.

Alan M. Fern wrote in *Library Quarterly* 37 (1967): 142, "The book is handsomely produced and richly illustrated, and the articles maintain a high level of scholarship and literary style."

_____. *Scribes and Sources: Handbook of the Chancery Hand in the Sixteenth Century*. Boston: David R. Godine, 1980.
"This books aims to admit a wider public to an insufficiently familiar facet of European culture by giving some description of the [sixteenth century] writing masters and their works, together with an English translation of selected passages from their works" (preface). Osley admires the cursive hands of the sixteenth century, when bureaucracies arose and secretaries were needed. Hence, writing masters also were in demand, and many used that enemy of the scribe, the printing press, to spread their ideas and demonstrate their skills. Osley examines some twenty writing masters who left behind records of their work; Berthold Wople contributed the chapter on John de Beauchesne. With twenty-one illustrations, most of them reproducing chancery hands.

Parkes, M. B. *English Cursive Book Hands, 1250-1500*. London: Scolar Press, 1979.
In the twelfth century, the demand for books increased markedly. In response, scribes developed new forms of writing. To increase speed, scribes adopted a more rounded letterform and sought to remove pen from paper as infrequently as possible, so that by the mid-thirteenth century a distinctly cursive script had emerged. Following the lead of Neil R. Ker, Parkes calls this English script "Anglicana." More elaborate hands were reserved for deluxe volumes, but even these letters show cursive influences by the fourteenth century. Parkes argues that in the later 1300s a new script, probably introduced to England from Italy by way of France, again altered the form of letters. This new script became the secretary hand, which, by the second half of the fifteenth century, became the dominant English bookhand. Parkes examines the various forms of cursive and includes twenty-four plates showing forty-eight manuscripts that illustrate distinctive characteristics and scribal practices. This Scolar Press edition updates the bibliography in the 1969 Clarendon Press edition, makes a number of corrections, and adds two indexes.

Powell, Barry B. *Homer and the Origins of the Greek Alphabet*. Cambridge, England: Cambridge University Press, 1991.
In Chapter 1 Powell reviews the literature on the subject of the origins of the Greek alphabet—where it came from, when it was adopted, and

what it looked like. The second chapter examines different writing systems. In logographic systems, one sign represents one word. Other systems are syllabic (Phoenician, Linear B). According to Powell, the Greeks were the first to introduce alphabetic writing, and in Appendix I, Powell presents I. J. Gelb's concurring view that West Semitic writing was a syllabary, not a true alphabet. Chapter 3 looks at the early surviving examples of Greek writing to determine why the alphabet was adopted. Chapter 4 attempts to pinpoint the date of Homer (800-750 B.C.), and Powell concludes that someone wrote down the *Odyssey* and *Iliad* for himself. This transcription, when circulated, spread the use of the alphabet. As Powell states,"Homer sang his song and the adapter took him down. From this momentous event came classical Greek civilization and its achievements." Whether or not one shares Powell's views on the predecessors of Greek writing or its Homeric origins, one will find much sound information here on the development of the Greek alphabet and writing systems in general.

Roberts, C. H. *Greek Literary Hands, 350 B.C.-A.D. 400.* Corrected impression. Oxford, England: Clarendon Press, 1956.
"This volume aims at providing an elementary guide to the development of Greek literary handwriting in the Hellenistic and Roman periods." Roberts rejected all undated materials, thereby limiting his selection but making it more useful for those seeking to determine when an undated manuscript probably was written. Roberts notes that early extant Greek bookhands do not differ as markedly from documentary scripts as do later examples, which resemble print in their regularity. Most of the surviving examples are on papyrus and so derive from Egypt, but the few manuscripts with other provenances indicate that the bookhands shown here were universally used. With fifty-seven facsimiles, for each of which Roberts provides brief but informative annotations.

Sampson, Geoffrey. *Writing Systems: A Linguistic Introduction.* Stanford, Calif.: Stanford University Press, 1985.
Begins with the premise that all writing systems are glottographic (reproduce speech). These systems may be logographic or phonographic (record whole words or sounds). The rest of the book examines writing systems, beginning with Sumerian, the oldest written language. Minoan Linear B exemplifies a syllabic system; Semitic writing typifies consonantal writing. The Greco-Roman alphabet introduced vowels as equal to consonants. Korean presents features of sound (as does shorthand); Chinese is logographic; Japanese is a mixed system. The final chapter defends English spelling. Sampson always presents con-

crete examples to illustrate his theoretical reflections, and the book provides a solid survey of the subject.

Senner, Wayne M., ed. *The Origins of Writing*. Lincoln: University of Nebraska Press, 1989.

Brings together twelve essays that deal with the development of writing in the Middle and Far East, Europe, and Mesoamerica. Senner begins the volume with a survey of how various cultures have conceived of the origins of writing. *The Book of Jubilees* (135-105 B.C.) claims that Enoch was the first to write; *Sepher Yetzirah* credited Abraham with the invention of the alphabet. Diodorus Siculus claimed that Zeus gave the alphabet to the Greeks, but the Great Flood destroyed this knowledge. Denise Schmandt-Besserat looks at small clay tokens used for accounting in the fourth millenium B.C. in the Middle East. The plain tokens are precursors of numerals; the complex ones led to pictographs and an alphabet. M. W. Green carries on the story of the development of cuneiform. The origin of Egyptian hieroglyphics is the subject of Henry George Fischer's contribution. Frank Moore Cross treats the creation of the alphabet in the Middle East. He argues that all alphabets derive from "an Old Canaanite alphabet and its immediate descendant, the Early Linear Phoenician alphabet." Among the descendants of this alphabet was Arabic writing, which James A. Bellamy discusses, as well as the Greek and Latin, the subjects of chapters by Ronald S. Stroud and Rex Wallace. Elmer H. Antonsen and Ruth P. M. Lehmann respectively consider runes and ogham, used by the Germanic tribes and Celts. Chinese writing is the subject of David N. Keightley's contribution, and the final chapter, by Floyd G. Lounsburg, considers the Mayan hieroglyphics. All the essays are well-illustrated, and all include bibliographies for further study. Though intended for the general reader, these pieces are likely to interest the specialist as well.

Shepherd, Margaret. *Calligraphy Now: New Light on Traditional Letters*. New York: Putnam, 1984.

In the first section, "New Pens and Pen Strokes," Shepherd advocates new techniques and writing implements to supplement the traditional fixed angle use of the broad-edged pen. Section 2, "New Visual Purposes," applies the ideas of Section 1 to new uses, some of them alphabetic, some not. The third section examines some unorthodox scribes, such as graffiti artists and children, as well as amateur antiquarians. Section 4 shows how over the centuries lettering has incorporated illusionistic elements. "New Dimensions" (Section 5) explores three-dimensional lettering and the use of color; Section 6, "New Configurations," discusses layouts. Shepherd offers many examples and illustrations and sources for further study. She also notes what materials the would-be graphic artist will need, and she provides clear instructions. Throughout, Shepherd examines historical examples to show that her avant-garde ideas rest on traditional practices.

Standard, Paul. *Calligraphy's Flowering, Decay, and Restauration: With Hints for Its Wider Use Today.* Chicago: Society of Typographic Arts, 1947.

As in printing, the earliest calligraphy—which for Standard means the writing presented in Ludovico degli Arrighi's *La operina* (c. 1523)—was the best, and by the early nineteenth century commercialism had caused a decline in the art, since beauty was less important than speed. Standard believed that at least in the book arts, if not in the schools, calligraphy was enjoying a revival. He cites the work of T. M. Cleland and W. A. Dwiggins, among others, as examples of the renewed skill and interest in good penmanship joined to book production. Filled with early and more modern examples of attractive calligraphy and of printing incorporating calligraphic elements. Concludes with a plea for the teaching of good penmanship.

Stiennon, Jacques, and Geneviève Hasenohr. *Paléographie du moyen âge.* Paris: A. Colin, 1973.

The introduction looks at the very act of writing, which is at once physical, psychological, and social; at the ways to approach ancient documents (patiently, meticulously); and at the contributions of paleography to other disciplines. The first chapter traces the history of the subject, which may be said to begin with Jean Mabillon's *De re diplomatica* (1681). Chapter 2 traces the history of Latin script, and the third chapter deals with scriptoria, scribes, materials, and instruments for writing. Relates writing to its philological, cultural, and historical milieu. Includes a hundred pages of facsimiles. The first appendix provides transcriptions from medieval texts dealing with writing (among them an excuse for slow copying); includes French translations for Latin texts. Other appendices suggest exercises for students of paleography and provide a glossary of French and Latin technical terms, as well as a bibliography.

Tannenbaum, Samuel A. *The Handwriting of the Renaissance: Being the Development and Characteristics of the Script of Shakespeare's Time.* New York: Columbia University Press, 1930.

In his first chapter, Tannenbaum traces the development of the Latin alphabet from its origins to the Renaissance. He then describes general aspects of the secretary hand, which is the basic cursive script of the period he considers. Chapter 3 looks at lowercase letters (minuscule), giving a letter-by-letter analysis; Chapter 4 does the same for the majuscules. Subsequent chapters consider abbreviations, punctuation, and numerals. Following the bibliography, Tannenbaum offers fourteen examples of the Renaissance secretary hand and provides transcriptions.

Taylor, Isaac. *The History of the Alphabet: An Account of the Origin and Development of Letters*. New ed. 2 vols. London: Edward Arnold, 1899.

A pioneering study first published in 1883. Volume 1 deals with the Semitic alphabets, Volume 2 with the Aryan scripts. Taylor takes an evolutionary view of the alphabet. He maintains that the letter "M," for example, began in Egypt as an ideographic for Mulak (owl). The letter then became a syllabic representation for Mu, and finally "M." The two peaks of the letter are the ears of the original ideograph, the dip in the letter the beak. Similarly, "A" began as the picture of an eagle, "D" as a hand, and "F" as an asp. Taylor concentrates on Egyptian, cuneiform, and Chinese alphabets in his first volume, saying less about Mesoamerican and Hittite writing because less was known about these. Greek and Latin alphabets are the focus of the second volume. Taylor traces the Semitic alphabet back to Egyptian hieroglyphics, an idea developed by Emmanuel de Rouge and published in 1874. Taylor's idea of acrography is correct, though the sounds probably are based on Semitic rather than Egyptian words, and the shapes of the letters on Semitic pictographs. The Semitic debt to Egyptian writing remains a matter of debate, though the hieroglyphic system did include some phonetic characters.

Thompson, Edward Maunde. *An Introduction to Greek and Latin Paleography*. Oxford, England: Clarendon Press, 1912.

A classic. Thompson traces the development of Greek and Latin alphabets from their origins through the seventeenth century. He looks at how political events affected handwriting, and he traces the rise of national Latin book hands and cursive scripts in the Middle Ages. This scholarly treatment includes 250 examples of handwriting, beginning with fourth century B.C. papyrus and ending with a document from 1673. In addition to discussing the different forms of letters Thompson examines writing surfaces and writing implements.

Thomson, S. Harrison. *Latin Bookhands of the Later Middle Ages, 1100-1500*. Cambridge, England: Cambridge University Press, 1969.

Intended "as a sort of guide to the perplexed who have to work with the bookhands of the last four centuries of the middle ages." Most of the book consists of 132 facsimiles arranged geographically (France, Germany, Great Britain, Italy, and Iberia) and then chronologically. By 1100, Carolingian was in many places yielding to Gothic; by the later fifteenth century humanistic scripts were exerting a strong influence on bookhands throughout Europe. Thomson notes the peculiarities of each bookhand reproduced, making this work an excellent introduction to paleography, the more so because the author avoids highly technical terminology. Lawrence S. Thompson called this "the best available guide for identifying and dating later medieval manuscripts," and he concluded his review in *The Papers of the Bibliographic Society of America*, "Here is a basic work for the classical scholar, the medieval historian, the paleographer, and the collector of manuscripts (64, 1970, 384). James A. Brundage wrote in *The Classical Journal* 67 (1971): 78, "Every scholar who works seriously with Latin manuscripts of the high and later middle ages will need to use this book."

Ullman, Berthold Louis. *Ancient Writing and Its Influence*. New York: Longmans, Green, 1932.

A succinct, learned survey of "the history of the alphabet, Greek paleography and epigraphy, Latin paleography and epigraphy, and the origin of printing." Although much scholarship has appeared since the publication of Ullman's book, his observations remain sound, and the selective bibliography remains useful. Includes sixteen plates that illustrate the transformation of Greek and Latin scripts from the classical world to the end of the Middle Ages.

_____. *The Origin and Development of Humanistic Script*. Rome: Edizioni di Storia e Letteratura, 1960.

Ullman argues that Coluccio Salutati first created a version of the humanistic alphabet, drawing on Carolingian manuscripts that he owned. Poggio Bracciolini worked for Coluccio, and Poggio is generally recognized as a creator of the humanistic script, though others share this honor. Stanley Morison has proposed Niccolò de' Niccoli as the father of humanistic handwriting, and Ullman agrees that Niccoli did develop a new script. Poggio's would lead to Roman typefaces, while Niccoli's cursive was the forerunner of the italic. Ullman follows the early spread of this new writing, whose founders called it old because it resembled models predating the "new" Gothic forms. He discusses those scribes especially involved in the diffusion of this writing. With sixty-eight plates illustrating the humanistic hand.

Wardrop, James. *The Script of Humanism: Some Aspects of Humanistic Script, 1460-1560.* Oxford, England: Clarendon Press, 1963.
The text of the lectures Wardrop gave at King's College, London, in 1952 to advanced students of paleography. Wardrop observes that "the ultimate value of paleography . . . lies in just what it has to tell us about people and things." He remarks that the early Renaissance looked back to Rome, and the first humanists chose to adopt Carolingian minuscule not for its beauty but its antiquity. They called their writing "lettera antica"—the old script—in contrast to the "lettera moderna," or Gothic. Using fifty-eight plates Wardrop traces the development of humanistic script as it moved away from a revival of the Carolingian form to incorporate elements of classical inscriptions and the informal cursive. The *Times Literary Supplement* praised the book as one "which will surely remain a classic study of Renaissance paleography" and admired "the precision and elegance of its writing and the sparkle of its incidental biographical and critical aperçus" (May 6, 1965, 360).

Whalley, Joyce Irene. *English Handwriting, 1540-1853.* London: Her Majesty's Stationery Office, 1969.
A collection of facsimiles based on the holdings of the Victoria and Albert Museum. Many of the illustrations show actual letters and notebooks, such as a letter from Queen Elizabeth I. She signs her name in italic; the text of the letter is in the secretary hand. Other reproductions come from engraved copybooks; the earliest example in the collection is Martin Billingsley's *The Pen's Excellence*, first published in 1616. Writing masters quarreled over the desirability of ornamentation. By the end of the eighteenth century, the plain style in calligraphy had triumphed, though ornamental scripts were still taught as exercises. By the mid-nineteenth century, writing had become so widespread that teachers of the subject were no longer required. Universal penmanship tended to create uniformity: *Cassell's Popular Educator* (1853) included only three basic scripts. For each example Whalley provides an informative caption, and she places calligraphy in its historical, social, and economic contexts. For example, expanding commerce required a simple, rapid, legible handwriting and so contributed to the decline of elaborate scripts.

——————. *The Pen's Excellence: A Pictorial History of Western Calligraphy.* New York: Taplinger, 1982.

Drawing on the resources of the Victoria and Albert Museum, Whalley has produced an illustrated survey of the Latin alphabet from classical antiquity and early Christianity to the modern period. The book contains over 400 illustrations (only nine in color). For each, Whalley provides an informative analysis. At the end Whalley presents some exciting—or egregious—examples of "applied calligraphy" in commerce.

_____. *The Student's Guide to Western Calligraphy: An Illustrated Survey*. Boston: Shambhala, 1984.
Uses 172 black-and-white plates to demonstrate the history of Western scripts. Each section begins with an instructive essay, and appendices treat technical elements and terminology. Like *The Pen's Excellence*, this work draws on the resources of the Victoria and Albert Museum, where Whalley served as Assistant Keeper of the Library. Whalley shows the forms of the Latin alphabet and explores reasons for changes in the appearance of the letters.

_____. *Writing Implements and Accessories from the Roman Stylus to the Typewriter*. Detroit: Gale Research, 1975.
The ten chapters examine the stylus, the quill pen, steel pen, fountain pen, ink and ink holders, typewriters, pencils, the ballpoint pen, writing surfaces, and miscellaneous writing materials. The focus is on England. About half the 142-page volume is devoted to black-and-white illustrations that show how the implements work or that present especially fine examples. Raymund F. Wood commented in the *Journal of Library History* 12 (1977): 205 that Whalley's work "will provide students of the history of written communication at least a cursory, and even an interesting, survey of the commonest writing instruments of the past two thousand years." Includes a bibliography.

Williams, Henry Smith. *Manuscripts, Inscriptions, and Muniments, Oriental, Classical, Medieval and Modern, Described, Classified, and Arranged, Comprehending the History of Writing*. 4 vols. London: Merrill and Baker, 1902.
These oversize portfolios present more than 200 full-color facsimiles with commentaries tracing the development of writing around the globe. Volume 1 contains the Oriental series, with the story of deciphering cuneiform and hieroglyphics. The second volume deals with the classical period, including the origins and development of Greek and Latin scripts. The third volume treats Latin scripts in medieval Europe, and the fourth looks at illuminated manuscripts of the East and also modern scripts.

Wilson, Nigel. *Mediaeval Greek Bookhands*. 2 vols. Cambridge, Mass.:
Medieval Academy of America, 1973.

Volume 1 presents brief comments about the eighty-eight plates reproduced in Volume 2. The facsimiles range from the fourth to the
sixteenth century, most of them depicting medieval Greek minuscule.
The text of Volume 1 is brief—thirty-eight pages—because the book
was designed for Wilson's Harvard seminar on Greek paleography and
so was supplemented by his lectures. Because Wilson selected some
examples for which dating remains speculative, his comments about
some of the illustrations will not be accepted by all scholars. Nonetheless, Aubrey Diller wrote that "this work will be used with pleasure
and profit by students of Greek paleography" (*Speculum* 51, 1976,
158).

Zapf, Hermann. *Pen and Graver: Alphabets and Pages of Calligraphy*.
New York: Museum Books, 1952.

An attractive reissue of the first limited (1950) edition published in
Germany. Zapf studied the work of Edward Johnston and Rudolf Koch
to teach himself calligraphy as a way to improve typography. The book
includes twenty-five plates. These are followed by short discussions
that explain the development of the Latin alphabet. The earliest example shows a Greek hand; Zapf then progresses through the various Latin
bookhands to the script-like type of Giambattista Bodoni in the late
eighteenth century, and to modern German script. Zapf credits
Johnston, Koch, and Rudolf von Larisch with bringing "a vital impulse
to contemporary letter forms."

Chapter 6
TYPOGRAPHY, PRINTING, AND BOOK DESIGN

Arnold, Edmund C. *Ink on Paper 2: A Handbook of the Graphic Arts.* New York: Harper & Row, 1972.

In twenty-one chapters, Arnold surveys all facets of printing and bookmaking, including typesetting, computerized texts, layout, proofreading, ink, paper, binding, and planning a project. He includes a glossary of technical terms, and each chapter concludes with a bibliography. A useful, clearly written introduction for anyone seeking an overview of the processes involved in creating a book.

Barker, Nicolas. *Aldus Manutius and the Development of Greek Script and Type in the Fifteenth Century.* New York: Fordham University Press, 1991.

The first printers in Italy, Sweynheym and Pannartz, created a Greek font for their Lactantius (1465-1467), but Aldus replaced the earlier, monumental, antiquarian typefaces with a cursive Greek modeled on Cretan calligraphy. The new typeface suggested modernity. Greek was no longer an ancient language, but the working vocabulary of the fifteenth century humanist. The smaller Aldine typeface, combined with the absence of notes, allowed for more compact books—octavos that could be carried and read anywhere, not folios designed exclusively for the study. Barker explores the cultural milieu that prompted Aldus to undertake his program of Greek publishing and examines Aldus' typographical predecessors and successors. Barker also identifies Immanuel Rhusotas as the scribe who most influenced Aldus' first Greek font. George and Manuel Gregoropoulos suggested modifications for the second Aldine Greek type. The third derives from the script of Marcus Musurus, and the fourth, used for the 1502 Sophocles, resembles Aldus' own handwriting. Aldus' Greek types, based on scribal practice, influenced the handwriting of his contemporaries such as Angelo Vergecio, whose Greek characters later served as the model for Claude Garamond's *grecs du roi.* An appendix provides "Documents Relating to the Development of Greek Type in Venice." The first (1985) edition of Barker's study, limited to 200 copies, included four original Aldine leaves providing examples of the four Greek typefaces Aldus used.

Bennett, Paul A., ed. *Books and Printing: A Treasury for Typophiles.*
Cleveland: World, 1951.

Not all of the more than forty essays in this collection deal with
typography; Anne Lyon Haight, for example, offers her thoughts on
the question, "Are Women the Natural Enemies of Books," a response
to Andrew Lang's observation in *The Library* (1881) that women are
"the natural foes of books." Many of the pieces here, however, address
typographical matters. Holbrook Jackson comments on William Morris' efforts with the Kelmscott Press, which Jackson maintains produced books more pleasant to look at than to read. Stanley Morison's
"First Principles of Typography," often reprinted, appears here, arguing
for readability rather than eccentricity, however artistic the latter may
be. Eric Gill's "Typography" distinguishes between industrial and
humane printing. The aim of the former is plainness and uniformity;
the purpose of the latter in the expression of individuality. Gill objects
to mingling the two and concludes, "The beauty that Industrialism
properly produces is the beauty of bones; the beauty that radiates from
the work of men is the beauty of the living face." Among the other essays
included here are Frederic W. Goudy's "Type and Type Design," Paul
A. Bennett on Bruce Rogers, Daniel Berkeley Updike's "Some Tendencies in Modern Typography," and Theodore Low DeVinne's "The
Old and the New: A Friendly Dispute between Juvenis & Senex," in
which the latter's support for older typefaces confronts Juvenis' fondness for innovation. Altogether a delightful and informative volume.

_____. "On Recognizing the Type Faces." *The Dolphin* 2 (1935):
11-59.

Bennett begins with a brief survey of the five basic divisions among
typefaces: Venetian, Old Style, Transitional, Modern, and Contemporary. He also presents an anatomy of the letters, identifying serif, spine,
bowl, spur, tail, kern, and other features. Most of the article considers
specific twentieth century renditions of various types, many based on
older models. Thus, the American Type Founders Company Cloister
Old Style derives from Nicolas Jenson's fifteenth century Venetian
fonts; Jan van Krimpen's Romanee was inspired by the Aldine Bembo
and seventeenth century Dutch italic. A useful guide through the maze
of modern type.

Biggs, John R. *An Approach to Type.* 2d ed. London: Blandford Press,
1961.

Based on Biggs's addresses to students at the London School of
Printing and the Central School for Arts and Crafts, this book provides

a useful introduction for those involved in printing or those seeking to understand typography. Biggs begins by identifying the elements of type, explaining the point system by which type is measured, and discussing various sizes of type. He notes, for example, that different designs will appear to differ in size even though all may be twelve-point. Other matters addressed in Part 1 concern legibility and read-ability, classification of type, typographical decoration, and paper. Part 2 presents a historical overview of typography, and part 3 offers advice and further reading for the student. Biggs also shows many type specimens. Well illustrated.

_____. *Basic Typography*. New York: Watson-Guptill, 1968.
Examines "some of the fundamentals of typographic design that en-dure through all the vagaries of fashion in the hope that the student will develop first an analytic approach to design and second create solutions that grow out of the nature of the problem instead of trying to impose a preconceived formula." In "Principles," Biggs traces the elements of typography from the letter to the design of an entire book. "Mechanics" addresses technical aspects, and "The Practice" deals with layout. With a short glossary and bibliography.

_____. *Letter-Forms and Lettering: Towards an Understanding of the Shapes of Letters*. Poole, England: Blandford Press, 1977.
Written for those who wish to make letters. Chapters discuss the history of letterforms, legibility, "A Method of Practice" in making letters, the structural elements of the Latin alphabet, and variations of the basic design. Biggs argues for experimentation: "In order to shape letters well we must understand them, and in order to understand them we must make them." Focuses on the Latin alphabet but briefly discusses Cyrillic, Hebrew, Arabic, and Oriental writing systems. Concise and well-illustrated, with practical exercises and good advice about tools, materials, and techniques.

Binns, Betty. *Better Type*. New York: Watson-Guptill, 1989.
Intended for graphic designers, but useful for anyone seeking an introduction to typography and printing. Binns first explains basic terminology, such as stroke, space, and serif. The following chapters look at legibility and readability; letter design; line, word, and charac-ter spacing and how these are affected by the lightness or heaviness of the type; unjustified typesetting; and other matters. With many exam-ples of columns or pages of type to show readers the effect of a particular choice. Includes a brief bibliography.

Brewer, Roy. *An Approach to Print: A Basic Guide to the Printing Process.*
  London: Blandford Press, 1971.
  The first six chapters discuss printing methods. Chapter 7 deals with
  composition, Chapter 8 with typography and design. Illustration and
  reproduction are the subjects of Chapter 9; Chapter 10 considers
  computers. Chapters 11 and 12 concentrate on binding and ink. The
  volume concludes with a look towards future trends; it also includes a
  bibliography. Brewer offers an accessible text that is complemented by
  numerous illustrations. A good introduction to the technology and
  business of printing.

Bringhurst, Robert. *The Elements of Typographic Style.* Vancouver,
  British Columbia: Hartley & Marks, 1992.
  Bringhurst argues that "the typographer's one essential task is to
  interpret and communicate the text." The book is filled with maxims:
  "Read the text before designing it"; "balance facing pages by moving
  single lines"; "don't permit the titles to oppress the text." For each rule,
  Bringhurst includes discussion and explanation as he takes the typographer through the stages of creating a printed page. The book
  includes many examples of typefaces, arranged alphabetically within
  the categories of serifed, unserifed, scribal, titling and display faces,
  black letter, uncial, Greek, and Cyrillic. Appendices cover "Sorts and
  Characters," terms of the trade, and references for further study. Filled
  with insights and practical instructions; useful for the novice and
  veteran alike.

Bruce, David, Jr. *The History of Typefounding in the United States.* Edited
  by James Eckman. New York: Typophiles, 1981.
  Although Douglas C. McMurtrie prepared an edition of Bruce's manuscript in 1925, the Typophiles' version offers a more accurate text.
  Bruce, whose life spanned most of the nineteenth century, invented a
  number of improvements in typecasting, and this little volume, based
  on his holograph and typescript, describes his observations on changes
  in the industry, together with his contributions to these developments.
  Also discusses a number of individuals and firms important in the field.

Burns, Aaron. *Typography.* New York: Reinhold, 1961.
  Intended "for the student, professional and lay person, for anyone who
  wishes to learn more of the new function of modern typography—and
  the factors that contribute to its development." Concerned mainly with
  advertising that attracts consumers. Explores how typeface and layout
  combine to create design. Most of this oversize book is devoted to

examples, but Burns offers some of his own thoughts. For example, he maintains that "'perfect' typography must be unorthodox. It may mean using wrong fonts, cutting hyphens in half, using smaller punctuation marks, in fact, doing anything that is needed to improve the appearance of typography."

Burt, Cyril. *A Psychological Study of Typography*. Cambridge, England: Cambridge University Press, 1959.
An attempt to determine how such aspects as letter size and form, spacing between words and lines, texture and color of paper, ink, and press work affect legibility and readability. Burt concludes that these factors operate together. More space between lines is desirable for a wide or heavy typeface, for example. Burt also found that students and faculty in the arts prefer old style typefaces, whereas those in the sciences favor modern fonts. Readers in general prefer what they are used to, and negative associations with a typeface can turn readers against the text. Ordinarily, 10-point type with 2-point leading will provide adequate readability.

Carter, Harry Graham. *A View of Early Typography up to About 1600*. Oxford, England: Clarendon Press, 1969.
The 1968 Lyell Lectures. In his first lecture, Carter addresses "The Technicalities of Type." He then discusses the diversity of letterforms, particularly during the third quarter of the fifteenth century. By 1490, as Carter's third lecture observes, uniformity was becoming the rule, as printers adopted a limited number of typefaces. The fourth lecture traces the triumph of Roman over Gothic, and Carter concludes with a history of typefounding and punch-cutting. Well illustrated, with a supplement on italic type. The noted bibliographer Philip Gaskell called Carter's book "stimulating in its range, shrewd in its judgments, and full of fascinating technological detail" (*The Book Collector* 21, 1972, 562). Similarly, the *Times Literary Supplement* for August 7, 1970, maintained that Carter's book "is a work that every student of typography should read and reread; no one with any interest in the history of the printed book should ignore it" (p. 895).

Craig, James. *Designing with Type: A Basic Course in Typography*. Edited by Susan E. Meyer. New York: Watson-Guptill, 1971.
Intended for students, this spiral-bound book provides a sound introduction for the lay person or would-be typographer, yet even the professional will find it useful as a reference work. Craig's first chapter discusses the origin of the alphabet. The second addresses the anatomy

of the letter and the different methods of textual reproduction. Chapter 3 discusses measuring type; Chapters 4 and 5 look at various book and display fonts. In Chapter 6 Craig talks about the materials necessary for designing a book; later chapters treat designing with type, copyfitting, and page layout. Each chapter concludes with design projects, and the book provides a brief bibliography and glossary.

_____. *Production for the Graphic Designer.* New York: Watson-Guptill, 1974.
According to Fridolf Johnson, this "is easily the best book on production we have ever seen, and the most comprehensive and understandable with respect to the spectacular and revolutionary innovations in typesetting. This is a book that even experienced professionals will want and find enormously useful" (*American Artist* 38, October, 1974, 20). Covers printing and engraving, book papers, ink, color printing, imposition, and binding. Also includes type specimens of five popular fonts. Enriched with reproductions of many historical and modern examples of printing.

Dair, Carl. *Design with Type.* Toronto: University of Toronto Press, 1967. Begins with a discussion of the basic elements of typography, the characters. Dair explores the formation of words, lines, and blocks of text, offering advice along with 150 illustrative examples. Dair's primary concern is with displays and advertising rather than with text, and he has introduced the annoying "fracture," a hyphen turned ninety degrees, to replace the standard hyphenation at the end of a line. Much of the book focuses on creating contrasts within the text by using different typefaces or colors in the printing, and it considers innovations from the fifteenth century onward. The *Times Literary Supplement* for August 15, 1968, calls this "a useful primer, full of interesting illustrations and sensible comments, with a certain bias towards the avant-garde" (p. 875).

Day, Kenneth, ed. *Book Typography 1815-1965 in Europe and the United States of America.* Chicago: University of Chicago Press, 1966. Originally published in the Netherlands to celebrate the 150th anniversary of NV Drukkerij G. J. Thieme of Nijmegen, the volume contains nine essays—two devoted to typography in France, and one each to developments in Belgium, Germany, Britain, Italy, Holland, Switzerland, and the United States. The survey includes nearly 200 plates and provides a good overview of book production, showing the transformations that have resulted from new theories of art and new technology. Although the essays limit their focus to a particular country, one can see international influences such as the effect of the work of William Morris and Stanley Morison or the impact of printing in one country on that of another (for example, the connection between a Swiss copy of Dante and William Pickering's "Wreath" editions). Fridolf Johnson wrote in *American Artist* 32 (February, 1968): 56, "Besides being eminently readable, each essay is crammed with pertinent details on leading designers, typographers, and presses, making it invaluable as a reference book."

Denman, Frank. *The Shaping of Our Alphabet: A Study of Changing Type Styles.* New York: Alfred A. Knopf, 1955.
Traces the shape of the Latin alphabet from its origins to the twentieth century, using many illustrations to support the text. Denman notes the influence of important typefounders such as Garamond, who refined sixteenth century printing and whose influence remains pervasive, though he died in poverty in 1561. Among those who drew on Garamond's designs was Christoffel van Dyck, who created types for the Elzeviers and whose work served as a model for Caslon. Giambattista Bodoni and the Didots pioneered modern typefaces in the late eighteenth century age of revolution. The nineteenth century appears to Denman as a typographical wasteland until the emergence of William Morris. The book is printed in different types. Thus, Chapter 5, "Georgian Charm," dealing with the eighteenth century, appropriately uses Caslon Old Style; Chapter 11, "It's A Modern World," uses a sans serif font. An appendix explains how type is made by hand.

DeVinne, Theodore Low. *Historic Printing Types.* New York: DeVinne Press, 1886.
Written to provide a succinct account of book types, those who designed and cut them, and the history of these fonts. Chapters treat typefaces chronologically, beginning with early German printing and proceeding through early roman and italic types, French and Dutch typography of the sixteenth and seventeenth centuries, English black letter, the types of Caslon and Baskerville, Bodoni, Fournier and later French founders, the revival of old style letters, and, finally, American typefounders. With over fifty useful illustrations. Still a standard work by one of America's leading graphic artists.

Dowding, Geoffrey. *An Introduction to the History of Printing Types: An Illustrated Summary of the Main Stages in the Development of Type*

Design from 1440 up to the Present Day: An Aid to Type Face Identification. London: Wace, 1961.

"Intended simply as an introduction to the subject . . . to familiarize students with the various categories or groups of printing types. We hope that it will also introduce them to wide reading in a fascinating subject." Part 1 presents types for books, showing the different styles in chronological order, beginning with Gothic. The second section treats display types, again starting with Gothic. Dowding offers brief, generalized comments on type characteristics but does not attempt detailed analysis. With many examples nicely reproduced in 117 illustrations. Includes a three-page bibliography.

Dreyfus, John. *Bruce Rogers and American Typography.* New York: Cambridge University Press, 1959.

A fond reminiscence concerning an important figure in type design. In the 1890s Rogers began working for George Mifflin at the Riverside Press, where Rogers fought to produce beautiful books. Dreyfus cites August Bernard's *Geoffrey Tory* and Isaac Walton's *The Compleat Angler* (both 1907) as examples of Rogers' artistic achievement. In 1912 Rogers left Riverside, and in 1916 he joined Emery Walker. Later Rogers worked for Cambridge University Press, Harvard University Press, and William Edwin Rudge. In 1928 he oversaw the production of his Centaur type, which was used in the Oxford Lectern Bible. He also designed *Aesop's Fables*, Shakespeare's plays, and other titles for the Limited Editions Club. Throughout his career he sought to follow traditional models, and his credo was, "The success of printing lies in never for one instant relaxing in the inspection of details, until the book is actually bound."

_____. *Type Specimen Facsimiles . . . Sixteenth and Eighteenth Centuries.* London: Bowes & Bowes, 1963.

Part of a project intended to reproduce all of the approximately 500 known type specimens sheets issued before 1800. The first volume presents fifteen. The earliest is an anonymous sheet from the Netherlands (c. 1565); this type was used for the King James Bible and Shakespeare's First Folio. The most recent example reproduced here shows Van Dijck types of about 1765. Preceding the sheets is an essay by Stanley Morison on the classification of type and brief discussions about each of the specimens. Of this effort to reproduce type specimens Morison writes, "The facsimiles and the annotations here provided should prepare the way for the greatly needed general manual . . . of the history of the most powerful of all the developments, after that of alphabetical writing, which in the past not only recorded but accelerated the process of civilization." A second volume, edited by Hendrik D. L. Vervliet and Harry Carter, presents two specimen books of Christophe Plantin's types (1567 and 1585) and one incomplete specimen sent to Plantin's son-in-law, Jan Moretus, by Guillaume II Le Be of Paris (1599). Philip Gaskell observed of this second volume, "The editors have an unrivaled mastery of their material, their exposition is clear and sensitive, the notes are of the right length and weight; the value of the whole enterprise is great and obvious" (*The Book Collector* 21, 1972, 566).

Gates, David. *Type.* New York: Watson-Guptill, 1973.
Presents more than 850 typefaces arranged by style, such as Modern, Sans Serif, or Calligraphic. Part 1 offers one-line specimens, and Part 2 presents fuller illustrations of these same fonts. For the major typefaces Gates provides complete alphabets in many point sizes; other typefaces are presented in complete alphabets but only in one or a few sizes. Includes historical information about the types and an analysis of their peculiar characteristics.

Gill, Eric. *An Essay on Typography.* London: Sheed and Ward, 1931.
Gill began designing type in 1925; among his creations was Joanna, which he used in his own printing firm of Hague and Gill. In the nine essays in this volume, Gill offers theoretical. historical, and practical insights into the nature of typography. He objects to uneven spacing between words, preferring an unjustified right margin. He recognizes the need for the mass-produced book but sees work emanating from a hand press as "more humane and livelier." Gill advocates spelling reform and the use of shorthand notation in the printing of books, but most of his arguments are more reasonable. The book's typography demonstrate Gill's theories of printing but not, happily, his fondness for shorthand.

Goudy, Frederic William. *Types of the Past, Type Revivals, with a Few Words on Type Design in General.* Syracuse, N.Y.: Syracuse University Press, 1936.
In the foreword to this published address, delivered at the New York Press Association Dinner on September 12, 1936, Howard Loggeshall wrote, "In all the history of printing from movable types there has not been a more sincere student, a more tireless worker, or a more potent stimulator of improvement in printing that Frederic W. Goudy." Goudy designed over one hundred typefaces. In his remarks he advocates type

that reveals "invention, novelty, style, beauty, and distinction." He also discusses his approach to designing type and concludes that he has never allowed his craft to "become an end in itself instead of a means only to a desirable and useful end."

_____. *Typologia: Studies in Type Design and Type Making with Comments on the Invention of Typography, the First Types, Legibility, and Fine Printing*. Berkeley: University of California Press, 1940.
"*Typologia* presents more or less graphically my work in type design and describes my own methods of type production" (preface). Goudy begins with a chapter on the manuscript book, the model for early printers. He then looks at the first types before he turns to his philosophy of type design. Goudy denounces imitation but emphasizes tradition. "The Story of a Type" tells of Goudy's designing the University of California Old Style (in which *Typologia* is printed). Other chapters address the problems facing a type designer and the question of legibility. A work at once delightful and informative.

Hammer, Victor. *Those Visible Marks . . . . : The Forms of Our Letters*. Lexington, Ky.: Anvil Press, 1988.
The text of a short talk that Hammer presented at Transylvania University, Kentucky. Hammer observes that most letters, especially in cursive and minuscule, are asymmetrical, and they point in the direction of reading. He argues that the Latin alphabet is ideal for representing the Latin language but assumes a degree of awkwardness when used for any other. Hammer also maintains that "'designed' letters reproduced by mechanical means" lack the life of the earlier typefaces created by Caslon, Garamond, and Bodoni because "only life generates life." The Anvil Press edition, limited to fifty copies, is printed in American uncial, a typeface of limited readability. The Typophiles reissued the book in 1989.

Hansard, Thomas Curson. *Typographia*. London: Baldwin, Cradock, and Joy, 1825.
The subtitle indicates the work's contents: "An historical sketch of the origin and progress of the art of printing; with practical directions for conducting every department in [a printing] office: with a description of stereotype and lithography." After a lengthy historical introduction, Hansard examines the work of some noted typographers. He then considers the practice of printing, exploring the techniques used and equipment necessary. Especially fascinating is his inclusion of the scale of prices for typesetting and presswork in the early nineteenth

century and his suggestions for calculating the cost of a printing project. Thus, he estimates that 500 copies of an octavo of 416 pages would cost the publisher 50 pounds, 14 shillings. *Typographia* remains particularly valuable for the glimpses it affords into printing practices of the first quarter of the nineteenth century.

Harrop, Dorothy A. *Modern Book Production*. Hamden, Conn.: Archon Books, 1968.
Harrop describes her book as providing "a simple outline of all the major modern processes involved in the making of books, periodicals, and newspapers, together with some guidelines to sound design, for the use primarily of students of librarianship, publishing and printing, practicing librarians, and others interested in the background to the printed material which they handle." She begins with a discussion of papermaking by hand and machine. The second chapter deals with type, the third with composition, and the fourth with methods of illustration. Subsequent chapters treat printing in color, printing of books and non-book material (newspapers, magazines, maps, and music), new technologies for reproducing texts, binding, make-up, and design. Concludes with a section on amateur printing. With a bibliography, three color plates, and sixty-eight black-and-white line drawings.

Hart, Horace. *Notes on a Century of Typography at the University Press, Oxford, 1693-1794*. Oxford, England: Clarendon Press, 1900.
Hart served as printer to Oxford University and Controller of the Oxford University Press from 1883 to 1915. He issued his book in 1900 in a limited edition of 150 copies, which he gave away. Hart concentrates on the Fell and Junius types. Appendix III reprints the correspondence of Dr. John Fell of Oxford that led to the acquisition of the Dutch types that bear his name. Hart also reproduces the Oxford University specimen sheets showing the typefaces and ornaments used in the century covered. The 1693 specimen is reproduced in its entirety; thereafter only the supplements appear. *The Nation* commented, "The total product is an honor to the press, and Mr. Hart's part in editing, composing, and printing it is beyond praise" (71, 1900, 176-177). Oxford University Press reprinted the volume, with some additions, in 1970.

Hlavsa, Oldrich. *A Book of Type and Design*. Translated by Silvia Fink. 2d ed. New York: Tudor, 1960.
Though the focus is on contemporary types and practices, Hlavsa offers

examples of earlier fonts as well. In the introduction, the book explores
the evolution of type from fonts based on scribal hands to more modern
styles, and this section also looks at such keys to type design as the use
of serifs, or the shape and slant of the letters. The main part of the book
presents over 250 typefaces clearly reproduced, and the book is well
indexed.

Hutchings, Reginald Salis. *The Western Heritage of Type Design.* London:
Cory, Adams & Mackay, 1963.
The subtitle describes this volume as offering "a treasury of currently
available type faces demonstrating the historical development and
diversification of form of printed letters." Hutchings provides a kind
of type specimen book, together with historical information on "the
derivation, inter-relationship, and representative status of the alphabets
shown." Though all the typefaces here are modern in that they are
twentieth century creations, many derive from older models. Hutchings arranges his alphabets to show the development of typography.
Hence, he begins with Goudy Text 292, designed in 1927 but based on
sixteenth century Gothic models. The final example is a font imitating
informal brush strokes; it was created by Peter Schneidler in 1955.

Isaac, Frank. *English Printers' Types of the Sixteenth Century.* London:
Oxford University Press, 1936.
A learned discussion of English typography in the 1500s. Isaac includes eighty pages of type specimens to demonstrate the variety of
fonts used during the period. He finds, for example, that Richard
Pynson introduced the roman typeface to England in 1508; all earlier
English printing had been in Gothic (black letter). Under Elizabeth,
partly because of the influx of continental refugees, English typography improved. Isaac's study can help date a book and identify its
printer(s) when this information does not appear on the title page.

Jackson, Holbrook. *The Printing of Books.* 2d ed. London: Cassell, 1947.
A collection of pieces by the always-entertaining Jackson. The three
essays in the first unit argue for the importance of keeping the reader
in mind in designing a book: "If at any time the printer asserts himself
at the expense of the reader, becomes puffed up with pride at his own
artistry so that his work struts between what the author has written and
what the reader would read, he must be put back into his proper place."
The eleven pieces in the second unit explore how authors have influenced the printing of their works. Their intervention has not always
been beneficent. George Moore, for example, created some books that

Jackson calls "uncomfortable . . . , rather snobbish and, perhaps, a little meretricious." Others, like John Ruskin, advanced typographic practice. The final section treats diverse subjects: the typography of William Morris (which Jackson dislikes), William Caslon, Claud Lovat Fraser, the Double Crown Club (which Jackson helped organize to encourage fine printing), the Curwen Press, and John Johnson's "Sanctuary of Printing" at Oxford, where the University Printer established a typographical museum.

Jaspert, W. Pincus, William Turner Berry, and Alfred Forbes Johnson. *Encyclopaedia of Type Faces.* 4th ed. New York: Barnes & Noble, 1970. An extensive selection of fonts, divided into roman, sans serif (here called lineales), and script. Provides a brief history of each typeface and notes distinctive characteristics. Useful as a pattern book for the designer, but anyone trying to identify a particular typeface must pore over many pages of examples because within each of the three large divisions the examples are arranged alphabetically without subcategories. Focuses on modern types, for which the volume serves as "the standard international index of western type faces in general service" (*Times Literary Supplement*, June 20, 1958, 352).

Jennett, Sean. *The Making of Books.* 5th ed. London: Faber & Faber, 1973. A standard on the subject of modern book production, divided into two major sections. The first part deals with the actual printing and binding of books and includes discussions of printing machinery, illustration, the making of paper, and machine- and hand-binding. Part 2, which occupies two-thirds of the volume, devotes a chapter to each aspect of book design, treating such matters as the selection of type, with examples of different typefaces. Jennett argues that ideally all the components of a book—paper, binding, typeface, dust jacket—will unite in a harmonious whole consistent with the text.

Johnson, A. F. "The Classification of Gothic Types." *The Library* 9 (1929): 357-380. Surveys attempts to catalog Gothic fonts and recommends dividing these typefaces into four categories. "Text" would embrace the traditional English black letter. A second category, "Fere-humanistica" (or "Gothico-antiqua") lacks serifs but is rounded. "Rotunda," or "Round-Text"—the term Johnson would substitute for Italian Gothic—and "Bastard," like roman italic, have the quality of script and suggest informality. The article includes illustrations of all four types, and Johnson explores a number of technical differences among them.

_____. *Decorative Initial Letters*. London: Cresset Press, 1931.
Johnson writes in his introduction: "The history of the mechanically reproduced initial is almost a history in miniature of wood-cutting and engraving. . . . National and provincial styles are readily evident, and an initial is frequently an easily recognized indication of the country or the town of origin of a printed book." Early initials derive from calligraphic models. Indeed, many of the initials in early printed books were supplied by hand. Fust and Schöffer's Mainz Psalter of 1457 contains printed, colored initials. Around 1470, Gunther Zainer of Augsburg also introduced decorative printed initials that served as models for William Morris and the Kelmscott Press. Pictorial or historiated initials were especially popular during the incunabular period. Although engraved title pages appear as early as 1550, engraved initials came into common use only in the seventeenth century; nearly all of these are pictorial. Woodcut initials remained popular, though, even after engraving supplanted woodcut illustration. After 1800, the decorated initial declined in popularity, and efforts to revive it have not proved altogether successful. The brief text is followed by many examples of printed initials, with short explications, covering five centuries of printing.

_____. *Type Designs: Their History and Development*. 3d ed., rev. London: André Deutsch, 1966.
An account of the typefaces that appeared from 1450 to the Victorian era. Johnson begins with Gothic, which he divides according to the fourfold scheme he proposed in "The Classification of Gothic Types" (1929), though here he further subdivides the Bastard fonts. Johnson next looks at roman fonts and traces the movement from old style to modern and back to old style again in the nineteenth century, a revival sparked by Charles Whittingham and William Pickering and later adopted by William Morris and other private presses. Italic is the subject of two chapters. Chapter 7 looks at script types designed to imitate handwriting, and Chapter 8 examines display types for advertising. With a twelve-page bibliography. A readable and sound introduction by a leading authority. The *Times Literary Supplement* for June 8, 1967 calls the book "invaluable" (p. 502).

Johnson, John. *Typographia*. 2 vols. London: Longman, Hurst, Rees, Orme, Brown & Green, 1824.
The subtitle declares that these volumes include "an account of the origin of printing, with biographical notices of the printers of England, from Caxton to the close of the sixteenth century: a series of ancient

and modern alphabets, and Domesday characters: together with an elucidation of every subject connected with the art." An early but still important work. Johnson rejects the claims of Laurens Coster of Holland to the title of proto-printer, and he denies that Oxford was the first site of an English press. In both cases Johnson has been vindicated. With much material on early English printing, and a vivid portrait of printing in the early nineteenth century.

Karch, Robert Randolph. *Graphic Arts Procedures: Basic*. 4th ed. Chicago: American Technical Society, 1970.
Intended for graphic artist trainees but useful for anyone interested in the subject, because the book clearly explains techniques. It is also well-illustrated and includes a glossary of technical terms. Chapter 1 examines the different methods of printing: relief, planographic, intaglio, collotype, and electronic. Chapter 2 deals with type, Chapter 3 with layout. Other chapters cover typesetting, paper, and binding. The book concludes with a discussion of job opportunities in the graphic arts.

_____. *How to Recognize Type Faces*. Bloomington, Ill.: McKnight & McKnight, 1952.
Presents examples of 1,475 typefaces, arranged in six large groups: serifed, black letter, stencil, script, square serif, and sans serif. To help the user, Karch further subdivides the first and last categories based on their treatment of the lower case "g." Karch does not include entire alphabets but rather presents the letters G, E, d, e, t, a, and g because these reveal the essential characteristics of each font. A long first section preceding the specimens deals with such matters as design, size, darkness, and weight of letters.

Krimpen, Jan van. *On Designing and Devising Type*. New York: Typophiles, 1957.
Krimpen disagrees with Stanley Morison on appropriate models for type. Morison rejects calligraphic influence, whereas Krimpen would draw from calligraphy, sculpture, and engraving. The body of the book is devoted to Krimpen's explanation of how he came to create his typefaces. He also offers his ideas on what constitutes good type design. For example, he does not favor "the copying or adapting of historical type-faces." He urges suiting the typeface to the purpose and argues that the best-designed fonts don't call attention to themselves.

Lawson, Alexander S. *Anatomy of a Typeface*. Boston: David R. Godine, 1990.

Lawson taught typography for thirty years at the Rochester Institute of Technology. In this volume he follows the classification scheme he presented in his *Printing Types: An Introduction* (1971) as he discusses thirty modern typefaces that allow a historical survey of printing. Thus, he begins with Goudy Text, a Gothic design. In this chapter, Lawson treats the medieval manuscript tradition, Gutenberg's imitation of the fifteenth century German bookhand, and subsequent typographical variations on black letter scripts. The book is well illustrated with contemporary and historical examples. It concludes with an account of how type is manufactured and the recognition that the computer has revolutionized printing.

———————. *Printing Types: An Introduction*. Rev. and exp. ed. Boston: Beacon Press, 1990.

The first chapter presents a historical survey of type. Chapter 2 offers a glossary. Lawson then turns to various classification schemes, including his own, which uses eight basic divisions (black letter, old style, transitional, modern, square serif, sans serif, script/cursive, and display/decorative). He offers examples of each type but does not attempt an exhaustive catalog. Especially useful for the historical overview. Fridolf Johnson, reviewing the first (1971) edition, praised the book's appearance and called the contents "excellent in every way; it is invaluable to anyone working with type by virtue of its clear and full outlining of the subject" (*American Artist* 35, October, 1971, 10).

Lawson, Alexander S., Archie Provan, and Frank J. Romano. *Primer of Typeface Identification*. Arlington, Va.: National Composition Association, 1976.

Presents twenty-six common typefaces. Discusses key characteristics as well as the history of each type and provides illustrations of peculiar features. At the back of the book is a chart noting what different manufacturers call a particular design. Arrangement is alphabetical rather than historical, but the first two pages discuss the eight basic categories of type: black letter, old style, transitional, modern, sans serif, square serif, script/cursive, and display/decorative.

Lee, Marshall. *Bookmaking: The Illustrated Guide to Design/Production/Editing*. 2d ed. New York: R. R. Bowker, 1979.

A practical handbook for the novice but useful for anyone seeking information on how a book is produced. Part 1, "Design and Production," begins with a short history of bookmaking and then examines in detail composition (preparing a manuscript for printing), typography, illustration, paper, binding, cost, and design. Part 2 deals with editing. *Wilson Library Bulletin* 40 (1966): 642 praised the first edition's "clarity of informative text and the quality and pertinence of its 300 illustrations." Richard K. Gardner, in *College and Research Libraries* 41 (1980): 166 wrote of the author's "clear style [that] holds the reader's interest throughout some very technical and detailed material." Gardner concluded his review by calling Lee's "the best book currently available on bookmaking in the U. S."

Legros, Lucien Alphonse, and John Cameron Grant. *Typographical Printing Surfaces: The Technology and Mechanism of Their Production.* London: Longmans, Green, 1916.
Although there are many ways to create an impression on a surface, the authors concentrate on metal type. They present a detailed anatomy of type and discuss design. They then turn to the manufacture of type, tracing the history of typecasting from the earliest days of printing to the twentieth century. Appendix II is especially useful: It lists and briefly describes British and American patents relating to typography. Appendix I provides a brief bibliography; Appendix III gives French and German equivalents for technical terms in English.

Lewis, John Noel Claude. *Anatomy of Printing: The Influences of Art and History on Its Design.* New York: Watson-Guptill, 1970.
Traces the history of printing and book illustration from Gutenberg to the twentieth century to show the "interaction between the printing press and the artistic, social, religious and economic backgrounds of the Western world." Lewis notes, for example, that Renaissance typography sought to create letters mirroring the proportions of the human body. The rococo was a reaction against Palladianism. Horace Walpole's Gothicism influenced the content of what he printed at his private press at Strawberry Hill but not in the manner of his printing, which was chastely neoclassical for the most part. The Gothic revival that Walpole fostered would, however, encourage the use of black letter and pseudo-medieval ornamentation. In the late nineteenth century, art nouveau and the Arts and Crafts movement each influenced the making of books, as did later trends such as the Bauhaus aesthetic, with its new vision of typography exemplified in Jan Tschichold's *Die neue Typographie* (1928). Beautifully illustrated; informative and attractive.

_____. *Typography: Design and Practice.* New York: Taplinger, 1978.

A revision of Lewis' *Typography: Basic Influences and Trends Since the Nineteenth Century* (1963). In the first part of the book, Lewis examines changes in typography since the Victorian era. James McNeill Whistler's concern with the design of his books influenced space and layout but did not affect the choice of typefaces. William Morris created new fonts based on fifteenth century models and so anticipated later typographical changes. Lewis notes how modern movements in art and architecture such as Dadaism or the Bauhaus have been reflected in the appearance of the printed page. The second part of the book deals with such practical matters as preparing a manuscript for the printer, the economic aspects of book production, and electronic modes of reproducing text.

Lieberman, J. Ben. *Type and Typefaces.* 2d ed. New Rochelle, N.Y.: Myriade Press, 1977.

Lieberman calls the vast array of typefaces the "Typorama." In the first three of twenty-six chapters (lettered rather than numbered) he provides a brief introduction to type design. Part 2 deals with fifteen important inventions that influenced typography. Lieberman begins with the development of a written alphabet and continues through "cold type" processes such as electronic and photocomposition. Part 3 deals with classification and identification of typefaces, and Part 4 explores some applications of the information presented earlier. Appendices provide type specimen pages. With a brief bibliography. Originally published as *Types of Typefaces* (1967).

Mackay (W. and J.) and Company. *Type for Books: A Designer's Manual.* London: Bodley Head, 1976.

This reference to the typefaces used by Mackay and Company can serve as a type specimen book for designers and editors. Following the extensive sampling of types are nearly 100 specimen pages showing how a text would look with different typefaces of various sizes. Also provides word and letter counts for some of the most commonly used types. John Ryder's *Flowers and Flourishes* (London: The Bodley Head, 1976), the companion volume, offers a comprehensive guide to printers' ornaments.

McLean, Ruari. *Modern Book Design: From William Morris to the Present Day.* Fair Lawn, N.J.: Essential Books, 1959.

Focusing on literature (books to be read, not just consulted), McLean argues for design that at once serves the author by not interfering with meaning and also exhibits grace and aesthetic beauty. In the nineteenth century, industrialization led to a deterioration in the design quality of the average book, though some good work continued to be done. William Morris prompted a revival of fine printing when he founded his Kelmscott Press. Francis Meynell of the Nonesuch Press and Allen Lane's Penguin and Pelican books encouraged other commercial presses to produce handsome books. McLean traces the resurgence of typographical excellence, and the book warns against sacrificing function for form. Nicely illustrated and well-written.

Melcher, Daniel, and Nancy Larrick. *Printing and Promotion Handbook*. 3d ed. New York: McGraw-Hill, 1966.
Intended for those "who have to buy printing and direct mail services; for those who have to plan or prepare advertising, publicity, or information material of any kind . . . ; for anyone, in fact, who attempts to influence others by the printed or duplicated word." The authors might add that this alphabetically arranged encyclopedia of printing design will prove useful to anyone seeking an understanding of the issues involved in preparing a pamphlet, editing a text, illustrating a book, or creating greeting cards—any aspect, in short, of printing. Appendix I offers a generous sampling of typefaces; Appendix II provides a bibliography. The postal information in Appendix III is sadly dated. A standard reference.

Moran, James. *The Composition of Reading Matter: A History from Case to Computer*. London: Wace, 1965.
Traces the methods of composing type, focusing on mechanized developments. Moran begins with a clear, concise discussion of creating, setting, and distributing type by hand, then turns to nineteenth century advances, beginning with an 1806 patent and David Bruce's typecasting machine (1838). Moran explores Ottmar Mergenthaler's invention of the linotype and Tolbert Lanston's of the monotype machine at the end of the nineteenth century, and he concludes with phototypesetting and computers. The book is especially useful for its discussion of machines that failed, such as the Young and Delcambre "Pianotyp."

_____. *Stanley Morison: His Typographic Achievement*. New York: Hastings House, 1971.
Morison was a leading typographical authority of the first half of the twentieth century. Moran discusses Morison's achievement against the background of the age. Largely self-educated, Morison possessed

the virtues and flaws of that condition. Though sometimes critical of his subject, Moran observes that "Morison will be remembered as the man who put the study of typographical history firmly on the map," and as the inspiration for text types that revolutionized and improved the level of book design. *RQ* 11 (1972): 277 called the book "masterly."

Morison, Stanley. "Decorated Types." *The Fleuron* 6 (1928): 95-130.
Although decorated types seem to belong to the nineteenth century, Morison shows that around 380 an inscription used an open letter designed by Philocalus. The Fust and Schöeffer 1457 Psalter used floriated initials; writing masters' elaborate scripts influenced French typographers of the sixteenth and seventeenth centuries. Around 1690 the firm of James and Thomas Groven produced the first English decorated type, Union Pearl. Using numerous examples, Morison follows the decorated letter to the late 1920s. He concludes that "a letter cannot live by ornament alone—... decoration is a condiment and not an aliment," especially for book type.

_____. *First Principles of Typography*. New York: Macmillan, 1936.
A brief but important statement by a leading typographer. Morison defines typography as "the art of rightly disposing printing material in accordance with specific purpose; of so arranging the letters, distributing the space and controlling the type as to aid to the maximum the reader's comprehension of the text." Thus, black letter, however pleasant for a Christmas card, will not work for a modern book. Morison cautions against excessive artistry, against typeface or layout that calls attention to itself because these distract the reader from the subject matter. The preliminary section of a book will provide sufficient scope for the typographer's ingenuity. The text itself should serve the reader, not the printer.

_____. *Letter Forms, Typographic and Scriptorial: Two Essays on Their Classification, History, and Bibliography*. New York: Typophiles, 1968.
Reprints two pieces not readily available elsewhere. The first is a lengthy consideration, "On the Classification of Typographical Variations," which served as a preface to *Type Specimen Facsimiles* (1963) edited by John Dreyfus. The second essay, "On Some Italian Scripts of the XV and XVI Centuries," appeared in an Italian bookseller's catalog in 1962. The former traces the history of typography and its study and urges the adoption of precise methods of describing type-

faces. In the second piece Morison stresses the importance of Giovan Francesca Cresci and Luca Horfei, who broke with earlier practices. Horfei created what Morison calls "a Christian revision of the pre-Christian Roman Capital."

_____. *On Type Faces: Examples for the Use of Type for the Printing of Books*. London: Medici Society and The Fleuron, 1923.
A limited edition type facsimile book illustrating "a range of good types available to the public" in the early 1920s. In his introduction, Morison criticizes the typographic experimentation of such private presses as Essex House, Eragny, King's, and Vale. "The letters simply must not come between the writer and his reader," Morison writes. The type also should suit the material; the beautiful letters of the Doves Press would not be appropriate for a modern novel. Morison's essay also provides a summary history of type design.

_____. *Selected Essays on the History of Letter-Forms in Manuscript and Print*. 2 vols. Edited by David McKitterick. Cambridge, England: Cambridge University Press, 1981.
Nineteen essays divided into four units: "The Design of Types," "Letter-forms," "Newspapers," and "The Learned Press." Chronologically they range from "Towards and Ideal Type" (1924) to "The Learned Press as an Institution" (1963). Some of the pieces had never been published before; others had appeared only in limited editions. Though Morison's typographical knowledge cannot be confined to two volumes, this welcome collection indicates the range of his interests and the extent of his learning.

_____. *A Tally of Types*, edited by Brooke Crutchley. Cambridge, England: Cambridge University Press, 1973.
Type production became mechanized in the late nineteenth century, but the typefaces so created were generally mediocre. In 1923, Morison was appointed adviser to the Monotype Corporation to develop more attractive type, based largely on older models. Morison discusses the historical background of this effort, noting the influence of such turn-of-the-century figures as William Morris and Edward Johnson. Morison then shows the typefaces that resulted from his work with the Monotype Corporation, types that drew on Italian Renaissance, French Renaissance, and eighteenth century examples. Each section is printed in the typeface it discusses. An appendix deals with types manufactured by the Monotype Corporation after Morison completed his text. Though Morison exaggerated his role in the reformation of twentieth century

typography, the volume demonstrates that his influence was still great. Fridolf Johnson called this "an eminently readable account [and] a handsome addition to printing history" (*American Artist* 38, May, 1974, 16).

_____. "Towards an Ideal Type." *The Fleuron* 2 (1924): 57-75. Dissents from the then-popular admiration of Nicolas Jenson's roman types. Morison argues for a type in which "the essential form corresponds with that handed down; and . . . the letters compose agreeably into words." He finds Jenson's upper and lower cases incompatible. Morison regards the Carolingian book hand as better than Jenson's typefaces and praises the letters Aldus Manutius used in his *Hypnerotomachia Poliphili* (1499) because the capitals are not as high as the ascenders of the lower case letters. Morison objects to "arrogant capitals," which he finds in certain twentieth century designs. He advocates a return to the principles of the *scittura umanistica* of the Italian Renaissance, a hand modeled on the Carolingian.

_____. *Type Design of the Past and Present*. London: The Fleuron, 1926. Morison begins his survey with book hands of the Middle Ages, especially Carolingian and the humanistic adaptation of that script in the fifteenth century. Only in Italy did that style challenge the Gothic, so Gutenberg and other German printers adopted the national hand for their printed books. Johann and Wendelin de Spira created the first roman typeface (Venice, 1469), and Nicolas Jenson perfected it. Morison defends Aldus Manutius' typefaces but sees him as more the scholar than the typographer, though Garamond in the sixteenth century copied Aldus rather than Jenson. Aldus also invented the italic type, but Morison prefers that created by Ludovico degli Arrighi of Rome. In the seventeenth century, Holland produced the best type; hence in 1660 Bishop Fell secured Dutch type for the Clarendon Press, Oxford. The eighteenth century witnessed the introduction of modern typefaces. Morison calls the types created between 1810 and 1850 "the worst that have ever been"; the revival of old typefaces later in the century led to improved bookmaking. Morison offers a vigorous, concise history with ample illustrations of the various types.

_____. *The Typographic Arts: Two Lectures*. Cambridge, Mass.: Harvard University Press, 1950. Morison delivered "The Typographic Arts" at the Royal College of Art, Edinburgh, in 1944, and "The Art of Printing" at the British Academy, London, in 1937. In the former, Morison surveys the history of printing to show how typography mirrors the sister arts such as architecture. The latter piece looks at the way printing has been regarded over the centuries and makes a case for clarity and consistency, qualities that will gain printing the recognition as one of the arts. With thirty-two illustrations.

_____. *The Typographic Book 1450-1935: A Study of Fine Typography through Five Centuries.* Chicago: University of Chicago Press, 1963.
This revision of *Four Centuries of Fine Printing* (1924) presents 377 examples of fine printing from Gutenberg to 1935, arranged chronologically. The book was intended to encourage study of these models and to foster the printing of more attractive, more readable books. Morison's introduction emphasizes the need for unobtrusive type and printing. Morison also surveys the history of printing. The examples reproduced can serve as an encyclopedia of type and design. David Kaser wrote in *College and Research Libraries* 26 (1965): 156, "The book is nicely designed and beautifully printed on fine paper. The facsimiles are excellently reproduced. . . . All-told, *The Typographic Book* succeeds very well."

Moxon, Joseph. *Mechanick Exercises: On the Whole Art of Printing.* Edited by Herbert Davis and Harry Carter. London: Oxford University Press, 1958.
Originally published in the seventeenth century, Moxon's was the first practical treatise on the art of printing and so serves as an invaluable source for studying the industry during that period. Moxon offers numerous details on the outfitting of a printing office and the steps involved in producing a printed page. He regards every operation as important and warns against shortcuts such as buying rather than making ink. He advocates the use of the improved wooden hand press developed in Holland and provides details about its construction and operation. Includes a glossary of printing terms. The editors have provided a biography of Moxon, and have added copious notes and illustrations that enhance the volume's usefulness.

Myers, Robin, and Michael Harris, eds. *Aspects of Printing from 1600.* Oxford, England: Oxford Polytechnic Press, 1987.
Brings together seven essays. Sheila Lambert looks at the efforts of the Stationers' Company to limit competition through government regulations in the early seventeenth century. Derek Nuttall examines typefaces used by seventeenth century English printers; most were im-

ported, but a number were of domestic production, and these indige-
nous products exhibit features that anticipate alphabets created by
Didot, Bodoni, and other late eighteenth century typographers. Peter
Isaac argues that Joseph Banks, among others, was crucial to the
success of William Bulmer's efforts to produce well-printed books.
Provincial printing in Warrington in the late eighteenth century is the
subject of Michael Perkin's essay; Michael Henry deals with the life
of a nineteenth century printing apprentice. Ian Maxted's contribution
explores the role of Friedrich Johann Justin Bertuch (1747-1822) in the
literary life of Weimar. The last piece, by Michael Treadwell, draws on
lists of master printers to arrive at some idea of the size of the London
printing trade between 1637 and 1723.

Ovink, G. W. *Legibility, Atmosphere-Value, and Forms of Printing Types.*
Leiden, Netherlands: A. W. Sijthoff's Uitgeversmaatschappij, 1938.
Examines "our psychological knowledge of modern printing type" and
seeks to add to that knowledge. Ovink argues that familiarity with a
typeface greatly influences legibility, so that a German can read fraktur
as readily as roman. The book discusses how letter size, space between
lines, length of the line, and paper color and surface affect reading. In
Part 2, Ovink turns to the feeling that a particular type evokes, the
psychological rather than the physical effects of typography addressed
in Part 1. The final section offers a brief historical survey of modern
typography and includes a list of the major modern typefaces. With an
eight-page bibliography.

Peignot, Jerome. *De l'écriture à la typographie.* Paris: Editions Gallimard, 1967.
Traces the history of letter shapes in the west from Phoenician and
Etruscan forms, through classical inscriptions and medieval manuscripts, to old style and modern type. Peignot argues that printing,
unlike writing, imposes a barrier between author and text. He also notes
that while early printers sought to imitate script, they could not; hence,
type fundamentally altered the shape of letters. Concludes with a
biographical dictionary of important typographers and a glossary of
technical terms.

Pottinger, David. *Printers and Printing.* Cambridge, Mass.: Harvard
University Press, 1941.
Pottinger seeks to enlighten the lay reader about the nature of printing.
The first two chapters talk about the origins and development of
printing. Chapter 3 deals with the printer's equipment. Type design is

the subject of the fourth chapter, and Chapter 5 continues this topic with an analysis of what makes a type suitable for a book. Jenson, Caslon, Baskerville, and Scotch appeal to Pottinger for their clarity, beauty, and power. The volume concludes with an discussion of book design. Every book should exhibit unity, just proportion, and clarity. Pottinger does not reject modern efforts to redesign the book but prefers the more traditional formats.

Provans, Archie, and Alexander S. Lawson. *100 Type Histories.* 2 vols. Arlington, Va.: National Composition Association, 1983.
The authors examine 100 typefaces. They have chosen "not . . . to portray the best available styles, but [those] most likely to be encountered not only by the personnel of typographic establishments but by all those engaged in the production of the printed word." For each typeface the authors provide a brief history, a sample alphabet, and a short analysis of distinguishing features. For example, the sans serif Antique Olive lower case letters have short ascenders and descenders. The dots of Artcraft's i and j are tear-shaped, and the ear of the g curves backward. At the beginning of each volume, Provans and Lawson explain terms like "x-height," "tail," "arm," and "ear."

Reed, R., ed. *Symposium on Printing.* Leeds, England: Leeds Philosophical and Literary Society, 1971.
A collection of eight pieces presented to celebrate the 150th anniversary of the publisher. J. M. Kerby's "Caxton to Computers" traces the development of printing over five centuries and notes the rise of automation. Roy Wisbey examines the use of the computer in literary studies to create concordances or to analyze a writer's style. Peter Waters' "Problems of Restoring Old Books" argues for new methods of training conservationists to cope with the increasing number of books that are deteriorating because of acid paper and natural and man-made disasters. R. C. Alston discusses the printing of facsimiles; John Dreyfus deals with "The Design of Type Faces," mainly through illustrations of different alphabets. "Chinese Prints and Printing" by I. Manton gives a brief historical survey of the subject. The volume concludes with D. J. G. Holroyde's essay on the role of television in communication. A wide-ranging, informative work.

Reiner, Imre. *Modern and Historical Typography: An Illustrated Guide.* New York: P.A. Struck, 1946.
Reiner offers selected examples of printed title pages, trade and business cards, printer's ornaments, cartouches and vignettes, calligraphic

type, printed bookplates, billheads, advertising, labels, and trademarks. Two short chapters discuss the work of the typographer Michael Fleischmann (1701-1786) and the illustrator/wood-engraver Thomas Bewick (1753-1828). Each section includes brief comments by the author. Reiner advocates simple title pages and simple designs for ornaments, and the book argues against "extremes of fanfare on the one hand or aesthetic over-refinement on the other" in advertising. Attractively printed and filled with common-sense advice.

Rice, Stanley. *Book Design: Text Format Models.* New York: R. R. Bowker, 1978.
Intended for the trade but useful for anyone involved or interested in publishing. Rice divides his book into various facets of design, such as main text setting, starting text, lists, plays, and mathematical theorems; and he then offers a number of options for dealing with these printing problems. A starting text might be indented or not; the first few words could be capitalized. Rice recommends specifying to the publisher the desired typeface, type size, type body (type size plus leading), width of the line, and amount of indentation. An appendix provides a glossary of technical terms.

Savage, William. *A Dictionary of the Art of Printing.* London: Longman, Brown, Green, and Longmans, 1841.
Offers insights into printing practices of the nineteenth century and before. Some of the entries remain current (e.g.,"broadside," "cancel," "specimen page"). Others, such as "newspapers," include valuable historical information. Still others, such as "price of pages," reveal much about printing practices of the early nineteenth century.

Scarfe, Laurence. *Alphabets: An Introductory Treatise on Written and Printed Letter Forms for the Use of Students.* London: Batsford, 1954.
Intended to introduce "the student to alphabets, so that he may in some measure see the over-all scheme of the evolution of design from the traditional starting-point of Roman Capitals to the present-day machine-set typefaces." In his introduction, Scarfe reflects on differences between writing and printing but concludes that calligraphy influences typography. He then presents a quick outline of the Latin alphabet before he gives historical examples of script and printing. Another brief chapter traces the decline and revival of attractive typography, and the book concludes with a large sampling of typefaces.

Scholderer, Victor. *Greek Printing Types, 1465-1927*. London: Trustees of the British Museum, 1927.

A beautifully printed guide to sixty examples displayed in an exhibition at the British Museum. In 1465, both Peter Schöeffer in Germany and the partners Konrad Sweynheym and Arnold Pannartz in Italy developed Greek typefaces. Schöeffer's efforts were not altogether satisfactory; Sweynheym and Pannartz, though they created only a lowercase font without accents or breathings, were more successful. Nicolas Jenson's Greek type was as skillful as his roman. Aldus Manutius was the first to model his Greek type on contemporary script rather than on the formal bookhands. Under the auspices of Francis I, the French Royal Greek types appeared, combining the skills of the calligrapher Angelus Vergetius (Angelo Vergecio) and the typecutter Claude Garamond. The French Royal Greek served as the standard for the next two hundred years. Baskerville and Bodoni attempted new Greek types but with unhappy results. Not until the late nineteenth century did designers create a practical and attractive new type for Greek. The facsimiles show the changes in type and also the spread of Greek printing in Europe. Nicolas Barker's *Aldus Manutius and the Development of Greek Script and Type in the Fifteenth Century* (cited earlier) challenges some of Scholderer's observations about Aldus, but the book provides a concise, generally accurate, and attractive survey.

Silver, Rollo Gabriel. *Typefounding in America, 1787-1825*. Charlottesville: University Press of Virginia, 1965.

Begins with the activities of John Baine, who came to America with his grandson in 1787 and began making type in Philadelphia. The first chapter, "Typefounding as a Permanent Industry," concentrates on the work of Archibald Binny and James Ronaldson, who also came from Scotland. "Some Minor Typefounders and Punchcutters" notes that among those involved in the fledgling industry were Benjamin Franklin and his grandson Benjamin Franklin Bache. "Growth and Expansion" traces the industry's development through the efforts of men like E. W. White and William Hager. "Inventions and Patents" considers efforts to improve typefounding; the fourth patent issued in the United States was granted to Francis Bailey for "a mode of forming types." Despite American progress in typefounding, "The Importation of Type" notes that the United States continued to rely on foreign suppliers throughout the period covered; but tariff protection allowed the American industry to grow, so that by 1825 it was sufficiently well established to make importation unnecessary. Includes thirty-two type specimen pages to illustrate the work of several American foundries.

William Charvat observed in *American Literature* 38 (1966): 423, "The book is meticulously researched [and] richly illustrated."

Simon, Herbert. *Introduction to Printing: The Craft of Letterpress.* London: Faber & Faber, 1968.
Intended to offer "some help to those who wish to acquire practical skills and by so doing gain an enduring interest in printing and typography." Discusses typesetting, proofreading, design, and other technical details. The *Times Literary Supplement* for February 22, 1968 remarked, "The book is clearly written and beautifully produced and should be equally valuable for beginners and experts" (p. 190). Because of technological developments since 1968, the volume is more appropriate to amateurs still using type than to commercial presses, but the principles presented remain relevant.

Simon, Oliver. *Introduction to Typography.* 2d ed. Edited by David Bland. London: Faber & Faber, 1963.
Provides guidance in all aspects of preparing a book and presents numerous examples of what Simon regards as good models. For example, Simon recommends smaller type for poetry, to avoid broken lines and to preserve the shape of the poem. He recommends centering a title on the total poem, not on the first line. Though intended for the typesetter, the book serves as a good introduction for the lay reader. Provides an extensive glossary of printing terms and a brief bibliography. Fridolf Johnson called the book "a classic text on typography and book design [that] should be in the library of every school and designer interested in fine typography" (*American Artist* 34, October, 1970, 65).

Smith, Adele M. *Printing and Writing Materials and Their Evolution.* Philadelphia: By the author, 1901.
Presents "in succinct form the leading facts relating to the history of printing, writing materials, and of bookbinding, and the processes by which they are made ready for general use." About half of the book is devoted to the history of printing, beginning with ancient relief processes such as those used to create cuneiform tablets, stamps, and brands. Smith examines blockbooks and broadsides before she discusses some early master printers. This section also discusses various presses. The second unit looks at writing and printing surfaces (such as rocks and paper), writing implements, and ink. The final section provides a brief history of bookbinding from antiquity to the end of the nineteenth century.

Spencer, Herbert. *Pioneers of Modern Typography*. London: Lund Humphries, 1969.

On February 20, 1909, Emilio Filippo Tommaso Marinetti published his "Manifesto of Futurism" in *Le Figaro*. Futurism revolted against the status quo in typography as well as in painting. Marinetti wrote, "The book will be the futurist expression of our futurist consciousness. . . . A new, painterly, typographic representation will be born on the printed page." Futurism and other modern movements—Dadaism, suprematism, constructivism—converged in Germany in the early 1920s. In October, 1925 a special issue of *Typographische Mitteilungen*, written by Jan Tschichold, introduced modern typography to a large audience of printers. In a book filled with samples of modern typefaces, Spencer discusses the careers of El Lissitzky, Theo van Doesburg, Kurt Schwitters, H. N. Werkman, Piet Zwart, Paul Schuitema, Alexander Rodchenko, Laszlo Moholy-Nagy, Herbert Bayer, and Tschichold, all important figures in establishing modern printing styles. Fridolf Johnson called the book "stimulating, valuable" (*American Artist* 34, October, 1970, 65).

Strauss, Victor. *The Printing Industry: An Introduction to Its Many Branches, Processes, and Products*. Washington, D.C.: Printing Industries of America with R. R. Bowker, 1967.

In his foreword to this work, Bernard J. Taymans, then president of the Printing Industries of America, Inc., remarked, "Victor Strauss has produced the most comprehensive book ever written on the printing industry. . . . It removes the mystery from printing and opens the gates of knowledge to everyone." The text can be very technical at times, but it offers comprehensive coverage of all facets of the industry, including presswork, paper, ink, and binding. An important reference, with much information on the role of computers in printing.

Sutton, James, and Alan Bartram. *An Atlas of Typeforms*. New York: Hastings House, 1968.

An illustrated history of 500 years of type, focusing on roman letters. The *Atlas* juxtaposes historical types such as Caslon in their original form, as shown in books and specimen sheets, with modern machine-made adaptations. Authorial comment is limited largely to the captions, leaving the reader to find the differences among various forms of a typeface. At the beginning of the book, the authors present medieval bookhands, which served as the models for the earliest typefounders. Attractive and informative, with many facsimiles.

_____. *Typefaces for Books*. London: British Library, 1990.

Most of this book is devoted to displaying over 100 digitized book typefaces in various sizes and spacings. Before presenting the specimens, the authors discuss technological and historical developments, type families, and principles of bookmaking. The volume concludes with short chapters on points of style, copyfitting, rules, signs and symbols, and a bibliography. Intended for type designers and professionals, but even the general reader will find material of interest here. For example, Sutton and Bartram present a succinct survey of changes in type from 1450 to the twentieth century, and the section on bookmaking provides a condensed version of Stanley Morison's *The Typographic Book* (1963). Ruari McLean wrote, "This book provides an immense and scholarly catalogue of options for today's typographers. . . . The design of this book is itself a model of elegant practicality" (*Times Literary Supplement*, January 11, 1991, 22).

Tanselle, G. Thomas. "The Identification of Type Faces in Bibliographical Description." *Papers of the Bibliographical Society of America* 60 (1966): 185-202.

Making the case for identifying the typeface of a book in a descriptive bibliography, Tanselle urges the recording of both size and style. He prefers measuring ten lines rather than twenty and recording the measurement in millimeters rather than inches. He also urges the adoption of the British standard for typeface nomenclature and suggests different levels of description. "Roman" might suffice in some cases, "Roman Baroque" in others, while others still might call for more detail, such as "Walbaum, Monotype 374 (DIN 1.34)," where DIN refers to a German classification system.

Tinker, Miles Albert. *Legibility of Print*. Ames: Iowa State University Press, 1963.

A scientific exploration of the elements that affect legibility. For example, italic is harder to read than roman lowercase; so, too, is text printed in all capitals, probably because then words lack conventional form. Tinker found that readers prefer types with serifs, though the absence of serifs does not affect reading speed. Mixed type retards reading speed, and readers prefer a single typeface. The book also discusses such matters as type size, width of line, layout, and use of color printing. An important book for any typographer or anyone concerned with making a text readable and pleasing.

Tracy, Walter. *Letters of Credit: A View of Type Design*. Boston: David R. Godine, 1986.

In the first part of the book, Tracy discusses elements of type design such as legibility and readability (Chapter 4), proportion (Chapter 6), and character spacing (Chapter 10). The second part looks at specific designers and types—Jan van Krimpen, Frederic Goudy, Rudolf Koch, W. A. Dwiggins, and Stanley Morison's Times Roman. Tracy calls this last "the most remarkable typographic phenomenon of the twentieth century." Also includes a good discussion of the technological revolution wrought by the computer. Tracy laments the transformation that allows for enlarging or shrinking any typeface because changes in size can distort the proper balance of thick and thin strokes. The book embodies half a century of study and thought, and it will inform as well as entertain the reader. James R. Kelly wrote that "For bibliographers and historians of the future, *Letters of Credit* will constitute an invaluable historical document; for readers today, it provides a glimpse of the dizzying transformation that is rapidly turning Gutenberg's world on its head" (*Papers of the Bibliographical Society of America* 83, 1989, 253). Ruari McLean called this "a thoroughly well-informed and wise guide" (*Times Literary Supplement*, December 5, 1986, 1388).

_____. *The Typographic Scene*. London: Gordon Fraser Gallery, 1988.

Tracy begins this pleasant survey of twentieth century typography by discussing the revival of fine printing in the 1890s and early 1900s. While many typographers looked to earlier models, some created new designs, especially for display type. In "Mentors," Tracy examines some important texts in the field, beginning with Theodore Low DeVinne's *The Practice of Typography* (1900-1904) and his 1885 Grolier Club lecture, "Historic Printing Types." The chapter on "Design: Conservative and Radical" argues for a commonsense approach. Tracy maintains that typographers should use fonts and format appropriate to the readership and subject. He concludes that electronics will not supplant the printed word, and he quotes John M. Strawthorn's "Future Methods and Techniques" (1981), "No matter what kinds of exotic technology we employ, people will *still be reading*."

Turnbull, Arthur T., and Russell N. Baird. *The Graphics of Communication—Typography—Layout Design*. 4th ed. New York: Holt, Rinehart and Winston, 1980.

A well-designed text, treating all facets of planning, preparing copy, and printing a visual message in any form, including the use of computers. The authors integrate communication theory with their discussions of design. Without discouraging creativity, they warn that the primary function of printing is the "clear exchange of information and consequently meaning." With special sections on magazines and newspapers. An appendix presents samples of commonly used typefaces, and the volume concludes with a bibliography and glossary.

Updike, Daniel Berkeley. *Printing Types: Their History, Forms, and Use: A Study in Survivals.* 3d ed. 2 vols. Cambridge, Mass.: Belknap Press, 1962.
A standard in the field since its first publication in 1922. Updike explores not only what printers and typographers have done since the mid-fifteenth century but also why certain experiments have succeeded. For example, he observes that Caslon's type surpassed its Dutch models because the letters work well together despite individual flaws. In the preface to the third edition, Lawrence C. Wroth wrote, "Those who have come after Updike in the writing of typographical history have in many instances enlarged areas with which he was imperfectly acquainted . . . ; these and others have set him right where occasionally he went off the course; and more than once certain of his judgments have been questioned. But one thing remains clear: it was he who put the thread into the hands of the new generation of typographical historians." William M. Ivins, in his review of the first edition, commented, "It is a book which should find interested readers among all people who like to look at books as well as read them, and there is no printer who takes his calling seriously who will not find that somewhere within its covers there is something especially for him. It is that pleasantly odd combination, a guide to the amateur and a sharp commentary for the professional" (*Yale Review* 12, 1923, 874). David Traister, commenting on a Dover reprint, observed that despite more recent scholarship, Updike "is still the place where a reader must begin" (*American Book Collector* 2, January/February, 1981, 56). This comprehensive study is enriched with 367 illustrations.

Warde, Beatrice. *The Crystal Goblet: Sixteen Essays on Typography.* Edited by Henry Jacob. Cleveland: World, 1956.
The collection takes its title from the opening piece, which is based on a lecture that Warde gave to the British Typographers Guild in 1932. She compared good typography to a fine "crystal-clear glass, thin as a bubble, and as transparent," and hence not interfering with the text. Such a requirement does not demand a dull typeface, though. Throughout the volume, Warde urges typographers to suit the font to the work,

to consider readability—how long one can continue to read a text—as well as legibility. The final essay presents what Warde regards as the most important thirty-two dates in the history of printing. Among these are 1814, when *The Times* (London) introduced Koening's cylinder flat-bed steam-powered press, and 1891, when William Morris began the Kelmscott Press.

_____. "Type Faces, Old and New." *The Library* 16 (1936): 121-143.
A survey of the revival of old-face type and an exploration of ways to classify various typefaces. Warde provides a clear explanation of key terms such as "face" and "family" and "size," offers a simple classification scheme, and presents some examples of typefaces with and without leading (separation of lines of print).

Williamson, Hugh. *Methods of Book Design: The Practice of an Industrial Craft.* 3d ed. New Haven, Conn.: Yale University Press, 1983.
Follows a manuscript through the steps that turn it into an edition, covering such aspects as composition, printing processes, illustration, paper, binding, dust jacket, and pricing. In addition to explaining the technicalities of book production, Williamson offers advice on design that will create a harmonious whole. Editorial planning, visual planning, and technical planning must function together. Reviewing the second edition, M. H. Black observed, "The text is uniformly clear and judicious; at all points the main problems are identified, and rational solutions advanced. Simply taken as a store of hints to the practitioner, based on practical experience, the book is almost inexhaustible" (*The Library* 23, 1968, 88).

Wilson, Adrian. *The Design of Books.* New York: Reinhold, 1967.
The author writes in his introduction that he intends "to show how the designer goes about preparing his layouts and following the book through the production processes." Wilson traces the history of book design and offers the first published illustrations of the first known example of layouts, which were prepared for the 1493 *Nuremberg Chronicles.* Chapters discuss typography, printing methods, paper, the parts of a book, design decisions (such as which typeface to use, how large to make the book, how wide to leave the margins; Wilson includes a useful checklist of twenty-four questions for the designer to consider), binding, and dust jacket. The last three chapters treat trade books, textbooks and reference material, and limited editions. The *Times Literary Supplement* for May 23, 1968, commented, "Mr. Wil-

son's book deserves a wide and sustained success because it delivers
so much practical advice with such an endearing mixture of enthusiasm
and enjoyment" (p. 536).

Zachrisson, Bror. *Studies in the Legibility of Printed Text.* Stockholm:
Almqvist & Wiksell, 1965.
A series of experiments reported here reveals that legibility remains
unaffected by many features of typography and layout. Right margins
justified or unjustified, letters with or without serifs, large or small
fonts play only minor roles in legibility, according to objective tests of
reading. Readers tend to prefer what they are accustomed to seeing on
the page. Yet readers and typographers generally agree on the appro-
priateness of certain typefaces for certain functions, perhaps because
of habit and custom. The experiments also reveal that general readers
and even specialists "are less sensitive and capable than is often
believed, when confronted with definite decisions about the aesthetics
of typography."

Zapf, Hermann. *About Alphabets: Some Marginal Notes on Type Design.*
Rev. ed. Translated by Paul Standard. Cambridge, Mass.: MIT Press,
1970.
Zapf served as art director for the Stempel type foundry, Frankfurt,
Germany, and published much about typography. The attractive *About
Alphabets* presents his autobiography, in the course of which he
explains his approach to type. He notes that modern type must be
suited to a variety of papers and mechanical printing processes that
did not concern typefounders in previous centuries. Though older
typefaces serve as Zapf's models when he designs letters, he argues
that new typefaces are as essential as new designs anywhere else. A
shorter version of the autobiography was published by the Typophiles
in 1960.

_____. "Printing Types and Books: An Expression of Their
Times." *Penrose Annual* 56 (1962): 47-53.
Until the nineteenth century, books reflected the spirit of their age. The
printing of Pierre-Simon Fournier, like a painting by Boucher or
Chardin, reveals the elegance, luxury, and splendor of the French court
of the 1760s. Giambattista Bodoni at first imitated Fournier, but after
the French Revolution he broke with tradition to create his own
typefaces. Gothic lettering demonstrates the same verticality as the
Gothic cathedral; the rounded humanist script of fifteenth century Italy
suggests the architecture of that country. Zapf urges the same consid-

erations for modern book production, which should reflect contemporary civilization; he dislikes self-conscious revivals. "Modern industrial designs—expressing our time and our philosophy—should be reflected in books and printed material by means of typefaces which have been designed according to the same concepts."

The Printing Press

Harris, Elizabeth M., and Clinton Sisson. *The Common Press*. 2 vols. Boston: David R. Godine, 1978.
Volume 1 provides the discussion, Volume 2 the plans of the early eighteenth century press housed at the Smithsonian Institution. Harris describes its construction to allow others to create a copy. She also considers the legend that this press once was used by Benjamin Franklin, and she traces the press's history until it reached the Smithsonian in 1883. In 1901 the Smithsonian secured ownership. A good anatomy of the wooden handpress as it existed for some 350 years.

Moran, James. *Printing Presses: History and Development from the Fifteenth Century to Modern Times*. Berkeley: University of California Press, 1973.
Lawrence S. Thompson called this work "indispensable for the student of books in the last two centuries" (*Papers of the Bibliographical Society of America* 68, 1974, 464). This handsome book treats "the development of the relief printing press from its inception in the middle of the fifteenth century until approximately 1940." It begins with the wooden press and its improvements. In the early nineteenth century, the wooden press yielded to metal models; the first of these was developed by the third Earl Stanhope (1753-1816). The cylinder press marked an advance over the older forms and became popular in the late nineteenth century. This technology was replaced in turn by the rotary press. Moran explains the history and operation of each of these machines. Appendix I discusses amateur and miniature presses; Appendix II deals with special presses for making a proof or trial impression. The *Times Literary Supplement* for December 8, 1973, commented that the text "is admirably comprehensive and well illustrated (the plates in particular are well chosen) from contemporary sources" (p. 1500).

Saxe, Stephen O. *American Iron Hand Presses*. Council Bluffs, Iowa: Yellow Barn Press, 1991.

The fourteen chapters of the book treat the various iron presses that were developed or used in America in the nineteenth century: Stanhope, Columbian, Ruthven, Wells, Stansbury, Smith, Washington, Albion, Philadelphia, Bronstrap, Foster, Ruggles, Union, and Tufts. Saxe explains the history of these presses and discusses their uses and method of operation. With wood engravings of the presses; these attractive illustrations were executed by John De Pol.

Lithography

Antreasian, Garo Z., and Clinton Adams. *The Tamarind Book of Lithography: Art and Techniques.* Los Angeles: Tamarind Lithography Workshops, 1971.

In Part 1 the authors deal with the practical considerations of lithographic printmaking, from planning the lithograph and selecting a stone to signing and numbering the edition. This section also considers the use of a metal plate rather than a stone, color lithography, and transfer lithography (which requires transferring a lithographic image to a second surface before printing; the image is first drawn on transfer paper and then moved to the printing surface). Part 2 examines the more technical aspects of lithography, such as the chemical processes involved, the papers suitable for the process, and the kinds of presses available. A detailed, informative account that *Choice* (8, 1972, 1441) called "The most comprehensive, thoroughly illustrated, and beautifully produced book on the art of lithography ever to appear. . . . The authors provide expertise, advice, and instruction on all practical aspects of the medium." Fridolf Johnson similarly praised the book in *American Artist* 36 (November, 1972): 34-38.

Cliffe, Henry. *A Complete Handbook of Modern Techniques of Lithography.* New York: Watson-Guptill, 1965.

Cliffe directs his volume to the "artist printer." After a short definition of the process, Cliffe explains how he creates a three- color lithograph. Subsequent chapters provide more detail about each step in the process: preparing the surface of the stone (or metal), rolling up the image (inking), and printing. Also briefly treats presses, inks, and papers. The book concludes with a discussion of necessary equipment and a list of suppliers as of 1965. A useful feature of the book is the inclusion of many illustrations, including some in color, produced by lithography. These demonstrate the wide range of effects achievable through this mode of printing.

Griffits, Thomas Edgar. *The Rudiments of Lithography*. London: Faber & Faber, 1956.

Griffits was a practitioner and advocate of lithographic printmaking. He begins by tracing the history of the process. In Chapter 3 he discusses preparing the lithographic surface. Chapters 4 and 5 deal with the use of colored inks, Chapter 6 with artistic techniques. Chapter 7 explains what equipment is necessary, Chapter 8 treats presswork, and the book concludes with a discussion of register marks (to determine true color), paper and imposition, shading, and photolithography. In under a hundred pages Griffits offers much useful advice. Attractively illustrated.

Hirsch, S. Carl. *Printing from a Stone: The Story of Lithography*. New York: Viking, 1967.

An elementary presentation, especially suitable for high school and even junior high school students. Hirsch begins his study with a discussion of stone rubbings and quickly surveys other forms of reproducing a text. In Chapter 3 Hirsch turns to the lithographic process developed by Aloys Senefelder, and subsequent sections consider important figures who used the process: Honoré Daumier, Nathaniel Currier and James Merritt Ives, Joseph-Nicephore Niepce, and Alphonse Louis Poitevin. These last two were pioneers in photolithography. Hirsch traces the development of lithography from its invention to the middle of the twentieth century.

Loche, Renée. *Lithography*. Geneva: Éditions de Bonvent, 1971.

Loche writes that her book "is not a technical manual for specialists." Instead she seeks "to provide art-lovers, visitors to museums and exhibitions[,] and collectors with a full description of the technique and history of lithography." Yet the fledgling artist, too, will find the discussion useful as Loche traces the creation of a lithographic image from the preparation of the stone to the printing of the work. Loche also explores variations on lithography—the use of color, transfer lithography, the substitution of zinc for a stone, and lithographic engraving. Chapter 8 provides a historical overview of the process, and Chapter 9 deals with collecting lithographs. The book concludes with a glossary and brief bibliography. Includes numerous examples of the art and some illustrations showing how a lithograph is made. *Choice* observed that "this handbook combines articulate prose with provocative illustrations to reveal the unsurpassed vitality of lithography" (11, 1975, 1618). Fridolf Johnson praised the volume's beauty and called it "an unusually good book for its size" (*American Artist* 37, November, 1973, 22).

Miles, Russell L., ed. *The Encyclopedia of Lithography*. Chicago: Printed for the Editor, 1938.

Combines brief entries with more extensive essays, in a single alphabet, on such subjects as the use of color, dot etching, the history of lithography, papermaking, photocomposing, and typography for lithographers. The short definitions are unsigned, but the longer pieces carry the names of the authors. These longer essays can be both technical and highly informative, while the shorter pieces will be especially useful to the novice.

Pennell, Joseph, and Elisabeth Robins Pennell. *Lithography and Lithographers: Some Chapters in the History of the Art*. London: T. Fisher Unwin, 1915.

A revision of a work first published in 1898. The opening chapters discuss the history of lithography from its invention in Germany. The focus of the book is on the use of lithography in France and England to create prints. Later chapters deal with technical matters: the stone or metal surface, materials for drawing, acids, papers, presses, presswork, and variations on the basic method. The oversized volume is filled with reproductions that in themselves comprise a history of the art.

Porzio, Domenico, ed. *Lithography: Two Hundred Years of Art, History, and Technique*. Translated by Geoffrey Culverwell. Secaucus, N.J.: Wellfleet Press, 1982.

A collection of eight essays. Porzio writes in his preface, "It is the intention of this book to provide a profile both of the technical evolution of the medium and of the actual history of lithographic art." Jean Adhemar's opening contribution surveys the art over the past two centuries. Porzio treats the technical aspects of lithography. This well-illustrated piece examines and demonstrates how great practitioners have used the medium. Alain Weill focuses on the poster; Michel Melot looks at the use of lithography in social satire. Jacqueline Armingeat discusses the illustration of books, and Porzio includes Aloys Senefelder's account of his discovery of the process of printing from a stone. The book concludes with a glossary by Rosalba and Marcello Tabanelli, biographical sketches of major artists, and a bibliography. An excellent historical survey, especially good on French and Italian lithographers of the nineteenth century. The text is enriched with nearly 300 illustrations, a third of them in color.

Senefelder, Aloys. *The Invention of Lithography*. Translated by J. W. Muller. New York: Fuchs and Lang, 1911.

In 1817 Senefelder, the inventor of lithography, wrote the story of his discovery; the book appeared in Munich in 1818, and an English translation followed the next year. Muller's version is more faithful to the original, though it omits the plates that accompanied Senefelder's first edition. Muller apparently used the 1821 second edition, which also reprints the text without the illustrations. The first part of the volume provides a history of the invention; the second describes the technical aspects of lithographic printing as it was practiced in its infancy. Senefelder's account offers fascinating glimpses into Bavarian life in the early nineteenth century. The instructions about lithography remain useful.

Theory and Practice of Lithography. Washington, D.C.: Government Printing Office, 1964.
A training manual designed for apprentices in the trade. The introduction provides a historical sketch of lithography and touches on the uses of the process in the Government Printing Office. Chapter 1 treats offset copy preparation and phototypesetting; Chapter 2 considers photographic processes. Lithographic platemaking and presswork are the subjects of the next two chapters, and the last unit discusses paper and ink. A good introductory text, with a brief bibliography and glossary.

Twyman, Michael. *Early Lithographed Books: A Study of the Design and Production of Improper Books in the Age of the Hand Press*. Williamsburg, Va.: The Book Press, 1990.
Aloys Senefelder's discovery of lithography in 1796 allowed for the inexpensive reproduction of all forms of material. The process proved especially useful for printing maps, music, illustrations, and non-Latin alphabets. Twyman looks at the early volumes produced through lithography. This volume lists 420 lithographed books and includes pagination and cost when this information is available. With a bibliography. John Lewis commented, "The whole work will be of value to anyone who cares about the production of books and its history" (*Times Literary Supplement* June 21, 1991, 24). An expanded version of Twyman's *Lithography, 1800-1850: The Techniques of Drawing on Stone in England and France and Their Application in Works of Topography* (London: Oxford University Press, 1970).

Weber, Wilhelm. *A History of Lithography*. New York: McGraw-Hill, 1966.
An informative and attractive volume that concentrates on lithography as a medium for illustration and printmaking. Weber is especially

concerned with the relationship between German and French artists. The oversize volume is filled with black-and-white and full-color examples. The text looks at technical advances over two centuries and also at the various uses of lithography. Weber notes that the art declined in popularity at the end of the nineteenth century but revived in France and Germany in the early 1900s.

Weddige, Emil. *Lithography*. Scranton, Pa.: International Textbook Company, 1966.

Weddige, a pioneer in twentieth century color lithography in America, wanted "to help make the medium understandable and usable for students and artists." Much of the book is devoted to an examination of lithographic artists. Weddige includes a portrait, brief biographical sketch, and sample of the person's work. He also deals with the technical aspects of lithographic illustration, from the equipment necessary to specific approaches to a particular problem. An attractive art book as well as a practical treatise.

Chapter 7
ILLUSTRATION

Bibliographies

Brenni, Vito J. *Book Illustration and Decoration: A Guide to Research.* Westport, Conn.: Greenwood Press, 1980.

An unannotated listing with over 2,000 entries divided into eleven categories: Reference Works, Book Decoration, Manuals of Illustration and Other Writings on Techniques, History of Methods of Illustration, History of Book Illustration from Ancient Times to the Present Day, History of Book Illustration and Decoration in the Countries of the World, Illustration and Decoration in Children's Books, Science and Technology, Medicine, Music, and Geography and History. The same title may appear in more than one category. With author and subject indexes. Covers works published from the sixteenth century to the late 1970s and includes many foreign-language titles.

Bridson, Gavin, and Geoffrey Wakeman. *Printmaking and Picture Printing: A Bibliographical Guide to Artistic and Industrial Techniques in Britain, 1750-1900.* Oxford, England: Plough Press, 1984.

As Bridson and Wakeman write in their introduction, "This bibliography is concerned with the processes of preparing printing surfaces, and the means of printing from them as practiced in Britain." The chapters cover printmaking and picture printing generally, intaglio, relief, lithographic, and photomechanical techniques. Each of these units is divided between books published before 1900 and those that have appeared more recently. In the first category, the authors have attempted to be comprehensive; the listing of more recent studies is more selective. Contains 1,754 entries; virtually all are English-language, and most were printed in Britain. Especially valuable for the essays that precede each section, and the annotations, when present, are informative.

Manuals

Biggs, John R. *Illustration and Reproduction.* New York: Pellegrini & Cudahy, 1952.

Intended for artists but useful for anyone interested in knowing how illustrations are produced. Biggs divides his text according to the three basic techniques for printing illustrations: relief, intaglio, and plano-graphic. The volume concludes with comments by a number of artists such as Ronald Searle and Noel Spencer. The text is enriched with nearly 150 illustrations that demonstrate the various processes and provide examples of what each technique can yield.

_____. *Woodcuts: Wood-engraving, Linocuts, and Prints by Re-lated Methods of Relief Print Making*. London: Blandford Press, 1958. Designed to help the would-be artist by describing "in detail the tools, materials and methods of both woodcutting and engraving and at the same time including a wide range of examples of prints." An introduc-tion provides a brief historical survey. The next two chapters discuss and illustrate woodcutting, linocutting, and wood engraving. Biggs then treats the printing of illustrations and explains which papers are best for the various types of work. The text concludes with chapters on stencilling and on Japanese color prints. Includes a bibliography and list of suppliers, both dated.

Brunner, Felix. *A Handbook of Graphic Arts Reproduction Processes*. New York: Hastings House, 1962. Intended for "art collectors, and dealers, librarians, booksellers, pub-lishers, artists, graphic designers, and the printing trade." Presents a "pictorial record of graphic processes from the earliest woodcuts and copperplate engravings down to the very latest example of the art." The three-language text (English, German, and French) explains the various techniques used to create illustrations and presents numerous important examples of each process. Other illustrations demonstrate tools, machines, and techniques. Useful for anyone wanting to under-stand how illustrations are produced.

Buckland-Wright, John. *Etching and Engraving: Techniques and the Modern Trend*. New York: Studio Publications, 1953. In his introduction Buckland-Wright defines the scope of his work: "Without being an exhaustive treatise . . . its aim is the simplification of the techniques with a view to encouraging artists and interesting students, amateurs and others in the possibilities inherent in the known processes and their contemporary adaptations." Buckland-Wright first discusses the theory and history of the various forms of etching and engraving and then offers some basic procedures. In each chapter he includes both historical and twentieth century examples to show the

Illustration 137

possibilities of the technique. The book demonstrates that etching and engraving need not be purely mechanical copying but can be vital forms of artistic expression.

Chamberlain, Walter. *The Thames and Hudson Manual of Etching and Engraving*. London: Thames and Hudson, 1972.
The book is divided into two sections. In the first nine chapters, Chamberlain presents a brief history of etching and then explores various techniques: soft ground, aquatint, open bite, deep etching, relief etching, and photoetching. He explores the different acids used (Dutch mordant, nitric acid, ferric chloride) and explains the virtues and drawbacks of each. Chapters 8 and 9 discuss methods of biting the metal plate and making corrections. Metal engraving is the subject of the second half of the book. Again Chamberlain first gives a historical survey before turning to techniques. Includes a bibliography, glossary, and list of suppliers. Well-illustrated. Useful for the practitioner and the student of the book arts.

_____. *The Thames and Hudson Manual of Wood Engraving*. London: Thames and Hudson, 1978.
Chamberlain begins with a brief discussion of the woodcut and metal engraving. Wood engraving combines elements of both, focusing on the line, like metal engraving, but using wood. The first chapter surveys the history of the art. Though examples date back to the fifteenth century, Thomas Bewick inaugurated the first great age of wood engraving in the late eighteenth century. A second flowering followed in the Victorian era, a third in the 1920s and 1930s. Chamberlain then turns to the practical aspects of the subject, treating materials, tools and other equipment, drawing and engraving on the wood block, necessities for and methods of printing in color. Also includes a list of suppliers, a bibliography, and a glossary. Thorough and well-illustrated. Like other manuals, this one will serve not only the would-be engraver but also anyone seeking a clear understanding of the processes involved.

Curwen, Harold. *Processes of Graphic Reproduction in Printing*. 4th ed. Revised by Charles May. London: Faber & Faber, 1966.
Curwen wrote this book for "those who are engaged in, or who intend to engage in making designs for reproduction, either by the small quantity methods usually thought of as fine arts, or by the more varied and mostly quite different methods used in the factories of printers." The volume is organized by technique, beginning with the easiest (and oldest)—the relief methods of wood engraving and woodcutting. Cur-

wen next moves to intaglio methods such as copper engraving and etching, stencilling, and lithography. He then turns to photographic reproduction. Part 3 is devoted to bookbinding. Well-illustrated. Includes a brief bibliography.

Hamilton, Edward A. *Graphic Design for the Computer Age: Visual Communication for All Media*. New York: Van Nostrand Reinhold, 1970.
Hamilton, who served as Art Director for Time-Life Books, explores various ways of using illustrations to convey information. He includes numerous examples that emphasize the power of the visual image and the variety of techniques and approaches available to the graphic artist. Chapters are short—only one exceeds ten pages—and concentrate on a limited number of fundamental points. For example, in "Color Versus Black-and-White" Hamilton cautions that color is essential in some cases but distracting in others, and he offers some examples to show what he means. Useful for graphic artists or those seeking to understand how illustrations can enhance or even replace a text.

Lamb, Lynton. *Drawing for Illustration*. London: Oxford University Press, 1962.
Treats the "theoretical, contractual, and technical aspects of drawing for illustration." Intended for the illustrator seeking information on dealing with "authors, publishers, blockmakers, and printers." Despite this intended audience, the book will be useful for anyone interested in illustration, because it explains the processes involved and also nontechnical elements that influence artists. For example, when publishers or editors want readers to imagine a character's appearance, the artist may be asked to leave features vague and to emphasize clothing or background. Lamb also notes that a picture that may be ideal for a cover may be too obtrusive in the text.

Leaf, Ruth. *Intaglio Printmaking Techniques*. New York: Watson-Guptill, 1976.
A step-by-step illustrated explanation, with a list of suppliers and bibliography. In Part 1, Leaf presents general information, explaining the necessary materials and equipment, tools, papers, presses, and workshop. In the course of the discussion she makes useful observations. For example, she writes that thicker paper is better for deeply etched plates; machine mold paper is better than handmade, but papers made without a mold usually are inferior. Part 2 looks at etching techniques, Part 3 at printing the illustration, and Part 4 explores other

Illustration 139

methods of reproducing an image: drypoint, engraving, collographs, tuilegraphs, and the Blake Transfer Method. Includes many examples of prints made with the techniques treated here.

Lewis, John Noel Claude. *A Handbook of Type and Illustration*. London: Faber & Faber, 1956.
A technical book intended for the printer. Deals with the processes involved in the making of illustrated books and reproductions of pictures in various media. Illustrated and indexed.

Histories

Bland, David. *A History of Book Illustration: The Illuminated Manuscript and the Printed Book*. 2d ed. Berkeley: University of California Press, 1969.
A survey enriched with over 400 examples of illustration, from an Egyptian papyrus roll from around 1980 B.C. to the 1960s. Covers Oriental as well as Western manuscripts and books. Bland's broad scope precludes detailed analysis of any topic; Hebrew book illumination, for example, receives less than a page of text. Bland does not seek to present new information but codifies existing knowledge. The book is well written and offers a fine overview. Ruari McLean praised the work as an ideal introduction for the general reader (*Connoisseur* 173, 1970, 278). Howard W. Winger concurred in *College and Research Libraries* 33 (1972): 65. "The first edition was a unique contribution to the history of book illustration. The second edition, though not greatly nor always carefully revised, is an improvement on the first."

_____. *The Illustration of Books*. 3d ed. London: Faber & Faber, 1963.
Less detailed than the previous title but still useful for the novice. In the first part of the book, Bland surveys the history of illustration. He concentrates on the printed book but notes that already in the Middle Ages the person who designed a manuscript and planned its illustrations was not necessarily the artist who executed the drawings. In Part 2 Bland examines the processes of illustration, especially relief, intaglio, lithography, and collotype. With forty-six illustrations.

Bliss, Douglas Percy. *A History of Wood-Engraving*. London: J. M. Dent & Sons, 1928.
Bliss first discusses the techniques of woodcutting and wood engraving

before turning to a historical survey. He notes that while woodblocks were used for printing cloth in the Middle Ages, paper had to be readily available before this art form could serve printmakers. By the early fifteenth century that condition had been met; pilgrimages and playing cards stimulated the development of woodcuts, as visitors to shrines eagerly bought "Helgen" (images of saints). Blockbooks also date from this period, and the advent of printing further encouraged the artist in wood. The chapter on the seventeenth and eighteenth centuries is brief because the woodcut served the uneducated; designs in this period were, according to Bliss, "simple, crude and inelegant." Thomas Bewick in the late 1700s revived the art. Bliss examines the revitalized woodcut in the nineteenth and early twentieth centuries. He concludes with advice to engravers to suit the woodcut to the typeface. A useful survey.

Blunt, Wilfrid. *The Art of Botanical Illustration*. London: Collins, 1950.
Blunt writes in his preface, "This book ... is the first attempt to present a general survey of the development of botanical illustration from the crude scratchings of paleolithic man down to the highly scientific work of the present day." Blunt notes that the Great Temple of Thutmose III at Karnak contains the earliest surviving florilegium: the bas-reliefs depict 275 plants. Egyptian, Cretan, Assyrian, Greek, and Roman artifacts show that pictures of plants were a popular form of decoration. A codex of Dioscorides of 512 A.D. demonstrates a naturalism not repeated until the Renaissance. Blunt cites the Master of Mary of Burgundy as a pioneer in reviving botanical accuracy. The survey highlights the work of important botanical illustrators, notes the influences of one country on that of another, the effect of technology (such as stipple engraving and photography) on artists' renderings of plants, and the relationship between science and art. Nicely illustrated with forty-seven color plates, thirty-two monochrome plates, and seventy-five drawings.

Calot, Frantz, L. M. Michon, and Paul Angoulvent. *L'Art du livre en France des origines à nos jours*. Paris: Delagrave, 1931.
"They order this matter better in France," Yorick observes in the first line of Laurence Sterne's *A Sentimental Journey* (1768). He might have been discussing book illustration. In various periods other countries have rivaled France, but none can show such consistency of exquisite bibliographic production. In lyrical prose, Calot surveys the history of French bookmaking, emphasizing the illumination of manuscripts and illustration from the Merovingian period to the twentieth century. The

Illustration 141

book is filled with fine black-and-white reproductions, though one misses color, especially in the manuscript facsimiles. Calot devotes a substantial chapter to bookbinding and another to French collectors and libraries. The bibliography, though dated, includes some works that remain classics, as Calot's own book has become.

Chatto, William Andrew, and John Jackson. *A Treatise on Wood Engraving, Historical and Practical.* London: Henry G. Bohn, 1861.
A history of woodcuts from antiquity to the nineteenth century, accompanied by over 400 illustrations from wood engravings prepared by the noted artist John Jackson. Chatto notes that Egyptian hieroglyphics were stamped into clay by means of intaglio woodcuts, and the earliest printed books were produced from woodblocks that incorporated text and illustrations. The Mainz Psalter of 1457 printed by Fust and Schöffer includes initials printed from woodcuts. Chatto calls these "the most beautiful specimens of this kind of ornament which the united efforts of the wood-engraver and the pressman have produced." By the end of the seventeenth century, the woodcut had yielded to the copper engraving, but the late eighteenth century witnessed a revival. The history concludes with a discussion of nineteenth century artists in the medium and a chapter on the technical aspects of illustrating with wood.

Cleaver, James. *A History of Graphic Art.* New York: Philosophical Library, 1963.
Explores prints and book illustration as a means of narrative, beginning with ancient Egyptian tomb paintings and Greek vases, medieval manuscript illumination and early printed woodcuts, to the private press books of the late nineteenth century and the prints of the twentieth. An appendix explains the four basic methods of creating an image (relief, intaglio, planographic, and silk screen). With over a hundred illustrations, a glossary, and a brief bibliography.

Corbett, Margery, and R. W. Lightbown. *The Comely Frontispiece: The Emblematic Title-Page in England, 1550-1660.* London: Routledge & Kegan Paul, 1979.
The authors discuss four types of illustrated title pages—those with "a single overall design," those divided into compartments, those with a cartouche, and those arranged architecturally. According to Corbett and Lightbown, these illustrations drew on the emblematic tradition and contributed to the interpretation of the text they introduced; the frontispiece usually was designed by the author. The work studies in

detail twenty examples, beginning with John Dee's 1577 *General and Rare Memorials* and concluding with Thomas Hobbes's *Leviathan* (1651). The authors note that the title page of Henry Peacham's *The Compleat Gentleman* (1622), for instance, depicts both Nobility and Learning, but assigns the former the more honorable left-hand side to show which is the more valuable for the gentleman. Hobbes's political views are summarized on the title page of his treatise. Gordon Williams called this "a valuable pioneering venture in the field of early book illustration" (*The Library* 2, 1980, 356).

Crane, Walter. *Of the Decorative Illustration of Books Old and New.* 2d ed., rev. London: George Bell & Sons, 1901.
The first four chapters examine the history of illustration from the earliest manuscripts to the end of the nineteenth century. A final chapter presents Crane's views on ornamentation and illustration. Crane argues that printing and illustration reached their peak in the Renaissance and then began a long decline, which was only beginning to be reversed by such enterprises as William Morris' Kelmscott Press (1891-1898). Extensively illustrated, especially with nineteenth century examples, including some of Crane's own work. Though *The Dial* 23 (1897): 68 presented an unfavorable review of the first edition, that same periodical observed four years later that the book "has come to occupy a place of authority in its own field; the wealth of illustrative examples, no less than the historical and critical value of the text, making it an indispensable handbook for the student or book-lover" (30, 1901, 379).

Dance, S. Peter. *The Art of Natural History: Animal Illustrators and Their Work.* Woodstock, N.Y.: Overlook Press, 1978.
Part 1 offers a chronological survey from prehistory to the twentieth century but concentrating on the period from the Renaissance to the end of the nineteenth century. Dance observes that the artists of the classical period rendered animals realistically, whereas most medieval representations are fanciful. Not until the sixteenth century did realism reappear. Part 2 examines specific aspects of zoological representation: anthropomorphism, attempts to show motion, illustrations of microscopic creatures, and efforts to appeal to a non-scientific audience. Appendices discuss techniques, offer suggestions for further reading, and provide brief biographical sketches of important figures. Lavishly illustrated in black-and-white and color. Gerald Carson wrote of the book's "easy erudition and literary grace" (*Natural History* 88, May, 1979, 86). Fridolf Johnson called it "most desirable and permanently valuable" (*American Artist* 43, August, 1979, 22).

Illustration 143

Daniels, Morna. *Victorian Book Illustration*. London: British Library, 1988.

During the Victorian era publishers used a variety of methods to illustrate their books—etching, aquatint, metal and wood engraving, lithography, and photography. Daniels explains each process in her introduction, and the following five chapters talk about illustrating works dealing with history, religion, natural history, the Orient and fantasy, and, finally, fictional and nonfictional portraits of the age. Using a rich assortment of color and black-and-white reproductions, Daniels examines the contributions of many illustrators. Some of these, like Cruikshank, have retained their popularity, while others have received less recognition than their talents merit. A pleasant, attractive introduction to a wonderful age of book illustration.

Darton, Frederick Joseph Harvey. Modern Book-Illustration in Great Britain and America. London: The Studio, 1931.

This special Winter number of *The Studio* begins with a brief retrospective of early book illustration and then examines the work of eighty-five artists, most of them from the late nineteenth and early twentieth centuries. Darton analyzes as well as describes, and he admires the illustrators who are most faithful to the text. He singles out Rockwell Kent as the person who "shows us what modern book illustration can be and do." Includes numerous examples of work discussed in the text, including pieces that Darton regards as flawed. A provocative survey of an important period.

De Bray, Lys. *The Art of Botanical Illustration: The Classic Illustrators and Their Achievement from 1550 to 1900*. Secaucus, N.J.: Wellfleet Press, 1989.

Despite its title, this work begins with botanical illustrations on the walls of the Temple of Tithmose III at Karnak, Egypt, dating from about 1500 B.C., and the lengthy concluding chapter examines twentieth century treatments. De Bray focuses on important artists such as Hans Weiditz (a.k.a. Johannes Guidictius), who provided the drawings for Otto Brunfels' *Herbarium Vitae Eicones* (1530). In this work Weiditz broke with the thousand-year-old tradition of copying Dioscorides and Apuleius, the exemplars from antiquity who had hitherto served as models for plant illustration. De Bray links artistic developments with other factors, such as economics and climate, which explain the flourishing Dutch and Flemish schools of flower painting in the sixteenth, seventeenth, and eighteenth centuries. Arranged chronologically and geographically, this book is filled with fascinating information and gorgeous reproductions, many of them in full color.

Ellis, Richard Williamson. *Book Illustration: A Survey of Its History and Development Shown by the Work of Various Artists, Together with Critical Comments*. Kingsport, Tenn.: Kingsport Press, 1952.
A collection of seventy-six short pieces that appeared originally in *Publishers Weekly*. Ellis' introduction briefly discusses the history and techniques of book illustration. The text itself focuses on the work of particular artists, providing an illustration and one-page discussion of the person's life and work. The emphasis is on nineteenth and twentieth century illustration, though Ellis includes an Egyptian relief carving, a page from the Chinese Diamond Sutra (the oldest dated blockbook, 868 A.D.), and some important examples from the fifteenth through the eighteenth centuries.

Eppink, Norman R. *101 Prints: The History and Techniques of Printmaking*. New ed. Norman: University of Oklahoma Press, 1971.
Eppink, a printer and printmaker, sought to provide "a single source to which one could turn to find explanations of all the processes and technical variations and which also included original prints to illustrate the methods under discussion." All the prints were made by the author, who discusses the techniques used and provides some historical background. In his treatment of the chiaroscuro woodcut, for example, Ellis notes that such illustrations were popular in Italy and Germany in the 1500s and 1600s. The book is arranged by process: relief, intaglio, intaglio and mixed media, planographic, stencil, photographic, and miscellaneous. A final section discusses techniques accessible to children. These include the potato print and rubbings. Offers a selective bibliography.

Felmingham, Michael. *The Illustrated Gift Book, 1880-1930: With a Checklist of 2500 Titles*. Aldershot, England: Scolar Press, 1988.
"This book describes the revolution in book illustration from 1880-1930, when photo-mechanic methods of reproduction created a 'golden age' of illustration." The author considers the technology of illustration, markets, and the lives of the illustrators and their methods. He discusses both the well-known artists of the day, such as Aubrey Beardsley, but also many unknowns, such as Alan Olde and Alice Woodward. The book examines how these people learned their craft. Includes a bibliography of the works of some eighty-five artists. Ruari Mclean's review in *The Book Collector* 38 (Spring, 1989): 122-124

Illustration 145

criticized the quality of the illustrations but observed that "the author gives a fascinating account of books and illustrators of a period which is only now coming into focus, and of which this is perhaps the first study in depth. . . . An excellent book."

Friedman, Joan M. *Color Printing in England, 1486-1870*. New Haven, Conn.: Yale Center for British Art, 1978.
An exhibition catalog that describes and illustrates almost 200 representatives of English color printing. The first example was produced around 1485 in St. Albans, ten years after William Caxton brought the printing press to England. Not until the eighteenth century would England again produce a book with color printing, John Baptist Jackson's *An Essay on the Invention of Engraving and Printing in Chiaro Oscuro* (1754). A useful historical survey that examines techniques and important artists. One wishes for more than the twenty-four color plates provided. Dame Juliana Berner's *Book of Hawking, Hunting, and Heraldry* (c. 1485), for example, appears here only in black-and-white.

Garrett, Albert. *British Wood Engraving of the Twentieth Century*. London: Scolar Press, 1980.
D. Nelson in *The Times Educational Supplement* for October 23, 1981, called this "an excellent introduction to the subject as well as a delightful and serious book in its own right" (p. 23). Garrett was president of the Society of Wood Engravers and here shares his observations and expertise. Attractively illustrated, and suitable for either the general reader or the connoisseur.

_____. *A History of British Wood Engraving*. Atlantic Highlands, N.J.: Humanities Press, 1978.
A survey of the subject from its beginnings, concentrating on the twentieth century. A good complement to the previous title. Garrett dismisses woodcuts as inartistic but praises wood engraving. Especially useful for the biographical sketches of those who have worked in this art form. Nicely illustrated and well-printed. Poorly indexed. A readable if opinionated history.

Garvey, Eleanor M. *The Artist and the Book, 1860-1960, in Western Europe and the United States*. 2d ed. Boston: Museum of Fine Arts and Harvard College Library, 1972.
Garvey prepared this important work in conjunction with an exhibition at the Boston Museum of Fine Arts. Arranged by artist. Each of the 324 entries provides a brief biography, a description of the illustration in

the exhibit (not all are reproduced in the book), and bibliographical references. In his introduction to this second edition, Philip Hofer noted that since the first edition appeared in 1960 *"the book has, in fact, become a major vehicle of artistic expression."* Many of the finest artists are represented here, including Paul Klee, Picasso, and Camille Pissarro. French artists have the most entries (182 in all) indicating the importance of the art book in that country. The United States lags well behind in second place with forty-seven examples.

George, Mary Dorothy. *Hogarth to Cruikshank: Social Change in Graphic Satire.* New York: Walker, 1967.
In over 200 illustrations George shows how William Hogarth, Thomas Rowlandson, James Gilray, George Cruikshank, and many of their lesser-known contemporaries depicted English society from about 1720 to 1830. The volume contributes as much to an understanding of English life as to an appreciation of the major graphic artists of the period. Howard Daniel called this "an exemplary work of its kind, lucid, beautifully written, its scholarly apparatus displayed helpfully and modestly. . . . Dr. George has produced a beautiful and useful book . . . and anyone interested in eighteenth century modes and manners will continue to be in her debt" (*The Studio* 175, March, 1968, 158-160).

Getlein, Frank, and Dorothy Getlein. *The Bite of the Print: Satire and Irony in Woodcuts, Engravings, Etchings, Lithographs, and Serigraphs.* New York: Clarkson N. Potter, 1963.
In their opening chapter the Getleins observe, "From the beginning of European printmaking in the fifteenth century until the present, the printmaker, in his work, has looked askance and looked askew at all the powers that govern man, at Church and State, at science and art, at justice and war, at love itself." Chapter 2 examines the various ways prints are made, and the rest of the book presents a historical survey from the fifteenth to the mid-twentieth century. Much of the story is told through an analysis of particularly important figures: Albrecht Durer, Rembrandt, William Hogarth, Francisco Goya, Honore Daumier, Georges Rouault, and Käthe Kollwitz all have chapters to themselves. More than half of the book's 272 pages are devoted to illustrations of the printmaker's art.

Gill, Bob, and John Lewis. *Illustration: Aspects and Directions.* New York: Reinhold, 1964.
In this short book the authors present their principles of illustration and demonstrate their views, using eighty-eight examples to support the

Illustration 147

text. Because photography provides precise documentation, the illustrator must go beyond reportage, must make a statement. Gill and Lewis praise Thomas Bewick not for his technical skill as a wood engraver but for his comments on country life. Similarly, Thomas Rowlandson, Honoré Daumier, Henri de Toulouse-Lautrec and Max Beerbohm earn accolades for their interpretation of human "frailties and follies." With a brief chapter on children's books.

Hamilton, Sinclair. *Early American Book Illustrators and Wood Engravers, 1670-1870*. 2 vols. Princeton, N.J.: Princeton University Press, 1968.

A catalog based largely on the Hamilton collection. Volume 2 appeared in 1958; it was reissued with the supplement ten years later. Part 1 in both volumes deals with the seventeenth and eighteenth centuries and includes both metal engraving and woodcuts. Because so much of this work was anonymous, arrangement here is chronological. Part 2, the larger section, deals with nineteenth century woodcuts and wood engraving and is arranged alphabetically by artist. Those who began working before 1870 are included, even if their careers extended beyond the title's terminal date. Hamilton provides an introductory essay that traces the development of illustration in America from John Foster's c. 1670 woodcut of Richard Mather (Item 1 in the catalog) to the late nineteenth century. For each entry, Hamilton provides attribution of the illustration, and he includes many reproductions. An important reference that covers over 2,000 examples of early American illustration. Excellent index.

Hammelmann, Hans A. *Book Illustrators in Eighteenth Century England*. Edited and completed by T. S. R. Boase. New Haven, Conn.: Yale University Press, 1975.

The volume contains Boase's essay on eighteenth century illustration, an annotated alphabetical list of illustrators, and forty-five black-and-white plates. Among the issues Boase treats are the influence of French illustrators on their British counterparts and the effects of the copyright laws on illustrations. For each artist the study provides a brief biography, an analysis of the work, and a bibliography listing where his or her illustrations appeared. Comprehensive but not encyclopedic. M. Rosenthal wrote in *Connoisseur* 192 (1976): 234, "This is a valuable volume. It will prove useful to both the bibliophile and the art historian. It is also the kind of work which is essential if serious study is at last to be paid to eighteenth-century England."

Hardie, Martin. *English Coloured Books*. New York: Putnam, 1906.
  The Book of St. Albans, published in 1485 or 1486, is the first example
  of English color printing. The next example dates from the eighteenth
  century. In the interim, handcoloring was the means used to add tints
  to illustrations, and this practice persisted into the nineteenth century.
  Hardie credits William Savage (1770-1843) with reintroducing color
  printing from woodblocks. George Baxter combined color from woodblocks with metal engraving. Jakob Christoph Le Blon pioneered color
  printing exclusively with metal (1722). Hardie examines the various
  processes employed and discusses those who made important contributions through the end of the nineteenth century.

Harthan, John P. *The History of the Illustrated Book: The Western Tradition*. London: Thames and Hudson, 1981.
  Although Harthan does not ignore technical or aesthetic considerations, he focuses on "the historical and cultural context in which the
  books were produced." Arrangement is chronological, and the text is
  enriched with 465 illustrations (thirty-three in color). Harthan notes
  how various elements fuse to create a particular style—classical and
  Oriental meld in Byzantine art; barbarian ornamentation influences the
  book in Merovingian Gaul, Visigothic Spain, and Celtic Britain. Later,
  in the early eighteenth century, English illustration was enriched by the
  influx of French, Dutch, and German engravers. Harthan's book provides an essential introduction and serves as an important reference.

Hind, Arthur M. *A History of Engraving and Etching from the Fifteenth
  Century to the Year 1914*. 3d ed., rev. Boston: Houghton Mifflin, 1923.
  Hind writes in his preface that he seeks to present "a descriptive survey
  of the history of engraving on metal throughout the various centuries
  and schools," from the mid 1400s onward. The first chapter discusses
  processes and materials. The remaining chapters offer a historical
  overview, and appendices provide a classified list of engravers by
  country, a lengthy bibliography, and an index to over 2,500 artists,
  together with references. Includes 110 black-and-white illustrations.
  The Bookman (64, 1923, 76) praised Hind's judgments and observed,
  "As an introduction to a knowledge of the history of the art, and as an
  encyclopaedic work of reference, Mr. Hind's book is one of the best
  that can be given an honoured place on the shelves of anyone interested
  in the subject."

_____. *An Introduction to a History of Woodcut*. 2 vols. Boston:
  Houghton Mifflin, 1935.

Illustration 149

Originally planned as a complete survey of the woodcut, this volume is limited largely to the fifteenth and early sixteenth centuries, though the first chapter discusses processes and materials and the second provides a quick overview of the subject since the invention of printing. Chapter 3 looks at early examples of woodcuts both Oriental and Western, and Chapter 4 treats the blockbook. Then in Volume 2 Hind presents his geographically arranged account of woodcut illustrations for books and broadsides in Europe. Hind champions the blockbook and woodcut, praising their simplicity that imparts to them a "noble and expressive character." Still an important history and reference. With almost 500 facsimiles.

Hindman, Sandra, ed. *The Early Illustrated Book: Essays in Honor of Lessing G. Rosenwald.* Washington, D.C.: Library of Congress, 1982. Rosenwald (1891-1979) was a great collector of illustrated books, and he donated his collection of over 2,600 volumes to the Library of Congress. The essays in this anthology look at these books and offer much information. Diane Scillia finds that the illuminator known as the Passional Master also made woodcuts in Utrecht in the 1470s. James Snyder looks at the woodcuts in six books published between 1484 and 1486 by Jacobus Bellaert of Haarlem, especially Bartholomaeus Anglicus' *De Proprietatibus Rerum* (1485). In "The Genesis Woodcuts of a Dutch Adaptation of the *Vita Christi*" Barbara Lane finds much freedom of invention, an independence linked to the religious movement known as the Devotio Moderna. Keith P. F. Moxey explores the literary, artistic, and historical background for *The Ship of Fools* by Sebastian Brant. Four other essays examine landscape in early illustrations. J. H. Perry observes, for example, that early representations of the New World often depict idealized scenery or European settings. Jane Cahill notes that the Jesuit missionaries brought to the Orient books with illustrations of European landscapes, and late Ming Chinese landscape albums reveal this Western influence. The three concluding essays consider illustrated printed editions of Virgil; the illustrations differ from those in classical and medieval versions. Ruth Mortimer finds that in the twentieth century the shorter poems seem more popular than the *Aeneid*, a preference reflecting nostalgia for country life. A well-illustrated volume, with eight color plates and some 175 black-and-white reproductions.

Hodnett, Edward. *Five Centuries of English Book Illustration.* Brookfield, Vt.: Scolar Press, 1988.
In 1481 William Caxton published the first illustrated book in England,

The Myrroure of the Worlde by Vincent of Beauvais. By 1500, six other English printers had issued books with illustrations. Etchings and engravings appeared in the next century; by the end of the seventeenth century, woodcuts had yielded to copper engraving and etching. These techniques in turn were supplanted by aquatint, wood engraving, steel engraving, and steel etching in the early 1800s, the era Hodnett regards as "the great period of English book illustration." The late nineteenth century saw the introduction of photoengraving and a revival of the woodcut. Private presses like William Morris's Kelmscott, the Golden Cockerell Press, and the Gregynog Press fostered improved illustration in trade editions, but many illustrations became decorative rather than interpretive. Hodnett presents an overview of each period and then offers brief sketches of important illustrators (or, for the earlier centuries, publishers of illustrated works, since many of the illustrators are unidentified). Though Hodnett's primary concern is with the artists, he touches on the relationship between art and socioeconomic factors. Thus, he notes that the Victorian vogue of genteel, static scenes reflects "the importance attached to middle-class respectability and upper-class leisure." Hodnett offers a checklist of 2,500 illustrated books and provides numerous bibliographic references. With 207 illustrations, six of them in color. In his review for *Apollo*, Christopher Newell spoke of Hodnett's "great erudition and enthusiasm" (130, 1989, 138).

_____. *Image and Text: Studies in the Illustration of English Literature*. London: Scolar Press, 1982.
Looks at the illustrations for books published by John Day (1522-1584), illustrations for Shakespeare's plays in the eighteenth and nineteenth centuries, William Blake as illustrator, John Martin's pictures for *Paradise Lost*, the work of Hablot Knight Brown ("Phiz"), Sir John Tenniel's illustrations for *Alice in Wonderland*, Edward Burne-Jones' designs for William Morris, and Aubrey Beardsley's pictures for four books published in the 1890s: Sir Thomas Malory's *Le Morte D'Arthur*, Oscar Wilde's *Salome*, Alexander Pope's *Rape of the Lock*, and Beardsley's own *Under the Hill*. Hodnett assesses the efforts of these artists as interpreters of the text. For instance, he sees Fuseli's illustrations of Shakespeare as vigorous but insensitive to the text. Though John Gilbert was a lesser artist, his illustrations are more effective. Hodnett praises John Martin's Miltonic sensibility but questions his selection of scenes to depict.

Hofer, Philip. *Baroque Book Illustration*. Cambridge, Mass.: Harvard University Press, 1951.

Illustration 151

Based on the collection in the Harvard Library Department of Graphic
Arts, Hofer's quick survey of seventeenth century book illustration
includes 149 black-and-white illustrations. Hofer was writing when
interest in this work was low; even Hofer speaks apologetically of the
art he is studying. Yet he also notes that royal and aristocratic patronage
prompted the production of many fine works, and during the seventeenth century mezzotinting was perfected. As in other aspects of the
baroque, illustrations struggle between formality and exuberance.
Hofer briefly examines the work done in specific European countries.
He finds many fine examples in England and France. Though Spain
and Portugal offer fewer outstanding baroque illustrations, Fernando
de la Torre Farfan's *Fiestas de la S. Iglesia . . . de Sevilla* (Seville, 1671)
shows what Iberian artists could accomplish. Much of Europe was
devastated by the Thirty Years War (1618-1648), and in the Netherlands the greatest artists of the period generally did not illustrate books,
so in many countries one sees a decline from the high standards of book
illustration of the previous century.

Holloway, Owen E. *French Rococo Book Illustration.* New York: Trans-
atlantic Arts, 1969.
Rococo illustration arose in France in the latter part of the eighteenth
century, though hints of the form appeared as early as the 1600s.
Holloway singles out the work of Hubert François Gravelot, Charles
J. D. Eisen, J. M. Moreau, Clement Pierre Marillier, and Pierre Philippe
Choffard as exemplifying the form and its variations. He especially
praises the *Decameron* (1757-1761), a 1762 edition of La Fontaine,
Choix de chansons (1773), and C. J. Dorat's *Fables nouvelles* (1773)
as masterpieces of the rococo and of book illustration. Hollaway links
the art form with the desire apparent among the upper class during the
reign of Louis XV for "perennial youth and charm." This obsession
explains for Holloway the proliferation of Cupids and children. The
period also is marked by an "epicurean pursuit of happiness" that is
again reflected in the rococo illustrations. With 283 black-and-white
illustrations reproduced in their original size.

Holme, C. Geoffrey, and E. G. Halton, eds. *Modern Book Illustrators and
Their Work.* London: The Studio, 1914.
M. C. Salaman provides an introduction to this collection of work by
fifty turn-of-the-century British artists. Salaman's text discusses the
progress of English book illustration during the nineteenth century and
provides brief comments about the people included. Salaman speaks
of the "graciousness of line and decorative design, with simplicity of

expression" that characterize the work of Robert Anning Bell, the unity of effect in books decorated by Charles Robinson. Most of the volume consists of representative samples of illustrations, arranged alphabetically by artist. A good visual study of a great age of British illustration.

Houfe, Simon. *The Dictionary of British Book Illustrators and Caricaturists, 1800-1914*. Rev. ed. Woodbridge, England: Antique Collectors' Club, 1981.

Much more than the title indicates, this volume provides a history of book illustration as well as an extensive annotated list of some 2,500 graphic artists of the nineteenth century in Britain. Each chapter concludes with bibliographic references, and the work also provides a general bibliography at the end. Houfe's observations are astute. He notes, for example, that the sculptor John Flaxman liked line drawings because they are "ideal for showing the clear profiles of neo-classical architecture and ornament." Though in 1865 Charles Knight complained of the failure of illustration to show the darker side of English life, Houfe finds a strong school of social realism in the latter half of the century, and the influx of radicals from failed Continental revolutions aided this movement.

Hunnisett, Basil. *Steel-Engraved Book Illustration in England*. Boston: David R. Godine, 1980.

Although examples of steel engraving date from the fifteenth century, the nineteenth century was the great age for this type of illustration. It stood between the cheap woodcut for the masses and the handcolored aquatints for the rich. Steel engraving persisted through the 1800s, but its heyday was 1825-1845. Hunnisett notes that the steel engraving (often actually steel etching because of the hardness of the metal) made possible the illustrated literary annual. By the 1880s steel engraving was in decline, and photography provided the last blow. With sixty-six facsimiles. An appendix reprints an article from *All the Year Round* of October 27, 1866 that explains the process of steel engraving. Tobin A. Sparling of the Yale Center for British Art wrote in *The American Book Collector* 2 (March/April, 1981): 78-79, "In *Steel-Engraved Book Illustration in England* Basil Hunnisett provides a comprehensive study of steel-engraving which ranks as a significant addition to the literature of British book illustration.... A pioneering work of high scholarship, [it] is destined to become a standard in its field."

Ivins, William Mills. *Prints and Visual Communication*. Cambridge, Mass.: Harvard University Press, 1953.

Illustration 153

For thirty years, Ivins served as curator of prints at the Metropolitan Museum of Art. He argues that prints, reproducible works of art, "are among the most important and powerful tools of modern life and thought." Ivins contrasts words, which require decoding, with the immediacy of images. He also notes that most theories of art were based on reproductions rather than actual paintings; only photography permits precise replication. Though Ivins offers a theoretical approach to the print, he surveys the history of visual reproduction and includes eighty-four annotated examples.

Jennings, O. *Early Woodcut Initials.* London: Methuen, 1908.
Looks at the use of woodcut initials in printed books of the fifteenth and sixteenth centuries and presents over 1,300 examples. The study is arranged geographically, beginning with Mainz and following the spread of printing. Jennings notes that Schoeffer used woodcut initials to imitate manuscript practice. Printers in Augsburg abandoned the manuscript model. Many of the letters are so elaborate that they seem mere ornament or illustration rather than part of the text. In the woodcuts used by Gerard Ponticus of Milan, for example, vines and flowers cover the letters like kudzu. In later German initials, pictures actually obscure the writing. Like other forms of woodcut, initials eventually disappeared at the end of the sixteenth century when copper engraving became the major form of book illustration.

Jussim, Estelle. *Visual Communication and the Graphic Arts: Photographic Technologies in the Nineteenth Century.* New York: R. R. Bowker, 1974.
A study of the effects of photography on the graphic arts, including book illustration, in the nineteenth century. Jussim discusses the various technologies available and looks at the work of three major illustrators, Howard Pyle (1853-1911), William Hamilton Gibson (1850-1896), and Frederic Remington (1861-1909). Jussim also seeks to apply information theory to the study of illustration and to examine the implications of photographic codification. She argues that for some artists photography was an aid, but William Hamilton Gibson offered a truer expression of "The Flume" through engraving, though he also was a photographer. She disagrees with Ivins' *Prints and Visual Communication* (cited earlier), which maintains that photography lacks syntax, and she notes how dependent many illustrators became on photographs as the basis of their illustrations. With 121 reproductions.

Kaden, Vera. *The Illustration of Plants and Gardens, 1500-1850*. London: Her Majesty's Stationery Office, 1982.

Kaden relates botanical illustration to developments in science and landscape aesthetics. Hence, her book serves as an introduction to both. The sixteenth century is the age of the woodcut and the herbal, and the focus of such books was medical. In the seventeenth century, flowers came to be appreciated for their beauty as well as their utility, and this trend gave rise to the florilegium, often with copperplate engravings. Kaden calls the 1700s "the botanist's century" because in 1735 Linnaeus published his *Systema Naturae*, classifying plants by genus and species. After 1850 new technology led to a decline in the quality of illustration, so the book ends at that date. The text is followed by 103 plates, many in full color, drawn from the collection in the Victoria and Albert Museum. A good overview.

Kastner, Joseph. *The Bird Illustrated, 1550-1900*. New York: Harry N. Abrams, 1988.

One volume of Conrad Gessner's *Historiae Animalium* (1551) was dedicated to birds and included over 200 woodcut illustrations. Kastner traces the depiction of birds beginning with that work to the end of the nineteenth century, using almost one hundred plates, many in color, to show how various illustrators have dealt with this subject. The book is arranged by type of bird: predators, game birds, waders, birds of the field and woodland, swimmers, and exotics. Each section includes a one-page discussion and a portfolio of prints. Along the way Kastner offers some fascinating observations. For example, he notes that early bird illustrators did not bother with realistic backgrounds. He also comments that because males are more colorful, some artists ignored the female of the species.

Kastner, Joseph, and Miriam T. Gross. *The Animal Illustrated, 1550-1900*. New York: Harry N. Abrams, 1991.

Written in conjunction with an exhibit at the New York Public Library, this work draws on that institution's extensive collection of illustrated volumes portraying flora and fauna. In "A Peaceable Kingdom of Books and Art," Kastner notes how natural history has depended on artists "to explain and illuminate its findings—and, just as important, to attract readers." The book is organized by type of animal—wild beasts, domestic creatures, birds, insects, reptiles, and, finally, imaginary and unusual animals. Kastner provides a brief introduction to each unit, and Gross has written short captions for the one hundred plates. An attractive volume that includes a bibliography of the works that provided the illustrations.

Illustration 155

Kingman, Lee, ed. *The Illustrator's Notebook*. Boston: Horn Books, 1978. A collection of essays by such leading illustrators as Fritz Eichenberg, Lynd Ward, Warren Chappell, and Ernest Shepard. Intended to encourage and guide the would-be illustrator of children's books. The artists discuss their philosophies of illustration, the history of illustration, its place in the arts, its function as a means of communication, and the contributors' experiences with various techniques. Betina Ehrlich warns against bright colors, which are more likely to appeal to adults than to children, and she urges illustrators to stress narrative. Several contributors emphasize the importance of technical virtuosity as well as creativity. With over one hundred black-and-white and color illustrations and a bibliography for further study.

Klemin, Diana. *The Illustrated Book: Its Art and Craft*. New York: Clarkson N. Potter, 1970. Deals with seventy-four twentieth century illustrators, most of them American. Arranged alphabetically, with examples of each artist's work, together with comments and a brief bibliography. In the chapter "The Art and Craft of Illustration," Klemin discusses the technical aspects of illustration.

Knight, David. *Zoological Illustration: An Essay Towards a History of Printed Zoological Pictures*. Folkestone, England: Dawson's, 1977. A concise survey of the subject from the invention of printing to the introduction of photographic illustration in the early twentieth century. The opening chapter looks at the functions of zoological illustration. In the next chapter, Knight discusses techniques. The subsequent three chapters offer a chronological overview that concentrates on historically significant works. Knight observes how various factors influenced the depiction of animals. Darwin's studies, for example, led to increased concern with habitat and individual variation.

Lejard, André, ed. *The Art of the French Book from Early Manuscripts to the Present Time*. London: Paul Elek, 1947. In his introduction, Philip James observes that far more than in England, illustration in France has been the focus of the well-made book. The great French artists have tended also to be illustrators. Although the halftone and four-color processes were less expensive, French publishers insisted on maintaining the high quality of their illustrations through line engraving, aquatint, and lithography. Even photography had a less deleterious effect in France than elsewhere. The text then discusses twelve centuries of French book illustration, from a seventh century lectionary to the early twentieth century. Many of the nearly 200 illustrations derive from the collection of the Bibliothèque Nationale. The volume concludes with a survey of French bookbinding, which, like illustration, offers some of the finest examples in the world.

Lewis, John Noel Claude. *The Twentieth Century Book: Its Illustration and Design.* 2d ed. New York: Van Nostrand Reinhold, 1984.
Looks at book design from the late nineteenth century to the mid-twentieth. Lewis sees two schools of thought among book designers, those influenced by art nouveau and those, like William Morris, who looked to the past for typographical and pictorial inspiration. The private press movement revived typography and raised the quality of commercial bookmaking. Lewis discusses trends that have shaped the modern book and looks at those who created or responded to these impulses. The volume is filled with reproductions of what Lewis regards as the finest examples of the twentieth century book. With separate chapters on children's books and paperbacks. Fridolf Johnson in *American Artist* 32 (January, 1968): 67 called Lewis' work "one of the most complete and informative on the subject yet produced." The *Times Literary Supplement* for December 21, 1967 described it as "scholarly and intelligent as well as beautifully illustrated" (p. 1230).

McLean, Ruari. *Victorian Book Design and Color Printing.* 2d ed. Berkeley: University of California Press, 1972.
Examines developments in English books of the nineteenth century. McLean considers not just illustration but also typography, binding, ornamentation, and presswork. Especially important in this period is color printing, which influenced all aspects of the book, from binding to illustration. McLean writes that "the Victorian period was one of rapid change, of fertile invention, and of enormous vitality, all of which is reflected in its books." The period saw great technological advances, but books, especially illustrations, were made by hand until the 1890s. Though admiring, McLean's study does not ignore the excesses and failures that the period witnessed.

MacRobert, Thomas Murray. *Fine Illustrations in Western European Printed Books.* London: Her Majesty's Stationery Office, 1969.
Drawing on the collection in the Victoria and Albert Museum, Mac-Robert presents 125 black-and-white reproductions that reveal the range and nature of book illustration from the Middle Ages to the mid-twentieth century. The brief text preceding the pictures discusses the ways in which illustrations have been produced and observes shifts

Illustration 157

in fashion. MacRobert writes, for instance, that the nineteenth century produced no finely illustrated Ovid, turning instead to Dante, Cervantes, Milton, and Goethe. English illustrators became prominent in the nineteenth century; in the 1700s the major British illustrators were almost all immigrants.

McTigue, Bernard. *Nature Illustrated: Flowers, Plants and Trees, 1550-1900. From the Collections of the New York Public Library.* New York: Harry N. Abrams, 1989.
The forty-four color plates and fifty-nine black-and-white reproductions focus on botanical illustrations of the eighteenth and nineteenth centuries; when scientific advances combined with new printing technology to produce beautiful books. The book ends with 1900 because photography by that date had reduced the quality of botanical illustration. McTigue observes that the great herbals of the sixteenth century relied on woodcuts for illustrations, which could be impressive but often were not. The seventeenth century introduced engraving and sought to convey "visual delight" as well as "scientific discovery." Artistry is most pronounced between 1700 and 1900, the period of Pierre Joseph Redouté, James Bateman, and Mark Catesby. With a list of the books from which the illustrations are drawn.

Mayor, A. Hyatt. *Prints and People: A Social History of Printed Pictures.* New York: Metropolitan Museum of Art, 1971.
A survey from antiquity to twentieth century lithographs and silk screening, enriched with 752 illustrations. Mayor discusses techniques but focuses on the role of prints in society. Though many fine artists have produced prints—Dürer, Picasso, and Matisse, for example—Mayor observes that the print is the medium for the masses. Prints have served to advertise the latest wares or latest advances in science; thus, Vesalius commissioned John Stephen to provide woodcuts for his anatomy text. Includes some astute analysis of individual prints, such as Rembrandt's *Christ Presented to the People.* Mayor finds the model of El Greco's *St. John Beholding the Wonders of the Apocalypse* in Dürer's woodcut "Agony in the Garden," and notes that Dürer's Adam is based on a Venetian drawing of the Apollo Belvedere. Lincoln Kirsten wrote that from Mayor's book "the reader gains a vivid, by no means cursory view of paper pictures (including photographs) in their extravagant technical variety, while he is guided as seldom before through the mechanism of connoisseurship" (*The Nation* 214, 1972, 219).

Melot, Michel. *The Art of Illustration*. New York: Rizzoli, 1984.

Art Decoration 36 (January, 1985): 92 called this volume, with its 110 color and 240 black-and-white reproductions, "an exquisite history of illustration." Melot observes that letters and pictures both serve as signs but differ; even the earliest pictographs no longer are figures but a more abstract code inaccessible to the illiterate. In the classical period illustration and text, though complementary, were separate. Islamic calligraphy, on the other hand, fused text and picture, as did insular and Merovingian decorative letters. In the later Middle Ages, text and image again diverge. Later still the illustration becomes a necessary adjunct to the word, especially in scientific works. In 1571 Bartolomeo Taegio observed, "Words and pictures separately have no meaning, but accompanying each other they manifest the secret of our soul." Melot argues that in the late twentieth century the word and image compete, but pictures also can enhance the power of the word.

Meyer, Susan E. *America's Great Illustrators*. New York: Harry N. Abrams, 1978.

Studies ten American artists active in the late nineteenth and early twentieth centuries, the period Meyer regards as "the Golden Age of Illustration." The artists are Howard Pyle, N. C. Wyeth, Frederic Remington, Maxfield Parrish, J. C. Lyendecker, Norman Rockwell, Charles Dana Gibson, Howard Chandler Christy, James Montgomery Flagg, and John Held, Jr. Meyer first surveys the period and then looks at each illustrator in a separate chapter. She discusses the influences that each reflects and notes the contributions that each made. Meyer observes, for example, that John Held at once looked back to the nineteenth century woodcut and forward to the poster-like illustrations of the 1920s. Frederic Remington adapted European artists' reporting techniques to portray the American West. With 417 illustrations, 186 in color.

Muir, Percy Horace. *Victorian Illustrated Books*. New York: Praeger Publishers, 1971.

A topical survey of English illustrated books during the reign of Victoria (1837-1901), with some retrospective glances. Muir first considers children's books. He then discusses the work of Thomas Bewick and George Cruikshank, line engraving, novels in parts and periodicals, the Dalziels (engravers, artists, publishers, and printers who greatly influenced book production in the mid-1800s), color printing, and the tendencies of the fin-de-siecle artists. Two concluding chapters treat foreign influences and the book in nineteenth century

Illustration 159

America. Nicely illustrated with nearly a hundred reproductions, almost all of them in black-and-white. Muir offers critical assessments along with his history. He condemns William Morris' Kelmscott Press productions as hard to read, and he credits Aubrey Beardsley with changing "the course of book illustration throughout the Western world." Among Muir's other enthusiasms are the illustrations of George Cruikshank and Charles Keene.

Nordenfalk, Carl. "The Beginning of Book Decoration." In *Essays in Honor of George Swarzenski*. Edited by Oswald Goetz. Chicago: Henry Regnery, 1951, pp. 9-20.

Nordenfalk argues that the earliest book illustrations served to orient readers of a scroll or codex, to act as a rubric. As he observes, "Book decoration is born because of the necessity for providing a dividing and supporting framework for tabular texts." Decorated canon tables appeared by the fourth century A.D.; the origin of such ornamentation remains obscure, but the models probably were not Christian.

Peppin, Brigid, and Lucy Micklethwait. *Dictionary of British Book Illustrators of the Twentieth Century*. London: John Murray, 1983.

Michael Patrick Hearn calls this bio-bibliography of some 800 British illustrators "an invaluable guide [that] provides an extraordinary amount of new information in a well-organized dictionary" (*American Book Collector* 5, May/June, 1984, 48). For almost every artist the authors have included a sample illustration, and they attempt in limited space to present some critical comments along with the biographical information. Also lists works illustrated and references for further research.

Pitz, Henry C. *A Treasury of American Book Illustration*. New York: American Studio Books and Watson-Guptill, 1947.

Essentially a picture book demonstrating the range of twentieth century American illustration. Pitz touches on earlier artists; he admires Howard Pyle, for example, and sees him as bestriding his age like a colossus. Pitz notes that in the twentieth century, American illustration has become international and so has muted its earlier Anglo-Saxon character. Includes short chapters on children's books, the increasing number of well-illustrated books, problems facing illustrators, and the dust jacket.

Pollard, Alfred W. *Early Illustrated Books: A History of the Decoration and Illustration of Books in the Fifteenth and Sixteenth Centuries*. 2d ed. London: Kegan Paul, Trench, Trubner, 1917.

Early printers drew on manuscript illuminators to embellish their books, but sometimes purchasers would engage illustrators. Later printers freed themselves from illuminators by using woodcut initials and other illustrations. The first example of a mechanically illustrated book according to Pollard appeared in Bamberg in 1461. After two general chapters, Pollard examines developments in particular countries. E. Gordon Duff supplied a chapter on England. A nicely illustrated, well-written study that remains a classic.

_____. *Fine Books*. London: Methuen, 1912.
Still useful for books from 1450 to 1780; a brief final chapter carries the history onward to the twentieth century. Pollard looks at fine printing as well as illustration but has much to say about this latter topic. He notes that too many artists have tried to create illustrations that are overly complex for the mode of reproduction being used, or have ignored the necessary harmony between print and picture. Most of the discussion of illustration deals with woodcuts; the penultimate chapter traces the use of engravings, a practice already in use in the fifteenth century but not popular until the mid-sixteenth, when Jerome Cook of Antwerp issued a series of plates. With forty black-and-white illustrations. Frederick W. Gookin called this "a volume which every collector of beautiful books and every student of the history of printing and of book illustration must find indispensable" (*The Dial* 54, 1913, 17).

Prideaux, Sarah Treverbian. *Aquatint Engraving: A Chapter in the History of Book Illustration*. London: Duckworth, 1909.
In 1775 Paul Sandby introduced the aquatint to England, where it enjoyed great popularity until about 1830. In France it had been introduced earlier, and Goya found the technique congenial. Prideaux seeks to provide "a guide to the student of aquatint engraving [and] to call attention to a mode of illustration which at its best has never been surpassed in the history of book production." She notes that aquatint was especially popular for works dealing with topography and architecture. The first two chapters focus on technical aspects. Prideaux then devotes Chapter 3 to Goya and to various French artists. The rest of the book concentrates on England. Appendix A lists books published before 1830 containing aquatint plates. Other appendices present biographical sketches of engravers, a list of artists, a special bibliography of the publications of Rudolph Ackermann (who published many important illustrated volumes in the early nineteenth century), a list of books with Thomas Rowlandson's aquatints, another of aquatint en-

Illustration 161

gravers and their books, and a bibliography for further study. *The Nation* 91 (1910): 226 commented, "For what she has done in a little-worked field, in this first separate study of aquatint, the author deserves the thanks of all interested. If she has not finished a complete history of the art, she has fully covered, for England, the period during which it had its greatest vogue."

Rainey, Sue, and Mildred Abraham. *Embellished with Numerous Engravings: The Works of American Illustrators and Wood Engravers, 1670-1880.* Charlottesville: Department of Rare Books, University of Virginia Library, 1986.

In 1986 the University of Virginia held an exhibit to show two centuries of American book illustration, from the late 1600s to 1880. In her introductory essay, Rainey traces the evolution from the woodcuts of John Foster to the sophisticated wood engravings of Alexander Anderson (1775-1870), known as "the American Bewick," and F. O. C. Darley (1822-1888). After the Civil War the demand for illustrated books and magazines increased and was answered by such periodicals as *Scribner's Monthly, St. Nicholas,* and *Picturesque America* (1872-1874). This last work won the praise of a French commissioner at the 1876 Centennial Exposition in Philadelphia. Rainey and Abraham concentrate on illustrations using wood rather than metal, though they note that the latter was used in nineteenth century America.

Ray, Gordon N. *The Art of the French Illustrated Book, 1700 to 1914.* 2 vols. New York: Pierpont Morgan Library, 1982.

French book illustration has long been outstanding, and that mastery characterizes the period Ray examines. The study reveals changes in taste and technique. In his introduction, Ray explains how he built the collection described in these volumes; most of the items here belonged to him. Arrangement of the text is chronological by artist, beginning with Charles Le Brun (1619-1690). Includes bibliographical references as well as examples of the artists' work and useful commentary. An essential reference that covers almost 400 books and magazines and includes over 600 illustrations, twenty-four in color. Dore Ashton commented, "*The Art of the French Illustrated Book, 1700 to 1914* . . . can be savored for both its erudition and the quality and quantity of its illustrations. . . . The inquisitive reader will learn about not only the techniques employed by artists . . . but also the circumstances, aesthetic and sociological, under which illustrators labored. . . . Ray offers rich, analytic and frequently witty commentary" (*The Nation* 235, 1982, 692).

_____. *The Illustrator and the Book in England from 1790 to 1914.* New York: Pierpont Morgan Library, 1976.

English book illustration of the eighteenth century was less impressive than its continental counterpart, but in the nineteenth century it achieved a level of excellence that continued until World War I. Ray describes 333 books and includes 100 plates (one for each of the more important volumes), along with numerous illustrations in the text. He excludes photographic illustration but discusses all other techniques. He also presents short essays on individual artists and important topics such as "Wood Engraving between Bewick and the Dalziel Brothers" and "The First Half Century of Lithography." The book serves as a history of illustration for the period, revealing shifts in technique. It also indicates that artists increasingly asserted their independence from the text. A standard reference. Glenn J. Shea, in *The American Book Collector* 26 (March/April, 1976): 8, praised Ray's study for its "lively, informal scholarship laced with beautiful pictures." Allen M. Samuels concurred: "If the joy of a study of the illustrator's work is the combination of fine scholarship, a handsomely produced book, a literate text, and an abundance of suggestive images, then Professor Ray's *The Illustrator and the Book* is certainly an occasion for happiness" (*The Library* 32, 1977, 292).

Reed, Walt, and Roger Reed, eds. *The Illustrator in America, 1880-1980: A Century of Illustration.* New York: Madison Square Press, 1984.

Divided into decades, this study presents annotated examples of the work of major artists. The book is richly illustrated with both black-and-white and color reproductions, and the comments provide biographical and bibliographical information. A one-page introductory essay by an illustrator precedes each group of pictures. The book shows that tastes and techniques have changed over time, but it also reveals certain perdurable aspects of illustration. For example, Frederic Remington and Walt Spitzmiller, though separated by almost a century, both show the fascination of the rodeo rider. An informative coffee-table book.

Roger-Marx, Claude. *Graphic Art of the Nineteenth Century.* Translated by E. M. Gwyer. London: Thames and Hudson, 1962.

A chronological survey of European illustration in the 1800s. Roger-Marx observes the shifts in taste from wood engraving to copper engraving, the revival of lithography at mid-century, and Gustave DorVe"'s revitalization of the wood engraving—he executed about 10,000 of them. This useful history provides brief biographies of important figures and includes many illustrations.

Illustration 163

Rumpel, Heinrich. *Wood Engraving*. Geneva: Éditions de Bonvent, 1972. Filled with illustrations from the fifteenth through the twentieth century, this book provides a survey of the woodcut and wood engraving. Rumpel first defines the woodcut, then offers technical information, including information on tools and processes. The history looks at social and political aspects of woodcuts as well as the aesthetics of the illustrations. For example, the woodcut was a powerful force in the ongoing religious controversies of the sixteenth century.

Sandford, Christopher. "The Aesthetics of the Illustrated Book." *The Dolphin* 2 (1935): 82-93. Offers thoughts on what a good illustration is and is not. Sandford objects to incongruities such as mismatched colors or bold type and weak illustrations. His standard of excellence is the harmonious blend of paper, type, binding, and illustration. As he writes, "The illustrations must not be strained into coordination with the book, nor vice versa." He finds that many expensive books do not meet his criteria. Includes some examples that show how harmony is achieved or violated.

Shikes, Ralph E. *The Indignant Eye: The Artist as Social Critic in Prints and Drawings from the Fifteenth Century to Picasso*. Boston: Beacon Press, 1969. Examines over 150 artists from western Europe, the United States, and Mexico who have through the their art commented "on human folly in its infinite variations," particularly social evils. Considers artists' social criticism from the mid-fifteenth century work of Master E. S. and Hieronymus Bosch to the twentieth century. Early chapters deal with the subject chronologically. Shikes then concentrates on specific countries for a particular period, for example, "France and Belgium after the Commune: From Pissarro to Rouault." Includes 405 black-and-white reproductions. Franz Schulze called the book "a lucid, highly readable, at times quite moving catalogue of six centuries of 'protest art'" (*Saturday Review* 52, November, 29, 1969, 34).

Simon, Howard. *Five Hundred Years of Art and Illustration from Albrecht Dürer to Rockwell Kent*. Cleveland: World, 1942. Simon seeks "to trace the development of the modern book artist through the men who influenced his growth." The first two hundred pages discuss twenty-two important figures, from Dürer in the sixteenth century to Gustave Doré in the nineteenth. The second half of the book looks at twentieth century book illustration geographically, with individual chapters devoted to France, Germany, Poland, Russia,

Italy, Belgium, Holland, Mexico, Great Britain, and the United States. Filled with black-and-white illustrations.

Sitwell, Sacheverell, and Wilfred Blunt. *Great Flower Books, 1700-1900: A Bibliographical Record of Two Centuries of Finely-Illustrated Flower Books.* New York: Atlantic Monthly Press, 1990.
Lists over 750 illustrated flower books from the great age of botanical illustration and offers fifty-two full-page color illustrations, including three reproductions from Pierre Joseph Redouté's *Les liliacées* (Paris, 1802-1816). Among these is the magnificent rendering of the Iris germanica. Sitwell discusses the history of botanical books, and Blunt provides an essay on "The Illustrators of the Great Flower Books." An expanded, affordable version of the sumptuous 1956 edition published by Collins (London).

Sitwell, Sacheverell, Handasyde Buchanan, and James Fisher. *Fine Bird Books, 1700-1900.* New York: Atlantic Monthly Books, 1990.
Sitwell provided the introductory essay; the other two authors compiled the bibliography, and Fisher added a list of species depicted in the fifty-two plates included in this volume. Sitwell stresses the importance of Audubon, whose illustrations surpassed those of his predecessors, and she notes that until the nineteenth century, botanical was superior to zoological illustration: many eighteenth century bird books were more entertaining than accurate. An important reference and a delight to read or just to look at. An expanded version of the luxurious 1953 edition published by Collins (London).

Slythe, R. Margaret. *The Art of Illustration, 1750-1900.* London: Library Association, 1970.
The first chapter provides an overview of the period, and the second discusses technical aspects. Slythe then devotes a chapter to each process: woodcut and wood engraving, etching, engraving on metal, and lithography. The volume concludes with a bibliography and index of names. With forty black-and-white illustrations. International in scope; considers Oriental as well as Western examples.

Strachan, W. J. *The Artist and the Book in France.* New York: George Wittenborn, 1969.
Strachan first surveys French book illustration before 1900. Most of the volume looks at the twentieth century *livre d'artiste*, and there is a bibliography of these works (arranged by artist). As Strachan observes, this kind of book, with autographic illustrations executed by artists

Illustration 165

important in other fields, is virtually unique to France and has attracted painters and sculptors of every school. He notes that French illustration has a long-standing tradition of excellence, and in the eighteenth century Fragonard and Boucher, David and Girodet were among the important painters who illustrated books. In the early 1900s the publishers Ambroise Vollard and Daniel Henry Kahnweiler promoted the *livre d'artiste*, employing Picasso, Juan Gris, Rodin, Braque, and others. Strachan explains how the books were made. With 181 facsimiles. Philip Jones observed that the book's "authority and completeness make it a standard work of reference. . . . No serious student of the subject can afford to be without it" (*Apollo* 90, 1969, 541-542).

Taft, Robert. *Artists and Illustrators of the Old West, 1850-1900.* New York: Scribner, 1953.
A standard reference work. The first part of the book surveys the history of the West, with its trappers, explorers, and Indian fighters. Taft provides ninety illustrations to show the richness of the material artists produced in the era before photography usurped the role of the illustrator. He is especially concerned with the contributions of unfamiliar artists like Heinrich Möllhausen and Albert Waud, giving limited space to better known figures like Frederic Remington. Taft also groups together artists treating a particular topic, such as Custer's Last Stand or the completion of the transcontinental railroad, so readers can compare renditions.

Vision of a Collector: The Lessing J. Rosenwald Collection in the Library of Congress. Washington, D.C.: Library of Congress, 1991.
Issued for the centenary of the birth of Rosenwald, who donated his collection of over 2,600 illustrated books to the Library of Congress. This volume contains one hundred essays, each dealing with a different book from the Rosenwald collection. The work begins with five essays on manuscripts. These are followed by twelve on early printing, typography, and writing manuals, thirty-nine pieces on illustrated books, six on eighteenth century French illustrated books, four on William Blake, seven on modern illustrated books, three on architecture, seven on binding, five on geographical works, three on herbals, and nine on scientific books. The essays are short—few exceed four pages—but filled with erudition. Egbert Haverkamp-Begemann observes, for example, that depictions of nature in the works of late fifteenth century artists from Haarlem reflect the beauty of the city's setting. Starr Siegele interprets Wassily Kandinsky's *Klange* (1912), a work of German expressionism by the Russian artist. The 1775 Phila-

delphia reprinting of Abraham Swan's *The British Architect* shows, according to James Gilreath, "that the steps toward a distinct national identity in the art of architecture [in America] were still hesitant, timid, filled with self-doubt." With one hundred illustrations, one for each of the books treated in the text. Also provides a biographical sketch of Rosenwald by William Matheson.

Wakeman, Geoffrey. *Victorian Book Illustration: The Technical Revolution.* Detroit: Gale Research, 1973.
During the Victorian era, photomechanical methods of illustration replaced autographic techniques, as photography, electrotyping, and cross-line screening emerged. Drawing on nineteenth century descriptions, Wakeman traces the technological changes that affected book illustration, noting the decline of certain types, such as aquatint, and the rise of other methods. Woodcuts, for example, remained popular until almost the end of the century, reaching a peak in the 1880s and then declining rapidly. Wakeman also discusses failed experiments, such as Godfrey Woone's efforts with plaster stereotyping. With forty illustrations showing machinery, tools, and examples of what the various technologies produced. James Wells commented in *Library Quarterly* 45 (1975): 215-216 that Wakeman's book "contains an enormous amount of information, written with great concision and clarity. . . . It is an important and valuable addition to the literature of the history of printing technology."

Ward, Gerald W. R., ed. *The American Illustrated Book in the Nineteenth Century.* Winterthur, Del.: Winterthur Museum, 1987.
Nine essays treating diverse aspects of the subject. Neil Harris looks at reactions to increased illustration; he argues that pictures challenge elitist and conservative values. Judy L. Larson discusses Thomas Dobson's edition of the *Encyclopaedia Britannica*, published in Philadelphia between 1790 and 1803. This eighteen-volume set was a landmark in American illustration, having more than 500 plates (compared to 200 in the British edition), and prompted others to imitate it. The great demand for engravers created by the project stimulated the growth of this trade in America. Georgia B. Barnhill's essay looks at illustrated Natural Histories published in Philadelphia between 1800 and 1850. John Sartain's illustrations for gift books is the subject of Katherine Martinez' essay; Sue W. Reed looks at four series of pictures executed by F. O. C. Darley. Neville Thompson examines architectural books in the nineteenth century, especially the vision that it offered of the ideal American home. Susan Otis Thompson reassesses the influ-

Illustration 167

ence of the British Arts and Crafts movement on American bookmaking. Elizabeth Hawkes analyzes the work of Howard Pyle, and the volume concludes with Lois Olcott Price's piece on photochemical book illustration. A well-illustrated volume.

Weitenkampf, Frank. *The Illustrated Book.* Cambridge, Mass.: Harvard University Press, 1938.
Deals with the printed book and notes changes in technology over the centuries. In the 1400s, printers used woodblocks that harmonized with letterpress, Indeed, woodblock books had preceded those printed from movable type. In the sixteenth century, artists sometimes forgot the text in a self-conscious effort to create elaborate illustrations. Although copper engravings appear as early as 1476, they supplanted woodcuts only in the sixteenth century, and in the nineteenth century etching and aquatint enjoyed great popularity. Wood engraving also was in favor in the 1800s, pioneered by Thomas Bewick. In the last quarter of the nineteenth century, pen-and-ink, halftone, and collotype illustrations emerged to rival the woodcut. As the halftone process improved, color illustrations became possible, allowing for the work of Edmund Dulac and Arthur Rackham, Howard Pyle and Maxfield Parrish. The twentieth century has seen the proliferation of techniques but also a desire for a harmonious relationship between text and picture. Well illustrated throughout; includes a useful though dated bibliography.

Weitzmann, Kurt. *Ancient Book Illumination.* Cambridge, Mass.: Harvard University Press, 1959.
Four lectures presented at Oberlin College. The first deals with scientific and didactic treatises, the second with epic poetry, the third with drama, and the fourth with literary prose. Although few examples of classical illustration survive because of the fragility of papyrus, Weitzmann argues that the tradition of illustration was widespread and may be recreated by looking at other artifacts such as vases, frescoes, textiles, sarcophagi, and the medieval manuscript illustrations that derive from classical models. Weitzmann maintains that a "continuous narrative style" of illumination was developed by illustrators of papyrus rolls in Hellenistic Egypt.

_____. *Illustrations in Roll and Codex: A Study of the Origin and Method of Text Illustration.* 2d printing, with addenda. Princeton, N.J.: Princeton University Press, 1970.
The Egyptians began illustrating papyrus rolls as early as 1980 B.C. The Greeks adopted Egyptian methods and even subject matter. When the

codex replaced the roll, little changed at first, since rolls already used columns that easily transferred to the design of the page. The parchment codex permitted more elaborate techniques than the papyrus roll, though, and encouraged larger, full-page illustrations. By 400 A.D. one finds full-page framed pictures, as in the Vatican Virgil. Weitzmann examines the relationship between text and illustration (sometimes tenuous) and the iconic significance of the pictures included. He explains incongruities in illustrations by positing a lineage of models that may distort or modify some features while retaining others, so that one cannot assume that different artists are responsible for variations in style. An important study.

_____. *Studies in Classical and Byzantine Manuscript Illumination*. Edited Herbert L. Kessler. Chicago: University of Chicago Press, 1971.

Twelve essays that reveal the range of Weitzmann's studies. He was especially interested in the transmission of illustrations, a subject addressed, for example, in the second piece here, "Greek Sources of Islamic Scientific Illustrations," and in "The Classical Heritage in the Art of Constantinople." In "The Illustration of the Septuagint," Weitzmann claims that the pictures from a manuscript served as models for paintings and mosaics in churches and that early biblical manuscripts were more heavily illustrated than later ones. The Cotton Genesis (fifth-sixth century A.D.) had over 300 miniatures, for example. The earliest Biblical illustrations probably were influenced by pagan examples. Another essay argues for a Byzantine Renaissance in the ninth and tenth centuries and claims that it helped make possible the later Italian Renaissance. Filled with illustrations (320) and erudition. Together the essays cover the period from antiquity to the thirteenth century.

Woodberry, George E. *A History of Wood Engraving*. New York: Harper & Bros., 1883.

Although the origins of the woodcut are obscure, single-page examples from early fifteenth century Europe have survived, and these coexist with blockbooks. Printers adopted woodcuts to illustrate their volumes. Italy refined the woodcut into an art, but Albrecht Dürer "was the first to discover the full capacities of wood-engraving as a mode of artistic expression." By the end of the sixteenth century, copperplate engravings had replaced woodcuts as the dominant form of illustration; Woodberry therefore skips over the seventeenth and eighteenth centuries until he reaches Thomas Bewick (1753-1828), the father of modern

Illustration 169

wood-engraving. Woodberry maintains that the early woodcut stimulated a sense of realism and secularism in art, and in the nineteenth
century it resurfaced as a democratic art form.

Children's Books

Bader, Barbara. *American Picturebooks: From Noah's Ark to the Beast
Within*. New York: Macmillan, 1976.
According to Bader, in the late nineteenth century children's picture
books became artistic. Her work examines twentieth century American
picturebooks, beginning with the work of E. Boyd Smith (b. 1860)
through the 1970s. Bader focuses on selected illustrators but also
discusses publishers and notes various technical, artistic, social, and
political factors that impinge on children's literature. For example,
Golden Books could appear in the numbers they did during World War
II because their publisher had a large allocation of rationed paper.
Profusely illustrated with nearly 700 reproductions, 100 of them in
color. Zena Sutherland praised the book as "a fusion of historical
overview, often brilliant graphic analysis, a broad and erudite knowledge of books, and a clear understanding of the forces that have
contributed to changes in the field of children's books" (*Library
Quarterly* 49, 1979, 108). Ethel L. Heins wrote in *The Horn Book* 52
(1976): 486, that Bader's "criticism is always thoughtful and often
keen and incisive." A sound history and important reference, despite
its selectivity.

Cianciolo, Patricia. *Illustrations in Children's Books*. 2d ed. Dubuque,
Iowa: Wm. C. Brown, 1976.
Written for those seeking information about "the varieties of illustrated
books that are available to children." The first chapter argues that
illustrations should not simply provide decoration but should "help tell
significant aspects of the story and . . . extend the text." Cianciolo also
wants text and illustration to "blend so well that it will seem as if one
person had been responsible for both." The second chapter surveys
various styles of illustration, such as expressionistic, cubist, or impres-
sionistic. The author next discusses different media and techniques and
concludes with a chapter on using illustrations to promote learning.
Each chapter contains a bibliography, and the volume provides a long
list of titles that Cianciolo regards as well illustrated. Each entry here
is briefly annotated. Also has the list of Caldecott Medal books from
1938 through 1969.

Dalby, Richard. *The Golden Age of Children's Book Illustration*. London: Gallery Books, 1991.

For Dalby the golden age of book illustration for children was the period between 1837 and 1939, though he begins his survey with George Cruikshank's pictures for the Grimm Brothers' *German Popular Stories* (1823-1826) and concludes with Ernest Howard Shepard's work, which continued into the 1970s. Altogether Dalby discusses fifty-six artists. most of them English or American. For each he provides a brief biography and a short discussion of important works, together with examples that reveal the artist's style. None of the artists receives in-depth analysis, but this attractive volume serves as a sound introduction to nineteenth and twentieth century illustrations for young readers.

Gottlieb, Gerald. *Early Children's Books and Their Illustration*. Boston: David R. Godine, 1975.

The first stories for children probably were fables like those of Aesop, and the first example included here is an unillustrated papyrus fragment with parts of three fables by Babrius; the manuscript dates from the third or fourth century A.D. The volume quickly arrives at the eighteenth century, a period so important that Gottlieb includes an essay by J. H. Plumb on this "First Flourishing of Children's Books." Most of the examples discussed in this volume date from the eighteenth and nineteenth centuries. Altogether 225 titles are included, the last being *The Little Prince* (1943). The book presents high spots, especially of English and American works, rather than a comprehensive survey. Arranged by type of book, such as Bestiaries, ABC's, Religious Books, or Fairy Tales. Nicely illustrated. David Preiss praised the work as "enticing and informative, delightfully designed, readably written, perfectly printed, and artfully arranged so that the grouping of the books illustrated also end up being miraculously chronological" (*American Artist* 40, December, 1976, 25).

Meyer, Susan E. *A Treasury of the Great Children's Book Illustrators*. New York: Harry N. Abrams, 1983.

Treats thirteen illustrators of children's books, each of whom typifies a particular style or trend. All were born in the nineteenth century, a great period for children's books and their illustrators. Meyer's introduction surveys the social, literary, and artistic background of the period. The rest of the book treats Edward Lear, John Tenniel, Walter Crane, Randolph Caldecott, Kate Greenaway, Beatrix Potter, Ernest H. Shepard, Arthur Rackham, Edmund Dulac, Kay Nielsen, Howard Pyle,

Illustration 171

N. C. Wyeth, and W. W. Denslow. By focusing on this limited number of illustrators, Meyer can provide detailed discussion of their contributions. Copiously illustrated throughout. Lamia Doumato called this "a useful, handsome volume on illustration" (*American Reference Book Annual* 16, 1985, 336).

Miller, Bertha Mahony, et al. *Illustrators of Children's Books.* Boston: Horn Book, 1947.
Miller first looks briefly at early illustrated books such as Aesop's *Fables* from William Caxton's press (1484), with its 185 woodcuts, and the New England primer with its quaint picture accompanying each letter. In 1744, John Newbery, issued his first "juvenile," *A Little Pretty Pocket Book*; Miller and company examine the history of book illustration from this date onward. The authors explore the various processes used, provide biographies of twentieth century illustrators, and include bibliographies of illustrators and of authors whose work has been illustrated for children. Also includes suggested readings and bibliographic notes. Carefully illustrated throughout. Supplemented by Ruth H. Vigeurs, Marcia Dolphin, and Bertha M. Miller's *Illustrators of Children's Books, 1946-1956* (Boston: Horn Book, 1958) and by Lee Kingman, J. Foster, and R. G. Lontoft, *Illustrators of Children's Books, 1957-1966* (Boston: Horn Book, 1968).

Pitz, Henry C. *Illustrating Children's Books: History—Technique—Production.* New York: Watson-Guptill, 1963.
A volume for the historian or the practitioner. David Preiss claimed that "no one interested in illustration should be without this book" (*American Artist* 41, November, 1977, 28). In under two hundred pages, Pitz first surveys the history of illustrated children's books from the fifteenth century onward. The second section discusses theoretical and practical issues that the illustrator must confront, and the book concludes with advice on how to handle an assignment and also how to get one. With a brief bibliography.

Ward, Martha E., and Dorothy A. Marquardt. *Illustrators of Books for Young People.* 2d ed. Metuchen, N.J.: Scarecrow Press, 1975.
With 750 entries, offering biographical information together with a list of works illustrated by the artists included. Despite the absence of illustrations and critical commentary, this remains a useful bio-bibliography that provides the basic facts about the prominent and lesser-known illustrators of children's books.

Whalley, Joyce Irene. *Cobwebs to Catch Flies: Illustrated Books for the Nursery and Schoolroom, 1700-1900*. Berkeley: University of California Press, 1975.

A well-illustrated survey of the topic, arranged by type of book, such as religious works, histories, and grammars. All the books examined here were intended to instruct as well as entertain. The title derives from a reader first published in 1783. Whalley notes how instructional materials evolved in the course of two centuries as publishers slowly accepted the notion that children's books should instruct through delight instead of delighting in instructing. Whalley relates the shift in texts to changes in society. She observes that children's books initially sought to save souls, then to teach manners, morals, and facts. In the eighteenth century publishers appealed to adult book buyers, but in the late nineteenth and twentieth centuries books for young readers have sought to appeal to children rather than their parents. *The Horn Book Magazine* 52 (1976): 70 called this "a substantial work of history and criticism with a fresh focus."

Whalley, Joyce Irene, and R. Chester. *A History of Children's Book Illustration*. London: Victoria and Albert Museum, 1988.

Because so much early illustration is anonymous, the first six chapters offer a chronological survey that focuses on trends rather than individuals. Later chapters deal with specific artists, mainly British. John Barr commented that "the authors have fitted a remarkable amount of information conveniently between two covers and placed it usefully within the wider histories of art and of publishing" (*The Library* 11, 1989, 287-288). With over 200 illustrations, thirty-seven of them in color. An important history and a useful reference.

Chapter 8
BOOKBINDING

Bibliographies

Brenni, Vito Joseph. *Bookbinding: A Guide to the Literature*. Westport, Conn.: Greenwood Press, 1983.

The first attempt at a book-length bibliography on the subject since Wolfgang Meyer's magisterial 1925 effort (see below). Topical arrangement, with emphasis on history rather than technique. Reviewers have criticized the work for various reasons. Mirjam M. Foot in *The Library* 6 (1984): 419 objected to the overly complex organization, to important omissions, to careless proofreading that failed to detect improper attributions, and to incorrect classification. Samuel Ellenport also complained about omissions and the limited glossary (*The Papers of the Bibliographical Society of America* 78, 1984, 106). Though not definitive, this remains a useful bibliography.

Breslauer, B. H. *The Uses of Bookbinding Literature*. New York: Book Arts Press, 1986.

This forty-four page book, international in scope, focuses on hand-bookbinding in the West, and its primary concerns are history and design. How-to manuals receive little attention. Helpful for the student seeking the best material available. The publication includes "Lists of Books and Articles Mentioned in the Text," compiled by Martin Antonetti. Paul S. Coda recommended the bibliography to anyone interested in the history of the book, "especially those whose inquiries send them into the study of early, international fields of bookbinding" (*Bulletin of Bibliography* 45, 1988, 67).

Meyer, Wolfgang. *Bibliographie der Buchbinderei-Literatur*. Leipzig: Karl W. Hiersemann, 1925.

Despite its publication date, still an excellent bibliography on the subject, with 2,691 entries arranged alphabetically under broad subject headings such as allgemeines (general works), geschichte (historical studies), and tecnik. The listing of books and articles is international in scope and provides full bibliographic information, but the entries generally lack annotation. Useful even for non-German speakers.

Schmidt-Kunsemuller, Friedrich-Adolf. *Bibliographie zur Geschichte von der Einbandkunst den Anfangen bis 1985.* Weisbaden, Germany: Dr. Ludwig Reichert Verlag, 1987.

The most comprehensive bibliography available, with 8,033 entries topically arranged. Sections cover bibliography, terminology, binding techniques, aesthetics, history, specific binders and historians of binding, and specific countries divided by chronological periods. Indexes allow access by author, binder, collector, location, and type of binding.

Manuals

Banister, Manly. *Bookbinding as a Handicraft.* New York: Sterling, 1975.

A well-illustrated manual showing the would-be home binder how to deal with magazines, books, and manuscripts. Includes instructions for leather bindings and information on the necessary materials and tools. Bannister shows the novice how to make some of his own equipment and thus save money. Also discusses which books are not good candidates for the binder's efforts.

Burdett, Eric. *The Craft of Bookbinding: A Practical Handbook.* Newton Abbot, England: David and Charles, 1975.

In his introduction, Burdett discusses equipment, tools, and the various steps necessary for different types of binding. Here he also suggests some improvised equipment for the amateur. The next four chapters present in detail the basic stages—preparatory work, forwarding, covering, and finishing. Chapter 5 treats cover design, Chapter 6 miscellaneous topics such as making slip cases or portfolio cases. In Chapter 7, Burdett deals with repairing books, and Chapter 8 offers a glossary of terms like "strawboard" and "foril." The book concludes with a list of suppliers and a brief bibliography. More detailed than many other introductions and hence more useful.

Clements, J. *Bookbinding.* London: Arco, 1963.

As Clements writes in his foreword, this work "introduces the reader to the fundamentals of bookbinding and includes a concise history of fine bindings, together with a short account of the early development of publishers' edition binding." Most of the book offers practical instruction, beginning with definitions of technical terms and a discussion of necessary tools and equipment. Clements then tells how to prepare a book for rebinding. Chapter 3 treats case binding, Chapters 4 and 5 binding a book out of or in boards. These are followed by chapters on other forms of binding, on repairing old bindings, finishing, letter-. ing, and making boxes and slipcases. Two historical chapters and a short treatment on design conclude the work. With line drawings to guide the binder, and a brief bibliography.

Cockerell, Douglas. *Bookbinding and the Care of Books: A Text-Book for Bookbinders and Librarians*. 5th ed., rev. London: Sir Isaac Pitman and Sons, 1962.
A standard since its first appearance in 1901. Cockerell's object was "to describe the best methods of bookbinding, and of keeping books when bound." Much here on what to avoid, such as "sprinkled" or "tree" calf, produced by using ferrous sulphate, which eventually destroys the leather. Much of Cockerell's advice remains sound, as when he comments, "It is far more pleasant to see an old book in a patched contemporary binding, than smug and tidy in the most immaculate modern cover." Similarly, his comments on the care of books are still timely, and occasionally they provoke a smile, as when he warns, "Cockroaches are very troublesome in libraries." Reviewing the first American edition, *The Nation* wrote, "The outsider will learn all that he need know from this volume, and even the practiced binder will, we should think, find much in the way of valuable hints, and still more in the way of encouraging insistence upon points which he is much too apt to forget" (75, 1902, 138). Utilitarian line drawings and twelve photographs of bindings accompany the text.

Corderoy, John. *Bookbinding for Beginners*. New York: Watson-Guptill, 1967.
A well-illustrated instruction manual with a (now-dated) list of American and English sources for equipment and material. Intended for the amateur working alone or in a class; Corderoy taught bookbinding for years. Corderoy first presents the necessary tools, materials, and equipment, and he tells the novice how to make some of these items. He then takes the would-be binder through the stages of the process, recommending that the beginner first use plain paper. A good book for the neophyte.

Diehl, Edith. *Bookbinding, Its Background and Technique*. 2 vols. New York: Rinehart, 1946.
See entry under "General Studies," below.

Dutton, Meirick. *Introduction to Book Binding*. London: Faber & Faber, 1965.

An amateur craft binder, Dutton has here written enthusiastically for beginners and has provided over forty line drawings to guide the novice. Dutton also includes reproductions of some important examples of fine bindings, including one by Roger Payne and another by Cobden-Sanderson. Though intended for the practitioner, the book provides much information for those seeking basic information on binding techniques. Covers making a notebook and a case for a book, rebinding an old book, and binding a book in leather. Also includes sixteen pages on machine binding. The *Times Literary Supplement* review for October 28, 1965, observed that the book "can be trusted implicitly by the beginner, and it can be read with profit by the more advanced. It deserves a place on any binder's shelf, not far from Douglas Cockerell's famous *Bookbinding and the Care of Books*" (968). Because of the book's brevity, beginners may need to consult other manuals when they confront certain problems.

Gross, Henry. *Simplified Bookbinding*. New York: Charles Scribner's Sons, 1976.
An amateur, Gross writes for other weekend binders who do not want to spend a lot of money on frames, presses, and tools. He shows how one can create a press simply and cheaply and notes that two bricks can suffice. The book offers clear, succinct instructions for dealing with tattered volumes and includes other projects, such as the manufacture of slipcases and book boxes. Provides a list of suppliers. A good introduction for the novice.

Hewitt-Bates, James Samuel. *Bookbinding*. 8th ed., rev. Leicester, England: Dryad Press, 1967.
In his preface, Hewitt-Bates states, "The aim of this book is to assist the teacher of arts and crafts in primary and secondary schools and training colleges, by presenting the subject from a simple and practical angle that will give due regard to the educational value of the processes described." Himself a master craftsman and teacher, Hewitt-Bates offers a series of clearly illustrated exercises to guide the would-be binder from the making of portfolios to the binding of a book and making marbled papers. Chapters 2-3 list necessary equipment and materials.

Johnson, Arthur W. *The Practical Guide to Craft Bookbinding*. New York: Thames and Hudson, 1985.
Designed for those seeking information about the structure of a book, whether or not they wish to bind. The volume is attractively printed,

with the text in black, marginal notes and line drawings in red. Recognizing that no book can provide all the information necessary for the would-be practitioner, Johnson advises the novice to seek professional instruction. Includes a glossary, list of suppliers, and suggested projects. Provides clear explanations and excellent illustrations.

_____. *The Thames and Hudson Manual of Bookbinding*. London: Thames and Hudson, 1978.
Following a brief history of English bookbinding decoration—some of the information here is erroneous—Johnson discusses the equipment and materials needed for binding and then offers illustrated instructions on the binding—or rebinding—of a volume. Includes a glossary and reproductions of some fine (and one gaudy) examples of hand-binding. Mirjam M. Foot, the doyenne of binding history, called Johnson's book "a serious teaching manual which describes in great detail and with excellent illustrations the various and variant processes of binding," though she objects to his occasional dogmatic pronouncements (*The Book Collector* 27, 1978, 581). Encyclopedic.

Johnson, Pauline. *Creative Bookbinding*. Corr. ed. Seattle: University of Washington Press, 1973.
Intended for the school teacher, for whom exercises have been devised, and for the novice who lacks access to professional instruction. The lengthy introduction gives a history of the book; this is followed by instructions in binding and a long discussion of decorated papers. Johnson suggests alternatives to expensive equipment, such as bricks or a C-clamp as alternatives to a press, and she notes that a chair turned sideways can serve as a sewing frame. With a brief bibliography. A 1990 Dover reprint offers an updated list of suppliers. Reviewing the first (1963) edition, Lawrence S. Thompson called Johnson's volume, "A lucid practical manual on the basic skills of hand binding.... Miss Johnson has written a well-balanced reference work on binding which is also an eminently readable book" (*The Papers of the Bibliographical Society of America* 59, 1965, 341). An excellent book for beginners or advanced amateurs.

Lewis, Arthur W. *Basic Bookbinding*. London: B. T. Batsford, 1952.
Offers "step-by-step instructions in the essential operations involved in the binding of books by hand in cloth and in library style." Intended for students and the neophyte working alone. Provides a list of necessary equipment and materials (Chapters 1-2) and then discusses basic operations (Chapter 3) before turning to actual binding. Lewis regards

cover decoration as beyond the scope of the work, but he does conclude with a chapter of lettering.

Muir, David. *Binding and Repairing Books by Hand.* New York: Arco, 1978.

A well-illustrated manual that offers step-by-step instruction on repairing heads and tails, corners and torn pages, rebacking, rebinding, and gold-finishing. Includes a list of necessary equipment, with suppliers, and a glossary of technical terms such as "capping" (forming the piece of material which covers the head band at the top and tail of the spine) and "head and tail" (the book's top and bottom). Muir warns that professional bookbinders apprentice for six years, so the reader should not expect instant success.

Perry, Kenneth F., and Clarence T. Baab. *The Binding of Books.* Rev. ed. Bloomington, Ill.: McKnight and McKnight, 1967.

The first part of this practical manual presents general information for the beginner. The five chapters in this section explain the parts of the book and how these are held together; types of bindings; tools and equipment needed, necessary materials and supplies; and machine binding. The second part of the book addresses specific binding tasks; for each the authors list the necessary materials and equipment and then explain the procedure. Though the book provides a number of good illustrations, the novice working alone may wish for more of these. As a textbook or supplementary reading for a class, the work will prove most helpful.

Robinson, Ivor. *Introducing Bookbinding.* New York: Watson-Guptill, 1968.

Provides an "introduction to tools, equipment, and materials of the craft together with sequential demonstration of basic book-binding skills likely to be within the scope of the average school, college, or similar miscellaneous hand bindery." Well-illustrated, with a brief bibliography and list of suppliers, mainly British.

Theory and Practice of Bookbinding. Rev. ed. Washington, D.C.: Government Printing Office, 1962.

A textbook intended for apprentices in the Government Printing Office. Begins with a short history of bookbinding, then turns to matters such as stitching and sewing or rebinding magazines. Good for definitions of terms and processes, but designed to accompany rather than replace instruction. The book lacks illustrations and step-by-step instructions.

Town, Laurence. *Bookbinding by Hand for Students and Craftsmen.* 2d ed. London: Faber & Faber, 1963.

Town, who teaches bookbinding, has "written primarily with the teaching of bookbinding in schools always in mind, and many of the processes have been modified slightly to fit the needs and ability of children, but without sacrificing the essential methods of the practical craftsman." A good introduction for the novice.

Vaughn, Alex J. *Modern Bookbinding: A Treatise Covering Both Letterpress and Stationery Branches of the Trade, with a Section on Finishing and Design.* London: C. Skilton, 1960.

An instruction manual for those with access to expensive and extensive equipment. The novice may have some trouble with instructions such as "the head and back are knocked square and the fore-edge gripped between the cheeks of a laying press while the back is being glued." The advanced student, even the practiced binder, may find some useful hints here.

Watson, Aldren Auld. *Hand Bookbinding: A Manual of Instruction.* New York: Reinhold, 1963.

A excellent guide for the beginner wishing to bind a book.

Young, Laura S. *Bookbinding and Conservation by Hand: A Working Guide.* New York: R. R. Bowker, 1981.

Young wrote in her preface, "This book is designed as a working guide in the field of hand bookbinding and book conservation. It is intended as a practical manual for teachers and their students; as an instruction guide to be followed by the beginner attempting to learn binding on his or her own; and as a ready reference for experienced binders, book collectors, book dealers, and librarians." Offers clear, step-by-step instructions, but the list of needed supplies may daunt the novice. Not as basic as Gross (cited earlier), but ideal for the serious amateur. Includes a list of suppliers, a glossary, and bibliography. Neal L. Edgar wrote in *ARBA* 13 (1982): 155 that this is "one of the best available primers on hand bookbinding in an attractive format which is easily read, well-illustrated, and organized by a master of the art."

Zaehnsdorf, Joseph William. *The Art of Bookbinding: A Practical Treatise.* 2d ed., rev. and enl. London: George Bell & Sons, 1890.

Written by a leading practitioner to help "the unskilled workman." Offers detailed instructions, from folding to applying end papers to gilding the edges and applying gold leaf. Concludes with a chapter of general information, such as repelling insects and removing various types of stain. Also provides a glossary of technical terms. Interesting to the historian and modern binder.

General Studies

Allen, Sue. *Victorian Bookbindings: A Pictorial Survey.* Rev. ed. Chicago: University of Chicago Press, 1976.
Covers the period from 1825, when cloth trade bindings were introduced, to the early 1900s; looks at both English and American examples. Short chapters, generally two pages long, cover such subjects as the use of gold and silver, the Japanese influence on bindings, art nouveau covers, and the role of illustrators like Hugh Thomson (1860-1920) and Charles Ricketts (1866-1930) on cover design. Three color microfiche accompany the book to illustrate 251 bindings. The technology reduces the cost of the book, but the quality of reproduction varies considerably, and the stability of the color film remains a question. In their review for *The Journal of Academic Librarianship* (3, 1977, 98) Betty Jo Irvine and Josiah Bennett praised the brief text but devoted most of their discussion to criticism of the microfiche.

Andrews, William Loring. *A Short Historical Sketch of the Art of Bookbinding: With a Description of the Prominent Styles by William Matthews.* New York: s.n., 1895.
Not seen.

Ball, Douglas. *Victorian Publishers' Bindings.* Williamsburg, Va.: The Book Press, 1985.
A discussion of the mass-produced binding, which was introduced in the 1820s. Ball concludes his book around 1880, when technical and aesthetic changes occurred in cloth bindings. Ball challenges the long-held tradition that Pickering's Diamond Classics were the first to be issued in publishers' cloth. He notes the introduction of cloth and casing (as opposed to binding) in the 1820s, and gold blocking in 1832. Although these nineteenth century bindings were produced en masse, major designers were involved, and Ball lists the work of many of them. The book is also useful for identifying types of cloth grains, seven of which are illustrated in Appendix B. Reviewing the book for *The Private Library*, Peter Stockham praised the study as "useful . . . to the specialist and to those who only rarely see such volumes. It is itself nicely bound in full cloth, with decorated endpapers, and well

designed and printed (10, 1987, 131). Paul S. Coda showed similar enthusiasm: "Chapters such as 'The Climate of Design' and appendixes such as 'Cover Designs by Major Designers' are invaluable compilations of information to aid historians and book collectors wanting to identify and describe decorative bindings. . . . No bibliographer or historian interested in nineteenth century books . . . should be without *Victorian Publishers' Bindings* (*Bulletin of Bibliography* 44, 1987, 298). Sue Allen's more guarded review appears in *The Papers of the Bibliographical Society of America* 83 (1989): 240-241.

Battershall, Fletcher. *Bindings for Bibliophiles*. Greenwich, Conn.: The Literary Collector Press, 1905.
A handsomely made (though unhappily not well-bound) volume aimed at the book collector. Not intended as a history or technical manual, the book seeks to explain to the collector what to look for—and ask for—in a binding. In the course of the short chapters, Battershall offers some practical advice; for example, he recommends silk thread and leather joints. The work also provides a brief history of gold tooling. A book that can be read at a sitting with both profit and amusement.

Brassington, W. Salt. *A History of the Art of Bookbinding with Some Account of the Books of the Ancients*. New York: Macmillan, 1894.
Not seen.

Carter, John. *Publishers' Cloth: An Outline History of Publishers' Binding in England, 1820-1900*. New York: R. R. Bowker, 1935.
A small pamphlet produced in conjunction with an exhibition at the New York Public Library. Begins with a discussion of the earlier practice of issuing books unbound or in trade bindings commissioned by the seller rather than the publisher. Carter divides the period under discussion into five eras: the primitive style, roughly covering the first decade; "the struggle for recognition" (1832-1840); "the establishment of supremacy" (1841-1855); "the expansion of the fabric range" (1856-1870); and three decades of modification (1871-1900). Carter observes that by 1870 the binder had all the machinery necessary, and changes thereafter occurred because of shifts in taste or desire for economy. A good brief survey.

Chalmers, John P., ed. *A Bookbinder's Florilegium*. Austin, Tex.: Press at the Humanities Research Center, 1988.
A collection of statements by thirty-eight twentieth century bookbinders, who provided their "credos" in 500 words or less. Philip Smith,

arguably England's preeminent late twentieth century binder, talks about some of his innovations, such as the single- post sewing frame, but concludes, "If I am using the book to make some statement or object, it should function as a book." For Jamie Kamph, bookbinding is "a subtle form of literary criticism." Despite the differences in age, nationality, and temperament, the binders agree on many points: the delight in craftsmanship, the love of books, and the desire to please others while pleasing oneself. An attractive book, though plainly bound.

Comparato, Frank E. *Books for the Million: A History of the Men Whose Methods and Machines Packaged the Printed Word.* Harrisburg, Pa.: Stackpole Books, 1971.
A nicely illustrated study of nineteenth and twentieth century developments in mechanical binding, especially in the United States, though the first third of the book discusses early industrialization in France, England, and Germany. Comparato notes that well into the twentieth century Europe clung more tightly to hand-binding than did America. Includes biographies of those who contributed significantly to machine-binding, such as David Smyth (inventor of a sewing machine) and Charles Juengst (who mechanized gathering). L. W. Griffin called this "an essential title in the literature of bookbinding and publishing" (*Library Journal* 97, 1972, 1008).

Darley, Lionel S. *Bookbinding Then and Now: A Survey of the First Hundred and Seventy-Eight Years of James Burn & Co.* London: Faber & Faber, 1959.
A history of a bookbinding firm begun by Thomas Burn in London in 1781. Traces developments in the industry, such as the introduction of William Burn's rolling press to flatten and consolidate the sheets before they are sewn (1827) and the advent of steam-powered machinery. A good history of bookbinding practices from the end of the eighteenth century to the middle of the twentieth.

Diehl, Edith. *Bookbinding, Its Background and Technique.* 2 vols. New York: Rinehart, 1946.
Volume 1 traces the history of binding from the making of papyrus rolls and clay tablets to the twentieth century, though the focus is on the past 500 years. Diehl includes nearly a hundred illustrations to show the evolution of binding styles. The first plate depicts a Babylonian clay cylinder (c. 2200 B.C.); Plate 81 shows a modern pigskin binding by the German Ignatz Wiemler. Volume 2 turns to the technical aspects of

hand-binding; this book can serve as an instruction manual and will give the reader a sound understanding of the techniques and processes involved. Though Diehl presents no new information, she has assembled a veritable encyclopedia on the subject. David A. Randall called Volume 2 "the best practical manual of the craft of bookbinding that exists in English, or, to this reviewer's knowledge, in any other language" (*New York Times Book Review*, January 12, 1947, 28).

Dutton, Meirick. *Historical Sketch of Bookbinding as an Art*. Norwood, Mass.: The Holliston Mills, 1926.
The five chapters discuss bookbinding in antiquity and the Middle Ages; binding in Italy, France, and England from the Renaissance onward; and binding in America (which receives little attention here). Dutton has undertaken no original research, but the book is pleasantly written and brings together much information. Dutton claims that Jean Grolier was the first collector to make extensive use of morocco leather and gold tooling, and Dutton observes that Venetian bindings reveal Oriental influences because of the city's extensive trade with the East.

Foot, Mirjam M. *A Collection of Bookbindings*. 2 vols. London: British Library, 1978-1983.
Describes bindings from the twelfth to the twentieth century; based on the collection that Henry Davis gave the British Library in 1968. In the first volume, Foot treats a number of these bindings in some detail, avoiding the better-known works, such as those done for Jean Grolier, in favor of more abstruse though equally fascinating work. Focusing on thirty-three representative bindings from the sixteenth through the eighteenth century, Foot can illuminate Dutch practices of a particular period or a hundred years of binding activity in Cambridge, England. Volume 2, arranged by country like Volume 1, presents some 400 bindings and offers brief notes. The black-and-white illustrations sometimes fail to convey the full effect of the craftsmanship. Nonetheless, Nicolas Barker in *The Book Collector* (29, 1980, 119) praised Foot's work as "a notable monument to the history of bookbinding" and admired the study's "substance, scope [and] judgment." Paul Morgan called the work "magisterial" (*The Library* 6, 1984, 96).

_____. *Studies in the History of Bookbinding*. Aldershot, England: Scolar Press, 1993.
Brings together sixty-four essays by the doyenne of bookbinding history. The articles are grouped under seven headings. Framing the anthology are Parts 1 and 7, which emphasize the importance of

binding history in the study of the book. Part 2 examines the craft of binding in the twentieth century. In Part 3 Foot turns to the medieval tradition. Other units deal with gold-tooled bindings (Part 4), unusual materials that have been used for bindings, such as an elaborately painted wood panel from 1488 on the account books of Sienna (Part 5), and important collections of bindings (Part 6). Most of the essays gathered here are brief and concentrate on a particular binding, yet they can illuminate an entire era. For example, Essay 38, "A London Rococo Binding, 1782" notes the similarity among tools used by different German binders and so suggests that in the latter half of the eighteenth century these craftsmen borrowed tools from each other.

Goldschmidt, E. P. *Gothic and Renaissance Bookbinding, Exemplified and Illustrated from the Author's Collection.* 2 vols. London: E. Benn, 1928.
Volume 1 contains the text; Volume 2 provides 110 illustrations of bookbindings from the fifteenth and sixteenth centuries. The early fifteenth century witnessed a revival of literary activity because of the religious impulses that led to stricter adherence to Benedict's Rule and hence more work in the scriptoria of monasteries. These efforts, in turn, led to a large number of stamped bindings. Goldschmidt seeks to determine regional styles to date and locate a binder's work. In the course of his discussion, Goldschmidt ranges widely through the book world of the late Middle Ages and early Renaissance. He notes, for example, that early printing centers were not binding centers; books traveled across Europe as unbound sheets until they found a buyer, usually in a university town. Thus, whereas Erfurt was not an important center of printing in the fifteenth century, many binders worked there, and a similar pattern prevails at Wittenberg and other cities with universities. A masterful study.

Harthan, John P. *Bookbindings.* 3d ed. London: Her Majesty's Stationery Office, 1985.
A short history of binding, followed by seventy-two black-and-white plates illustrating examples from the ninth through the mid-twentieth century. The oldest item is part of a blind-tooled goatskin cover over papyrus boards. Also from this period is an ornate ivory relief dating from the Carolingian Renaissance. Harthan includes good examples of the English "cottage" style, work by Edwards of Halifax and Roger Payne, Sydney M. Cockerell, and the Guild of Women Binders. The last ten plates show how a book is bound. Provides a brief glossary of binders' terms.

Hobson, Anthony. *Humanists and Bookbinders: The Origins and Diffusion of the Humanistic Bookbinding, 1459-1559*. Cambridge, England: Cambridge University Press, 1989.

A study of northern Italian and Parisian bindings from the mid-fifteenth to the mid-sixteenth century. Hobson relates these to the larger "cultural history of the period." He looks first at the beginning of this new binding style, with its peculiar motifs and gold tooling. He sees Padua as the origin of this *dolce stil nuovo*, drawing on Eastern as well as classical influences. The style became popular because it was at once beautiful and less expensive than gold cloth, velvet, or satin, and it was not associated with the medieval world that the humanists rejected. Hobson regards Felice Feliciano as the inaugurator of the humanist binding style. The book examines this style as it spreads from Italy to France, where it enjoyed the patronage of Francis I and Henry II. According to Hobson, Gommer Estienne, not related to the great printers, executed Henry II's bindings; Hobson thus rejects the claims of Claude Picard, once regarded as the royal binder responsible for most of the humanist bindings at Fontainebleau. The volume concludes with a census of 145 bindings incorporating plaquettes or medallions. In the seven appendices, Hobson addresses such matters as the use of pasteboard and the binders who worked for Jean Grolier, among whom Gommer Estienne again looms large. Nicolas Barker called this "a major contribution, not just to the history of bookbinding but to the history of an intellectual movement" (*The Library* 13, 1991, 161). The nearly 200 black-and-white reproductions are clear; the few color plates are less satisfactory.

Hobson, Geoffrey Dudley. *Studies in the History of Bookbinding*. London: Pindar Press, 1988.

Brings together fifteen of Hobson's articles treating bindings from the early Middle Ages to the seventeenth century. Hobson's versatility is evidenced in the languages represented—two of the pieces are in French, a third in German. Among the articles is "Further Notes on Romanesque Bindings," which is an extensive study and census of these products of the twelfth and thirteenth centuries. Two other articles treat the library of Jean Grolier, correcting many long-held views. For example, though Grolier's bindings assign ownership to friends as well as Grolier himself, Grolier did not own many duplicate copies for lending. Hobson also traces the origin and diffusion of Grolier's famous phrase "et amicorum." The volume includes numerous reproductions of the bindings discussed. A handsome and informative book.

Horne, Herbert Percy. *The Binding of Books: An Essay in the History of Gold-Tooled Bindings.* 2d ed. London: Kegan Paul, Trench, Trubner, 1915.

Alfred W. Pollard updated this work from the 1894 edition. The first chapter discusses binding techniques. Horne then looks at gold-tooling in Italy, France, and England, concentrating on the sixteenth and seventeenth centuries. Concludes with a plea for fine printing and fine binding. *The Nation* wrote that Horne's "knowledge is wide, and his understanding of the principles of the art thorough; and it is a pleasure to follow his clear account of the developments of gold-tooling in Italy and its transference to France" (59, 1894, 92). *The Dial* called the first edition "the most comprehensive and valuable essay on the decorative features of bookbinding that has appeared in English" (18, 1895, 217). Horne was a partisan of French binding, though he also admired early Italian examples. The book includes a dozen illustrations.

Kuhn, Hilda. *Wörterbuch der Handbuchbinderei und Einbandrestaurierung.* Stuttgart: Max Hettler, 1969.

A handy reference that provides the German, English, French, and Italian for 1,033 words and phrases used in "bookbinding and restauration [sic] of papyri, manuscripts, engravings, autographs, documents, bindings and globes." Arrangement of the body of the dictionary is alphabetical by German term, but Kuhn provides an alphabetical index for the three other languages. The words sometimes provide insights into the history of books and binding. For example, the German word for parchment is Pergament, a cognate that more closely suggests the first supposed site to substitute animal skin for papyrus. Similarly, "Prussian blue" in German is "Pariserbleau"; the French indifferently refer to the color as "bleu de Paris" or "bleu de Prusse."

Lewis, Roy Harley. *Fine Bookbinding in the Twentieth Century.* New York: Arco, 1985.

Lewis wrote in his introduction, "My intention is to illustrate some of the best work of the century, ranging from conventional to avant-garde. . . . This book pays tribute to some of the outstanding firms and individuals, illustrating highlights of the work that has emerged, as well as indicating trends and developments." Concentrates on postwar efforts in Britain, especially work by Philip Smith. Some of the examples discussed and illustrated are beautifully restrained, such as Douglas Cockerell's design, executed by his son, for an Apuleius *Cupid and Psyche* and Donald Glaister's gold-tooled outline of a whale for the covers of *Moby Dick*. Dee Odell-Foster's three-dimensional binding for *The Visual Dictionary of Sex*, with latex breasts and a bronze hand, and Peter Weiersmuller's design for *Fear of Flying*, with its flapping wooden wings, reveal other facets of modern style.

Miner, Dorothy. *The History of Bookbinding, 525-1950 A.D. An Exhibition Held at the Baltimore Museum of Art November 12, 1957 to January 12, 1958.* Baltimore: Walters Art Gallery, 1957.

This elaborate exhibition catalog, a landmark in the study of bookbinding, describes 718 items and includes 106 pages of plates. The earliest example is an ivory diptych from Constantinople used to cover a writing tablet. Includes examples of royal bindings as well as work done for commoners. Arranged chronologically, the volume demonstrates the changes in style over the centuries, and reveals much about the attitudes of the owners. For example, between the thirteenth and sixteenth centuries the city treasurers of Sienna bound their account books each year or half-year, regularly commissioning an artist to paint the wooden boards. These books thus record three centuries of Siennese painting and also show how highly the city regarded these reports.

Needham, Paul. *Twelve Centuries of Bookbindings, 400-1600.* New York: Pierpont Morgan Library, 1979.

Looks at one hundred bindings from the Pierpont Morgan collection. Most of the book consists of detailed discussions of specific bindings, but also included are essays on the earliest extant examples, medieval treasure bindings, and early leather bindings in Europe. All the bindings are illustrated, most in black-and-white but seven in full color. The book serves as an encyclopedia for the period covered. Paul Morgan's review for *The American Book Collector* 1 (May/June, 1980): 47-50 praises Needham's "high scholarly standard; the lucidity of the explanations; the clarity of the illustrations; the absence of misprints and errors . . . ; the evidence of research . . . ; and the ability to summarize and acknowledge the work of others." Giles Barber called the book "an excellent introduction to the history of Western bookbinding" (*Times Literary Supplement*, January 30, 1981, 123).

Nicholson, James Bartram. *A Manual of the Art of Bookbinding.* Philadelphia: H. C. Baird, 1856.

The first practical guide to bookbinding to appear in America. Nicholson, an important Philadelphia binder, drew from a number of earlier texts—indeed, plagiarized from them. After a history of bookbinding, Nicholson discusses sheet work, forwarding, half- binding, blank binding, boarding, clothwork, and finishing. Though intended as a practical guide for would-be binders, the volume is of more interest to the historian seeking to understand how craft binding was conducted in the mid-nineteenth century. Provides seven examples of marbled paper and illustrations of tools and techniques.

Nixon, Howard M. *The Development of Certain Styles of Binding.* London: Private Libraries Association, 1963.
An account of the development of the "center and corner piece" and "interlacing ribbon" styles of binding, supplemented with thirty-two illustrations. Both patterns began in the East. The former came to Europe through Venice, but by the late sixteenth century it had acquired the name it retains, the Lyonese style. Variations include the Cambridge and Harleian styles. The interlacing ribbons pattern characterizes Grolier bindings as well as cottage and fanfare bindings. Nixon ranges widely, touching on a number of important binders.

_____. *Sixteenth-Century Gold-Tooled Bookbindings in the Pierpont Morgan Library.* New York: Pierpont Morgan Library, 1971.
This catalog to a 1971 exhibition offers a study of sixty-six fine bindings. Nixon discusses them in detail and relates them to other, similar work. Includes biographies of the binders and those who commissioned their efforts. The bindings are clearly reproduced. Taken together, the discussions constitute a history of the subject. For example, in his treatment of a Spanish binding he notes that gold-tooling reached the rest of Europe through both Spain and Italy, though the earliest extant example comes from the latter country. The *Times Literary Supplement* refers to Nixon's work as "a survey of modern knowledge of Renaissance bookbinding. . . . This is scholarship at its best: learned, reasonable, humane" (July 2, 1971, 188).

_____. *Styles and Designs of Bookbindings from the Twelfth to the Twentieth Century.* London: For the Broxbourne Library, 1956.
Illustrates 119 bindings, most of them in full page reproductions. Though they are superb examples, they typify their place and time and so together provide a history of the subject. The oldest item, which dates from about 1150, is a fine example of blind-tooled Romanesque sheepskin binding. The collection includes a fourteenth century miniature girdle book, a sixteenth century Italian woodcut binding, a stunning Edward of Halifax transparent vellum over white pasteboard (c. 1783), and a vellum binding by Sydney M. Cockerell (1951). Nixon's comments illuminate the specific item illustrated and relate it to similar bindings.

Nixon, Howard M., and Mirjam M. Foot. *The History of Decorated Bookbinding in England.* Oxford, England: Clarendon Press, 1992.

This revision of Nixon's 1979 Lyell Lectures on English bookbinding examines "grand bindings made by top craftsmen, rather than the run-of-the-mill products of the trade." The account begins with what may be the earliest extant example of a decorated European binding, the St. Cuthbert Gospel, with covers that may date from 698, and the book concludes with the work of Edgar Mansfield, whom the authors call "the father of the modern movement in English binding design." The text includes twelve color plates and 128 in black and white. The focus of the book is on design and craftsmen rather than technique or commerce.

Pollard, Graham. "Changes in the Style of Bookbinding, 1550-1830." *The Library*, 5th ser., 11 (1956): 71-94.

Pollard discusses the various leathers used for binding and the treatment of these materials. He notes, for example, that gold-tooling on the backs of books began in Italy about 1535; lettering the spine in the second panel did not become regular practice in England until the Restoration period. Labels attached to the spine quickly became the fashion after their introduction around 1680; by 1700 lettering directly on the spine had become the exception. Contrasting title and volume number labels appear about 1730. In the early 1600s, the French were fond of flat-backed books, and the English retained this practice until about 1710. Hollow-backed books are rare in England before 1800. Placing the date at the foot of the spine was introduced in England as early as 1620 but was again unfashionable until the start of the nineteenth century. A fascinating, informative survey.

Prideaux, Sarah Treverbian. *Bookbinders and Their Craft.* New York: Charles Scribner's Sons, 1903.

A collection of eight articles that treat Roger Payne, modern French and early Italian binders, early stamped bindings, English and Scottish bindings, a review of Ernest Thoinan's *Les Relieurs Français* (1893), and notes on patternmaking and design. *The Dial* wrote of this book, "All in all the information contained is neither massive nor overwhelming, but the book has a distinct . . . quality, being written with that interest which comes when long years of acquaintance with a subject has developed a recognition of essentials. . . . It is very pleasant to find a specialist who can write about her subject with a modified rapture that maintains true values" (36, 1904, 91).

_____. *An Historical Sketch of Bookbinding.* London: Lawrence
& Bullen, 1893.
Includes a 45-page bibliography and a chapter on early stamped
bindings by E. Gordon Duff. In her survey, Prideaux includes essays
on embroidered book covers, the use of metal in bound books, and
decorated book edges. Lacks illustrations. *The Nation* for August 10,
1893 (57: 105) called this "probably the best English summary of the
history of the art," and it remains a good historical introduction.

Regemorter, Berthe van. "The Bound Codex from Its Origin to the Early
Middle Ages." Translated by Mary E. Greenfield. *Guild of Book
Workers Journal* 17 (1978-1979): 1-25.
Originally published in French in 1955, this essay examines how
gatherings were sewn together and attached to boards. Regemorter
argues that the earliest form of boards had cavities for wax because
they were modeled on diptychs used for correspondence. Leather was
introduced slowly, first to cover only the spine, then as half-binding,
finally as full leather binding cover the entire board. Regemorter
illustrates various forms of sewing. She notes that over time the cavities
in the boards vanished, and she shows various forms of decorating
boards. A technical but informative study of early binding practices.

Roberts, Matt T., and Don Etherington. *Bookbinding and the Conservation of Books: A Dictionary of Descriptive Terminology.* Washington,
D.C.: Library of Congress, 1982.
In the foreword, Frederick R. Goff praised the volume for its "succinct
definitions, as well as the biographical vignettes." Though the book is
not intended as a history of bookbinding, the approximately 4,000
definitions often include historical information. Provides clear definitions of such terms as "extra binding," "accordion fold," "Russia calf,"
and "Russian leather." With informative drawings and some color
illustrations of attractive bindings.

Sadlier, Michael. *The Evolution of Publishers' Binding Styles, 1770-1900.*
London: Constable, 1930.
Beginning with paper wrappers in the eighteenth century, publishers'
bindings evolved to stiff covers with a labelled spine. Then, in the
1820s, publishers began using cloth bindings. Sadlier examines these
changes and also the decoration of cloth bindings. Includes twelve
plates depicting bindings from the period treated. *The Bookman* (78,
1930, 178) called this "an extensive survey that will interest all who
are interested in books, and will be of special value to collectors in

helping them to recognize from the style of a book's binding the approximate date of its publication."

Shalleck, Jamie Kleinberg. "Identifying and Classifying Fine Bindings." In *A Miscellany for Bibliophiles*. Edited by H. George Fletcher. New York: Grastorf & Lang, 1979, 127-157.
Shalleck examines a number of issues that the historian must consider in the effort to date a binding or to attribute it to a particular workshop. tooling can be helpful but hardly definitive. Other considerations include title treatment (title labels did not appear until the late seventeenth century), shape of the spine, endbands, and sewing. Shalleck discusses various volumes in the Princeton University library to demonstrate her points, and she includes numerous illustrations to show how bindings changed over time.

Smith, Philip. *The Book: Art and Object*. Merstham, England: Philip Smith, 1982.
A collection of articles that Smith, a leading British binder, wrote for various occasions and publications. Smith favors innovation rather than imitation of past models, but he warns against bindings that ignore the books, that seek to be art objects without function. Much of the text is devoted to Smith's thoughts on design, and he discusses his own work to illustrate his principles. Includes a large sampling of Smith's bindings.

_____. *New Directions in Bookbinding*. New York: Van Nostrand Reinhold, 1974.
Smith, a binder with an international reputation, here offers his thoughts on the nature of the craft. The book illustrates various techniques and explains how Smith created some of his noted works, such as his famous binding for *King Lear* (1967-1968). The primary function of this work is, however, to explore and encourage innovation. Includes illustrations of Smith's work, though many of the bindings shown are by his contemporaries. Dorothy A. Harrop wrote, "This book is a masterpiece of organization, mentally stimulating and visually exciting, and as a piece of special pleading it deserves a place on the shelves of all who are interested in the craft" (*The Book Collector* 25, 1976, 277).

Uzanne, Octave. *L'Art dans la décoration extérieure des livres, en France et à l'étranger: Les Couvertures illustrées, les cartonnages d'éditeurs, la reliure d'art*. Paris: Société Française d'Éditions d'Art, L. Henry May, 1898.

A lavishly illustrated book concerned with the aesthetics and history of bookbinding. Uzanne writes, "The book, like women, is made to please and to be decorated . . . ; it is created to seduce the eye before it charms the spirit." After a brief introduction on the philosophy of book decoration, Uzanne turns to late nineteenth century illustrated covers, mass-produced bindings, and craft binding of the period. Though Uzanne offers retrospective glances towards earlier centuries. his primary concern is with the tendencies of his own day.

Wakeman, Geoffrey. *Nineteenth Century Trade Bindings.* 2 vols. Oxford, England: Plough Press, 1983.
Begins by noting the shift in the nineteenth century from leather to cloth as a binding material. Companies emerged that specialized in these cloths; in 1865 there were seven firms in this field, and twenty years later there were twelve. Wakeman discusses the machinery used to mass-produce bindings, lists cost, and examines the working conditions of those engaged in the trade. In 1843, women employed by Westley, the largest commercial binder in Britain, worked from 8:00 AM to 8: 30 or 9:00 PM, with an hour for dinner (i.e., lunch) and half an hour for tea. Men worked fourteen hours, with two hours off for meals. A woman would earn twelve shillings a week. By 1866, hours had been reduced from fourteen to twelve for men, to eleven for women. Volume 2 contains examples of materials and types used.

Zaehnsdorf, Joseph William. *A Short History of Bookbinding.* London: Chiswick Press, 1895.
Not seen.

American Bindings

French, Hannah D. *Bookbinding in Early America: Seven Essays on Masters and Methods.* Worcester, Mass.: American Antiquarian Society, 1986.
Five of the essays explore the work of Andrew Barclay, Henry B. Legg, Caleb Buglass, John Roulstone, and Frederick Augustus Mayo. The opening piece discusses Scottish-style bindings in America, and another treats gilding. Enhances knowledge of American bindings in the colonial and early national period. Includes many useful illustrations. Frank Broomhead commented, "All who are interested in the study of American bookbinding and the biography of its practitioners, are likely to welcome this collection of articles" (*The Private Library* 9, 1986, 187). *The Virginia Quarterly Review* was equally enthusiastic: "Han-

nah French's seven essays on early American bookbinders are illuminating and enjoyable; her extensive research brings these masters to life while her clear, incisive and elegant prose makes the lengthy descriptions of their work a joy to read" (62, 1986, 138).

French, Hannah D., and William Spawn. *Early American Bookbindings from the Collection of Michael Papantonio.* 2d ed., enl. Worcester, Mass.: American Antiquarian Society, 1985.

In 1948 Michael Papantonio, co-founder of the legendary Seven Gables Bookshop in New York City (1946-1979), acquired a handsomely bound copy of the *New York Mirror and Ladies Literary Gazette*; the purchase stimulated his interest in American bindings. Over the next thirty years he collected nearly a thousand examples, almost all of which he gave to the American Antiquarian Society. The catalog provides sixty-one full-page illustrations, beginning with a John Ratcliffe binding from 1669 and concluding with a sample of the work of Pawson and Nicholson (Philadelphia, 1864). The catalog concludes with a checklist, by city, of the books in the Papantonio bequest. This listing shows the shift in binding centers (as in publishing centers), first from Boston to Philadelphia in the eighteenth century, then to New York in the nineteenth. Frank Broomhead called this "a useful reference volume" (*The Private Library* 9, 1986, 185).

Lehmann-Haupt, Hellmut, ed. *Bookbinding in America: Three Essays.* Rev. ed. New York: R. R. Bowker, 1967.

Begins with Hannah Dustin French's "Early American Bookbinding by Hand," which explores the age of craft binding between 1636 and 1820. An appendix to this sections lists, by city, American binders active during this period. Joseph W. Rogers' "The Rise of American Edition Binding" treats the shift from craft binding to industrial processes, showing how America emerged as a leader in binding technology. Rogers also looks at various binding cloths. In the concluding essay, "On the Rebinding of Old Books," Lehmann-Haupt discusses the "ethics and aesthetics of rebinding." He surveys earlier bookbinding practices and urges that a book not be rebound unless it must be, since old bindings provide important historical information about bookmaking, and any restoration should do as little damage as possible to the original. The style of a new binding should mirror the age of the book. This revised edition updates the bibliography of the first (1941) version.

Samford, C. Clement, and John M. Hemphill II. *Bookbinding in Colonial Virginia.* Williamsburg, Va.: Colonial Williamsburg, 1966.

Although court records show that a bookbinder, John Hill, was living in Virginia in 1647, the first binder discussed is the eighteenth century printer William Parks. Whereas in the northern colonies by the eighteenth century binding and printing had become separate occupations, in the south the two remained linked. Most of the bindings were utilitarian, but the authors show that craftsmen like John Stretch and Thomas Brend could embellish their work with gold tooling. Despite the title, the work focuses on Williamsburg and extends beyond the colonial period to the death of Brend in 1799. Contains some discussion of eighteenth century binding in Richmond and Annapolis. An important study for anyone concerned with early American bindings.

Tanis, James, and John Dooley. *Bookbinding in America, 1680-1910, from the Collection of Frederick E. Maser*. Charlottesville: University Press of Virginia, 1983.

The sixty-two examples in the catalog complement those in the Papantonio catalog prepared by Hannah D. French and William Spawn (discussed earlier). To the extent possible, each entry includes place of binding, name of binder, date, materials used, decoration, provenance, and references. Includes an essay on eighteenth century American binding. The essay notes the growing uniformity in style. Early eighteenth century New York bindings had more in common with seventeenth century British work than with bindings executed at the same time in Boston or Philadelphia, but by the 1740s these distinctions are becoming blurred. In the 1760s, emphasis shifted from decorated boards and plain spines to decorated spines and plain boards, as books began to be shelved with spines showing and as more British binders came to America. Frank Broomhead called the catalog "an outstanding addition to the literature of American bookbinding" (*The Private Library* 9, 1986, 184).

Wolf, Edwin, II. *From Gothic Windows to Peacocks: American Embossed Leather Bindings, 1825-1855*. Philadelphia: Library Company of Philadelphia, 1990.

An excursion into a fascinating byway of American bookbinding. During the second quarter of the nineteenth century, ornate leather bindings were popular for gift books. Woolf discusses the techniques and artistic influences and lists all books with embossed leather bindings of this period. Includes 226 illustrations, 66 of them photographs and the remainder rubbings that Woolf made. David McKitterick praised the work in *The Book Collector* 41 (1992): 409, commenting, "This is a book of which the Library Company can be proud, beautifully presented by [the printers] Meriden-Stinehour and one that will take its place confidently on that short but growing shelf of reliable books on nineteenth-century trade binding."

Arabic Bindings

Gratz, Emil. *Islamische Bucheinbande, des 14 bis 19 Jahrhunderts, aus den Handschriften der Bayerischen Staatsbibliotek ausgewahlt und beschrieben.* Leipzig: Karl W. Hiersemann, 1924.

Essentially an annotated catalog of Islamic bindings beautifully reproduced in the book's twenty-four plates, many of them in color. Among the most striking is Plate 15, showing a lavishly gold-tooled binding from sixteenth century Persia. Plate 7 shows an ornately gold-tooled cover from Syria or Egypt from the Mamluk period. The floral binding shown in Plate 23 comes from nineteenth century Persia. The volume testifies to the high level of skill evidenced in Arabic bookbindings, which deeply influenced western techniques and designs.

Haldane, Duncan. *Islamic Bookbindings.* London: Scorpion Communications and Publications, and the World of Islam Festival Trust, 1983.

A fine survey of the subject from 1400 to 1900, based on the holdings of the Victoria and Albert Museum. Arranged by region of origin: Arab, Persian, Turkish, and Indian; Persian bindings occupy the largest section. Most of these bindings are leather, tooled or painted, but some are made of papier-mâché or wood. Includes 175 plates and forty-five figures, many of these in color. Also provides an extensive bibliography. Henry O. Thompson described the volume as "a beautiful book of art that will grace anyone's coffee table, while the text is a solid scholarly work" (*Middle East Journal* 39, 1985, 190).

Sarre, F. *Islamic Bookbinding.* Translated by F. D. O'Byrne. London: K. Paul, Trench, Trubner, 1923.

British Bindings

Davenport, Cyril. *English Embroidered Bookbindings.* London: Kegan Paul, Trench, Trubner, 1899.

Embroidered bindings appear in England early; Davenport discusses and shows a thirteenth century English psalter bound in canvas, perhaps by Anne de Felbrigge, a late fourteenth century nun in Suffolk.

In the Renaissance, Tudor princesses created embroidered bindings using gold and silver thread; Queen Elizabeth and Mary Stuart were both accomplished needlewomen. The vogue of embroidered bindings persisted into the seventeenth century; more than half of the fifty-two examples illustrated here were produced after 1600. Davenport notes that embroidered bindings are uniquely English. He divides the designs into four classes: Heraldic, Figure, Floral, and Arabesque. The heraldic designs tend to be earlier, but materials, too, indicate date. Velvet was popular during the Tudor age, satin in the early seventeenth century. Includes suggestions for those interested in making modern embroidered bindings in the old style.

_____. *Royal English Bookbindings*. London: Seeley, 1896.

Hobson, Geoffrey Dudley. *Blind Stamped Panels in the English Book Trade, c. 1485-1555*. London: Bibliographical Society, 1944.
A detailed investigation of the subject, discussing the bindings and their makers. Concludes that blind stamping was introduced into England by foreigners, and after about 1557, with the death or retirement of Martin Dature, probably a Dutchman, a new style emerged. Gold rather than blind stamping now became popular, and the designs, smaller than those of the earlier period, reflected Islamic influence.

_____. *English Bindings Before 1500*. Cambridge, England: Cambridge University Press, 1929.
The text of a series of lectures Hobson gave at Cambridge in 1927, together with fifty-five plates. The earliest binding covers a copy of St. John's Gospel of the seventh century. The decoration here is carved rather than tooled; not until the twelfth century are bindings decorated with special tools. In the fourteenth century, English tooling apparently was in abeyance—Hobson could find no examples—but the practice resurfaced in the 1400s. An Oxford example of the fifteenth century shows the return to twelfth century style. Strickland Gibson commented, "Mr. Hobson's lectures have entailed much research on the history and culture of the twelfth century, and a minute investigation into the designs used by the early die engravers. In their published form they definitely place him as the chief authority on English bindings" (*London Mercury* 20, 1929, 309).

McLean, Ruari. *Victorian Publishers' Book-Bindings in Cloth and Leather*. London: Gordon Fraser, 1974.
With 200 plates, many of them in color, this is an important work on

the subject, especially for the 1860s. McLean writes in the introduction, "This is a picture book showing the richness of publishers' bindings principally in cloth and leather, produced in Britain during the nineteenth century." The text is limited. The earliest binding illustrated dates from 1826 (*The Poetical Rhapsody*). McLean discusses technical aspects, designs, and contemporary reactions to the innovation of publishers' bindings—before about 1820 books were issued in boards to be rebound by the purchaser. McLean notes that in the nineteenth century a new class of book-buyers emerged. These people could not afford custom binding but wanted their volumes held together in some permanent way. Throughout the century, the bindings exhibit elaborate decoration, often incorporating many colors. The bindings thus exemplify the same Victorian love of ornament that one finds in architecture and furniture of the age. Complementing this work is McLean's *Victorian Publishers' Book-Bindings in Paper* (London: Gordon Fraser, 1983).

Middleton, Bernard C. *A History of English Craft Bookbinding Techniques.* 3d supplemented ed. London: Holland Press, 1988.
Middleton trained in the British Museum Bindery before establishing his own bindery, and so brings much technical expertise to his book. Chapters are arranged by topic, such as sewing, end papers, gluing the spine, and finishing. Middleton discusses developments in each area. Thus, for sewing he traces the movement from passing thread through holes near the back folds (stabbing) to tape-slotting, tacketing, raised-thong sewing, oversewing, and the use of adhesive, first rubber and later polyvinyl acetate. He illustrates and explains each process. Includes six appendices covering the London book trade around 1800, working conditions and hours for binders, the growth of fine and wholesale binderies, the development of specialization in book-edge gilding, the effect of the Arts and Crafts movement on binding, and a warning against the use of sulfuric acid in preparing leather for binding. Mirjam M. Foot wrote of an earlier edition that Middleton offered "an inspiring book . . . which no one who is interested in bookbinding as a craft should miss" (*The Book Collector* 27, 1978, 582).

Nixon, Howard M. *Five Centuries of English Bookbinding.* London: Scolar Press, 1978.
A chronological arrangement of one hundred short pieces that Nixon wrote for *The Book Collector* between 1952 and 1977. The earliest binding here dates from 1483 and is the work of the binder whom William Caxton brought with him from Bruges. The most modern is a

Cosway binding from around 1928, designed by J. H. Stonehouse and executed by Riviere and Son. The names of many early craftsmen have been lost, and so they have been designated as the "squirrel binder" or "flamboyant binder for Henry VIII." Each binding is reproduced in black and white on the recto of a page; facing the illustration are Nixon's informative comments. Taken together, these pieces constitute a history of English binding since the end of the fifteenth century. *The Book Collector* observed, "No bibliopegic scholar, no reader of this journal, and no one who expects to handle an English bookbinding can afford to be without" Nixon's book (27, 1978, 388). Giles Barber called the work "a most useful contribution to scholarship" (*English Historical Review* 95, 1980, 645).

Nixon, Howard M., and Mirjam M. Foot. *The History of Decorated Bookbinding in England.* Oxford, England: Clarendon Press, 1992.
Based on Nixon's 1979 Lyell Lectures, which he was unable to revise before his death in 1983. The historical survey concentrates on what Mirjam M. Foot, who prepared the manuscript for publication, calls "the bindings . . . at the top end of the market: presentation copies, collectors' items, grand bindings made by top craftsmen." Nixon notes that England can claim the first known decorated European binding, likely dating from 698. Gold-tooling came late to the country; the earliest known example was made about 1519. By the 1650s, England was imitating the French style that employed tooling with dotted outlines. During the late seventeenth century, Samuel Mearne's workshop produced excellent bindings, and in the next century Edward of Halifax extended the practice of fore-edge painting. He also introduced Etruscan bindings and vellum bindings with scenes painted on the underside. The advent of publishers' bindings in the 1820s did not challenge fine binding; indeed, publishers themselves sometimes produced elaborate covers. Nixon's account ends with Edgar Mansfield, whom he calls "the father of the modern movement in English binding design." The book contains twelve color plates and 128 black-and-white illustrations of bindings.

Oldham, James Basil. *English Blind-Stamped Bindings.* Cambridge, England: Cambridge University Press, 1952.
E. P. Goldschmidt, writing in the *Spectator* (184, August 8, 1952, 196) called this "a splendidly produced volume with sixty-one plates which will indubitably stand as the authoritative reference book for anybody curious to discover whether any particular bookbinding belongs to a group of which specimens have been recorded and of whose origin,

period and localisation something more or less definite is known." The book presents the text of the Sanders Lectures for 1949. Continues G. D. Hobson's study of English bindings (cited herein), looking at tooled bindings from the fifteenth to the seventeenth century. *The Times Literary Supplement* for September 19, 1952, called Oldham's study "the most important . . . yet published on the earlier English bookbindings, and is the foundation on which any further research should be based" (p. 620). Reproduces over 1,000 rubbings, identifies some sixty binderies, and classifies over 400 rolls used for tooling.

French Bindings

Devauchelle, Roger. *La Reliure en France de ses origines à nos jours.* 3 vols. Paris: J. Rousseau-Girard, 1959-1961.
Volume 1 extends from the Middle Ages to the end of the seventeenth century, Volume 2 covers the period 1700-1850, and the final volume treats bindings from 1850 onward. Containing 250 illustrations of bindings, this is a comprehensive examination of the topic. Also includes an illustrated guide to binding a book.

Devaux, Yves. *Dix siècles de reliure.* Paris: Éditions Pygmalion, 1977.
A lavishly illustrated volume treating binding in France from the Middle Ages to the twentieth century, with most of the book devoted to the period after 1470, when printing came to France and when French binding established itself as pre-eminent in Europe. Brief sections at the end of the work discuss techniques of binding and decoration and present a biographical dictionary of binders, authors, and collectors not treated in the main text. Informative, entertaining, and visually pleasing.

Duncan, Alistair, and Georges De Bartha. *Art Nouveau and Art Deco Bookbinding: The French Masterpieces 1880-1940.* London: Thames and Hudson, 1989.
Primarily a study of forty-eight binders active between 1880 and 1940. The introduction offers a survey of the period. Art nouveau binding came into vogue coincidentally with the death of the great Second Empire binder George Trautz. Henri Marius Michel championed the effort to integrate a book's binding and content; therefore, he used laurel motifs for poetry, the rose for romances. Until World War I, binders used traditional materials; thereafter Pierre Legrain and others introduced more exotic bindings that used such items as nickel and shark-

The History of the Book

skin. Legrain viewed the cover as a whole and used lettering as part of his designs. By the eve of World War II, French binding was the most creative in the world, and its new approach was widely recognized and praised. The book includes 252 illustrations, 202 of them in color.

Fletcher, W. Y. *Bookbinding in France*. London: Seeley, 1894.

Fournier, Edouard. *L'Art de la reliure en France aux derniers siècles*. 2d ed. Paris: E. Dentu, 1888.

Michon, Louis-Marie. *La Reliure française*. Paris: Larousse, 1951.
A survey of bindings from the Middle Ages to the mid twentieth century. Michon begins with a short discussion of gold covers enriched with ivory or enamels; he suggests that an ivory relief now covering a twelfth century manuscript in the Bibliothèque de l'Arsenal dates from the third century; another example from the fifth century covers a Gospel of the ninth. Blind-tooled leather also was used in the Middle Ages, probably beginning in the eighth century. Most of the book is devoted to leather bindings from the fifteenth century onward and treats various binders and changing styles. Commercial binding, though mentioned, receives little attention. With sixty-four black-and-white illustrations.

Uzanne, Octave. *The French Bookbinders of the Eighteenth Century*. Translated by Mabel McIlvaine. Chicago: Caxton Club, 1904.
In the first chapter, Uzanne quickly surveys the history of binding through the Middle Ages and Renaissance. The second chapter treats legal matters affecting binders of the eighteenth century. Uzanne notes the popularity of mosaic designs and gold-tooling, but he prefers the tooling that imitates the ironwork of the period. Chapter 3 discusses various binders such as the Padeloup and Derome families. Technical aspects and prices are the subject of Chapter 4, and Chapter 5 examines the use of materials other than leather for covers, especially for almanacs and other small books. The volume includes twenty plates illustrating bindings of the period. An important study that fostered new interest in the subject.

Italian Bindings

Nardelli, Franca Petrucci. *La legatura italiana: Storia, descrizione, techniche*. Rome: La Nuova Italia Scientifica, 1989.

Covers Italian bookbinding from the fifteenth through the nineteenth century and explains how to describe a binding. Illustrates twenty examples, which are discussed in detail. Though intended as an introductory guide, it is useful for anyone seeking information on Italian bindings of the period or anyone wanting a model of how to write about bindings. *The Book Collector* calls this "a modest but extremely useful manual" (39, 1990, 318).

Quilici, Piccarda. *Legature dal quattrocento al novecento.* Brindisi, Italy: Amici della 'A. de Leo,' 1988.

An illustrated catalog of 109 bindings housed in the Brindisi Cathedral Library. Two chapters deal with early manuscripts, the rest with printed books from 1512 to 1900.

PART III
HISTORY

Chapter 9
GENERAL WORKS

Avrin, Leila. *Scribes, Script, and Books: The Book Arts from Antiquity to the Renaissance.* Chicago: American Library Association, 1991.
Traces the history of the book in the Orient and the West until the advent of printing. A well-illustrated volume on the hand-produced book. Intended for the general reader; offers no original research and contains some minor errors but still presents a sound synthesis of scholarship. Fred W. Jenkins wrote in *College and Research Libraries* 53 (1992): 89, "Avrin's work is a remarkably readable synthesis of the vast scholarly literature on the development of the book . . . before Gutenberg. It will provide a real service to the non-specialist reader and student and will undoubtedly be widely used as a basic text in book history courses."

Balsamo, Luigi. *Bibliography: History of a Tradition.* Translated by William A. Pettas. Berkeley, Calif.: Bernard M. Rosenthal, 1990.
"The chief purpose of this book is to explain in greater depth than has previously been done the circumstances and the objectives which fostered the evolution of the various tools of cultural information . . . known as bibliographies" (Author's Preface). Like Theodore Besterman's *The Beginnings of Systematic Bibliography* (cited in this chapter), this study begins with Galen but extends to the twentieth century. Balsamo examines the motivations of bibliographers, who sought to promote the knowledge of books for a variety of purposes, often political or religious. Balsamo also traces changes in the form and content of bibliographies as compilers tried to make their works more accessible. Balsamo gives much credit to booksellers as innovators in the field of enumerative bibliography.

Barker, Nicolas, ed. *A Potencie of Life: Books in Society, the Clark Lectures, 1986-1987.* London: British Library, 1993.
The volume begins with Barker's essay, co-authored with Thomas R. Adams, on the nature of the discipline of the history of the book, and it concludes with a short piece praising libraries such as the William Andrews Clark (Los Angeles), where these lectures were presented. In between are pieces by R. H. and Mary Rouse on book production in late medieval Paris and Lotte Hellinga's discussion of the effects of

printing on books and readers in the fifteenth century. Other contributors include Mirjam Foot, who writes on "Bookbinding and the History of Books," and W. B. Carnochan on authorship in eighteenth century Britain. John Bidwell treats the effects of the 1819 Panic on American papermakers, and Thomas B. Adams looks at the London publishing firm of Mount and Page, which specialized in maritime books in the eighteenth century.

Besterman, Theodore. *The Beginnings of Systematic Bibliography*. London: Oxford University Press, 1935.
A study of the origins of systematic bibliography as far back as Galen's second century A.D. *De libris propriis liber*, but emphasizing the fifteenth and sixteenth century contributions to the field. Besterman discusses some fifty bibliographies that appeared during the first 150 years of printing, beginning with the work of Johannes Tritheim (1462-1516), whom Besterman regards as the father of bibliography. By 1600, bibliographies had largely assumed the form and content that they would maintain thereafter.

Binns, Norman E. *An Introduction to Historical Bibliography*. 2d ed., rev. and enl. London: Association of Assistant Librarians, 1962.
Although the opening chapter deals with handwriting and manuscripts, Binns concentrates on the printed book, tracing the advance of printing from its invention in Germany to its introduction into the British colonies of North America. After this chronological survey Binns turns to specific subjects: type, the title page, illustration, binding, publishing, bookselling, book collecting, and copyright. Includes a bibliography after each chapter. A good history of the printed book.

Blumenthal, Joseph. *Art of the Printed Book, 1455-1955: Masterpieces of Typography Through Five Centuries from the Collections of the Pierpont Morgan Library*. New York: Pierpont Morgan Library, 1973.
A catalog based on an exhibit that Blumenthal organized to "illustrate the highest achievements in printing in the western world." Blumenthal provided a fifty-page essay on "the great printers and their books" to accompany the 125 black-and-white illustrations drawn from 112 examples of outstanding typography. In effect an illustrated history of the printed book.

Bornstein, George, and Ralph G. Williams, eds. *Palimpsest: Editorial Theory in the Humanities*. Ann Arbor: University of Michigan Press, 1993.

A collection of fourteen essays divided into three sections. The four articles in Part 1 address issues of editorial theory. Five contributions in the second part consider editorial problems of literary works, and in the last unit the authors explore problems of editing the Bible, Benjamin Franklin's correspondence, operatic texts, and the papers of Martin Luther King, Jr., as well as the restoration of the Sistine Chapel ceiling. Despite their diverse concerns, all the contributors observe that the notion of a stable text has yielded to a recognition of the text's fragility and the indeterminacy of textual boundaries. Editorial considerations segue into questions of context and the sociology of literature.

Carpenter, Kenneth E., ed. *Books and Society in History: Papers of the Association of College and Research Libraries Rare Books and Manuscripts Pre-Conference.* New York: R. R. Bowker, 1983.

A collection of nine essays, with an introduction by G. Thomas Tanselle. Robert Darnton leads off the volume with an attempt to define the field of the history of the book. His definition focuses on "how ideas were transmitted through print and how exposure to the printed word affected human thought and behavior during the last 500 years." Darnton notes the importance of authors, publishers, printers, shippers, booksellers, and readers. Elizabeth L. Eisenstein then examines the fifteenth century transition from the scriptorium and the hand-produced book to the printing office. Henri-Jean Martin's contribution focuses on publishing in the France of the *ancien régime*. The printing of English laws between 1484 and 1640 is the subject of Katharine F. Pantzer's essay. Richard III was the first monarch to print statutes; and he had the laws printed in French, Pantzer argues, to show continuity with his predecessors even though Parliament was using English. For the same reason, when Henry VII succeeded Richard III, the Tudor monarch also had the statutes of his first two Parliaments printed in French. Bernhard Fabian deals with English language publishing in eighteenth century Germany, where English books cost less than in Britain. Raymond Birn returns to the *ancien régime* to discuss book production and censorship in the last fifteen years of the reign of Louis XIV (1700-1715). Religious books were particularly liable to censorship (thirteen percent were censored, as opposed to ten percent of books in other categories). Stylistic infelicities provided at least a pretext for some censorship. John Feather considers English government involvement with printing in the eighteenth century; Frédéric Barbier looks at nineteenth century French publishing, and the volume concludes with James J. Barnes's study of the British and American book trade, 1819-1939. In a short conclusion Paul Raabe suggests areas of future investigation in library history and the history of the book. Tanselle observes, "Taken together [the essays] suggest the wide range of problems that book history must investigate, and they illustrate a number of ways of tackling those problems."

Carter, Thomas Francis, and L. Carrington Goodrich. *The Invention of Printing in China and Its Spread Westward.* 2d ed. New York: Ronald Press, 1955.

Block-printing in China dates back to at least 698, by which time the techniques for reproducing text and illustrations were more sophisticated than those exhibited in European blockbooks nearly a thousand years later. Carter argues that European block-printing was inspired by Oriental examples. He notes that China and Korea also developed movable type before Gutenberg. Korea even created metal type and type molds. Carter does not see any evidence that Europe knew of these inventions, but he emphasizes the importance of the Chinese invention of paper (which reached the West through the Arabs) in the development of printing. A good introduction to Oriental printing.

Chappell, Warren. *A Short History of the Printed Word.* New York: Alfred A. Knopf, 1970.

A well-written account enriched with personal anecdotes from a leading printer. Intended for the lay reader. Begins with block- printing that preceded movable type, and traces the art and technology that have affected the book over the past five centuries. Provides a good account of important printers and type designers, methods of illustration, and the book market. Chappell is especially fond of, and informative about, early printers, who saw themselves as artists. He is less enthusiastic about modern mass-produced books. With many fine illustrations. The *Times Literary Supplement* for August 18, 1972, lamented the lack of footnotes but concluded, "*A Short History of the Printed Word* will provide the general reader with a clear and endearing personal view of the development of type design and illustration. The explanations of technical matters are admirably lucid" (p. 976).

Chartier, Roger, ed. *The Order of Books: Readers, Authors, and Libraries in Europe Between the Fourteenth and Eighteenth Centuries.* Translated by Lydia G. Cochrane. Stanford, Calif.: Stanford University Press, 1994.

In the three chapters of this short book, Chartier examines the issues of reading, authorship, and the creation of libraries and bibliographies in early modern Europe. Chartier is more concerned with raising questions than in answering them. Thus, he warns that in dealing with literacy and readership the historian of the book must recognize that each person finds particular meaing in a text. The form of the book contributes to but does not completely determine how any individual will read a text. In his second chapter, Chartier draws on Michel Foucault's "Qu'est-ce qu'un auteur?" (*Bulletin de la Société française de philosophie* 44, July-September, 1969, 73-104). Chartier notes how the history of the book can show the shifting relationship between author and text and so help answer the question Foucault poses. The third chapter explores various attempts to create a universal library such as that described in a short story by Jorge Luis Borges, "The Library of Babel." These attempts were sometimes physical, but this impulse lies behind many bibliographies, such as the *Bibliotheca universalis* (Zurich, 1545) of Conrad Gesner and various journals of the seventeenth and eighteenth centuries. An important work by a leading historian of the book.

_____. *The Culture of Print: Power and the Uses of Print in Early Modern Europe*. Translated by Lydia G. Cochrane. Princeton, N.J.: Princeton University Press, 1987.
The essays collected here seek "to reconstruct the multiple uses of the many forms of print" in the fifteenth through eighteenth centuries. The first contribution examines the ways saints' lives could be used polemically. Other marvelous tales and folklore also can reveal the impact of print on attitudes of the reading public. The next section examines the uses of religious materials to confirm or subvert orthodoxy. The final group of essays examines the effects of political imagery and texts. These studies reveal that the printing press affected all segments of society and was as important for the dissemination of images as it was for the spread of words.

Clair, Colin. *A History of European Printing*. New York: Academic Press, 1976.
This general history is especially useful for its discussion of the fifteenth and sixteenth centuries, to which over half the book is devoted. Conversely, it is weak on the nineteenth and twentieth centuries. Because Clair had already written a similar volume devoted to Britain, he gives less space to Britain here. Good treatment of technical matters, though the focus is on the major printers who advanced the development of the book, particularly the early scholar printers like Christophe Plantin (about whom Clair wrote a book) and type designers like Granjon. Ignores the business of book production. With an

extensive bibliography and an index with some 3,000 items that makes this a handy reference guide, especially for early printing.

_____. *A History of Printing in Britain*. New York: Oxford University Press, 1966.
"This book is an attempt to provide an outline history of the development of printing in Great Britain since the time of Caxton" (preface). Clair devotes little attention to the economics of the book trade but focuses on significant figures and their contributions. He also examines technological changes and the effects of legislation on the printing industry. Unlike *A History of European Printing*, this book is especially good on the nineteenth and twentieth centuries. Bill Katz lamented Clair's dull prose but praised his scholarship and accuracy in his review in *Papers of the Bibliographical Society of America* 60 (1966): 487-488.

Dahl, Svend. *History of the Book*. Metuchen, N.J.: Scarecrow Press, 1968.
Despite the publication date, this book is based on lectures delivered in the 1920s, though it incorporates some more recent scholarship. Dahl is especially good at linking the book to larger social and cultural movements. Thus, he notes that in post-Revolutionary France, the reaction against the refinements of the *ancien régime* banished elaborate illustration, and favored stark typography and bindings with "warlike emblems" that harkened back to republican Rome. About two-thirds of the volume deals with the printed book; the rest considers the manuscript.

Davenport, Cyril. *The Book: Its History and Development*. New York: Van Nostrand, 1908.
Davenport begins with the earliest inscriptions in stone and metal, palm leaf books, and other such means of recording information. He then deals with manuscript rolls and codices; here he also traces the history of bookbinding. Subsequent chapters take a thematic approach, dealing with paper (Chapter 3), printing (Chapter 4), and illustrations (Chapter 5). The final four chapters return to Davenport's primary interest, bookbinding, to discuss materials other than leather (Chapter 7), leather bindings (Chapter 8), blind and gold-tooling (Chapters 9 and 10). Each chapter concludes with a bibliography. A good overview, pleasantly written.

Davis, Donald G., ed. "Libraries, Books, and Culture." *Journal of Library History* 21 (Winter/Spring, 1986).

The Winter issue opens with two general pieces: John Feather's "The Book in History and the History of the Book" and David D. Hall's "The History of the Book: New Questions? New Answers." Other papers deal with such matters as book ownership among German artisans in the sixteenth century, the growth of public libraries in mid-nineteenth century America, and the importance of private libraries for the early English Dissenting academies (1663-1730). An enlightening collection of essays.

Diringer, David. *The Hand-Produced Book*. London: Hutchinson's Scientific and Technical Publications, 1953.
An authoritative history of the book before printing, enhanced by 185 black-and-white illustrations. Intended for the general reader, the work begins with the earliest written records, such as Stone Age paintings and carvings. Diringer looks at all forms of writing and drawing, including those of the Maya, Toltecs, and Aztecs as well as the more familiar cuneiform of the Assyrians and Egyptian hieroglyphics. Most of the work traces the development of the book in the Orient and the West until the advent of printing. An appendix treats inks, pens, and other writing implements.

Eisenstein, Elizabeth. *The Printing Press as an Agent of Change*. 2 vols. Cambridge, England: Cambridge University Press, 1979.
Frances Yates wrote in the *Times Literary Supplement* for November 23, 1979, "This is an important book, concerned with root problems in the dissemination of culture" (p. 5). Drawing on a wealth of scholarship, Eisenstein traces the effects of the printing press from 1450 to the eighteenth century. She is especially concerned with the role of the press in promoting humanism, the Reformation, and the scientific revolution. In this last area, for example, Eisenstein notes that printing insured the preservation and dissemination of classical scientific treatises and also spread the news of each discovery. Print fostered the Reformation by promulgating Luther's ideas (small wonder that Luther regarded the press as a divine gift) but also highlighted differences among Catholic texts and theologians and so inspired reformers. Protestantism in turn tended to be more friendly to the press than were Catholics. Copernicus' *De Revolutionibus*, Vesalius' landmark anatomical drawings, and Galileo's last works were all printed in Protestant cities. Eisenstein's work is important not only for what it says but also for stimulating a sharp debate on the extent to which printing was itself an agent of change. This controversy encouraged greater interest in the entire area of the history of the book.

Esdaile, Arundell. *Esdaile's Manual of Bibliography.* 5th rev. ed. Metuchen, N.J.: Scarecrow Press, 1981.

Edited by Roy Stokes, this edition of a book first published in 1931 offers useful instruction for the librarian, collector, and student of literature. The first chapter defines the field of analytical bibliography. The next provides an anatomy of the book from preliminaries to endpapers. Chapter 3 quickly surveys the history of the book, and subsequent chapters treat writing surfaces, typography, presswork, illustrations, and bindings. Collation and description are covered in the last two chapters. Each chapter includes a list of suggested readings, and the work includes a glossary. A clear presentation, rich in historical examples.

Feather, John P. *A History of British Publishing.* London: Routledge, 1988.

"My objective has been to show how British publishing has developed over the last five hundred years and to explain why it has taken the directions in which it has travelled." Four themes intersect in this account: the role of the publisher in organizing the creation and distribution of printed matter, copyright, "commercial imperatives," and censorship. Although Feather devotes a brief introduction to the book trade before printing, the focus is on the period since Caxton, who established the primacy of London which it retains in British publishing. The first section, "The Press in Chains," extends the story to 1695, when the Licensing Act expired. Part 2 covers the eighteenth century; Part 3 considers the effects of the Industrial Revolution on nineteenth century publishing, and Part 4 examines the twentieth century. With extensive notes and a solid bibliography.

Feather, John P., and David McKitterick. *The History of the Book and Libraries: Two Views.* Washington, D.C.: Library of Congress, 1986.

The text of the addresses presented in March, 1985 by these two scholars. In the first, Feather explores the relationship between the history of the book and politics, economics, social conditions, technology, and culture. McKitterick, rare book curator at the Cambridge University Library, argues for the integration of library history into the larger contexts of the history of the book and history generally. He observes that libraries can reveal much about book-buying and collecting, scholarship, and society. Together these papers provide an overview of the state of the discipline of book history in the mid-1980s.

Febvre, Lucien, and Henri-Jean Martin. *The Coming of the Book: The Impact of Printing, 1450-1800.* Translated by David Gerard. Atlantic Highlands, N.J.: Humanities Press, 1976.

A landmark study. Focusing on France and Germany, the authors argue that the printed book was "one of the most potent agents at the disposal of western civilisation in bringing together the scattered ideas of representative thinkers." Printing served not only as a means of recording and transmitting ideas; it also "created new habits of thought." The opening chapters set the stage for the arrival of printing; they discuss the world of manuscripts, the introduction of paper into Europe, and the technical advances that allowed for multiple copies of a single work. The authors then examine the printed book as physical object and as a commodity. The makers of books—printers, publishers, and authors—are treated in Chapter 5. Chapter 6 looks at the diffusion of printing; Chapter 7 considers the book trade, and Chapter 8, occupying nearly a third of the volume, discusses the book as an agent of change. According to Febvre and Martin, the printing press shattered the unified Latin culture of Europe, allowed the Reformation to sweep across the continent, and, by multiplying copies, rendered the individual book less of an icon.

Gaskell, Philip. *A New Introduction to Bibliography*. 3d printing with corrections. New York: Oxford University Press, 1972.
Focuses on the printed book. The first unit deals with printing on a handpress and examines type, typesetting, paper, presswork, storing unbound books, and binding. The second unit treats machine printing and explores similar subjects. In this section, Gaskell devotes two chapters to the book trade. The third unit applies historical background to bibliographical identification, description, and editing. Provides an extensive reading list. A solid introduction to book production from 1500 to 1950. Norman Russell, in *The Review of English Studies* 24 (1973): 526-529, praised the work as "a masterly consolidation of the results of authoritative bibliographical research during the past half century,... an invaluable work of reference which no library concerned with literary studies, printing history, or librarianship can afford to do without." Fredson Bowers, that grand old man of bibliographical studies, demonstrated less enthusiasm in "McKerrow Revisited" (*Papers of the Bibliographical Society of America* 67, 1973, 109-124).

Gold, Leonard Singer, ed. *A Sign and a Witness: 2,000 Years of Hebrew Books and Illuminated Manuscripts*. New York: New York Public Library and Oxford University Press, 1988.
An exhibition catalog for the New York Public Library. The volume traces the development of Hebrew books from the Dead Sea Scrolls to the twentieth century. Twelve essays by noted scholars explore such

aspects as "Early Hebrew Printing" and "Publishing and the Rise of Modern Hebrew Literature." With many illustrations and a twenty-page bibliography.

Greetham, D. C. *Textual Scholarship: An Introduction.* New York: Garland, 1992.

Greetham's nine chapters explore all facets involved in producing an edition and seek to acquaint the reader with the terms and processes of textual scholarship. Greetham begins with "Finding the Text," in which he examines the nature (and importance) of enumerative bibliography. Chapters 2 and 3 discuss how manuscripts and printed books are produced. Chapter 4 is devoted to descriptive (analytical) bibliography, Chapters 5 and 6 to paleography and typography. In Chapter 7, Greetham considers textual history, including stemmatics. Textual criticism and scholarly editing comprise the subject matter of the final two chapters. Appendices reproduce pages from the Shakespeare First Folio and different kinds of scholarly editions. With 160 illustrations and a "Selected Bibliography" covering eighty pages. A fine introduction, at once learned and accessible.

Handover, P. M. *Printing in London from 1476 to Modern Times.* Cambridge, Mass.: Harvard University Press, 1960.

This well-illustrated series of lectures looks at the book trade in the sixteenth and seventeenth centuries (Chapters 1-2), the Bible patent (Chapter 3), the periodical press from the sixteenth to the twentieth century (Chapters 4-6), jobbing (Chapter 7), and the decline of book production in London (Chapter 8). Particularly concerned with the business of early publishing. J. C. Wyllie noted some factual errors but praised the book for its "handy summary of English publishing monopolies since the sixteenth century, with some discursive comments on the English periodical press" (*Shakespeare Quarterly* 12, 1961, 335). Fredson Bowers was not impressed (*Modern Language Quarterly* 22, 1961, 214).

Jennett, Sean. *Pioneers in Printing.* London: Routledge & Kegan Paul, 1958.

Jennett's nine chapters deal with eight people who greatly contributed to the development of the printed book. Jennett's account appropriately begins with Johannes Gutenberg and moves to William Caxton, England's first printer. Jennett then writes about William Caslon, the first important English typefounder. John Baskerville, the eighteenth century printer, is included as the creator of modern typefaces, and Aloys

Senefelder follows for his invention of lithography. Frederick Koenig's chapter discusses improvements in the printing press, such as the introduction of cylinders. Two other chapters consider Ottmar Mergenthaler, developer of a practical Linotype machine, and Tolbert Lanston, who created the Monotype. Chapter 7 does not deal with a particular individual but instead discusses attempts to produce machines like the Linotype and Monotype. Together these chapters constitute a history of the technology and business of printing from the mid-fifteenth to the mid-twentieth century.

Johnson, Elmer D. *Communication: An Introduction to the History of the Alphabet, Writing, Printing, Books, and Libraries.* Metuchen, N.J.: Scarecrow Press, 1973.
A history of books and libraries. Johnson begins with the development of written communication and then explores libraries in the classical world. The fourth chapter deals with medieval book production and preservation. The rest of the volume considers printing in Europe (Chapters 5-6), England (Chapter 7), and America (Chapters 8-11, 14); "Books and Printing since 1775" (Chapter 12); "Modern Foreign Libraries" (Chapter 13), the library profession (Chapter 15), and new developments in books and libraries (Chapter 16). Each chapter includes a bibliography. Intended primarily for librarians, the work will appeal to all seeking a good survey of book production.

Labarre, Albert. *Histoire du livre.* Paris: Presses Universitaires de France, 1970.
Begins with prehistoric records on stone and wood but proceeds rapidly to papyrus rolls in the Greco-Roman world. The third chapter examines the medieval book. Labarre notes the transition at the end of the twelfth century from monastic to lay book production, and he rightly observes that scribes and illuminators were not immediately displaced by the printing press. In the fourth and fifth chapters, Labarre deals with early printing. Here he comments that the early presses produced works that had been popular in the Middle Ages, with the Bible, St. Augustine and other Church Fathers, Cicero, Aristotle, Virgil, Aesop, Cato, and Ovid among the most frequently reprinted. In Chapter 6, Labarre considers the effects of the Counter-Reformation and Enlightenment on the book, and the study concludes with a chapter on the book in the age of the Industrial Revolution. A good brief history that relates the book to economic, social, and cultural conditions. With a brief bibliography.

Lejard, A., ed. *The Art of the French Book from Early Manuscripts to the Present Time*. London: Les Éditions du Chêne, 1947.

Philip James observes in his introduction, "To turn the pages of this book is to realise at once and for ever that the art of the book in France is the inevitable triumph of the illustrator." The nearly 200 illustrations, many in color, emphasize this aspect of French bookmaking. Figures like Fournier and Didot receive brief mention for their typographic innovations, but artists and illustrators are the primary concern of the brief essays that precede each portfolio of reproductions. Even the volume's ratio of text to pictures highlights the concern with the latter. A lovely illustrated history of the French book from the ninth to the twentieth century.

Levarie, Norma. *The Art and History of Books*. New York: James H. Heineman, 1968.

This richly illustrated, well-researched account begins with the clay tablets of the Babylonians and Assyrians and the papyrus fragments of the Egyptians. Quickly moving through antiquity, Levarie devotes somewhat more attention to medieval manuscripts. About half the volume deals with the first two centuries of printing, which Levarie examines geographically. Subsequent periods receive substantial but less extensive treatment. With a useful bibliography. The *Times Literary Supplement* for July 17, 1969 commented, "This is a thoroughly sensible, generously illustrated, and attractively produced history of manuscripts and printed books and their illustration. . . . It is difficult to imagine an introduction to the subject which the general reader will find more infectious, or from which he will profit more" (p. 768).

McKerrow, Ronald Brunlees. *An Introduction to Bibliography for Literary Students*. Oxford, England: Clarendon Press, 1927.

An expert on English literature of the sixteenth and seventeenth centuries, McKerrow sets forth here his vast knowledge of the way books were produced with a handpress. Part 1 deals with book production, including presses, presswork, paper, and binding. Part 2 applies this information to a variety of bibliographical problems, such as determining priority of editions and dating undated imprints. Part 3 considers how closely typesetters tried to follow an author's manuscript and explains how errors arose in printing. Eight appendices deal with the beginning of printing, printing types, peculiarities of English printing, common abbreviations and contractions in early printed books, folding of leaves in 12mo and 24mo volumes, color printing, difficult Latin place-names, and Elizabethan handwriting. A pioneering effort and in many ways still the text of choice for those interested in book production in the Elizabethan and Jacobean periods.

McLuhan, Marshall. *The Gutenberg Galaxy: The Making of Typographic Man.* Toronto: University of Toronto Press, 1962.
Arguing that technology shapes individuals, McLuhan focuses on two developments that have particularly affected humanity. The first is the creation of the alphabet, which led to "detribalization" and culminated in the flowering of Greek culture. The alphabet also privileged sight over other senses. The invention of printing confirmed this "visual stress" and influenced all aspects of human endeavor. McLuhan concludes that advances in electronics have somewhat offset the effects of the Gutenberg Revolution by stressing nonvisual perception. An influential study.

McMurtrie, Douglas C. *The Book: The Story of Printing and Bookmaking.* New York: Oxford University Press, 1943.
A revision of McMurtrie's *The Golden Book* (1927) and still an authoritative history of the subject from prehistoric pictographs to twentieth century typography and illustration, written "from the viewpoint of the designer and printer." Emphasis is on the printed book, to which McMurtrie devotes over 500 of the volume's 600 pages. The list of illustrations runs to twelve pages, indicating the wealth of pictures that complement the text. Includes a lengthy bibliography.

McNally, Peter F., ed. *The Advent of Printing: Historians of Science Respond to Elizabeth Eisenstein's "The Printing Press as an Agent of Change."* Montreal: Graduate School of Library and Information Studies, McGill University, 1987.
Presents four responses to Eisenstein's landmark book. Philip T. Teigen, concerned with the history of medicine, questions Eisenstein's assumption that the Renaissance, the Reformation, and the Scientific Revolution can be subsumed under the larger rubric of a communications revolution. The philosopher and historian William Shea notes numerous factors, some technological (like the telescope), others conceptual (like the revival of the idea that the earth moves), that contributed to the Scientific Revolution but were independent of the printing press. Eisenstein discusses the importance of printing in circulating ideas, but Shea notes that before Galileo only ten astronomers in Europe had accepted the Copernican system. The press alone, then, did not lead to acceptance of a heliocentric universe. Susan Sheets-Pyenson looks at nineteenth century efforts to popularize science and agrees with Eisenstein that "changes in printing technology have

affected the dissemination of science which, in turn, seems to have affected the generation of scientific ideas." Through a study of the dissemination of Einstein's theory of relativity, Lewis Pyenson's concluding essay again supports Eisenstein's view of the printing press as an agent of change. Peter McNally's introduction lists fifty-two reviews that, whether favorable or not, illustrate the interest in and centrality of Eisenstein's work.

MacRobert, T. M. *Printed Books: A Short Introduction to Fine Typography.* London: Her Majesty's Stationery Office, 1957.
An illustrated history with forty-six plates tracing the changes in printing styles from Gutenberg to the 1920s. In the introduction MacRobert notes that not only were the first printed books modeled on manuscripts but so were the Aldine italic types and Philippe Grandjean's roman letters executed at the end of the seventeenth century. MacRobert briefly treats the development of many unattractive modern typefaces and the revival of fine printing at the end of the nineteenth century.

Olmert, Michael. *The Smithsonian Book of Books.* Washington, D.C.: Smithsonian Institution, 1992.
This well-illustrated, attractively printed book surveys the history of the book from the cuneiform tablets of Mesopotamia and hieroglyphics of Egypt to letterpress printing and the web press used to print *The Smithsonian Book of Books.* Later chapters deal with such special topics as the publishing of Shakespeare's works, bookbinding, important scientific works, the Kelmscott Press, book illustration, children's books, dictionaries, the book business, and unusual items found inside of books (including a page from a Gutenberg Bible discovered in a seventeenth century book and a "bibliofossil" crane fly preserved in the paper of a 1615 pamphlet). The volume concludes with a paean to books and reading. Though intended for a general audience, the work offers nuggets of information that even the scholar will value. Lacks a bibliography.

Orcutt, William Dana. *Master Makers of the Book.* Boston: Little, Brown, 1929.
In his opening chapter, Orcutt surveys the world of books before printing and the early history of the craft. The next chapter deals with Aldus, whom Orcutt calls "The great figure in the whole history of the Book." Orcutt discusses Aldus' achievements as printer, humanist, and scholar. Subsequent chapters look at the work of Robert Estienne and Geoffrey Tory, Christophe Plantin, the Elseviers, John Baskerville, the Didot family, Giambattista Bodoni, Joachim Ibarra, William Morris,

Thomas James Cobden-Sanderson, and Emery Walker. Through his biographical sketches Orcutt traces the development of the book and the printing industry from its birth to the early twentieth century.

Oswald, John Clyde. *A History of Printing: Its Development Through Five Hundred Years.* New York: D. Appleton, 1928.
About half the book deals with the first seventy years of printing, and here Oswald is both interesting and sound, incorporating fascinating anecdotes about the early printers. Oswald is also useful for his discussion of early American printing. Much of the more modern history receives cursory treatment. Nicely illustrated, with well over a hundred pictures, many of them in color.

Parkes, M. B. *Pause and Effect: Punctuation in the West.* Aldershot, England: Scolar Press, 1993.
Presents seventy-four pages of plates, with transcriptions and commentary, tracing the history of punctuation and the significance of these incidentals. Facsimiles of the same text as it was reproduced over time illustrate changes in scribal and printing practices, with emphasis on the former. Because the written text reflects reading practice, Parkes's study is not a trivial pursuit but rather a significant contribution to the understanding of texts and readers. For example, the introduction of spaces between words in a Latin text may suggest that the language was becoming less familiar, so that readers needed more help in dealing with the text. Rosamond McKitter wrote in the *Times Literary Supplement* for June 4, 1993, "*Pause and Effect* will be referred to henceforth as an invaluable compendium of evidence, by all those concerned with writing, reading and the uses of literacy in the Middle Ages."

Peddie, Robert Alexander. *An Outline of the History of Printing: To Which Is Added the History of Printing in Colours.* London: Grafton, 1917.
This brief history traces the development of printing from its inception in the mid-1400s to the early twentieth century. Despite the book's brevity—it devotes thirty-six pages to printing and covers color printing in another fifteen—it provides a wealth of factual detail, such as the dates and places of the first use of Greek (Subiaco, 1465) and Hebrew (Italy and Germany, around 1475) type.

_____. *Printing: A Short History of the Art.* London: Grafton, 1927.
In his preface Robert Peddie writes, "The present work has . . . been planned . . . to give in concise and handy form, . . . a general compre-

hensive survey of the development of printing in many lands from its invention up to comparatively recent times." The focus is on Europe and America, but the appendix devotes five pages to the appearance of printing in Asia, Africa, and Australia. Arrangement is geographical, based on the date of the first printed book in the country. Each section is written by an authority in the field. Thus, George Parker Winship writes about printing in Spanish America, Lawrence C. Wroth deals with British North America, and Henry R. Plomer provides the unit on Great Britain. Maurits Sabbe, in his section on Holland, credits his country with the invention of printing, but Peddie places this essay fourth, tacitly endorsing the conventional view of Gutenberg as first printer.

Plomer, Henry R. *A Short History of English Printing, 1476-1900*. 2d ed. London: Kegan Paul, Trench, Trubner, 1915.
  As A. W. Pollard observes in his preface, English printing before 1640 was much better documented than it has been subsequently. Plomer's book reflects this antiquarian orientation, with most of the book dealing with the earlier epochs of bookmaking. Hence, the volume is most useful for the period before 1640, though Plomer devotes fifty pages to the eighteenth century and thirty each to the late seventeenth and the nineteenth centuries.

Posner, Raphael, and Israel Ta-Shema, eds. *The Hebrew Book: An Historical Survey*. Jerusalem: Keter Publishing House, 1975.
  An edited collection of book-related articles in the sixteen volumes of the *Encyclopaedia Judaica*, with the addition to Ta-Shema's "The Science of the Hebrew Book" (Chapter 4) that surveys the field of Hebrew bibliography. Profusely illustrated. Charles Berlin found many faults in the work but conceded that it is "attractive, well-intentioned, and useful" (*Journal of Library History* 13, Spring, 1978, 211). Herbert C. Zafren's review in *Library Quarterly* 46 (1976): 307-308 also is largely negative but acknowledges, "It is the only book in English . . . that has brought so much material on the Hebrew book together in one place, and it does excel in illustrations."

Reynolds, L. D., and N. G. Wilson. *Scribes and Scholars: A Guide to the Transmission of Greek and Latin Literature*. 3d ed. Oxford, England: Clarendon Press, 1991.
  Despite its apparently limited focus, this study offers much information on the history of the book. The authors explore the creation and preservation of manuscripts in antiquity, the scriptoria of the Middle

Ages, the impact of printing on texts, and the rise of textual criticism as a discipline. Good discussion of bookhands, the popularity of certain authors at different times, and the manuscript tradition.

Rider, Alice Damon. *A Story of Books and Libraries*. Metuchen, N.J.: Scarecrow Press, 1976.
Intended for a high school audience. The first two chapters look at ancient writing and writing materials. Chapter 3 considers the libraries of antiquity. The next four sections present a historical survey, followed by a chapter on four great modern libraries (British Library, London; the Folger Shakespeare Library, Washington, D.C.; the Vatican Library; and the Pierpont Morgan Library in New York City). Concludes with a discussion of book collecting.

Schottenloher, Karl. *Books and the Western World: A Cultural History*. Translated by William D. Boyd and Irmgard H. Wolfe. Jefferson, N.C.: McFarland, 1989.
A translation of the second (1968) edition of *Bücher bewegten die Welt* by a noted scholar/librarian. Schottenloher's German title suggests his view of the centrality of the book in history; he saw the written and printed word as "das wesentliche geistige Agens der Weltgeschichte" (the essential spiritual force that moves world history). International and comprehensive in scope, moving from antiquity to the twentieth century, this study nonetheless emphasizes Germany. Such a focus is not inappropriate, given Germany's role in the Carolingian Renaissance, the incunabula period, and the Enlightenment. With over sixty pages of bibliographical notes. Norman Stevens called this "a valuable textbook and reference source" (*Wilson Library Bulletin* 64, December, 1989, 128).

Steinberg, S. H., and James Moran. *Five Hundred Years of Printing*. 3d ed., rev. Baltimore: Penguin Books, 1974.
A standard work that relates printing to the history and culture of each period and place and shows how printing changes lives. This long-lived book, first published in 1955, is a standard text in college and library school courses on the history of the book. It deserves this distinction because it provides a wealth of information in brief compass and in readable prose. Steinberg uses a chronological approach for the early period of printing, then shifts to a topical approach in what he calls "The Era of Consolidation" (1550-1800) and the nineteenth century. Unlike most historians of the book, Steinberg does not regard the incunabular period (to December 31, 1500) as a separate unit. Instead,

he sees the first century of printing as being of a piece, when "almost every single feature that characterizes" modern printing emerged.

Tanselle, G. Thomas. *The History of Books as a Field of Study.* Chapel Hill: University of North Carolina Press, 1981.
The text of the second Hanes Lecture. In this pamphlet, Tanselle argues the need to combine traditional bibliographic study of the physical book with social, economic, cultural, and intellectual history into a unified discipline. He criticizes historians like Robert Darnton for sometimes ignoring the physical features of the book, and he urges international cooperation. Tanselle also cautions against concentrating on only the great writers, since all books can reveal information about "the printing and publishing practices of the time." In his review, John Feather praised Tanselle's contributions to the field and this lecture in particular for "advanc[ing] the debate on book history" (*Journal of Library History, Philosophy, and Comparative Librarianship* 17, 1982, 467).

Thomas, Alan G. *Great Books and Book Collectors.* London: Weidenfeld and Nicolson, 1975.
An expanded version of Thomas' *Fine Books* (1967). Thomas, a London bookseller for more than fifty years, deals with twelve aspects of the book: manuscripts, early printing, bookbinding, the Bible, early books in Hebrew, herbals and colorplate books, English colorplate books, books on architecture, books about the New World, private presses, first editions and forgeries, and book collectors. Focusing on the high spots of each area, Thomas uses these subjects to survey the making and buying of books from antiquity to modern times. The book is well-written and sumptuously illustrated. An excellent introduction that will also interest the advanced student.

Twyman, Michael. *Printing, 1770-1970: An Illustrated History of Its Development and Uses in England.* London: Eyre and Spottiswoode, 1970.
Andrew H. Horn wrote in *Library Quarterly* 43 (1973): 421, "Anyone interested in typography and the graphic arts will find Twyman's *Printing, 1770-1970* an enlightening exposition and a very useful reference work." Twyman examines the modern age, when the Industrial and French Revolutions combined with increased population and expansion of trade to alter society and printing. The focus is on non-book materials, though Twyman's observations apply to all forms of print. The seven chapters deal in turn with the information explosion, new technology, color printing, the shift from hand-printing to me-

chanical and electronic methods, typography, illustration, and design. In a second section, Twyman explores how illustrations document such aspects of society as rural life or war. A nontechnical, amply illustrated text that provides a short list of suggested readings.

Vervliet, Hendrik D. L. *The Book Through Five Thousand Years*. London: Phaidon, 1972.
Issued as part of the celebration of International Book Year. An attractive eight-pound volume with 264 full-color illustrations, the work is aimed at "the educated amateur who wishes to extend his field of knowledge." Divided into four sections: the prehistory of books and printing; the book in the Orient; the manuscript in the West; the printed book in the West. Essays were prepared by two dozen experts. Thus, David Diringer deals with writing, Kurt Weitzmann with illustrated rolls and codices in the Greco-Roman world, and Otto Mazal with medieval bookbinding. Each unit includes a bibliography. David Coombs wrote in *Connoisseur* 183 (1973): 316, "For the information alone and certainly in combination with the wealth of illustrations, this book is likely to be invaluable to anyone seriously interested in the subject." If the book had an index it would be perfect.

Winckler, Paul A., ed. *Reader in the History of Books and Printing*. Englewood, Colo.: Information Handling Services, 1978.
An excellent anthology with useful suggestions for additional reading. The volume begins with Denys Hays's "Fiat Lux," from John Carter and Percy H. Muir's *Printing and the Mind of Man* (1967). Hays looks at the power of the book to defy time and to enlighten "the mind of man." The next unit deals with the elements required for books and printing, including the alphabet. This unit also deals with bookbinding and illustration. Unit 3 examines the manuscript book, and Unit 4 the printed page.

Wroth, Lawrence C., ed. *A History of the Printed Book*. New York: Limited Editions Club, 1938.
The third number of *The Dolphin*. The first unit traces the development of the book from manuscripts in antiquity to the twentieth century. Unit 2 deals with technical aspects, such as the history of the printing press and papermaking. Unit 3 treats illustration and bookbinding, and the work concludes with "A Summary of Printing History," a survey of important studies. Each chapter is written by an authority in the field. An attractive, informative, entertaining book that remains a classic.

Chapter 10
THE BOOK IN ANTIQUITY

Bischoff, Bernhard. *Latin Paleography: Antiquity and the Middle Ages.* Translated by Daibhi O'Croinin and David Ganz. Cambridge, England: Cambridge University Press, 1991. See entry under "THE ALPHABET."

Chiera, Edward. *They Wrote on Clay: The Babylonian Tablets Speak Today.* Edited by George G. Cameron. Chicago: University of Chicago Press, 1938.
In this short book written for a general audience, Chiera seeks to reconstruct the world of the Assyrians, Babylonians, and Sumerians. Much of the volume is devoted to the development of an Akkadian alphabet and the creation of clay tablets with cuneiform writing. Chiera traces the evolution of this writing system from pictographs to phonemes. At the end of the book, Chiera speculates on the relationship between cuneiform and Phoenician letters and also on the influence of Near Eastern writing on Asian systems.

Collon, Dominique. *First Impressions: Cylinder Seals in the Ancient Near East.* Chicago: University of Chicago Press, 1987.
Cylinder seals were invented, along with writing on wet clay tablets with a stylus, by the Sumerians or Elamites of Mesopotamia in the fourth millennium B.C. Sumerian pictographs developed into the cuneiform script used for Akkadian, Babylonian, Assyrian, Hittite, Old Persian, Elamite, Amorite, and other Middle Eastern dialects. Cuneiform, with its hundreds of symbols, yielded to an alphabetic system among Phoenician merchants, who also replaced the cylinder seal with a stamp seal, just as they substituted parchment and papyrus for clay tablets. The cylinder seal, clay tablets, and cuneiform were inextricably linked. Collon studies the seals for what they reveal about the cultures that produced them. Part 1 provides a historical survey. Part 2 looks at the seals in society, and Part 3 considers the subjects and themes depicted on these seals. With 966 illustrations of images on seals and clay tablets. Provides a substantial bibliography.

Dilke, O. A. W. *Roman Books and Their Impact.* Leeds, England: Elmete Press, 1977.

A beautifully produced volume with twenty-three plates (five in color) that explains the production of books in classical Rome. It also treats authorship, reading, and the survival of Latin texts into the Renaissance. Dilke notes that books in Rome were written on papyrus (later on parchment), and works could be published by being copied or by being read. Literacy appears to have been extensive, and book ownership may have been, too. The Villa dei Papiri discovered at Herculaneum housed some 800 papyrus rolls; large villas generally perhaps contained similar libraries. Augustus established two public libraries in Rome; in the fourth century A.D. the city had twenty-six of them (Kenney, below, says twenty-eight). Dilke suggests that the high cost of papyrus and labor in the fourth century helped establish the dominance of the vellum codex over the papyrus scroll. Dilke concludes by observing the still-powerful influence of the books produced in the Roman Republic and Empire. Herbert L. Kessler called Dilke's work "an erudite account of ancient Latin books, . . . an authoritative and readable introduction to a major manifestation of classical culture" (*American Journal of Philology* 100, 1979, 447-449).

Hadas, Moses. *Ancilla to Classical Reading.* New York: Columbia University Press, 1954.
The first part of this book deals with the production, reception, and preservation of books in the Greco-Roman world. Here Hadas addresses such questions as "What . . . were the physical resources of the writer—paper, alphabets, handwritings? How did he publish, and how make his living? How large was his public and what were his relations to it? . . . How was his work cared for, kept intelligible, transmitted through the ages?" Whenever possible, Hadas presents evidence from ancient texts themselves. Part 2 offers an anthology of gossip about classical authors, again drawn from Greek and Roman sources; these observations help bring the ancient authors to life.

Havelock, Eric A. *The Literate Revolution in Greece and Its Cultural Consequences.* Princeton, N.J.: Princeton University Press, 1982.
In this collection of his previously published essays, Havelock argues that "the introduction of the Greek letters into inscription somewhere about 700 B.C. was to alter the character of human culture, placing a gulf between all alphabetic societies and their precursors." Havelock looks at these consequences, which emerged slowly; only in the late fifth century B.C. were letters taught "at the primary level of schooling" and general literacy thus brought about. Even Greek drama of the Golden Age reflects oral rather than written culture; the latter comes

to the fore only in the fourth century B.C. Havelock is more concerned with the results of the introduction of the alphabet than with the alphabet itself, and he offers many insights into Greek culture and the differences between literacy and orality. Havelock maintains that the Greeks had the first true alphabet, since the Semitic precursors lacked vowels. John E. Rexine wrote in *Classical World* 76 (1983): 252, "No matter whether one is interested in the history of the alphabet, the Greek language, literature, philosophy, social, intellectual or cultural history, the history of human thought, anthropology, or the development of human culture over the ages, *The Literate Revolution in Greece and Its Cultural Consequences* is a book that must be read and considered seriously in any valid attempt to demand what Greek culture was really like from its preliterate to its highly literate stages, and what the consequences of this revolution were for the Greek and Western World."

Hussein, Mohamed A. *Origins of the Book: Egypt's Contribution to the Development of the Book from Papyrus to Codex*. Greenwich, Conn.: New York Graphic Society, 1972.
An accessible introduction that traces the evolution of the book in Egypt from papyrus roll to medieval Arabic codex. Although Hussein thus limits his account geographically, developments in Egypt are indicative of those throughout the Mediterranean world. Moreover, in antiquity Egypt was a major center of book production, a source of papyrus, and a source of binding and illustrations. This historical survey examines in turn the age of the Pharaohs, the Greco-Roman era, the Coptic book, and the book in Islamic Egypt to the fourteenth century. With forty-two color plates, eighty-four black-and-white illustrations, and a three-page bibliography.

Kenney, E. J. "Books and Readers in the Roman World." In *The Cambridge History of Classical Literature*. Vol. 2, *Latin Literature*, edited by E. J. Kenney. Cambridge, England: Cambridge University Press, 1982.
Sketches "the conditions under which books were composed, copied, circulated, preserved, studied, and used" in the Roman world (third century B.C.-fifth century A.D.). Kenney observes that Roman literature and education followed Greek models. While a book trade existed, formal publishing did not. Rich Romans had slaves who copied manuscripts. Kenney sees Atticus as arranging for the dissemination of the works of his friends but not acting as a true publisher. Yet Roman books traveled widely. Martial says that his poems were read as far away from Rome as Britain; Pliny the Younger speaks of a bookseller in Lyons.

Authors probably received no profits from the sale of their books. Instead they relied on patronage, though booksellers may have paid for an author's exemplum (copy text). G. Asinius Pollio established the first public library in Rome in 39 B.C. By the reign of Constantine, Rome had twenty-eight. The shift from roll to codex in the early centuries A.D. led to the loss of many manuscripts not copied onto parchment. Those thought worthy of being recopied had a far better chance of surviving into modern times. Kenney argues that the modern reader, provided with a well-edited text and reference works, can more easily read and understand Latin literature than could the Romans of antiquity.

Kenyon, Frederic G. *Ancient Books and Modern Discoveries*. Chicago: Caxton Club, 1927.
Most of this beautiful book examines the various materials used for writing surfaces, particularly clay, papyrus, and parchment. The focus is on "substances which have played [an important] part in the early history of our civilisation, and on which substantial works have been written." Kenyon provides good descriptions of books in antiquity, and the thirty plates following the text nicely illustrate his points. Kenyon also recounts the locating of such important items as the clay tablets at Knossos or the Oxyrhynchus papyri in Egypt.

_____. *Books and Readers in Ancient Greece and Rome*. 2d ed. Oxford, England: Clarendon Press, 1951.
A well-written, learned account. Kenyon first discusses the increase in reading in ancient Greece. Though the alphabet existed from the eighth century B.C. onwards, not until the age of Aristotle in the fourth century B.C. did reading and libraries proliferate. Books in this period consisted of papyrus rolls. Kenyon describes these in great detail. In the second and third centuries A.D., the papyrus codex began to supplant the roll for Christian literature, and soon the vellum codex became the dominant form of the book, though papyrus rolls persisted into the sixth century. In an appendix, Kenyon presents Pliny the Elder's discussion of papyrus (drawn from the *Natural History*), giving both the Latin and an English translation. Also quoted are other Latin comments that deal with the physical book. For these Kenyon offers no English equivalent.

Knox, Bernard MacGregor Walker. "Books and Readers in the Greek World." In *The Cambridge History of Classical Literature*. Vol. 1, *Greek Literature*, edited by P. E. Easterling and B. M. W. Knox. Cambridge, England: Cambridge University Press, 1985.

Greece had a literature before it had an alphabet to record it. By the late eighth century B.C. the works of Homer and Hesiod had been written down, though no books survive from before the late fourth century B.C. Earlier vase paintings provide evidence that Greek books resembled those of Egypt, the source for bookmaking material. Graffiti and other bits of writing suggest widespread literacy. Plato's *Apology* of Socrates and Aristophanes' *Frogs* talk about reading books; Xenophon mentions the book collector Euthydemus. Plato's Academy probably had a library; Strabo calls Aristotle "the first whom we know who collected books." Aristotle's works are filled with citations from other texts. Once one reaches the Hellenistic period evidence about books and the book trade markedly increases. There were no publishers, but authors, booksellers, and collectors arranged to have texts copied. The results were usually error-laden. Greek books spread throughout the known world, with their center in the vast Alexandrian library and museum (a research institute). Knox concludes his essay with observations about the survival of Greek texts through the Middle Ages and into the Renaissance.

Lewis, Naphtali. *Papyrus in Classical Antiquity.* Oxford, England: Clarendon Press, 1974.
Part 1 discusses the plant, Part 2 the writing surface made from it, and Part 3 the industry that this form of paper spawned. Lewis notes that papyrus was serving as a writing surface by 3000 B.C., and it was "the principal writing material of Western Civilization for over three millennia thereafter." By the sixth century B.C., the Greeks were using the material; later, Roman conquest spread papyrus to the entire ancient world. Egypt was the major supplier, with Alexandria at the center of production and trade. Lewis argues that prosperous villagers and laborers could not afford papyrus, but the upper middle class could. Lawrence S. Thompson called this "the definitive work on papyrus as a product and an article of commerce" (*Papers of the Bibliographical Society of America* 71, 1977, 408). *Choice* (12, 1975, 822) thought the book of "major interest to students of papyrology, ancient historians, students of library science, librarians concerned with the history of the book, and historians of paper."

Pinner, H. L. *The World of Books in Classical Antiquity.* Leiden, Netherlands: A. W. Sijthoff, 1948.
A brief and pleasant survey with bibliographic notes and fourteen plates depicting ancient libraries, scrolls and other writing materials, and people reading. Covering much the same ground as Frederic G.

Kenyon's *Books and Readers in Ancient Greece and Rome* (cited herein) but in less detail, Pinner devotes chapters to scrolls and parchment codices, the Greek book trade, publishing in Rome, bookshops in antiquity, and book collecting in the ancient world. He finds an active trade in books from the fourth century B.C. onward. Authors were not protected by copyright and apparently received no money for their writing. All profits went to the publishers, who had to supply the materials and the educated scribes. Even in Rome these scribes were apt to be Greek; hence, their transcriptions of Latin texts were not always reliable. *Greece and Rome* 6 (1959): 121 praised Pinner's work.

"Publishers Before the Age of Printing." *Cornhill Magazine* 9 (1864): 26-32.

Deals with publishing in Rome around the time of Caesar Augustus, when large enterprises existed for the copying of manuscripts. According to this article, "Roman publishers exhibited immense activity, issued large and cheap editions, and made large profits." Drawing on the literature of the period the article notes that publication occurred orally as well as in manuscript, there being many free public readings: In a letter, Pliny the Younger comments that there has been a reading every day for a month. Seneca mocked the bibliomaniacs of the age; Martial claimed to be in every Roman hand and pocket. Martial also talks about the relatively low cost of his works, though fine bindings could raise the price. Books could be plentiful and cheap because of slave labor. Because transcriptions were made from dictation, errors could arise to bedevil later editors.

Putnam, George Haven. *Authors and Their Public in Ancient Times.* 3d ed., rev. New York: G. P. Putnam's Sons, 1923.

Putnam begins this investigation into the business of books with an examination of the earliest forms of writing: clay tablets in Assyria, the Book of the Dead in Egypt, folk songs and epics in the Orient, and Hebrew religious works. Next he looks at Greek literature, published first orally and then in papyrus rolls. In the Hellenistic era Alexandria replaced Athens as the major book market; Rome in turn surpassed Egypt, and Constantinople succeeded Rome. Putnam offers a good study of literary property in antiquity, but his ignorance of Latin and Greek leads him into blunders. Some of these errors do not affect his arguments; others are more damaging, such as when he incorrectly claims that Greek dramatic poets earned money from the sale of theater tickets.

Roberts, Colin Henderson, and Theodore Cressy Skeat. *The Birth of the Codex*. London: Oxford University Press for the British Academy, 1983.

The authors trace the evolution of the codex from its origin as a wooden writing tablet. Parchment notebooks followed. In the first century A.D., Martial commended the codex, but his preference appears not to have been shared. Christianity, however, almost immediately adopted the codex, probably at Jerusalem and Antioch. The codex's compactness and convenience and the success of Christianity encouraged the shift from roll to codex. By 300 A.D., roll and codex had achieved parity, and thereafter the codex predominated. Still, the roll persisted well into the Middle Ages.

Thomas, Rosalind. *Literacy and Orality in Ancient Greece*. Cambridge, England: Cambridge University Press, 1992.

Thomas first examines recent theories of literacy and orality. She argues that orality and literacy are not mutually exclusive; in archaic and classical Greece the two modes coexisted. Indeed, she writes, "Most archaic writing was largely used in the service of the spoken word." Legal documents often depended on oral supplements. Similarly, inscriptions seem incomplete to modern readers, but the Greeks assumed that memory would piece out the compressed text. Writing thus served as a mnemonic aid, not as a substitute for memory. Written texts were transmitted orally, and texts were read to be memorized. Not until the third century B.C. was poetry fully written out; until then the written text was not as important as the spoken words it recorded. An epilogue considers the role of literacy in the Roman world. Thomas suggests that even here orality may have been more persistent than previously believed. A readable, informed study with an extensive bibliography.

Thompson, Edward Maunde. *An Introduction to Greek and Latin Paleography*. Oxford, England: Clarendon Press, 1912.

See entry under "THE ALPHABET."

Turner, Eric G. *Greek Manuscripts of the Ancient World*. Princeton, N.J.: Princeton University Press, 1971.

This companion volume to Turner's *Greek Papyri* (cited herein) presents a sampling of Greek papyri from about 350 B.C. to 600 A.D. The material is arranged by genre and fully described to demonstrate the appearance of ancient writing. The introduction explores various facets of the book in antiquity. For example, Turner denies an absolute division between bookhands and cursive writing, noting that scribes often combined the two forms. Whereas parchment is ruled before writing begins, papyrus apparently was not. Turner discusses the rudimentary punctuation and other markings and the use of writing style to help date a manuscript. J. Neville Birdsall commented, "Here is a wealth of learning presented with a very becoming modesty, but never without scholarly authority. . . . It is not only a study which immediately stimulates and instructs us, but one which arouses the confidence that it will continue to supply instruction and illumination to each reader for many a year" (*Library* 27, 1972, 59). The *Times Literary Supplement* was equally enthusiastic: "The introduction and the detailed commentary on the plates are a mine of information about how the Greeks wrote different kinds of books . . . , their equipment, their conventions, their aids to the reader, and their corrections and explanatory notes. . . . This is a work of great expertise" (September 3, 1971, 1066).

_____. *Greek Papyri: An Introduction.* Princeton, N.J.: Princeton University Press, 1968.
This superb work examines Greek and Roman texts from the fourth century B.C. to the eighth century A.D. Turner, a professor of papyrology and editor of the Oxyrhynchus papyri, considers the materials used to construct these manuscripts, their rediscovery in Egypt, geographical distribution, editorial practices, ownership of papyri in the ancient world, the significance of papyri to students of Greek literature, types of papyrus documents and the state of papyrology. He concludes with a list of major editions of papyri. With extensive bibliographical notes. John F. Oates called the opening chapter "the latest and best survey of the book in antiquity" and recommended the entire volume as "useful and interesting [to] all who have any interest in classical antiquity, whether curious layman, teacher, student, or scholar" (*The Classical Journal* 64, 1968, 187).

Weitzmann, Kurt. *Ancient Book Illumination.* Cambridge, Mass.: Harvard University Press, 1959.
See entry under "ILLUSTRATION."

_____. *Late Antique and Early Christian Book Illumination.* New York: George Braziller, 1977.
Illustrations in papyrus rolls resemble comic strips, depicting many events in quick succession. The codex eliminated the possibility for such serial depiction but allowed more scope for the individual picture.

Christian book illustration adopted pagan conventions. Most of the illustrated books of the early centuries A.D. were produced in major metropolitan areas: Rome, Alexandria, Antioch, and Constantinople. Towards the end of the period that Weitzmann examines, abstract form replaces the classical tradition of realistic representation. Includes seventeen black-and-white illustrations in the text and forty-eight full-page color plates, which Weitzmann analyzes on the facing page. An excellent introduction to a subject that no one knew better than Weitzmann. With a selective bibliography.

——————. *Studies in Classical and Byzantine Manuscript Illumination.* Edited Herbert L. Kessler. Chicago: University of Chicago Press, 1971.
See entry under "ILLUSTRATION."

Wiseman, D. J. *Cylinder Seals of Western Asia.* London: Batchworth Press, 1959.
Examines the cylinder seals that were used from the fourth millennium B.C. to the collapse of the Persian Empire in the fourth century B.C. Wiseman considers the ways these seals served as a means of writing and decoration. Most of the book presents photographs of seals owned by the British Museum. The text briefly examines the manufacture and design of these seals and traces their three-thousand-year history.

Chapter 11
THE MIDDLE AGES

Bibliography

Banks, Doris. *Medieval Manuscript Bookmaking: A Bibliographic Guide*. Metuchen, N.J.: Scarecrow Press, 1989.
A collection of bibliographic essays followed by an alphabetical listing of 1044 books and articles treated in the text. Chapters discuss books in the Middle Ages, medieval libraries, the manuscript book and the Church, universities and books, the impact of economic and social conditions on books, and science and technology. Seeks to place book production in its social, religious, and historical context. Includes maps showing monastic centers of book production and medieval universities. Ian Rogerson calls this "a most useful introduction for the layman or student" (*Library Association Record* 92, 1990, 860).

Histories

Alexander, Jonathan J. G. *Insular Manuscripts Sixth to Ninth Century*. London: Harvey Miller, 1978.
Volume 1 of *A Survey of Manuscripts Illuminated in the British Isles*, this study offers a catalog of seventy eight manuscripts, with descriptions and bibliography, together with 380 illustrations. The short introduction discusses the achievement of the Insular style, which persisted into the twelfth century. Alexander examines its break with classical ornamentation in favor of the abstract. Among the glories of this period are the Book of Kells, the Book of Durrow, and the Lindisfarne Gospels. As these works indicate, Christianity's emphasis on the book focused artistic efforts on text and illumination, and these two elements fuse in the historiated initial. *The Book Collector*, dealing with this volume and that by Elzbieta Temple covering the years 900-1066, observed, "The admirably comprehensive and thoughtfully arranged plates combine with the text to provide the best survey of this great period of British art yet produced" (28, 1979, 183). John Beckwith commented, "No student of early medieval art can possibly ignore" Alexander's study (*Apollo* 109, 1979, 328).

_____. *Medieval Illuminators and Their Methods of Work*. New Haven, Conn.: Yale University Press, 1992.

Covers the history of illumination from the fourth to the sixteenth century. In addition to treating techniques, Alexander considers the lives of the artists in their social and historical milieux. He observes that in the early Middle Ages, monks were the primary illuminators, making books for their own monasteries. By the thirteenth century, lay scribes and illuminators had become dominant, and among these were women. Alexander has looked at many manuscripts and at contracts revealing the concerns of patrons for whom the books were created. With 218 black-and-white illustrations.

Avril, Françoise. *Manuscript Painting at the Court of France: The Fourteenth Century (1310-1380)*. Translated by Ursule Molinaro, with the assistance of Bruce Benderson. New York: George Braziller, 1978.

French manuscript painting in the fourteenth century is largely Parisian, patronized by the monarchy and the court. Avril traces the shifting styles and those responsible for them. The century opens with the Master Honoré's plastic treatment and the solidity of the depictions by the artists who created *The Life of St. Denis* (1317). Jean Pucelle fused these two approaches around 1320, as is evident in *The Hours of Jeanne d'Evreux* (1325-1328), which includes the earliest medieval attempt north of Italy to recreate an interior in three dimensions. Pucelle's influence long survived the artist's death in 1334. Toward the end of the century, naturalism replaced the idealized portrayals of Pucelle and his immediate successors. Illustrated with forty color plates and thirteen black- and-white figures.

Backhouse, Janet. *The Illuminated Manuscript*. Oxford, England: Phaidon, 1979.

Presents seventy manuscripts from the collection in the British Library. Begins with the Lindisfarne Gospels (c. 698) and concludes with an atlas produced around 1558. In her discussion of these manuscripts, Backhouse presents a history of the book in the Middle Ages within the context of other developments. A fine introduction to the subject. Most of the illustrations are in black and white, but the slim volume includes some striking color reproductions, such as the full-page miniature of the Annunciation from the Hours of Henry VII (France, c. 1500).

Basing, Patricia. *Trades and Crafts in Medieval Manuscripts*. New York: New Amsterdam Books, 1990.

Illuminated manuscripts provide valuable information to students of art history and religion; they also reveal much about daily life in the Middle Ages. The Luttrell Psalter, for example, produced before 1340 for Sir Geoffrey Luttrell of Irnham, Lincolnshire, contains what Basing calls "the finest set of agricultural scenes in a medieval manuscript" and thus demonstrates farm practices of the early fourteenth century. Basing's chapters examine agriculture, trade, industry and crafts, and the professions as they appear in medieval illumination. She notes that realism increases in later medieval works. With sixty-five black-and-white and fourteen color reproductions.

Bologna, Giulia. *Illuminated Manuscripts: The Book Before Gutenberg.* Translated by Jay Hyams. New York: Weidenfeld & Nicolson, 1988.
A beautifully produced oversize volume concentrating on the thousand-year history of the medieval book. Opens with a discussion of the book in the ancient world. The majority of the volume is devoted to full-page color reproductions with brief annotations. The earliest example comes from the Vatican Virgil (c. 400), the latest from the sixteenth century. Concludes with a discussion of American and European libraries with important manuscript holdings, biographical sketches of illuminators, and a selective bibliography.

Bradley, John William. *Illuminated Manuscripts.* 2d ed. London: Methuen, 1920.
Still a useful survey despite its age. This well-illustrated volume presents a sound overview of the medieval book. Reviewing the first edition, *The Nation* observed, "Mr. Bradley has labored valiantly with the difficulties of his vast theme, and has assembled skillfully a great amount of literary and antiquarian information" (89, 1909, 582).

Branner, Robert. *Manuscript Painting in Paris During the Reign of St. Louis: A Study of Styles.* Berkeley: University of California Press, 1977.
An important study of "manuscript paintshops active in Paris in the middle half of the thirteenth century." Branner argues that each workshop developed its own style. He notes that the first half of St. Louis' reign is characterized by the number of manuscripts produced; later, quality becomes more remarkable than quantity. The Bible was the work most frequently illuminated; copies were smaller and less ornate than their twelfth century predecessors. Usually only the opening scene of a book was illustrated, but Branner finds enough variation to question the widespread use of model books. He examines the styles

of the various workshops and the more general shifts in illustration that characterize the period. Includes a list of illuminators, scribes, booksellers, and parchment makers known to be working in mid-thirteenth century Paris; identifies the scribal hands in a number of important manuscripts; and lists the subjects illustrated. With 438 reproductions, twenty-five of them in color.

Brown, Michelle P. *Anglo-Saxon Manuscripts*. Toronto: University of Toronto Press, 1991.
The seventy-seven illustrations in this slim volume demonstrate the beauty and variety of the English manuscript tradition from the fifth to the eleventh century. Texts and the methods of producing them reveal influences from classical antiquity, Christianity, Continental practices, even the Middle East. Brown's introduction offers an overview of the period. She then examines book production and use, materials and techniques, script, and illumination. Also provides a brief bibliography.

Browning, L. L., ed. *Medieval Book Production: Assessing the Evidence*. Los Altos Hills, Calif.: Anderson-Lovelace and the Red Gull Press, 1990. Presents eleven essays that examine "how medieval books were produced, where, for whom, and by whom." A. I. Doyle starts the discussion by looking at monastic book production to determine the extent to which manuscripts were produced in the monasteries and to what extent monks turned to lay writers and artists. Peter Jones collates two manuscripts to speculate on the practices of medieval translators and the relationshop between the two texts he examines. Lynda Dennison's contribution follows the creation of a deluxe Psalter; Michael Gullick considers the possible Norman origins of some late eleventh and early twelfth century manuscripts in the Durham Cathedral Library. The work of the scriptorium of Frankenthal (near Worms) during the twelfth century is the topic of Aliza Cohen-Mushlin. Richard and Mary Rouse deal with commercial book production in Paris in the late Middle Ages. Claudine A. Chavannes-Mazel discusses the aesthetic considerations of manuscript design. Margaret A. Smith moves to the world of printing to determine what incomplete rubrication tells about book production. Claire Donovan relates the format of the Book of Hours in England to their use, and Adelaide Bennett notes the important role woman played as patrons of manuscripts. The volume concludes with an essay by Lucy Freeman Sandler on how James le Palmer arranged for the creation of the elaborate late fourteenth century encyclopedic *Omne bonum*. This collection of essays is handsome and informative, reflecting the state of the art of manuscript studies in 1990.

Cahn, Walter. *Romanesque Bible Illumination*. Ithaca, N.Y.: Cornell University Press, 1982.
Begins with a discussion of the few examples of illustrated Bibles that predate the Carolingian Renaissance. The second chapter treats Bible illumination under Charlemagne and his successors, and Chapter 3 looks at developments among the Mozarabs of Spain, the Anglo-Saxons, and Ottonians. In Chapter 4 he comes to the main topic of the work, illumination in the eleventh and twelfth centuries, and he provides some 200 black-and-white illustrations together with sixty striking color plates to enrich his text. At the end of the book is a selective catalog of 150 Romanesque Bibles, with locations, descriptions, and sources for further study. Mark Stevens calls this "a serious, well-researched book about work that is not as well known as late medieval illumination" (*Newsweek* 100, December 13, 1982, 98).

Calkins, Robert G. *Illuminated Books of the Middle Ages*. Ithaca, N.Y.: Cornell University Press, 1984.
Focusing on religious books, Calkins, a professor of art history at Cornell University, first traces the earliest Biblical manuscripts. He then examines in detail three Insular Gospel Books (the Book of Durrow, the Lindisfarne Gospels, and the Book of Kells), the Carolingian Bible of Charles the Bald (846), the Codex Aureus of St. Emmeram, also created for Charles and completed in 870, the Periscopes of Henry II (c. 1010), a number of prayerbooks, the Windmill Psalter (English, late thirteenth century), and the "London Hours," which reveals both French and Italian influences. Calkins emphasizes the relationship between the purpose of the text and its illumination and notes how illuminations within a codex create "an appropriate decorative program." With twenty-four color illustrations and 158 in black-and-white and a ten-page bibliography. Rosamond McKitterick, in the *Times Literary Supplement* for December 30, 1983, calls this "a fine and lucid introduction. . . . An invaluable addition to studies of book illumination in the Middle Ages" (1468).

Camille, Michael. *Image on the Edge: The Margins at Medieval Art*. Cambridge, Mass.: Harvard University Press, 1992.
Examine manuscript and architectural ornamentation in the late Gothic period (1200-1400). Camille links the flowering of liminal art "to changing reading patterns, rising literacy, and the increasing use of scribal records as forms of social control. Things written or drawn in the margins add an extra dimension . . . that is able to gloss, parody, modernize and problematize the text's authority while never totally

undermining it." The first (and longest) chapter examines medieval manuscripts per se. The next four look at representational details in manuscripts and other art. Camille argues that because truth in the medieval world was firmly established, artists enjoyed the freedom to experiment on the margins.

Carr, Annemarie Weyl. *Byzantine Illumination 1150-1250: The Study of a Provincial Tradition.* Chicago: University of Chicago Press, 1987.
Carr looks at more than a hundred illuminated manuscripts from the eastern Mediterranean and provides twelve color fiche filled with illustrations. Most of the books are nonliturgical; sixty contain the four Gospels, ten are psalters, five include the New Testament, and ten others combine New Testament and Psalter. Carr discusses the manufacture, script, iconography, and style of illustration, seeking to understand the relationships among the manuscripts and their connection to Byzantine art. She also considers when, for whom, and where they were created. The text is informative but unattractive, having been reproduced from typescript.

Carruthers, Mary. *The Book of Memory: A Study of Memory in Medieval Culture.* Cambridge, England: Cambridge University Press, 1990.
Carruthers considers the medieval emphasis on memory rather than on documentation or imagination, and she explores how this mentality affected the book. Even when books became relatively abundant in the late Middle Ages, writing was regarded as an adjunct to memory, not a substitute; and illustrations served not to provide texts for the illiterate but as mnemonic devices for readers. Even the marginal grotesques acted as memory aids. Decorative marginalia of birds, coins, bees, fruit, flowers, and jewels serve as metaphors for memory. Carruthers writes that such illustrations are neither iconographic nor illustrative. Rather, "They serve the basic function of all page decoration, to make each page memorable, but they also serve to remind readers of the purpose of books as a whole—that they contain matter to be laid away in their memorial storehouse."

Cazelles, Raymond, and Johannes Rathofer. *Illuminations of Heaven and Earth: The Glories of the "Très riches heures du duc de Berry."* New York: Harry N. Abrams, 1988.
The *Très Riches Heures,* created for the fifteenth century French bibliophile Jean de Berry, has been called the "King of Illuminated Manuscripts." This volume reproduces all 131 miniatures and enlarges details, offering over 300 illustrations, of which 285 appear in full

color. In his introduction, Umberto Eco discusses the masterpiece as a medieval encyclopedia and as "a cinematic document, a visual presentation that reveals the life of an age. But no film could ever match the scrupulousness, the splendor, the moving beauty of its reconstruction." Cazelles and Rathofer then proceed through the Book of Hours, explaining the creation and significance of the art. Includes an extensive bibliography.

D'Ancona, Paolo, and Erardo Aeschlimann. *The Art of Illumination: An Anthology from the Sixth to the Sixteenth Century.* Translated by Alison M. Brown. London: Phaidon, 1969.
A beautifully illustrated survey of illuminated manuscripts from late classical antiquity to the Renaissance. The volume begins with a quick overview of the period, referring the reader to specific plates. These 145 full-page reproductions are followed by notes discussing the manuscripts and the specific examples depicted. Includes bibliographic references. *Connoisseur* regarded this volume as "a thoroughly useful and sensibly arranged introduction to the subject" (176, 1971, 292).

De Hamel, Christopher. *A History of Illuminated Manuscripts.* Boston: David R. Godine, 1986.
Eighty full-color and 140 black-and-white illustrations enrich this masterly survey by the longtime head of Sotheby's Western Manuscripts department (London). Instead of concentrating on the high spots only, De Hamel looks at a wide range of material, which he has grouped by purpose or customer. The large illustrations in the Insular Gospel Books served the same function that Bede ascribes to the pictures in the church at Wearmouth, "that all . . . even if ignorant of letters, might be able to contemplate . . . the ever-gracious countenance of Christ and His Saints." Emperors wanted books as treasure: the Vienna Coronation Gospels, supposedly buried with Charlemagne, is written in gold on purple vellum. The wide-ranging holdings of twelfth century monastic libraries reveal the effort to embrace all knowledge. The rise of the university called forth more books and stimulated the secular book trade. Aristocrats commissioned fine volumes for their libraries, and as literacy expanded the middle class needed and wanted books as well. The most popular of these volumes was the Book of Hours. Books for priests were of course liturgical, and the earliest printed works responded to the demand for lectern Bibles, Psalters, and sermons. Humanist collectors commissioned reprints of classical texts; since the earliest surviving manuscripts often dated from the Carolingian period,

humanists adopted a version of this minuscule scribal hand, which later influenced humanistic type. To expedite copying, scribes began to join letters and so created *italic*. Rich collectors like the Medici could afford whole libraries of elaborate manuscripts. Janet Backhouse called this "a lively, entertaining, and down-to-earth book which can be recommended without reserve to all who are interested in [the] subject, whether they be experienced specialists or novices" (*Library* 9, 1987, 282). Hope Mayo praised the study in *Library Quarterly* 57 (1987): 210-213; Bernard McTigue in *American Book Collector* 7 (October, 1986): 45 wrote that "all students of the illuminated book will find something of use and interest for them herein." Also recommended by Rosamond McKitterick in the *Times Literary Supplement* for July 11, 1986, 771.

Delaisse, L. M. J. *A Century of Dutch Manuscript Illumination*. Berkeley: University of California Press, 1968.
A study of Dutch miniaturists from the late fourteenth to late fifteenth century. Delaisse finds a realism in their work that foreshadows seventeenth century Dutch art. Whereas other national styles of the period are idealized, "many human representations among the Dutch miniaturists are so individualized that they strike us as having a portrait quality." Landscape, too, is realistic rather than stylized. Symbolism plays a less important role in Dutch illumination than elsewhere in Europe; Dutch manuscript painting humanizes religious scenes. This artistic tendency is related to the Modern Devotion, a powerful religious force in the Low Countries in the fifteenth century; the movement rejected mystery in an effort to humanize Christianity. The volume includes 161 illustrations.

Diringer, David. *The Illuminated Book: Its History and Production*. Rev. ed. New York: Frederick A. Praeger, 1967.
A standard, comprehensive study, full of learning but written for the layman, surveying the purpose of illumination from the Egyptian Book of the Dead (c. 2000 B.C.) through the eighteenth century, though the focus is on medieval manuscripts. Filled with illustrations, the volume explores the diverse styles of illumination and discusses specific examples. Diringer provides a bibliography at the end of each unit and also a general bibliography at the end of the book.

Donovan, Claire. *The De Brailes Hours: Shaping the Book of Hours in Thirteenth-Century Oxford*. Toronto: University of Toronto Press, 1991.

William de Brailes created the first surviving Book of Hours around 1240. This professional illuminator, active in Oxford, prepared the book for a woman named Susanna; the volume probably supplemented her Psalter, since this manuscript omits the calendar and the Office of the Dead. Donovan provides a tour through the manuscript, exploring the more than one hundred illustrations that accompany and comment on the text. Donovan argues for close collaboration between illuminator and patron. For example, this Book of Hours includes illustrations of the story of Susanna and the Elders, a tribute to the woman who commissioned the work. A concluding chapter discusses successors to the De Brailes Hours. Appendices provide a table of iconography, a summary of the contents (which shows that the manuscript follows the liturgical use of Sarum but with enough variation to suggest that the text for a Book of Hours had not yet been fully established by 1240), brief descriptions of the other eight known thirteenth century Books of Hours produced in England, a list of manuscripts illuminated at Oxford between 1200 and 1270, and documents referring to William de Brailes. T.A. Heslop wrote in the *Times Literary Supplement* for March 20, 1992, "The book deserves to reach a wide audience. . . . Claire Donovan's attempt to recreate for a modern audience the devotional round of a thirteenth-century lady is an enterprising stimulus to the historical imagination of a kind all too rarely found in studies of manuscripts" (p. 24).

Dupont, Jacques, and Cesare Gnudi. *Gothic Painting.* trans. Stuart Gilbert. Geneva: Skira, 1954.
Looks at all facets of art in the thirteenth and fourteenth centuries—murals, stained glass, painting, tapestries, and illuminated manuscripts—throughout Europe. The book thus notes how the various media interrelate. The Psalter of St. Louis (1256), for example, depicts pinnacles, rose windows, and other features of Gothic architecture. The Limbourg brothers copied one of Taddeo Gaddi's frescoes and duplicated Gothic architecture in their *Trés Riches Heures of Jean de Berry*, and the portrayal of fashionable lords and ladies in that work is echoed in frescoes and murals. The volume is enriched throughout with glowing color reproductions of the art of the period, many of these taken from manuscripts.

Ettinghausen, Richard. *Turkish Manuscripts from the Thirteenth to the Eighteenth Century.* New York: New American Library, 1965.
A study of Turkish manuscript painting from the Seljuks to the Ottomans. Though Turkish art derives from Persia, the former is more

realistic, more concerned with the present; and love, a central concern of Persian art, is absent. Also, Turkish illumination often concerns itself with the lower classes. Ettinghausen notes how Turkish artists drew on conventions of both the East and West to create their peculiar style. The short book includes twenty-one color plates and two black-and-white illustrations.

Gameson, Richard, ed. *The Early Medieval Bible: Its Production, Decoration, and Use.* Cambridge, England: Cambridge University Press, 1994.

"The [eleven] chapters in this book elucidate various aspects of Latin Bible manuscripts, their production, decoration, and interpretation, use and general cultural significance from Antiquity to the thirteenth century" (preface). The volume opens with Patrick McGurk's essay on the oldest known manuscripts of the Latin Bible, a study based on 363 surviving examples from before 800. Many are mere fragments, but these examples include the Book of Kells and the Lindisfarne Gospels, arguably the finest manuscript gospel books ever produced. Gameson then looks in detail at one such early gospel book as a way of understanding book production in Britain in the seventh and eighth centuries. Other studies examine Carolingian Bibles and Psalters as well as Bibles in Italy and France in the later Middle Ages. Erik Petersen writes about the Hamburg Bible, which contains illustrations of thirteenth century bookmaking. Lesley Smith concludes the collection by noting that for the medieval reader the Bible was Christ, not just about Christ: It is the Word made flesh. A good companion to Margaret T. Gibson's *The Bible in the Latin West* (cited in this chapter).

Ganz, Peter, ed. *The Role of the Book in Medieval Culture: Proceedings of the Oxford International Symposium 26 September-1 October 1982.* 2 vols. Turnhout, Belgium: Brepols, 1986.

The papers in these two volumes are divided into five sections: The Making of the Book, Preparation of the Text, The Book as Evidence of Literacy, the Collection of Books, and Glossed Books as an Instrument of Continuity and Change. Not all the articles are in English, and many deal with specialized subjects, such as ruling techniques for manuscripts. Some, however, are of more general interest. For example, R. M. Thomson discusses the effect of the Norman Conquest on English libraries; he sees the invasion as salutary, promoting book production and preservation. Also likely to appeal to a general audience are Paul Meyvaert's essay on medieval forgers and F. Mutherich's "The Library of Otto III."

Gibson, Margaret T. *The Bible in the Latin West*. Notre Dame, Ind.: University of Notre Dame Press, 1993.

Inaugurating a series of studies of the medieval book, Gibson's work examines the history of the chief text of the Christian West, the Vulgate and its variants. The introduction traces scribal practices from late antiquity to the sixteenth century. Cassiodorus (c. 530-580) described the typical Bible of his day as being divided into nine volumes, though he also knew of large one-volume pandects (complete texts). The Codex Amiatinus, produced in Northern England around 700, is modeled on such a manuscript. Gibson notes the contributions of monastic scriptoria, the Parisian book trade, and finally the printing press in shaping the form and content of the Latin Bible. Following this fifteen-page survey are 28 black-and-white plates illustrating the trends discussed in the text. Facing each full-page facsimile is an analysis of the manuscript.

Goldschmidt, Adolph. *German Illumination*. 2 vols. Florence: Pantheon and Casa Editrice, 1928.

Translated from the German, this volume has become a standard reference because of the more than two hundred excellent plates. Volume 1 deals with the Carolingian period, Volume 2 with Ottonian. Goldschmidt's text, though running only to thirty-four pages, provides much information in its sound overview. Bibliographic references appear at the end of Volume 2.

Grabar, André, and Carl Nordenfalk. *Early Medieval Painting from the Fourth to the Eleventh Century*. Translated by Stuart Gilbert. New York: Skira, 1957.

Grabar treats mosaics and murals, Nordenfalk the illuminated manuscript. Nordenfalk notes that illumination preserved the techniques of classical art and so transmitted them to the Middle Ages, contributing to the periodic renaissances—England in the eighth century, France in the ninth, Germany and England around 1000. He traces the development and styles of illumination from late antiquity to the Ottonians; the text is lavishly illustrated throughout with full-color facsimiles. Includes a bibliography.

_____. *Romanesque Painting from the Eleventh to the Thirteenth Century*. Translated by Stuart Gilbert. New York: Skira, 1958.

The sequel to the authors' *Early Medieval Painting* (1957), this volume retains the division of labor of the earlier work. Nordenfalk again focuses on the illuminated manuscript; he notes that in the twelfth and thirteenth centuries the quantity of manuscripts increased, but their quality declined: Illumination seems derivative of the sister arts. France assumes the leadership in Romanesque illumination, which becomes an international style, penetrating to Bohemia in the east, supplanting or at least altering native traditions in Spain and Britain. Whereas Carolingian Bibles tended to consist of one volume, Romanesque Bibles range from two to five, in part because of the larger script but primarily because of extensive illumination. The Codex Gigas requires two people to lift it. Capital letters become more elaborate, the work of artists now rather than of scribes. Indeed, the letter can disappear beneath the art. Romanesque art reveals the influences of Byzantium and the Greco-Roman world; the pictures become three-dimensional, vital. A richly illustrated and informative study.

Gumbert, J. P. *The Dutch and Their Books in the Manuscript Age*. London: British Library, 1991.

From the tenth century, when book production began in the province of the diocese of Utrecht, until the fifteenth century, most of the Dutch manuscripts were made for religious houses and were neither remarkable for their artistry nor easily distinguishable from work done in neighboring areas. Matters improved in the fifteenth century, for which period there are more complete records. Typical of Dutch manuscripts of this time are "rake ruling" (making several lines at once) and "the decoration of initial letters by thin lines without shading," usually in blue and red but sometimes enriched with gold. Gumbert notes that Thomas à Kempis produced a five- volume Bible (1427-1438) and that the father of Erasmus worked as a scribe. H.R. Woudhuysen commented that this study "is dense and richly annotated, but . . . never loses sight of [its] subject matter, or of the general reader's interest" (*Times Literary Supplement*, August 30, 1991, 24).

Gutmann, Joseph. *Hebrew Manuscript Painting*. New York: George Braziller, 1978.

A brief survey of Hebrew illuminated manuscripts from about 900 to 1700. Gutmann finds no peculiarly Jewish style but rather observes similarities between Hebrew manuscripts and those produced by the surrounding community. Indeed, many of the illuminations in Hebrew manuscripts were executed by Christians and Moslems. Yet Hebrew script did lead to unique elements, such as micrography (use of minute letters) to create flowers or animals or geometric patterns. Also, God is never depicted. Gutmann's book concludes with forty color plates, each given a full page and accompanied by a discussion of the illustration as well as the manuscript from which it is taken.

Harris, William V. "Why Did the Codex Supplant the Book-Roll?" In *Renaissance Society and Culture: Essays in Honor of Eugene F. Rice, Jr.* Edited by John Monfasani and Ronald G. Musto. New York: Italica Press, 1991.
Provides a good survey of research on this question and offers a number of answers. The codex proved more economical because it used both sides of the writing surface. The codex also was simpler to use for reference and could contain more text than a roll. As book owners came to rely more heavily on the written word and less on memory, the codex became more popular because of the ease of finding a particular passage.

Harthan, John P. *The Book of Hours*. New York: Thomas Y. Crowell, 1977.
An anthology of about a hundred facsimiles taken from thirty-four Books of Hours, almost all reproduced in full color, some familiar, such as Christ as the Man of Sorrows in the *Trés Riches Heures of Jean de Berry*, others less well known, such as the Black Hours of Charles the Rash, Duke of Burgundy, with its text in gold on vellum stained black; the acid dye has severely damaged the leaves. Harthan's lengthy introduction discusses the books' content, artistry, and religious and historical significance. Although the examples illustrated were commissioned by the rich and powerful, Harthan notes the widespread appeal of Books of Hours, so that many, much simpler, were created for the middle class. A good introduction that will appeal to both the neophyte and the scholar. Alan Borg remarked, "Mr. Harthan has written one of the most engaging, interesting, and enjoyable of recent books on Medieval art" (*Connoisseur* 197, 1978, 145). John Beckwith affords a similarly favorable review in *Apollo* 109 (1978): 76.

_____. *An Introduction to Illuminated Manuscripts*. London: Victoria and Albert Museum, 1983.
A survey of the topic based on the holdings of the Victoria and Albert Museum, where Harthan served as librarian. In fewer than fifty pages, Harthan discusses production of the manuscripts and styles of illumination. He observes that people specialized in particular skills and that in the later Middle Ages, lay workshops became more important than monastic scriptoria for the production of manuscripts. With some thirty illustrations, most of them in color. A good book for the novice.

Henderson, George. *From Durrow to Kells: The Insular Gospel-Books, 650-800.* New York: Thames and Hudson, 1987.

Henderson seeks "to combine critical appraisal of the art and imagery of the Insular Gospel-books with a consideration of their specific historical context." Looks at the seven surviving examples: the Book of Durrow (which he argues was produced in England); the Durham, Corpus, Echternach, Lindisfarne, and Lichfield Gospels; and the Book of Kells (which he assigns to Iona). Includes 263 black-and-white illustrations, most of them taken from the gospel books, but a number point out parallels between the ornamentation in the volumes and other artifacts of the period.

Herbert, John Alexander. *Illuminated Manuscripts.* London: Methuen, 1911.

Begins with a chapter on the illumination in the classical period; the rest of the book considers medieval manuscripts. The discussion is arranged geographically and chronologically. Though the black-and-white illustrations are disappointing, the text provides a solid history and a good analysis of diverse styles. Herbert is especially helpful in showing parallels among various national schools. *The Nation* praised Herbert's "scholarly accuracy and clearness" (94, 1912, 94).

Kauffmann, C. M. *Romanesque Manuscripts, 1066-1190.* London: Harvey Miller, 1975.

An illustrated catalog of 106 English illuminated manuscripts. Kauffmann traces the evolution of English Romanesque style, which shows much innovation and experimentation, and discusses Romanesque iconography. He finds that the twelfth century witnessed a renaissance that resulted in a great increase in manuscript production and prompted a new international style. The monasteries remained the major center of book production, but lay scriptoria gained in significance, and laymen often illuminated texts written by monks. An excellent survey of what the medievalist Neil Ripley Ker termed "the greatest [period] in the history of English book production." Alan Borg offers a warm review in *Connoisseur* 189 (July, 1975): 44.

Ker, Neil Ripley. *Books, Collectors, and Libraries: Studies in the Medieval Heritage.* London: Hambledon Press, 1985.

A collection of twenty-eight important pieces by this eminent historian of medieval books and libraries. The selections are divided into two groups; the first ten treat scribes and the making of books, and the remainder deal with specific manuscripts, libraries, and collectors.

Some of the essays range widely, such as a survey of cathedral libraries from their inception to the present. Others are highly focused, like the inventory of St. Paul's Cathedral library in the thirteenth century. Chronologically, these articles cover almost a millennium of the handwritten book, from a study of Aldred, who wrote the colophon of the Insular Lindisfarne Gospel-book, to considerations of the migration of manuscripts and of the Oxford College libraries in the sixteenth century.

_____. *English Manuscripts in the Century After the Norman Conquest: The Lyell Lectures, 1952-3*. Oxford, England: Oxford University Press, 1960.

Examines the changes in the appearance of English manuscripts in the wake of the Norman Conquest. In the hundred years following this eventm English scribal hands developed great clarity and accuracy, and far more manuscripts were produced than had been previously. Ker observes, though, that only at Durham, Canterbury, and Rochester did Norman script affect earlier scribal hands. Elsewhere the Carolingian hand already in use survived the Conquest until about 1170, when Gothic began replacing earlier letterforms. Among the changes after 1066 were the introduction of the two- column arrangement, the shortening of ascenders and descenders to allow closer spacing of lines, and the use of new forms of punctuation. Twenty-nine pages of facsimiles follow the text.

Lehmann-Haupt, Hellmut. *The Gottingen Model Book*. Rev. ed. Columbia: University of Missouri Press, 1978.

Together with the Berlin Model Book, this volume, reproduced in facsimile and translated, shows how illumination in Germany was done in the mid-1400s. Includes step-by-step instructions on the drawing and coloring of foliage, the making of pigments, the preparation of the manuscript to receive color, and the actual illumination. Decorations in the two printed Gutenberg Bibles, the Butzbach and Mainz manuscript Bibles (1454), and various prayerbooks show that illuminators used model books to produce work of high quality. *The Gottingen Model Book* places the reader back in the workshop of fifteenth century Mainz, where pigment is stirred with a clean finger and the vellum is prepared for painting with a rubbing of crumbs from rye bread.

Lowden, John. *The Octateuchs: A Study in Byzantine Manuscript Illumination*. University Park: Pennsylvania State University Press, 1992.

The Octateuch contains the Five Books of Moses, Joshua, Judges, and the Book of Ruth. The earliest extant manuscripts of these eight books in one volume date from the tenth century. Lowden focuses on five examples from the eleventh to thirteenth centuries, his interest prompted by their extensive cycle of illustrations. The five manuscripts illustrate some 550 scenes; Lowden includes nearly a third of these miniatures in his work. His examination of these manuscripts has led to him to challenge earlier assumptions about specific relationships and influences, such as Kurt Weitzmann's claim that the Joshua Roll was based on the Octateuch. Lowden also questions Weitzmann's broader contention that one can use illustrations to trace manuscripts back to common sources. Lowden maintains that scribes could create precise copies when they chose, but they also could innovate, so that "the relationships between images cannot be established beyond question on visual grounds alone." The book is useful for its information about the Octateuch and also for its larger implications for the study of medieval manuscript illumination.

McCracken, Ursula E., Lilian M. C. Randall, and Richard H. Randall, Jr., eds. *Gatherings in Honor of Dorothy E. Miner*. Baltimore: Walters Art Gallery, 1974.

Miner was for many years Keeper of Manuscripts at the Walters Art Gallery, a leading collection of medieval manuscripts. The essays in this volume explore various facets of these materials. Kurt Weitzmann examines a tenth century Greek New Testament, the earliest known example with evangelist portraits facing pictures of a feast. Francis Wormald discusses the monastic library; Rosalie Green looks at drawings in the margins of an Ottonian Gospel from around 1000; Carl Nordenfalk studies a tenth century Gospel-book and makes the case for its originating in the monastery of St. Benedict at Fleury-sur-Loire around 988. Among the other contributions is L. M. J. Delaisse's "The Importance of Books of Hours for the History of the Medieval Book." Because more of these survive than any other category of medieval manuscript, they can help localize a book, and they show how work was apportioned among various artisans—scribe, rubricator, and miniaturist.

McKitterick, Rosamond. *The Carolingians and the Written Word*. Cambridge, England: Cambridge University Press, 1989.

Argues for a high degree of literacy and book ownership in eighth and ninth century France and Germany and for widespread knowledge of Latin as a written and spoken language, not just in clerical circles but also among the laity and government officials. McKitterick first studies the writing of laws and finds "a widespread ability to communicate by means of the written word in the process of administration and government." Later chapters discuss the production and ownership of books, libraries and cataloging, and literacy levels among the laity. Marsha L. Dutton called this "an essential reference book for questions of medieval European literacy [and] invaluable in its wealth of information about manuscripts, scribes, monastic patrons, Carolingian nobility, and lay owners of books" (*Library Quarterly* 60, 1990, 257). Pauline Stafford observed that through McKitterick's efforts "the unpromising material of Carolingian library catalogues is made to yield a rich harvest, one to delight structuralists and enlighten all those interested in the construction of the western mind" (*History Today* 40, April, 1990, 58).

_____, ed. *The Uses of Literacy in Early Medieval Europe.* Cambridge, England: Cambridge University Press, 1990.

A collection of eleven essays on literacy in Europe between 400 and 1000. Jane Stevenson's opening essay argues for a native pre-Christian literacy in Ireland; this literacy fused with Christian emphasis on the book. By the seventh century, literacy in Ireland was widespread, as reflected in surviving Hiberno-Latin manuscripts. Susan Kelly then examines literacy among the Anglo-Saxon laity in England and finds that written documents played an important role in secular society before the Norman Conquest, even before Alfred the Great's efforts at lay education. Ian Wood looks at Merovingian Gaul, where he discovers a literate bureaucracy and aristocracy. Thomas F. X. Noble notes the papacy's reliance on written records. In Islamic Spain, the Caliph Al-Hakam II assembled an extensive library, and in late tenth century Cordoba, Jews and Christians as well as Moslems produced numerous texts, but even before the Arab invasion of Spain the Visigoth aristocracy maintained a high level of literacy. Roger Collins finds a modicum of literacy also among the Christian kingdoms of the ninth century in northern Spain. Jewish literacy under Islam between the sixth and eleventh centuries is the subject of Stefan C. Reif's essay; Reif claims that during this period Jewish literacy, already well established, increased. He suggests that the Hebrew codex first appeared in the eighth century. Subsequent articles examine writing in Byzantium (Margaret Mullett finds a variety of literacies, not necessarily the high level once attributed to this society), early ninth century inscriptions at the monastery of San Vincenzo al Volturno, the use of writing by the royal government in pre-Norman England and the Carolingian empire, and the relationship between word and image in Carolingian illuminated manuscripts.

Madan, Falconer. *Books in Manuscript: A Short Introduction to Their Study and Use.* 2d ed., rev. London: Kegan Paul, Trench, Trubner, 1927.
Intended as an introduction to the subject of manuscripts. Madan, who served as a lecturer in medieval paleography at Oxford and as bibliographer at the Bodleian Library, first discusses writing materials and the form of books before printing. He then surveys the development of writing and bookhands (including abbreviations), scriptoria and scribes in the Middle Ages, illumination, and errors in transcription. The book then presents short descriptions of important collections of manuscripts, of famous manuscripts such as the Codex Sinaiticus (the oldest surviving Biblical codex in Greek), and of forgeries. Madan concludes with advice on the treatment and cataloging of manuscripts and the importance of public and private records.

Marks, Richard, and Nigel Morgan. *The Golden Age of English Manuscript Painting, 1200-1500.* New York: George Braziller, 1981.
In the thirteenth century, manuscript production moved from the monastery to the town; patronage shifted from church to laity. These shifts coincide with the Gothic triumph and are reflected in the types of manuscripts illuminated. The great Bibles of the twelfth century yield to Psalters and Books of Hours; though some secular texts also were illuminated, English illumination of the period remained centered on religious works. This volume contains forty color plates and twenty-three black-and-white figures. In her review for *Burlington Magazine* (125, 1983, 364), Janet Backhouse regrets that the authors have tried to cover so much material in so short a volume, but she acknowledges their success in presenting important and new ideas and in reproducing some unfamiliar manuscripts in high-quality facsimiles.

Marrow, James H., et al. *The Golden Age of Dutch Manuscript Painting.* New York: George Braziller, 1990.
Published in association with a 1990 exhibit at the Pierpont Morgan Library, this sumptuous volume includes a number of essays enriched with 120 color plates and 162 black-and-white illustrations. Although French and Burgundian manuscripts from the fifteenth century are better known than Dutch examples, the latter, generally prepared for the urban middle class, reveal a realism absent from their Gallic counterparts and anticipate seventeenth century Dutch artists' treatment of Biblical scenes. Marrow provides a historical overview; other essays explore more specific topics, and the descriptions of the individual items depicted provide much information. With an extensive bibliography.

Mayr-Harting, Henry. *Ottonian Book Illuminations*. 2 vols. London: Oxford University Press, 1992.

While Carolingian and Ottonian manuscripts differ in some ways, Mayr-Harting emphasizes their similarities. He argues for a close connection between such works as the Gospel Book of Otto III and the court at Reichnau, just as Charlemagne and his immediate successors were involved with and patronized the production of manuscripts. Mayr-Harting also examines the interconnections among art, religion, and politics exemplified in Ottonian illumination, particularly in its emphasis on the figure of Christ. Part 1 looks at themes of the illuminations; Part 2 treats specific manuscripts. Focuses on the more elaborate examples of the period and so may distort the image of the age.

Meiss, Millard. *French Painting in the Time of Jean de Berry: The Boucicaut Master*. London: Phaidon, 1968.

Like the Duc de Berry, Jean le Meingre II, Marshall of France, was a great patron of the arts, and the Book of Hours he commissioned is one of the glories of medieval illumination. Meiss agrees with an earlier view that the master illustrator of this work is Jacques Coene of Bruges. Meiss discusses the political and iconographic significance of a variety of miniatures handsomely reproduced in this volume. Thus, the study will appeal not only to students of the book and medieval art but also to those concerned with political developments in early fifteenth century France.

_____. *French Painting in the Time of Jean de Berry: The Late XIV Century and the Patronage of the Duke*. 2 vols. London: Phaidon, 1967.

Focusing primarily on the period 1380-1400, Meiss presents the background to the great flowering of French manuscript illumination and then turns to the life of Jean de Berry. Chapters 4 and 5 of the first volume consider portraits of the duke and of his arms; Meiss then discusses specific manuscripts such as the Petites Heures, the Vatican Bible, and the Grandes Heures, though the study treats other art of the period as well, such as the *Parement de Narbonne* showing the Passion. The second volume contains 845 illustrations, most in black-and-white. Meiss stresses the duke's role in bringing the Italian style to France and in encouraging the creation of miniatures and small objets d'art. C. A. J. Armstrong called the work "an encyclopedia of the period around 1400 as regards art and culture" (*English Historical Review* 84, 1969, 578).

_____. *French Painting in the Time of Jean de Berry: The Limbourgs and Their Contemporaries.* 2 vols. New York: George Braziller, 1974.

Looks at manuscript illumination in the first two decades of the fifteenth century in France. Meiss first examines secular literature and then turns to the Limbourgs and the *Bible Moralisé.* First produced in the thirteenth century in France, these were richly decorated works with thousands of representations of Biblical scenes, and they served as model books for illuminators. In the early 1400s, the Limbourgs worked on such a Bible. Meiss identifies the contributions of the brothers. Chapters 5 and 6 discuss the Belles Heures and *Trés Riches Heures of Jean de Berry*; Chapter 7 summarizes the Limbourgs' achievement, and the volume concludes with a look at the Rohan Master. Meiss regards Paul as the best artist of the three brothers and seeks to determine which Limbourg painted what. For example, Meiss assigns to Paul the February, October, and December calendar pictures of the *Trés Riches Heures.* Jean's work is more elegant, as seen in his Coronation of the Virgin, and Herman is the most forceful in handling color and composition. Volume 2 includes some 900 plates. Most show work of the Limbourgs, but others offer examples that provide a context for the brothers' efforts.

Miner, Dorothy E. *The Development of Medieval Illumination as Related to the Evolution of Book Design.* Baltimore: Walters Art Gallery, 1958.

A pleasant, informative twenty-page survey of medieval illumination, accompanied by thirteen illustrations. Early medieval design combined classical style with intricate, unrealistic, nonclassical forms to create a sense of motion and asymmetry. Three-dimensional art yielded to the two-dimensional page; illustration became ornament. Lettering, too, grew fanciful; text and ornament fused in the historiated letter. The Romanesque style of the eleventh and twelfth centuries balanced "the representational and the decorative." In the thirteenth century, the stiff linear Romanesque became gentler as it yielded to Gothic influence. In the fourteenth century, realism and three-dimensional art reappear as illumination asserts itself as self-contained art. Though artists tried to reconcile their work to the page, the conflict led, according to Miner, to a rejection of ornament by the humanists of the fifteenth century. She sees early printing as seeking to imitate the high quality of manuscripts, so that early printers would settle for nothing less than a beautiful book.

Morgan, Nigel. *Early Gothic Manuscripts, 1190-1285.* 2 vols. London: Harvey Miller, 1982.

Volume 1 covers English manuscripts from 1190 to 1250; Volume 2 deals with the years 1250-1285. The catalog discusses nearly 200 manuscripts, and together the two volumes contain some 800 illustrations. Morgan maintains that a transitional style (1190-1220) yields to early Gothic during this period. In the thirteenth century, he finds that lay workshops supersede monasteries as the chief producers of books. The Psalter, already a popular text for illuminators of the twelfth century, emerges as "the most popular luxury private devotional book," but bestiaries and vernacular biographies of saints are in demand also. Bibles become smaller, reflecting private rather than communal use. Towards the end of this period Books of Hours and Apocalypses become major vehicles for illumination. The pictures in these manuscripts reveal medieval life and its concerns, so these volumes serve as a history of the age, not just a record of its art.

Mütherich, Florentine, and Joachim E. Gaehde. *Carolingian Painting.* New York: George Braziller, 1976.

Charlemagne's desire to revive learning affected the physical character of books produced under his reign and those of his successors. The Carolingian minuscule imposed "order and uniformity," according to Mütherich and Gaehde. Combined with the Roman majuscule it could create a logical arrangement on the page. In seeking to revive the classical age, Charlemagne turned to Hellenistic and Roman artistic models, reproducing three- dimensional figures; this influence fused with the Insular style from Britain. This volume discusses the spread and collapse of Carolingian illumination in the ninth and tenth centuries, and illustrates the style with six black-and-white and forty-eight color plates; Gaehde comments on each of these.

Narkiss, Bezalel. *Hebrew Illuminated Manuscripts.* New York: Leon Amiel, 1969.

Although the earliest known examples of Hebrew illumination date from the tenth century, the tradition probably dates from antiquity. The prohibition against graven images did not discourage certain forms of art among Jews, though that restriction did limit Islamic decoration. Hebrew illumination mirrors that of its Christian and Arab neighbors, but sometimes demonstrates peculiarities of its own, such as the use of script as illumination. Narkiss' introduction surveys Hebrew illumination in the Middle Ages and Renaissance; this discussion is followed by full-page color reproductions from sixty manuscripts, with descriptions facing each facsimile.

Nordenfalk, Carl. *Celtic and Anglo-Saxon Painting: Book Illumination in the British Isles, 600-800.* New York: George Braziller, 1977.
The Gospel Books of the British Isles incorporate pre-Christian artistic motifs; they also represent great artistic achievement. Nordenfalk discusses these important manuscripts. Forty-eight color plates reproduce examples from twelve books, and Nordenfalk comments on each illustration. His introduction examines various elements that characterize these masterpieces. Thus, he notes that the Cathach of Saint Columba reveals inventiveness in its treatment of initials that invade the text but also energetically expand into the margins. These initials reflect Celtic metal and stone work. With the Book of Durrow, the Insular style fully emerges; even the parchment is prepared in a manner unique to the British Isles, so that the material has a "surface highly receptive to ink and color." Nordenfalk observes that ornament takes a variety of forms: interlace, curvilinear, or rectilinear.

_____. *Early Medieval Book Illumination.* New York: Rizzoli, 1988.
Covers the fourth to eleventh century. Begins with late classical illustrations, with its illusionist techniques. Nordenfalk sees this art of late antiquity as the impetus behind the Carolingian and Ottonian renaissances. The text turns next to the great Insular manuscripts of the seventh and eighth centuries; Nordenfalk notes that from the Near East to Ireland, elaborate ornament characterizes the art of this period, and he compares Merovingian illumination on the Continent with the work of the Anglo-Irish monasteries. He then looks at the Carolingian era; subsequent chapters deal with Spanish illumination, Anglo-Saxon work before the Norman Conquest, and illumination in Germany in the tenth and eleventh centuries. Lavishly illustrated throughout with sixty-one color reproductions.

Oliver, Judith H. *Gothic Manuscript Illumination in the Diocese of Liege (c. 1250-c. 1330).* 2 vols. Louvain, Belgium: Uitgeverig Peeters, 1988.
Looks at Psalters, Psalter-Hours, and Books of Hours. M. Smeyers writes in the foreword, "The study is important in describing and interpreting the nature of the religious, social, and cultural framework in which all these manuscripts functioned, especially taking into account thirteenth-fourteenth century spirituality, the beguine and begard movement, the part of women in the growth of popular devotion, and

also economic and political circumstances in the Mosan Valley." The first part of the study looks at the "textual and iconographic contents," the second at stylistic questions, such as the connection with Parisian illumination. Oliver finds diversity of text and artistic influence, but in general the manuscripts reveal a prosperous middle class; aristocratic patronage played a small role in book production of the region. Most of the Psalters were made for beguines, and these devout women may also have produced these books. Oliver connects the Psalters with the Modern Devotion movement of the next century. Volume 2 catalogues the Psalters and Books of Hours and contains the plates. Oliver also includes a selected bibliography. Scholarly and specialized, but accessible to the lay reader.

Pacht, Otto. *Book Illumination in the Middle Ages: An Introduction.* Translated by Kay Davenport. London: Harvey Miller and Oxford University Press, 1986.
The reviewer for *The Burlington Magazine* (127, 1985, 719) commented, "I can think of no comparable work which I would sooner offer to an intelligent newcomer to the subject. Its value lies in its potent mix of muscularly speculative thought, wide learning and patient, empirical observation. Everywhere telling, concrete examples are found to illuminate general principles, whether of a technical or ideological kind." Pacht observed that in the Middle Ages the book was both object and symbol and might be preserved in an elaborate shrine as a relic. He notes the integrity of text and decoration and discusses in detail initials, illustration of Bibles, the Apocalypse, and Psalters, and the ongoing conflict between two-dimensional surface and three-dimensional space. Includes 210 black-and-white illustrations, thirty-two in color, and a short bibliography. Bernard McTigue wrote of Pacht's study, "Informed by over sixty years of research, this work . . . belongs in the collection of anyone with an interest in the history of the book" (*American Book Collector* 8, April, 1987, 44).

Parkes, M. B., and Andrew G. Watson, eds. *Medieval Scribes, Manuscripts, and Libraries: Essays Presented to N. R. Ker.* London: Scolar Press, 1978.
A collection of twelve pieces on medieval manuscripts and libraries. Pierre Chaplais opens the collection with an essay arguing for the authenticity of an early eighth century letter from Bishop Wealdhere of London to the Archbishop of Canterbury; his defense of the document highlights details of Anglo-Saxon scribal practice. John C. Pope follows with a discussion of the Exeter Book of Old English Poetry;

again, in examining possible gaps the article reveals much about bookmaking before the Norman Conquest. Other essays consider such subjects as William of Malmesbury's book collecting, an article that also discusses his supervision of a scriptorium; the method of book production in medieval universities; monastic libraries at Durham and St. Albans; and the manuscript tradition of Cicero's "Posterior Academics," which survived as part of the author's *De finibus bonorum et malorum*. P. J. Croft wrote of this festschrift, "No one concerned with any aspect of the medieval book could fail to acquire new facts and fresh stimulus from the volume as a whole" (*Review of English Studies* N.S. 30, 1979, 444).

Pirani, Emma. *Gothic Illuminated Manuscripts*. Translated by Margaret Crosland. London: Hamlyn, 1970.
Focuses primarily on Italian manuscripts, with little attention to French illumination and even less to German, English, and other traditions. Examines Italian approaches to Gothic illumination, with sections devoted to the Bolognese, Florentine, Jienese, Venetian, Lombard, and Neapolitan styles. Contains sixty-nine color facsimiles.

Popova, Olga. *Russian Illuminated Manuscripts*. Translated by Kathleen Cook, Vladimir Ivanov, and Lenina Sorokina. New York: Thames and Hudson, 1984.
Russia became Christian late in the tenth century; the earliest surviving illuminated manuscripts date from the eleventh. Just as Russian Christianity came from Constantinople, so the early manuscripts reflect Byzantine influence, though modified by local characteristics, such as the angular figures in the Mstislav Lectionary (1103-1117). The thirteenth century Mongol invasions isolated Russia; during this period, miniatures became "simpler and more severely ascetic," according to Popova. As contact with Constantinople increased in the fourteenth century, so did Byzantine influence. Many Greeks began working in Russia, and Serbs brought with them yet another style of illumination. Andrey Rublyov of Moscow created in the early fifteenth century a style that was so much imitated that it became identified with Russian art. Popova provides sixty-nine reproductions, forty-eight of them in color, to illustrate her points.

Porcher, Jean. *Medieval French Miniatures*. New York: Harry N. Abrams, 1959.
A sumptuous colorplate book with ninety full page reproductions as well as numerous facsimiles in the text. Porcher concentrates on the later

Middle Ages, from the end of the tenth century to the sixteenth. The book contains two major units, the first devoted to Romanesque, the second to Gothic. In the first section Porcher emphasizes the foreign contributions that sharped French manuscript art. By the thirteenth century France was itself the maker of fashion, and book production was centered in Paris. Includes discussions of individual artists.

Putnam, George Haven. *Books and Their Makers During the Middle Ages: A Study of the Conditions of the Production and Distribution of Literature from the Fall of the Roman Empire to the Close of the Seventeenth Century.* 2 vols. New York: G. P. Putnam's Sons, 1896.
Cassiodorus, Saint Benedict, and Saint Ferreol imposed upon monasteries the obligation to copy manuscripts; Italy, Germany, France, Holland, and Ireland had scriptoria soon after the fall of Rome, and by the end of the seventh century Wearmouth and Yarrow in England also had emerged as centers of book production. Putnam followed the secularization of bookmaking in the later Middle Ages, as universities attracted scribes and booksellers. He also traces the development of xylography and then printing from movable type, giving more credit to Jan Koster than most believed due him. Putnam noted how early printers sought to imitate manuscripts, and how some copyists and engravers objected to the new technology. The vogue for theological works yielded to a demand for the classics by the end of the incunabular period. In the second volume, Putnam pursued printing during the Reformation. He observes that printing and religion interacted: the press democratized religion. He also discussed the problems facing early publishers and booksellers. He found that some printers, like Froben and the Estiennes, were careful with their texts, but many were not. James Westfall Thompson, reviewing the second volume, wrote, "throughout there is evidence of scholarship, industry, and that sympathy for his subject without which no writer can be at his best. Mr. Putnam has been at his best. *Palmam qui meruit, habeat*" (*The Dial* 22, January 16, 1897, 51).

Randall, Lilian M. C. *Images in the Margins of Gothic Manuscripts.* Berkeley: University of California Press, 1966.
Examines this fascinating facet of illustration for the period 1250 to 1350. Randall looked at 226 manuscripts and classified the images. According to her, the years 1250-1300 witnessed much experimentation, especially in England, where marginal illustration could expand to become full-fledged illumination. Perhaps because of English influence, Jean Pucelle extended this practice to French manuscripts, which

in the early fourteenth century present many odd marginal creatures. As the fourteenth century progressed, such figures lost their originality. Many of these illustrations have iconographic significance; others merely reflect the exuberance of the artist. Over seven hundred black-and-white reproductions reveal the range, humor, and skill represented in the margins of these manuscripts, which range from such homely scenes as a mother bathing her child to a surrealistic academy taught and attended by apes. Nicolas Barker observed, "Mrs. Randall's is a careful and generally accurate piece of work, which will commend itself to all those to whom the workings of the medieval imagination are of interest" (*The Book Collector* 17, 1968, 91). Lawrence S. Thompson called the study "essential to a full understanding of the history and literature of Western Literature during the period covered" (*Papers of the Bibliographical Society of America* 62, 1968, 155).

Robb, David Metheny. *The Art of the Illuminated Manuscript*. New York: A. S. Barnes, 1973.
A heavily illustrated survey of the subject, this book begins with classical antiquity but quickly moves to the Middle Ages; it concludes with an epilogue treating the fifteenth century. Robb's introduction discusses the manufacture of illuminated manuscripts, and he makes a number of important observations. For the early Middle Ages in the West, little art remains outside Italy. The illuminated manuscript marks the spread of Christianity and the high regard in which books were held. Books of the Carolingian Renaissance demonstrate the effort to revive classical culture, and the eclectic nature of Carolingian illumination reflects Charlemagne's drawing on England and Italy for scholars to reform and educate his empire. Robb discusses the development of Romanesque and Gothic styles and the influence of Jean Pucelle in the fourteenth century; Robb perceptively likened Pucelle to Giotto. A fine account, especially useful for the general reader. Reviewers complained about the quality of the plates but praised the text (see *The New York Times Book Review* for December 2, 1973, 90, and the *Times Literary Supplement* for May 3, 1974, 480).

Rothe, Edith. *Medieval Book Illumination in Europe: The Collections of the German Democratic Republic*. New York: W. W. Norton, 1968.
A study of 160 manuscripts, mostly from ecclesiastical libraries, covering the period 400-1600. Because so many countries and schools are represented, the volume serves as an introductory history. The oldest surviving examples of Christian manuscript illumination are Italian but are housed in Germany; Plate 1 shows illustrations of 1 Samuel 15 from

around 400. Other examples depict the Insular style of Britain; the products of the Carolingian Renaissance; Ottonian manuscripts that integrate script and illustration and use gold for background; late Romanesque art aiming at greater naturalism; Gothic Books of Hours; and the sixteenth century flowering, when artists like Albrecht Dürer and Lucas Cranach the Younger were involved in book production. Rothe provides brief notes on each of the plates and a historical commentary that traces the development of styles of illumination.

Rouse, Mary A., and Richard H. Rouse. *Authentic Witnesses: Approaches to Medieval Texts and Manuscripts.* Notre Dame, Ind.: University of Notre Dame Press, 1991.
Contains thirteen essays on medieval manuscripts from the eleventh to the fifteenth century. In the opening piece, the Rouses argue that the codex did not render the roll obsolete; medieval poets used rolls because they were less expensive and more portable than the codex. This article expresses the authors' fundamental principle: In the book, form follows function. Thus, increased reliance on books rather than memory led to new ways of organizing the text on the page for faster reference, and to the creation of concordances and indexes. Other chapters discuss the thirteenth century Parisian book trade, which they again relate to developments that affected book use, and the role of florilegia (anthologies of quotations). The volume concludes with an examination of how printing mirrored and also changed the medieval concept of the book.

Salmi, Mario. *Italian Miniatures.* New York: Harry N. Abrams, 1954.

Sandler, Lucy Freeman. *Gothic Manuscripts, 1285-1385.* 2 vols. London: Harvey Miller, 1986.
Volume 1 contains the text and 419 illustrations; Volume 2 presents a catalog of 158 English manuscripts with discussion and bibliography. Though styles change over the century covered, Sandler finds certain persistent characteristics: "a consistent taste for the heterogeneous as opposed to the homogeneous, the multiple as opposed to the unified . . . a strong sense of visual humour, a taste for the grotesque, . . . for detailed pictorial narrative, for depiction of the particularities of nature, often made more piquant or dramatic by juxtaposition or intermingling with representations of stylized, non-natural fantasies and hybrids." Sandler challenges the assumption that English style in this period derives from French and other Continental models; she sees "parallels rather than influences." She distinguishes six styles among

the manuscripts she examined: Court, Tickhill (named for John Tickhill and his Psalter), East Anglian, London, Bohun (after the Bohun family), and Litlyngton (for Nicholas Litlyngton, Abbot of Westminster). Liturgical texts—Bibles and prayerbooks—contain the vast majority of the best illumination, and only one literary text appears here, though on the Continent, secular literature was widely illuminated. As the subject matter suggests, most of the manuscripts were produced by the Church. Again, on the Continent by the fourteenth century, secular booksellers had assumed a more important role in manuscript production. M.A. Michael wrote that "the introduction provides the most detailed scholarly analysis of the main research on English Gothic manuscripts yet to be produced," and he praised Sandler's "enthusiasm and scholarship" (*Burlington Magazine* 129, 1987, 670).

Saunders, O. Elfrida. *English Illumination*. 2 vols. Florence, Italy: Pantheon, 1928.
Volume 1 contains the text and the first fifty duochrome reproductions; Volume 2 adds some eighty more. Saunders begins with Celtic illumination and proceeds through the fifteenth century. The study traces changes in style from Celtic to Anglo-Saxon, then to Romanesque and Gothic. It also examines the various local styles that developed and how these eventually yielded to a national and international art as each patron chose the best illuminator regardless of geographical origin. Saunders finds that throughout the thousand years covered, English art tended to be more decorative than representational. She also makes the point that though British illuminators produced no manuscripts to rival those commissioned by the Duc de Berry, they retained a high level of excellence through the Middle Ages.

Scott, Kathleen. *Later Gothic Manuscripts*. London: Harvey Miller, 1993.
Examines 140 fifteenth and early sixteenth century manuscripts illuminated in the British Isles, among them such outstanding examples of medieval bookmaking as the Bedford Hours.

Shailor, Barbara A. *The Medieval Book*. New Haven, Conn.: Yale University Library, 1988.
Written to accompany an exhibit of the Beinecke Rare Book and Manuscript Library's fine collection of medieval and Renaissance material. Shailor looks first at how manuscripts were produced; she discusses materials used, pricking and ruling, bookhands, decoration, binding, and finishing. The study then treats various types of books, showing how content affected form. Thus, a late thirteenth century

Aristotle intended for university students provides ample room at the bottom of each page for annotation. The more than 160 miniatures and historiated initials in Guillaume de Termonde's *Le Livre de Lancelot du Lac, Part III* allow even the illiterate to enjoy the romance. Concludes with a discussion of the shift from manuscript to printing. Well-illustrated.

Sweeney, James Johnson. *Irish Illuminated Manuscripts of the Early Christian Period.* New York: New American Library, 1965.

Temple, Elzbieta. *Anglo-Saxon Manuscripts, 900-1066.* London: Harvey Miller, 1976.
Describes all Anglo-Saxon illuminated manuscripts of the century and a half preceding the Norman invasion and presents 370 illustrations. Included here is Temple's discovery, a Gospel Lectionary housed in Warsaw. She observes that the wars with the Danes in the ninth century temporarily ended English book production. Under Alfred the Great, book production revived, especially at Canterbury and Winchester, each with two scriptoria. Manuscripts of this era reflect Continental and Byzantine as well as Insular influences. By the end of the tenth century, Anglo-Saxon art began in turn to influence Continental style, especially in the Franco-Flemish area and Scandinavia. The catalog discusses 106 manuscripts and provides bibliographic references. John Beckwith declared, "Mrs. Temple's scholarship is exemplary and her book will become a standard source of reference. . . . The illustrations are lavish, well-printed and well arranged. . . . The book is a tribute to the elegance, sophistication and sheer beauty of Anglo-Saxon art" (*Apollo* 104, 1976, 515).

Thomas, Marcel. *The Golden Age: Manuscript Painting at the Time of Jean, Duke of Berry.* New York: George Braziller, 1979.
Concentrates on the manuscripts produced in Paris between 1380 and 1420, especially those commissioned by Jean, Duc de Berry, whose books are among the glories of medieval artistry. Thomas notes that Paris drew illuminators from across Europe and so engendered an international style that in turn spread across the continent. He observes, too, that because images often are so similar, influence is difficult to determine. Includes a selective bibliography, forty color plates, and nineteen black-and-white figures.

Thompson, Daniel Varney. *The Materials and Techniques of Medieval Painting.* London: Allen & Unwin, 1956.

Though not limited to manuscript illumination, this book offers many details relevant to that topic. Thompson discusses the preparation of parchment and vellum, media used to bind pigment, the pigments themselves, and the use of metals. The study shows that medieval painters and illuminators drew on a wide range of materials. For example, blue could be derived from azurite, indigo, woad, ultramarine, copper, or silver. Thompson also indicates that the illuminator had to be more than just a trained draftsman: "The skill of medieval writers and painters in design is fairly obvious; but it was backed up by technical knowledge and devotion and perseverance which only those who have attempted to match it can comprehend with any fair degree of completeness." *The London Mercury* described the first edition as "a useful handbook for the student of the technique of medieval painting, manuscript illuminating, fresco and oil painting" and praised the clear, comprehensible presentation (34, 1936, 380).

Thompson, Daniel Varney, Jr., and George Heard Hamilton, trans. *De arte illuminandi: The Technique of Manuscript Illumination.* New Haven, Conn.: Yale University Press, 1933.
Translation of an anonymous fourteenth century Italian instruction manual on the art of illumination. The author, an illuminator, discusses all the elements of his art. Thus, the text notes the eight colors used—black, white, red, yellow, blue, violet, rose, and green—and the sources of these pigments. White, for example, comes from white lead or animal bones. The translators provide extensive notes that enhance the value of the book for anyone seeking an understanding of the methods used in medieval illumination.

Turner, D. H. *Early Gothic Illuminated Manuscripts in England.* London: British Museum, 1965.
Covers the period 1220-1285. Around 1220 Robert de Lindesey, Abbot of Peterborough, commissioned a Psalter; another in the Fitzwilliam Museum, Cambridge, England, appears to contain illumination by the same artist. These Psalters, in Late Transitional Style, reflect the beginning of a shift from the Romanesque to the Gothic, from stylized to more natural representation. Turner finds that in the thirteenth century professional scribes and illuminators become increasingly important, as individual patrons replaced institutions as the chief commissioners of books. Turner discusses a number of important manuscripts and illuminators (such as Matthew Paris, c. 1200-1250) in this short pamphlet, which includes four color and sixteen black-and-white illustrations. Although some critics discount the artistry of

English illumination of this period, Turner praises the "freedom of spirit" exemplified in the manuscripts. If they do not equal those executed in Paris at the same time, they nonetheless remain "of the greatest importance."

_____. *Romanesque Illuminated Manuscripts*. London: Trustees of the British Museum, 1966.

Treats the period 1049-1180. Romanesque art is international in style and was created for and by churchmen. The first great Romanesque illuminated manuscript in England is the Albani Psalter, probably produced at St. Albans around 1123. It reveals Ottonian and Byzantine influences. The Shaftesbury Psalter (c. 1130-1150), with its statuesque figures, artificially arranged draperies, and stylized expressions, further develops the Romanesque mode. The angularity of the illuminations in Henry of Blois's Psalter (1140-1160) is more typical of English Romanesque than the rounded figures of the Shaftesbury Psalter. Because the British Library's collection includes fine examples of Continental Romanesque manuscripts, Turner does not limit his discussion to England but surveys work from various European centers. He concludes that "the Romanesque period was the golden age of book illustration in Europe. Never before or after did it rank so high and independently as a form of art, enjoy such widespread cultivation and excellence and so respond to the spirit of the times." With four color and sixteen black-and-white illustrations.

Twitchett, Denis Crispin. *Printing and Publishing in Medieval China*. New York: Frederic C. Beil, 1983.

In the foreword to this brief book, Twitchett observes, "Paper and printing are two Chinese inventions that have had an immeasurable effect upon our own western culture. Without them the cheap and widespread dissemination of books and of knowledge that was one of the preconditions for the development of our modern world would have been impossible." China was using paper by the beginning of the second century A.D.; printing from wooden blocks dates from the ninth century (the "Diamond Sutra," the earliest dated printed book, was produced in 868). Woodblocks were used for illustrations as well as for text. By the eleventh century, the Chinese had developed movable type, which might be made of ceramic, wood, or tin. Such printing was not, however, popular in China, perhaps because of the language's multiplicity of characters. Korea adopted the use of movable type, though, and in 1403 the government produced several hundred thousand bronze characters.

Unterkircher, Franz. *A Treasury of Illuminated Manuscripts: A Selection of Miniatures from Manuscripts in the Austrian National Library.* New York: G. P. Putnam's Sons, 1967.

Reproduces illustrations from fifty-eight volumes, the earliest dating from the eighth century, the most recent coming from the mid-sixteenth. Unterkircher, Keeper of Manuscripts, discusses the volumes. Some of the items here are familiar; others, like the examples of ninth century astronomical illustrations from Salzburg, will prove new to most readers. Though many of the manuscripts are Austrian, a number come from Germany, Italy, France, England, or the Netherlands. A useful history of illumination.

Voelke, William M., ed. *Masterpieces of Medieval Painting: The Art of Illumination.* Chicago: University of Chicago Press, 1980.

A listing, accompanied by fifteen colored microfiche, of about twenty percent of the extensive holdings of the Pierpont Morgan Library collection of illuminated manuscripts from the sixth to the sixteenth century. The list notes where the manuscript originated, the date, scribe and illuminator when known, and details such as length, size in millimeters, and illustrations. The fiche provide some 1,200 high-quality reproductions, many of these not readily accessible elsewhere.

Walters Art Gallery. *Illuminated Books of the Middle Ages and Renaissance: An Exhibition.* Baltimore: Trustees of the Walters Art Gallery, 1949.

An important exhibition catalog, richly illustrated in black-and-white. The catalog describes 233 manuscripts, most of them the gift of Henry Walters, others from major collections such as the Pierpont Morgan Library. The earliest is a Psalter from eighth century England, probably Canterbury; the latest is a mid-seventeenth century example of calligraphic art. Even after the invention of printing, many fine manuscripts, especially Books of Hours, continued to be produced. Following each description is a bibliography for further study.

Weitzmann, Kurt, et al. *The Place of Book Illumination in Byzantine Art.* Princeton, N.J.: Art Museum, Princeton University, 1975.

A collection of four essays. Weitzmann begins the book by discussing characteristics of Byzantine illumination and ways to study this subject. He observes that Byzantine illumination quickly developed great narrative skill. It also stresses the dignity of religious figures, drawing on Oriental style but also looking back to classical models. The eleventh century reacted to this latter influence and so added a spiritual dimension. Byzantine art skillfully depicts dogma, and towards the end of the Middle Ages it added emotion. To study this art, Weitzmann speaks of looking at documentary evidence, reconstructing fragmentary manuscripts, examining other media such as mosaics, and studying the influence of Byzantine motifs on other cultures as well as Jewish and Greco-Roman influence on the Byzantine style. William Loerke and Ernst Kitzinger compare Byzantine illumination to monumental compositions and murals; Hugo Buchtal concludes the book with a study of manuscripts produced in fourteenth century Constantinople. Well-illustrated.

Wieck, Roger S. *Time Sanctified: The Book of Hours in Medieval Art and Life.* New York: George Braziller, 1988.
Drawing on some three hundred Books of Hours in the Walters Art Gallery in Baltimore, Wieck, with help from Lawrence R. Poos, Virginia Reinburg, and John Plummer, discusses these works as art and as social documentation. The prominence of women in the works from the later Middle Ages shows their growing importance and increasing literacy. The Black Death brought a new consciousness of mortality that is reflected in the Office of the Dead, a section of the prayerbook devoted to funerary and memorial services. In the unit on "The Book of Hours and Medieval Art," Wieck offers a guided tour through these works, which he compares to a Gothic cathedral. Lavishly illustrated and clearly written; includes a brief bibliography.

Williams, John. *Early Spanish Manuscript Illumination.* New York: George Braziller, 1977.
Traces the history of illumination in Spain from the seventh to the twelfth century; most of the examples come from north-central Spanish monasteries of the tenth century. Under the Visigoths, Spain developed a "distinctive provincial style," according to Williams. This style included Visigothic minuscule, which survived until the twelfth century. Williams questions the influence that Arabic art supposedly had on illumination of the tenth and eleventh centuries; he finds pre-Carolingian styles more important, at least initially. When Fernando I (1037-1065) accelerated the pace of Christian conquest in Spain and created close ties with France, he set in motion forces that would supplant a uniquely Spanish style with European Romanesque. Well-illustrated.

Chapter 12
THE FIFTEENTH CENTURY

Bibliographies

Besterman, Theodore. *Early Printed Books to the End of the Sixteenth Century: A Bibliography of Bibliographies.* 2d rev. ed. New York: Rowman & Littlefield, 1969.

A comprehensive, international listing with 2,389 entries in various languages. Covers the first 150 years of printing, including a unit on blockbooks. Treats both bibliographies of bibliographies and bibliographies. Well indexed, but items listed generally are not annotated, although Besterman does indicate the number of entries in each work.

Heilbronner, Walter Leo. *Printing and the Book in Fifteenth Century England.* Charlottesville: Bibliographical Society of the University of Virginia, 1967.

Includes over 400 works dealing with English incunabula, and provides helpful annotations as well as an analytical index. The first section treats catalogs and checklists, arranged chronologically; all but three date from the twentieth century, indicating the growth of interest in the subject. The second and larger section examines books and articles in the field. The *Times Literary Supplement* for April 18, 1968, observed, "Anyone working on English incunabula will find this a most useful and time-saving work to have close at hand" (p. 405). For a less favorable commentary see *Modern Language Review* 64 (1969): 630-631.

McMurtrie, Douglas C. *The Invention of Printing: A Bibliography.* Chicago: Club of Printing House Craftsmen, 1942.

More than three thousand items appear in "the first attempt, within the past half century to compile a comprehensive bibliography of published materials on the invention of printing with movable types." The work begins with such antecedents to the printed book in Europe as textile printing, playing cards, blockbooks, and binders' stamps. McMurtrie also devotes sections to rival claimants to the title of first printer and treats specific works such the Gutenberg Bible, the Missale Speciale, and the 1457 Psalter. Lists books and articles and provides full bibliographic information. Annotations are limited.

Peddie, Robert A. *Fifteenth Century Books.* London: Grafton, 1913.
An annotated listing of selected books. Intended to assist in identifying and studying incunabula. The sections are short but treat a wide range of topics, including Hebrew printing, music printing, maps, color printing, and book illustration. Especially helpful is the list of Latin place-names (Appendix I), since readers may not know that Hispali in a colophon is Seville.

Studies

Alexander, J. J. G. *Italian Renaissance Illuminations.* New York: George Braziller, 1977.
The invention of printing was not the only important development in book history in the fifteenth century. Alexander shows how manuscript illumination in Italy in the early 1400s reflects the "intellectual, moral, spiritual, and artistic rebirth of Europe, the revival of ancient classical influences, the rise of a new impulse in culture, in literature, and in art." A beautiful volume with many full-color illustrations. Includes suggestions for further reading.

Barker, Nicolas. *Aldus Manutius and the Development of Greek Script and Type in the Fifteenth Century.* New York: Fordham University Press, 1991.
See this entry under TYPOGRAPHY, PRINTING, AND BOOK DESIGN.

Bennett, H. S. *English Books and Readers 1475 to 1557.* Cambridge, England: Cambridge University Press, 1952.
In his preface, Bennett speaks of his book's "fourfold purpose." He begins by examining the book market and literacy before Caxton introduced the press to England, and Bennett proceeds to examine how Caxton and his successors established the culture of print. Looking at some 5,000 volumes printed during the first eighty-two years of printing, Bennett studies "the conditions which gave [the book] significance and . . . the readers whose support was essential to its success." Bennett's final chapters consider the actual making of a book, from manuscript to final printed form. This volume ends in 1557 with the establishment of the Stationers' Company, marking the coming of age of the printing industry. An informative, highly readable account.

Blades, William. *The Life and Typography of William Caxton, England's First Printer, with Evidence of His Typographical Connection with Colard Mansion, the Printer of Bruges*. 2 vols. London: Joseph Lilly, 1861-1863. Still an authoritative work. Blades's was the first important biography of England's proto-typographer. As James Moran wrote in the introduction to the 1971 Rowman and Littlefield reprint, "William Blades's published researches on William Caxton represent a landmark in bibliographical history and [have] not been superseded as a record of Caxton's life and achievement." Moran notes the praise Blades received from two of England's leading students of bibliography, A. W. Pollard and E. Gordon Duff. Blades is not infallible. He believed, for example, that Caxton learned to print in Bruges rather than Cologne and that Caxton discarded one typeface when he secured another. This latter view led Blades to construct a questionable chronology of Caxton's imprints. Blades is right, though, to credit Caxton with promoting English literacy, and he notes that Caxton was concerned with the accuracy of his texts. As a printer, Blades brought important technical knowledge to his study.

Blake, Norman Francis. Caxton: England's First Publisher. New York: Barnes & Noble, 1976.
Enriched with sixty-three illustrations, this volume examines the technical aspects of the books William Caxton produced. The first chapter looks at Gutenberg and the dawn of European printing. Blake then deals briefly with Caxton's life as a merchant before turning to his work as a printer, first at Bruges, then at Westminster. Subsequent chapters examine printing, layout, illustration, the book trade, and Caxton's publishing methods (which contrast with those of his successor, Wynkyn de Worde). The book concludes with a bibliography of Caxton's imprints, notes on the plates, and a selective secondary bibliography. Blake sees Caxton's printing as another facet of his mercantile interests, and his decision to print in English as a clever business ploy that would expand the market for books. Complements Blake's *Caxton and His World* (London: Deutsch, 1969), which examines the literary aspects of Caxton's imprints. John Richardson wrote in *College and Research Libraries* 38 (1977): 64 that Blake offers "a fascinating, insightful volume necessary for understanding Caxton and the publishing and book trades in England and the Low Countries during the fifteenth century."

Buhler, Curt F. *The Fifteenth Century Book: The Scribes, the Printers, the Decorators*. Philadelphia: University of Pennsylvania Press, 1960.

In the fifteenth century, the making of manuscripts and the printing of books coexisted, and scribes were as apt to copy printers' work as the reverse. The printing press thus did not end the production of handwritten books, and scribes served as editors for printers. Both printed and manuscript volumes were decorated by hand. About half the volume consists of notes to the three lectures, and Buhler includes a number of facsimiles that complement the text.

Butler, Pierce. *The Origins of Printing in Europe*. Chicago: University of Chicago Press, 1940.

In his opening chapters, Butler examines the impact of printing on scholarship; he also discusses the technology that underlies movable type. His central concern, however, is to dispel what he regards as the Gutenberg myth. Rejecting the notion that printing from movable type emerged full-blown from the mind of Gutenberg like Athena from the head of Zeus, he argues that the technology of printing developed slowly and in various places. He concedes that at Mainz printing may have been "first organized into an industry," perhaps by Johann Fust, perhaps by another. Gutenberg appears as only one of the inventors of a technology to which many contributed. Butler's thesis is not widely accepted, but his book is useful for reproducing in English a number of important documents relating to the invention of printing from movable type in Europe.

Carlson, David R. *English Humanist Books: Writers and Patrons, Manuscript and Print, 1475-1525*. Toronto: University of Toronto Press, 1993.

Although printing came to England with William Caxton about 1476, manuscripts continued to be produced throughout the period covered in this study. One purpose of the manuscript was to secure patronage for those who hoped to earn a living from their writing. Carlson's first chapter discusses the unsuccessful attempt of Filippo Alberici to gain the patronage of Henry VII by presentng him with an ornate manuscript of poems and prose. The second chapter looks at Pietro Carmeliano's more profitable efforts in getting royal support. Carlson notes that the benefit was not all one-sided; Henry VII was able to show himself a humanist and patron of the arts, and he gained a propagandist. Bernard Andre, the subject of the third chapter, also traded support from Henry VII for his support of the Tudor monarch. Carlson shows how Andre used various means of publication, both manuscript and print, to maintain his reputation and royal patronage. In Chapter 4, Carlson considers the most successful of the humanist authors, Erasmus, who could manipulate publication in a way that guaranteed the maximum return for his efforts. He would sell the same text to different printers, and he would present potential patrons with manuscripts of previously published work. The humanist grammarian Robert Whittington also used different modes of publication for different purposes, giving Thomas Cardinal Wolsey a manuscript copy of poems previously printed. Carlson writes, "In the period of transition from manuscript to print . . . it seems that 'manuscript' meant one thing, and 'printed book' meant another. Whittington and his humanist contemporaries were attuned to the difference." The expensive manuscript became a more obviously magnificent gift when compared with the less elaborate printed book. In Chapter 6, Carlson notes that Wynkyn de Worde's decision to print William Lily's poetic anthology Epigrammata in 1522 without a subsidy indicates that by that time there was a market for humanist works. In the final chapter, Carlson shows how different modes of publication of Thomas More's poems altered their meaning. A learned acount with more than sixty pages of notes, nicely illustrated with thirty-two facsimiles, this volume contributes to a clear understanding of both humanism in England and the way the book as physical object conveys meaning.

Claudin, Anatole. *The First Paris Press: An Account of the Books Printed for G. Fichet and J. Heynlin in the Sorbonne, 1470-1472.* London: Bibliographical Society, 1898.
Wanting to bring the art of printing to France, Johann Heynlin invited three printers from Basel and secured financial support from Guillaume Fichet. Claudin examined the various Parisian imprints to determine their sequence. The printers left the Sorbonne in April, 1473, and shifted from the Italian humanist type that Heynlin admired to the Gothic. Instead of printing classical works, they turned to theology. This study is especially useful for its detailed bibliography of early Paris imprints.

_____. "Private Printing in France During the Fifteenth Century." *Bibliographica* 3 (1897): 344-370.
Claudin discusses eleven presses that he regards as private. The first, patronized by Guillaume Fichet, Johann Heynlin, and Cardinal Rolin, established at the Sorbonne, was the first press in all of France. In the course of the incunabular period Poitiers, Metz, Chartres, Brehan-Loudeac, the abbey of Lantenac, Embrun, Goupillieres, Dijon, Narbonne, and the monastery at Cluny also had private presses, most of them operating for a year or less, but some enduring for a longer period. Claudin presents a history of these presses and discusses their output.

Davies, W. H. *Devices of the Early Printers, 1457-1560: Their History and Development.* London: Grafton, 1935.

This volume is divided into three sections. In the first part, Davies discusses the history of printers' devices—their origins, significance, and development. Davies notes that early devices often reflect other forms of medieval art, whereas by the sixteenth century they suggest the Renaissance style. He observes that printers' devices persisted well beyond 1560, but these later examples demonstrate less artistic skill. Because the "orb and four" symbol appears so often in early devices, Davies devotes a special chapter to that particular symbolic representation. Its source remains obscure, but Davies offers some insights into the question. The second and longest part of the book reproduces and discusses some 250 devices, and the third section presents contemporary portraits of early printers. Includes a bibliography.

DeVinne, Theodore Low. *The Invention of Printing.* 2d ed. New York: Francis Hart, 1878.

After examining the various forms of printing, including engraving, lithography, xylography, and typography, DeVinne looks at ancient forms of creating impressions, such as stamps and brands. He regards the real achievement of the fifteenth century as the discovery of a way to reproduce letters with molds, a process DeVinne, a printer, clearly explains and illustrates. The book then turns to the uses of print in the fifteenth century. Among these were the manufacture of playing cards and religious prints. Other chapters treat the introduction of paper into Europe and its effect on the mass-produced book, scribal practices in the centuries before printing, and blockbooks. DeVinne examines the rival claims of Gutenberg and Jan Koster, rejecting the legend of the latter. He also considers and rejects other contenders for the distinction of proto-printer. DeVinne looks at the works of Fust and Schöffer and traces the early spread of printing. An important early study.

Dreyfus, John. *William Caxton and His Quincentenary.* New York: Typophiles, 1976.

Dreyfus argues that when Caxton retired as Governor of the English Nation in Bruges, he went to Cologne to learn the business rather than the craft of printing. Dreyfus claims that Caxton returned to England in the summer of 1476. This attractive book discusses Caxton's achievements, which included introducing a table of contents and the first use of an index in a printed English book. More important, Dreyfus credits Caxton with making English "a vehicle for literary expression";

the *Oxford English Dictionary* cites Caxton a number of times as the first to use a particular word.

Duff, Edward Gordon. *Early English Printing: A Series of Facsimiles of All the Types Used in England During the XVth Century, with Some of Those Used in the Printing of English Books Abroad.* London: Kegan Paul, Trench, Trubner, 1896.

Drawing largely on the collection of the Bodleian Library, Duff has reproduced entire pages, generally full-size, that illustrate fifteenth century English type. Preceding the reproductions are short biographies of those who printed in England during the period: William Caxton, Wynkyn de Worde, Julian Notary, John Lettou, William de Machlinia, the anonymous printer of *The Siege of Rhodes*, Richard Pynson, Theodoric Rood, and the St. Albans printer. Duff also provides brief descriptions of the forty plates, which include no examples of roman type.

_____. *William Caxton.* Chicago: Caxton Club, 1905.

Though drawing heavily on William Blades's *Life and Typography of William Caxton* (cited earlier), Duff supplied new information as well. For example, Blades rejected the view that Caxton learned printing in Cologne, though Wynkyn de Worde said that Caxton had printed a Latin book there. Duff traces this work. Duff believed that *The History of Jason* was Caxton's first folio printed in England; more recent scholars have awarded that distinction to *The Canterbury Tales*. Duff offers useful commentary on Caxton's imprints and includes twenty-five facsimiles, all reproduced full-size. In addition, 148 of the 250 copies of this book include a page of the rare first edition of *The Canterbury Tales*, taken from an imperfect copy in Lord Ashburnham's library. Includes a list of Caxton's books, with collations, and notes five books that Wynkyn de Worde executed using Caxton's types. Duff rightly stresses Caxton's resolve to print in English rather than Latin and to offer popular literature rather than theology and learned treatises.

Feld, Maury D. "The First Roman Printers and the Idiom of Humanism." *Harvard Library Bulletin* 36 (Winter, 1988).

The entire issue is devoted to this exhibition catalog, which includes a substantial introduction. Although printing began in Germany, it quickly spread to Italy under the aegis of Roman humanists associated with the Papal curia. Feld observes that the three books known to have been printed by Konrad Sweynheym and Arnold Pannartz at Subiaco— Cicero's *De oratore* (1465), Lactantius' *Opera* (1465), and Augustine's

De civitate Dei (1467)—reflect the humanistic fusion of pagan and theological writings. The learned and lucid introduction is followed by a discussion of some forty humanist texts printed in Italy between 1465 and 1607.

Gerulaitis, Leonardas Vytautas. *Printing and Publishing in Fifteenth Century Venice*. Chicago: American Library Association, 1976.
In the first chapter, Gerulaitis examines the economic and technical conditions that allowed Venice to become Europe's leading producer of incunabula. Chapter 2 examines efforts by early printers to gain a monopoly, and Chapter 3 considers legal aspects of the trade, such as censorship and privileges. Gerulaitis then turns to a study of the books published in Venice, Florence, Bologna, and Nuremberg. He concludes that humanism was not a strong force among middle-class readers; rather, a small elite bought and read many books. The information here is useful, but the conclusions have been challenged by other scholars.

Goldschmidt, E. P. *Medieval Texts and Their First Appearance in Print*. London: Bibliographical Society, 1943.
An examination of what early printers chose to issue reveals the tastes of early modern readers. Goldschmidt notes that readers came from several segments of society: the university, the church, the court, the aristocracy, the professions, and the schools. The New Devotion, a religious movement of the late fifteenth century, encouraged the printing of mystical works by medieval authors. Classical texts enjoyed popularity, but so did obscure Christian works that might serve in the schools as alternatives to pagan authors. Books that were "discovered" by the Romantics enjoyed an earlier revival in the fifteenth century, but some writers that now appear important, such as Roger Bacon, Matthew Paris, and Peter Abelard, were not reprinted until the sixteenth or seventeenth century. Some were not published until much later.

Gordan, Phyllis Walter Goodhart, ed. and trans. *Two Renaissance Book Hunters: The Letters of Poggius Bracciolini and Nicolaus de Niccolis*. New York: Columbia University Press, 1974.
Poggio Bracciolini (1380-1459), a member of the Papal curia for fifty years, traveled throughout Europe searching for classical texts. This volume presents ninety-two letters addressed to the Florentine humanist and bibliophile Nicolò de Niccoli. Covering a thirty-year period, they tell of the recovery of lost learning, though they also discuss politics, religion, and literature. Gordan includes nine other letters

dealing with the recovery of manuscripts. The annotations, which occupy about half the volume, provide important background information that immerses the reader in the book culture of the fifteenth century.

Haebler, Konrad. *The Early Printers of Spain and Portugal.* London: Bibliographical Society, 1897.
Examining a much-neglected area, Haebler presents a good history of printing in the Iberian peninsula. Printing arrived in Spain by 1474. Haebler discusses the imprints of Valencia, Saragossa, Seville, Tortosa, Lerida, Salamanca, Zamora, Mallorca, Burgos, Toledo, and elsewhere. Arrangement is chronological by press rather than by location. Although the account sometimes extends to the sixteenth century, the focus remains on fifteenth century printers and their work. Includes a bibliography of Spanish incunabula and thirty-three facsimiles.

Hall, Edwin. *Sweynheym and Pannartz and the Origins of Printing in Italy: German Technology and Italian Humanism in Renaissance Rome.* McMinnville, Oreg.: Philip J. Pirages, 1991.
Konrad Sweynheym and Arnold Pannartz were the first printers outside the German-speaking world. Over a period of ten years (1464-1473), these partners produced fifty editions of more than thirty titles, many of these first editions of essential humanist writings. Their two typefaces are elegant. E. Gordon Duff called their productions on vellum "the most beautiful books that exist," and C. H. St. John Hornby used the Subiaco type as the model for his printing at the Ashendene Press between 1902 and 1925. Hall provides a detailed study of the men, their printing, and the humanistic milieu in which they worked. The book was beautifully produced by the Bird & Bull Press and was issued with a leaf from the Sweynheym and Pannartz edition of *Postilla super totam bibliam* by Nicholas of Lyra, the longest work (1,832 leaves) printed in the fifteenth century.

Hellinga, Lotte. *Caxton in Focus: The Beginning of Printing in England.* London: British Library, 1982.
Hellinga looks at Caxton's early printing by studying his types. Combining her evidence with Paul Needham's study of Caxton's paper, she argues that Caxton's earliest major book was *The Canterbury Tales.* She also discusses patronage of the press and Caxton's efforts as a missionary of the printing press in England. Much here, too, on Caxton's life in the Netherlands before he returned to his homeland to become England's first printer. Hellinga examines comments about

Caxton from the fifteenth century onward. Well-illustrated with numerous facsimiles of Caxton's typography. Elizabeth Armstrong wrote that this work "will be of great use to all those who are interested in the early history of printing in England" (*English Historical Review* 100, 1985, 881).

Hellinga, Lotte, and John Goldfinch. *Bibliography and the Study of Fifteenth-Century Civilisation*. London: British Library, 1987.

In the early 1980s, Lotte Hellinga inaugurated the Incunabula Short-Title Catalogue (ISTC) as an on-line data base. This volume contains sixteen essays that deal with the capabilities of her data base, information that it might one day include, and the uses to which this information can be put. Severin Corsten, for example, found that students at the University of Cologne needed copies of Petrus Hispanus' *Summulae logicales*, but most editions were printed at Deventer for export. Commentaries, however, were published at Cologne. More generally, textbooks were published at major printing centers, whereas commentaries for local use were not. Ursula Altmann notes that some of the incunabula editions of Cicero were bilingual, intended for the lay reader rather than the humanist scholar, and so suggest that Cicero's influence was not limited to the academy. Martin Lowry's "Diplomacy and the Spread of Printing" examines the role of patronage in book production. A number of contributors note the importance of precise bibliographical information because apparently identical copies can present important differences, and a single volume may contain more than one work.

Hellinga, Lotte, and Helmar Hartel, eds. *Buch und Text in 15. Jahrhudert: Book and Text in the Fifteenth Century*. Hamburg, Germany: Dr. Ernst Hauswedell, 1981.

A collection of essays in English and German exploring various facets of fifteenth century printing. Paul Needham examines the use of paper as evidence in dating a book. Hans-Joachim Koppitz and Ursula Altmann consider readership; Altmann notes the efforts of Lukas Brandis of Rostock to reach an audience generally unable to afford books. Adrian Offenberg discusses Hebrew incunabula, a neglected area of research. David M. Rogers offers insights into the workings of the print shop of Gunther Zainer of Augsburg around 1475. A number of the essays treat the enduring manuscript tradition, though print appropriated manuscript conventions at the same time that it marginalized the handwritten book itself.

Hellinga, Wytze, and Lotte Hellinga. *The Fifteenth Century Printing Types of the Low Countries.* Translated by D. A. S. Reid. 2 vols. Amsterdam: Menno Hertzberger, 1966.

Volume 1 surveys Dutch printing in the incunabula period and describes all the presses and printers in the Netherlands, together with the various types that they used. In Volume 2, the authors present 291 plates showing each type and discussing its use. Essential for anyone seeking information on the subjeci. George D. Painter commented in *The Book Collector* 16 (1967): 228, "One does not know whether most to admire the new discoveries made by the Hellingas, or the scholarly method, the honesty, sobriety and expertise of judgment, the rigorous application to primary evidence, with which they set down, order, modify and illuminate what seems to be known already."

Hindman, Sandra, ed. *Printing the Written Word: The Social History of Books, Circa 1450-1520.* Ithaca, N.Y.: Cornell University Press, 1991.

A collection of ten essays divided into three sections: Printers, Authors and Artists, and Readers. Sheila Edmund's essay opens the work with a discussion of scribes who became printers, most notably Peter Schöffer. Martha Tedeschi considers the career of Leinhart Holle, and Hindman looks at the Paris printer Guy Marchant, whom she sees as more conventional than others have regarded him. Cynthia Brown's contribution seeks to understand how printing affected authorial self-consciousness. Eberhard König's essay examines illustrated incunabula from Mainz. Using illumination as a guide, he finds that Mainz was the source of Bibles for much of fifteenth century Europe. Lilian Armstrong observes that printing actually increased the demand for miniaturists in Venice. The book trade between the Continent and England and Scotland is the subject of Lotte Hellinga's essay. Paul Saenger and Michael Heinlen consider how individual differences among copies of an edition can reveal readers' habits and interests. For Michael Camille, the illustrations of Guillaume de Deguileville's *Pelegrinage de la vie humaine* reveal a shift in reading habits occasioned by print. The volume concludes with Tobin Ivelhaus' study of the blockbook *Biblia pauperum*, which he sees as mediating between oral and print cultures. Well-illustrated throughout in black and white.

Hindman, Sandra, and James Douglas Farquhar. *Pen to Press: Illustrated Manuscripts and Printed Books in the First Century of Printing.* College Park: University of Maryland Press, 1977.

Published to coincide with an exhibition of manuscripts and early printed books. Chapter 1 discusses the making of a book, with details about materials, gatherings, bookhands (or type), ruling, illustration, and binding. Chapter 2 considers experiments that combined print and manuscript. For example, the Nonnberg Passion manuscript, c. 1460, includes a series of eighteen woodcuts printed directly on the parchment leaves. Hindman finds frequent examples pointing to "the bivalent character of book production [in the incunabular period], at once responding to the advantages of the press and maintaining the personalized qualities of the pen." The third chapter looks at the audience for illustrated books. Only the rich could afford a fifteenth century illuminated manuscript, but by the mid-1500s an artisan could buy an illustrated book of emblems. With eighty-nine black-and-white and four color reproductions.

Hirsch, Rudolf. *Printing, Selling and Reading, 1450-1550.* Weisbaden, Germany: Otto Harrassowitz, 1967.

Hirsch examines the effects of the invention of printing, especially in Germany and Italy. The first chapter presents an overview of the subject. Hirsch then considers printers and printing, noting that the absence of a guild system in the trade allowed for rapid expansion and for the entry of printers from diverse social backgrounds. Hirsch also distinguishes between the shy, retiring scribe and the boastful printer. The next two chapters consider the economics of book production. Venice emerged as the leading producer of incunabula because of its commercial connections with the rest of Europe. In Chapter 5, Hirsch looks at the selling of books, a task generally handled by the printers themselves in the early incunabula period. To market their wares, printers travelled widely. Hirsch also notes that while printing lowered the cost of books, they remained relatively expensive. He examines regulations that helped or harmed the new industry (Chapter 6), "National and Local Characteristics of the Book Trade" (Chapter 7), and reading habits (Chapter 8). J. M. Edelstein praised the work as "encyclopedic . . . , rich and useful" (*College and Research Libraries*, 28, 1967, 448).

Ing, Janet. *Johann Gutenberg and His Bible: A Historical Study.* New York: Typophiles, 1988.

This attractive volume surveys what the late twentieth century knows about Gutenberg and his Bible and those issues which remain unresolved. Despite centuries of scholarship, the latter category is by far the larger. Ing explains in nontechnical language how traditional scholarship and modern approaches such as proton analysis of ink have provided insights into the making of the first book in the West printed from movable types; she also notes that theories still frequently outrun data. Includes an excellent list of references for anyone seeking to pursue questions touched on in the text. As Paul Needham commented in the preface, "Janet Ing has provided a valuable and original service to both specialist and general reader."

Johnson, Alfred Forbes. *The First Century of Printing at Basle*. London: Ernest Benn, 1926.
Johnson divides the first century of printing at Basel into three periods. Printing was introduced to Basel by Berthold Ruppel of Hanau, who learned his craft from Gutenberg. Most of the printing in the incunabular period in Basel was not distinguished, and despite the presence of a university few humanist texts were reproduced there. Johann Froben, who had begun printing in the 1490s, revolutionized printing in Basel in the second of Johnson's periods (1510-1540). Froben "made Basle the centre of the German book trade for Latin works and editions of the classics." His association with Erasmus contributed to Basel's importance as a center of humanist publishing. Urs Graf and Hans Holbein provided excellent illustrations at this time. The third period for Johnson begins in 1540, with the introduction of French types and the decline of the printing trade in Basel. With fifty plates illustrating the shifting style, content, and quality of printing in Basel in the fifteenth and sixteenth centuries.

Johnson, James Sydney. *The Press of the Renaissance in Italy*. San Francisco: Windsor Press, 1927.
Johnson argues that printers did not attempt to rival the art of the manuscript because they recognized the superior quality of hand-illumination. Early printers therefore continued to rely on the same artists who had decorated the manuscripts. By the end of the fifteenth century, though, woodcuts and typography melded to yield beautiful printed books that no longer required illumination. In the sixteenth century, "rampant commercialism cut down margins and squeezed italic letters in unreadable proximity on overcrowded pages." A paean to the works of Nicolas Jenson and Aldus Manutius. The book includes illustrations drawn from Aldus' *Hypnerotomachia Poliphili* (1499), often considered the most beautiful incunabulum. The borders of Johnson's book reproduce Renaissance motifs.

Kren, Thomas, ed. *Renaissance Paintings in Manuscripts: Treasures from the British Library*. New York: Hudson Hills Press, 1983.
Looks at twenty-four manuscripts and printed books from Belgium, France, and Italy from about 1450 to the mid-sixteenth century. The

items selected are sumptuous, having belonged to the richest and most powerful figures of the Renaissance: Charles the Bold, Isabella of Castille, Ludovico Sforza, and their ilk. The St. Augustine manuscript of 1480 commissioned by the King of Naples cost almost sixty ducats, the equivalent of five horses or two houses. The volume is arranged geographically, with an introductory essay preceding the entries for each area. The Flemish manuscripts, which Kren treats, receive the most attention. Nicely illustrated with thirty-two color reproductions and 184 in black and white. These not only show the manuscript being discussed, but also relate it to other works. With an extensive bibliography. Lilian Armstrong praised the exhibition catalog for creating "a deeper appreciation [for a] still little understood period of illumination" (*Renaissance Quarterly*, 38, 1985, 139).

Lehmann-Haupt, Hellmut. *Gutenberg and the Master of the Playing Cards*. New Haven, Conn.: Yale University Press, 1966.

This attractively printed volume argues that in addition to being the first in the West to print from movable type, Gutenberg played an important part in the invention of copper engraving. According to Lehmann-Haupt, Gutenberg created a set of illustrations that he had intended to use in the 42-line Bible (c. 1450). When he went bankrupt, these prints were used for the earliest known printed playing cards. These illustrations would have made the printed Bible even more closely resemble the manuscripts that Gutenberg was imitating. Lehmann-Haupt offers much information about early engraving, the use of model books, and the widespread copying of decorative motifs, but the central argument remains unproven and largely unaccepted.

Lowry, Martin. *Nicholas Jenson and the Rise of Venetian Publishing in Renaissance Europe*. Oxford, England: Basil Blackwell, 1991.

Jenson's Venetian printing was initially supported by a small group of patricians educated at the University of Padua. These men wanted to foster printing, and in 1469 they arranged a five-year monopoly for John of Speyer. He died soon afterwards, and by 1470 three other presses were active in Venice. By 1472, Jenson had earned the favor of the city's patrician intellectual elite. Lowry examines how this association influenced the appearance and content of Jenson's early works. Lowry rejects the notion, fostered by Jenson himself, that these texts were less corrupt than those of his rivals. Jenson's real skill, according to Lowry, lay in his ability "to get closer to well-springs of patronage, and turn them to better commercial use, than any of his competitors." After a financial crisis in 1473, Jenson sought to appeal to the market for law books, again adjusting his typefaces and texts to attract customers. Jenson continued to influence the world of printing after his death, and William Morris imitated Jenson's typography at his Kelmscott Press (1891-1898). Appendix 1 reprints Jenson's will, Appendix 2 compares Jenson's types with others being used in Venice in the 1470s, and Appendix 3 presents a short bibliography of Jenson's imprints. Also includes an extensive bibliography of sources consulted and a judicious selection of thirteen plates in black and white. Learned, readable, informative, and enjoyable.

_____. *Venetian Printing: Nicolas Jenson and the Rise of the Roman Letter Form*. Herning, Denmark: Poul Kristensen, 1989.
Lowry's brief essay seeks to deny Jenson the title of the creator of the humanist book and to award this distinction to Aldus Manutius. According to Lowry, Jenson's beautiful Roman fonts represent a commercial experiment (which failed), not an attempt to imitate humanist scribal practices. Lowry notes that Jenson produced books for the Venetian humanists but remained on the periphery of that circle. A beautiful book printed in a Jenson-style typeface designed by George Abrams for Poul Kristensen, the Danish royal printer. These views are refined, though not much modified, in Lowry's *Nicholas Jenson and the Rise of Venetian Printing in Renaissance Europe* (cited herein).

_____. *The World of Aldus Manutius: Business and Scholarship in Renaissance Venice*. Ithaca, N.Y.: Cornell University Press, 1979.
Placing Aldus within the Venetian world of commerce and humanism, Lowry offers a balanced assessment of the printer's achievements. Lowry shatters a number of myths about Aldus: He was not as careful an editor as tradition suggests, nor was he the creator of inexpensive editions for poor scholars. Yet this study demonstrates Aldus' significance in gathering manuscripts and diffusing classical, especially Greek, learning. Lowry also discusses Aldus' unsuccessful efforts to found a Greek academy. When one matching his ideas was established in Rome, Aldus was not invited to participate. In addition to extensive notes, Lowry provides a 22-page bibliography. Dennis E. Rhodes described the book as "a most competent, much needed, highly readable volume on a subject of great importance and eternal fascination" (*The Library* 2, 1980, 228). The *American Book Collector* 1 (May/June, 1980): 57 called it "superb."

McMurtrie, Douglas C. *The Gutenberg Documents*. New York: Oxford University Press, 1941.

Translates and annotates twenty-eight documents that illuminate the invention and inventor of printing. Includes two other documents dismissed here as spurious. Document XVI lists Gutenberg among the goldsmiths of Strassbourg; Document XXII shows that by 1457 he faced economic difficulties and defaulted on payments of interest to the St. Thomas Chapter of Strassbourg. Appendix A presents a handwritten notice giving Gutenberg's date of death as February 3, 1468. The note appeared in a book printed after 1470; this volume has disappeared. The date must be close to correct because document XXVII, dated February 26, 1468, speaks of the death of Gutenberg and the return of certain printing equipment lent him by Dr. Konrad Humery, who agreed to use these items only in Mainz.

Masson, Irvine. *The Mainz Psalters and the Canon Missae, 1457-1459.* London: Bibliographical Society, 1954.
The 1457 Psalter produced by Johann Fust and Peter Schöffer is a masterpiece of printing. Masson examines this work and also the twelve-leaved Canon Missae, which he dates between August, 1457, and sometime in 1458, based on a careful examination of the types. The discussion also considers the 1459 Benedictine Psalter. In his analysis, Masson explains how the two-color initials were produced. Masson provides a detailed explanation of a method important in dating early printed volumes, and he reveals much about early printing practices. With six large plates.

Needham, Paul. "Johann Gutenberg and the Catholicon Press." *The Papers of the Bibliographical Society of America* 76 (1982): 395-456.
The first edition of Jonathan Balbus' *Catholicon* states that the book was printed at Mainz in 1460. A number of students of early printing ascribe the work to Johannes Gutenberg. Needham agrees and attributes to Gutenberg "all Mainz printing before 1468" (the year of Gutenberg's death) not executed by Fust and Schöffer. Needham also argues that Gutenberg developed the technique of casting slugs containing two lines of type rather than individual letters. Here was a primitive method of stereotyping, a way of cheaply reprinting a work without having to reset type. The *Catholicon* was indeed reprinted with these slugs. The same technique was employed for Thomas Aquinas' *Summa de articulis fidei*, which exists in 36- and 34-line Mainz editions, and for the Mainz printing of Mattaeus de Cracovia's *Dialogus rationis et conscientiae*. A fascinating piece of bibliographical detection that adds important information about Gutenberg and early printing.

Orcutt, William Dana. *The Book in Italy During the Fifteenth and Sixteenth Centuries Shown in Facsimile Reproductions from the Most Famous Printed Volumes.* New York: Harper & Bros., 1928.
The 128 full-size facsimiles illustrate the early history of Italian printing. Arrangement is chronological by city, beginning with Subiaco. According to Orcutt, the earliest dated item from the press of Konrad Sweynheym and Arnold Pannartz, Italy's first printers, is the *Opera* of Lactantius, a page of which is reproduced here. (The Cicero, also reproduced in this volume, may predate Lactantius). Accompanying the plates is a brief discussion of printing in each city and of the particular items depicted. Handsome and informative.

Painter, George D. *William Caxton: A Quincentenary Biography of England's First Printer.* London: Chatto & Windus, 1976.
Unlike a number of other biographies, including Norman Francis Blake's *Caxton: England's First Printer* (cited earlier), Painter's argues that Caxton was a skilled author, and Painter accepts Caxton's explanation that printing served as a means of satisfying the demand for the translation of *The History of Troy.* Drawing on documents of the period, Painter helps situate Caxton in the English political and intellectual landscape of the late fifteenth century and offers some new ideas about Caxton's birthplace in Kent and his training as a printer in Cologne. Includes a useful list of Caxton's imprints and a solid bibliography of secondary sources. Curt Buhler considered this "a brilliant study, . . . a remarkable and distinguished achievement" (*Times Literary Supplement* July 29, 1977, 944). Doris Grumbach concurred: "Lovers of printing history, English history and the book as work of art will be delighted with what Painter has done to uncover the shadowy Caxton" (*New York Times Book Review*, April 24, 1977, 16).

Pearsall, Derek, ed. *Manuscripts and Readers in Fifteenth-Century England: The Literary Implications of Manuscript Study.* Dover, N.H.: Boydell & Brewer, 1983.
The nine essays here consider what the physical features of manuscripts reveal about the way texts are transmitted and read. Julia Boffey looks at courtly love lyrics. A. S. G. Edwards examines the production of and errors in manuscripts of the works of John Lydgate. Scribal editing of John Gower's works is the focus of Kate Harris' contribution. Lesley Lawton examines the illustrations of medieval texts, especially Lydgate's *Troy Book*. C. W. Marx writes about the relationship between two religious texts (*Complaint of Our Lady* and the *Gospel of Nicodemus*) sometimes linked in manuscripts. Carol M. Meale and John J.

Thompson deal with compilers, Jeremy J. Smith looks at mixed dialects in the manuscripts of Gower, and Thorlac Turville-Petre discusses the literature of the Northeast Midlands. A. I. Doyle's conclusion places these essays in the larger context of manuscript studies. Specialized, but useful as examples of textual study and important for those concerned with medieval books and literature.

Proctor, Robert. *The Printing of Greek in the Fifteenth Century*. London: Oxford University Press for the Bibliographical Society, 1900.

Focuses on the use of Greek type in Italy. The first chapter looks at "the history of Hellenic culture in Italy" before the advent of printing. Proctor then considers the appearance of Greek fonts in Latin texts to 1476, when Dionysius Paravisinus of Milan printed the *Erotemata* of Konstantinos Laskaris. This work bears the date of January 30, 1476, but may have been printed the following year. Proctor next deals with a number of other Greek books from Italian presses, and concludes with a discussion of early Greek printing in Germany, the Netherlands, France, Spain, and England. The text is supplemented by numerous facsimiles; taken together they purport to show "every known type used in a Greek book . . . up to the year 1500."

Redgrave, Gilbert R. *Erhard Ratdolt and His Work at Venice*. London: Bibliographical Society, 1894.

Redgrave first discusses the beginnings of Venetian printing. He observes that fifty printers were active in the city between 1470 and 1480. In 1476 Ratdolt issued his first imprint, the *Kalendarium* of Johann Müller of Konigsberg. Twelve years later he left Venice to print religious works at Augsburg, where he remained until his death in 1527 or 1528. While in Venice, Ratdolt created the first ornamental printed title page and extensively used woodcut initials. He was also the first to use several different colored inks simultaneously. Redgrave examines Ratdolt's Venetian imprints and presents a bibliography of the printer's work in Italy. With numerous facsimiles.

Rhodes, Dennis Everard. *Studies in Early Italian Printing*. London: Pindar Press, 1982.

Contains fifty-six pieces, eighteen in Italian and the rest in English, that Rhodes published between 1952 and 1978. Excludes his work on Florentine printing. The book is divided into six sections: Venice, Milan and Lombardy, Mantua, Southern Italy, smaller Italian cities, and seventeenth century Italian bibliography. The essays range widely—sometimes examining a particular volume, sometimes the career of a printer, sometimes the early history of printing in a particular city. The discussions always illuminate the issues they address. For example, Rhodes argues that Sienna produced about a hundred incunables, though only seventy-one are known; the majority of these deal with legal matters. Two pieces examine the brisk seventeenth century book trade between England and Italy to show the Italian interest in English science and the English interest in Italian antiquities, including religious books. John Tedeschi commented that *"Studies in Early Italian Printing* . . . provides an eminently readable and fascinating guide into the world of the bibliographer of early printing. It also raises . . . the larger historical questions that bear directly on the transmission of knowledge in Renaissance and early modern Europe" (*Papers of the Bibliographical Society of America* 78, 1984, 500-501).

Scholderer, Victor. "The Beginning of Printing at Basel." *The Library* 3 (1949): 50-54.
Basel experienced a printers' strike in 1471, so the trade must have been established in the city by then. Yet the earliest dated colophon from the city is from 1474. Scholderer argues that a Latin Bible, Nicolaus of Lyra's *Postilla super Evangelia*, and Gregory's *Moralia in Job* were the first three books published in Basel, and that printing there may have begun as early as 1468, as Dr. Kurt Ohly of Frankfurt University suggested in 1940. These books, Scholderer writes, may have come from the press of Berthold Ruppel, once an assistant to Gutenberg.

_____. *Johann Gutenberg: The Inventor of Printing*. London: Trustees of the British Museum, 1963.
An attractively illustrated, brief account of Gutenberg's life and work. Scholderer presents as fact much that is conjecture, and the bibliography is sparse, but the pamphlet provides a good starting point for the novice. Should, however, be read in conjunction with Janet Ing's *Johann Gutenberg and His Bible* (cited earlier).

_____. *Printers and Readers in Italy in the Fifteenth Century*. London: Geoffrey Cumberlege, 1949.
Although printing did not come to Italy until nearly a decade after the appearance of the Gutenberg Bible, the art found a welcome home there. Scholderer contrasts the works printed in Italy with those produced in Germany, observing that classical texts and vernacular literature enjoyed greater popularity south of the Alps. This lecture also examines the output of various cities and presses to arrive at some

understanding of the interests of the book-buying public. A readable survey. As R. Weiss commented in *Modern Language Review* 45 (1950): 401, "Dr. Scholderer's fine lecture . . . will doubtless be read with absorbing interest by everyone interested in incunabula or in Italian literature."

Schulz, Ernst. *The Study of Incunables: Problems and Aims.* Translated by Glenys Waldman. Ed. Rudolf Hirsch. Philadelphia: Philobiblon Club, 1977.

A translation of an address that Schulz gave in 1924. He notes that the printing press revived ancient notions of publishing and of literary property. He reminds his audience that publishers wanted to make money, so their products reveal the taste of the time, a taste that favored late medieval authors. A study of incunabla can contribute to an understanding of fifteenth century mentalities. In urging the unification of the study of the book with such disciplines as intellectual history, reading tastes, and other cultural investigations, Schulz was well ahead of his time. Curt F. Buhler called this work "required reading for anyone interested in incunabula" (*Renaissance Quarterly* 31, 1978, 345).

Slater, John Rothwell. *Printing and the Renaissance: A Paper Read Before the Fortnightly Club of Rochester New York.* New York: William Edwin Rudge, 1921.

Most of the paper considers five major Renaissance printers: Aldus Manutius of Venice, Robert Estienne of Paris, Johann Froben (Basel), Anton Koberger (Nuremberg), and William Caxton (London). According to Slater, "Taken together, the books issued from their presses at the end of the fifteenth and the beginning of the sixteenth century form a sort of composite picture of the Renaissance." Unlike some more recent historians of the book, Slater maintains that "printing did not make the Renaissance; the Renaissance made printing." Yet he acknowledges that printing "accelerated enormously the process of enlightenment."

Stillwell, Margaret Bingham. *The Beginning of the World of Books, 1450 to 1470.* New York: Bibliographical Society of America, 1972.

The first part of this book lists by date 215 items that appeared in the first two decades of printing. Stillwell provides "brief statements of author, title, place, printer and date, . . . bibliographical references . . . ; the location of rare and unique copies . . . ; various annotations," together with information about studies and facsimiles of the item. Supplementary sections list authors; commentators, editors, and translators; subjects; printers and places; and undated imprints. Appendix A summarizes documents relating to Gutenberg, and Appendix B lists undated imprints from the Netherlands, some of which have been used in the past to support the claim of Laurens Janszoon Koster of Haarlem to be the inventor of printing. Nicolas Barker remarked that *The Beginning of the World of Books* "is an invaluable summary of all the wealth of work that has been poured into the study of . . . the printed books and other matter datable to 1470 or earlier. . . . Only a scholar with long and deep knowledge and experience of the subject could have compiled such a work" (*The Book Collector* 23, 1974, 579-580).

_____. *Incunabula and Americana, 1450-1800: A Key to Bibliographical Study*. New York: Columbia University Press, 1931.
Intended to teach bibliographers how "to identify and collate a fifteenth century book" as well as Americana. The volume is useful for its discussion of the introduction and spread of printing during the first fifty years of printing. Stillwell also provides a list of some 600 reference works dealing with early printing, and a briefer bibliography for early illustration and engraving. Like Robert A. Peddie's *Fifteenth Century Books* (cited earlier), Stillwell's offers the modern equivalents of fifteenth century Latin names and explains Latin contractions and abbreviations popular in early printed books.

Todd, William Burton. *The Gutenberg Bible: New Evidence of the Original Printing*. Chapel Hill: University of North Carolina Press, 1982.
In the copy of the Gutenberg Bible at the University of Texas, lines 3 and 4 of folio 40 (recto) of Volume 1 are transposed in both columns. Todd argues from this mistake that the compositors arranged the type not by column but directly across the page. The accident was quickly noticed and corrected, so that no other copy exhibits this anomaly. To set type as Todd suggests, the compositors must have worked from a copy text, of which the Gutenberg Bible is a facsimile. In a review essay longer than Todd's lecture ("The Compositor's Hand in the Gutenberg Bible," *Papers of the Bibliographical Society of America* 77, 1983, 341-371), Paul Needham argues against Todd's hypothesis. Both pieces make important contributions to the ongoing study of early printing.

Trapp, Joseph Burney, ed. *Manuscripts in the Fifty Years After the Invention of Printing*. London: Warburg Institute, 1983.
The advent of printing did not at once destroy the manuscript tradition. M. D. Reeve observes in "Manuscripts Copied from Printed Books"

that a handwritten copy might be less expensive, a printed version might not be available for purchase, and some, like the Duke of Urbino, despised printed volumes. C. F. de Hamel examines the continuing trade in liturgical works in the late fifteenth century. Even into the early 1500s, lavish Books of Hours and Breviaries were produced by hand in Flanders. Eberhard König notes that the multiplicity of copies of the Gutenberg Bible provided work for many illuminators, though woodcuts eventually supplanted them. Lilian Armstrong comments on the persistence of a cycle of historiated initials in Pliny's *Historia naturalis*. Venetian illuminators of incunabular editions copied the series from fourteenth century Italian manuscripts, and the 1513 edition contains woodcuts based on these two-century-old illustrations. Other contributors focus on specific individuals or manuscripts, but all show the continuing viability and influence of manuscripts in the late fifteenth and early sixteenth centuries.

Wilson, Adrian. *The Making of the Nuremberg Chronicle.* Amsterdam: Nico Israel, 1976.

Hartman Schedel's The Nuremberg Chronicle was published in German and Latin in 1493 by Anton Koberger. Wilson looks at the production of this profusely illustrated volume to determine how a printer/publisher dealt with contemporary problems of book production. His intention is "to reconstruct the making of *The Nuremberg Chronicle*; the compilation of manuscript sources by its author; the artists' first concepts for the illustrations; the patrons' agreements for financing the publications; the layouts; the printing; the advertising; the distribution, and the final settlement." Some of the primary materials reproduced here had already been published elsewhere, but Wilson brings them together and offers useful comments. With many woodcuts and a bibliography. James E. Walsh wrote in *Papers of the Bibliographical Society of America* 72 (1978): 149, "Mr. Wilson and his publisher . . . are both to be congratulated on an outstanding contribution both to the history of the book and to the art of bookmaking."

Winship, George Parker. *Gutenberg to Plantin: An Outline of the Early History of Printing.* Cambridge, Mass.: Harvard University Press, 1926.

Though some of the material here reappears in Winship's later *Printing in the Fifteenth Century* (cited herein), this brief survey of early printing includes information not found in that later work and serves as a pleasant introduction to the subject. Winship notes, among other things, that economic expansion in the Rhine Valley promoted the development of printing to satisfy an increased demand for books. By 1480, Venice had become Europe's largest producer of books because of the proliferation of paper mills in Italy and the city's extensive commercial dealings that allowed it to export books cheaply. Winship describes the sixteenth century rise of the publisher as the major figure in book production, supplanting the printer and ending an era in the history of the book. In the course of his discussion, Winship considers early book illustration, scholar/printers, and patronage. R. B. McKerrow wrote in *Review of English Studies* 3 (1927): 248, "Altogether the book is one which can be warmly recommended to the notice of all literary students who desire a general view of the way in which printing began."

_____. *John Gutenberg.* Chicago: Lakeside Press, 1940.
This lecture, given at the University of Pennsylvania to celebrate the 500th anniversary of Gutenberg's invention, offers much speculation based on the limited documentary evidence available. Winship suggests that early printing in Strasbourg is less sophisticated than that of Mainz because Strasbourg printers used Gutenberg's early ideas, not the ones he later developed when he moved to Mainz from his native city. Winship suggests that as early as the 1430s, Gutenberg was working on an edition of the popular *Speculum humanae salvationis* to sell to pilgrims going to Aix, but a plague led to the abandoning of the pilgrimage and a financial loss. Winship is on more solid ground in noting the shift from forty to forty-two lines in the text of the Gutenberg Bible, and he observes that in the *Catholicon* of 1460 Gutenberg shrank the size of type even more.

_____. *Printing in the Fifteenth Century.* Philadelphia: University of Pennsylvania Press, 1940.
A collection of five lectures Winship delivered as Rosenbach Fellow in Bibliography. The first two deal with early German printing, the third with printing in Italy. In the fourth lecture, Winship traces the spread of printing in the later fifteenth and early sixteenth centuries, and in Chapter 5 he looks at particular facets of his subject, such as the first university press (Paris), luxury book production in France, and Caxton's press. A well-written introduction.

_____. *William Caxton and His Work.* Berkeley: Book Arts Club, University of California, 1937.
Contains two pieces, one a lecture that Winship gave to the Club of Odd Volumes in 1908, the other a letter addressed to the Book Arts

Club of the University of California in 1937. Much new information has come to light since 1937 about Caxton's printing, but Winship's short account remains a useful introduction. Reprints a number of important documents, including a long extract from Caxton's preface to his translation of the *Aeneid*, in which he speaks of his effort to standardize the English language. Winship's summary of Caxton's achievement is still sound: "He had introduced printing into England: he had given to English readers the best of foreign literature: he had increased a thousand fold their familiarity with the poetry of [John] Lydgate, of [John] Gower, and of Geoffrey Chaucer."

Chapter 13
THE SIXTEENTH AND SEVENTEENTH CENTURIES

Allen, Don Cameron. "Some Contemporary Accounts of Renaissance Printing Methods." *The Library* 17 (1937): 167-171.

Allen presents highlights from three "out-of-the-way books" that discuss printing in the sixteenth and seventeenth centuries. Leonardo Fioravanti's *Dello specchio di scientia universale* (Venice, 1567), Loys le Roy's *De la vicissitude ou variété des choses en l'univers* (Paris, 1579), and René François' *Essay des merveilles, de nature et des plus nobles artifices* (Rouen, 1622) all speak of the technical aspects of printing. Robert Ashley's 1594 English translation of le Roy's work, for example, noted that a pressman could produce 1,250-1,300 sheets in a day. He claims that printers used at least two presses—one for proofs, the other for the actual copy. He also said that some printers had experimented with copper letters, but these "pierce the paper."

Armstrong, Elizabeth. *Robert Estienne, Royal Printer: An Historical Study of the Elder Stephanus*. Cambridge, England: Cambridge University Press, 1954.

In 1504 or 1505 Henry Estienne, university printer, established his press "near the college of Beauvais opposite the School of Canon Law." Robert, his son, also became a printer, though his connections were closer to the court than to the university, and in 1550 religious disputes caused him to flee to Geneva, where he became Calvin's printer. Armstrong examines Estienne's work as scholar and printer, first for the king of France and then for the religious reformers. This detailed biography places Estienne's activities within the social and political movements of the period and pays particular attention to censorship. J. M. T. Charlton commented in *Classical Review* 6 (1956): 64, "Students of bibliography, of French social history, and of the history of biblical criticism, will find this book of great interest. So, too, will classical scholars."

Ascarelli, Fernanda, and Marco Menato. *La tipografia del '500 in Italia*. Florence: Leo S. Olschki, 1989.

An updated, corrected version of Ascarelli's 1953 *La tipografia cinquecentina italiana*, long the standard reference on sixteenth century

Italian printers. Arranged alphabetically by region and then chronologically by when printing arrived in a particular town. Each section provides biographical and bibliographical information. Most of the sixty-five plates reproduce rare title pages. Dennis E. Rhodes praised the book as "a magnificent reference tool which could hardly be bettered" (*The Library* 12, 1990, 350).

Avis, F. C. *Printers of Fleet Street and St. Paul's Churchyard in the Sixteenth Century.* London: Glenview Press for F. C. Avis, 1964.

Samuel Johnson, the essential bookman, loved Fleet Street, which was associated with printing from the industry's earliest days in England. John Lettou in 1480 opened a printing shop near Fleet Bridge; by 1500, when Wynkyn de Worde located at the lower end of Fleet Street, it was already a center of printing. Avis notes that the Fleet River in the sixteenth century provided transportation, and the street was surrounded by "the legal, learned, and religious professions," all needing books. Avis lists and briefly discusses the Fleet Street printers and then does the same for nearby St. Paul's Churchyard, which was a center of bookselling even before the advent of the press. A pleasant, informative pamphlet.

Baillie, William M. "Early Printed Books in Small Formats." *The Papers of the Bibliographical Society of America* 69 (1975): 197-205.

Looking at the *Short Title Catalogue of English Books* entries for 1600, 1620, 1640, and 1660, Baillie finds that no more than twenty percent of the books printed in England in those years appeared in duodecimo or smaller size; generally, the average was closer to ten percent. Yet important literary works were published in these formats. Baillie analyzes the *Gratiae theatrales* (London, 1662), a collection of three pre-Restoration plays, to understand how these small books were produced. For example, Baillie argues that the book was printed in stages between other tasks. He also finds that two typesetters, with different spelling preferences, worked on the project. Helps illuminate printing practices of the period.

Bennett, H. S. *English Books and Readers, 1558-1603; English Books and Readers, 1603-1640.* Cambridge, England: Cambridge University Press, 1965, 1970.

These two volumes continue Bennett's earlier account of the book trade in England from the establishment of the Stationers' Company to the eve of the English Civil War—and the end of the *Short-Title Catalogue of English Books.* Together they examine the variety of publications that appeared from the accession of Elizabeth onward and discuss the audiences that publishers hoped to attract. Bennett's books offer a panoramic view of the print culture in England during the period, showing increasing literacy, increasing book production, and a decline in the role of patronage as writers begin to rely more fully on readers and publishers for support. Through these years, religious works remain a major component of the trade, though chapbooks, almanacs, and other inexpensive ephemera assume a growing share of the market. The *Times Literary Supplement* for December 16, 1965, observed of *English Books and Readers, 1558 to 1603*: "The material is so skillfully selected, and so well presented, that not merely the specialist but anyone interested in the social history of the age of Elizabeth will here find much to satisfy curiosity and stimulate thought" (p. 1188). The same might be said of the later volume.

Bernard, August. *Geoffrey Tory, Painter and Engraver, First Royal Printer, Reformer of Orthography and Typography Under François I: An Account of His Life and Works.* Translated by George B. Ives. Boston: Houghton Mifflin, 1909.

The first section presents biographical information about Tory, who was born around 1480 at Bourges. In 1504 he went to Paris as a professor and editor. He became an engraver in 1518; the death of his daughter Agnes in 1522 led him to adopt his famous pot cassé as his printer's mark. His *Champ Fleury* praised the French language; the volume also dealt with typography. Tory became royal printer in 1531 and died in 1533. Bernard next provides a bibliography of Tory's work, and the section on iconography discusses his engravings and illustrations. Bernard explores Tory's vast influence, especially in ornamentation, contributing to the movement away from medieval to Renaissance motifs. Frederick W. Gookin praised Bernard's "accurate scholarship and . . . minute and painstaking research" (*The Dial* 46, 1909, 402). The volume is a masterpiece of typography and bookmaking by Bruce Rogers at the Riverside Press.

Bliss, Carey S. *Some Aspects of Seventeenth Century English Printing with Special Reference to Joseph Moxon.* Los Angeles: William Andrews Clark Memorial Library, 1965.

Bliss defends seventeenth century English printing, arguing that the presses produced a large number of editions—about 93,500—and that among these are such monuments of typography as Topsell's *Foure-Footed Beastes* and Jacob Tonson's 1697 *Virgil*. Bliss claims that the Samaritan, Syriac, Arabic, and Ethiopic types used for the Polyglot

Bible (printed in London) were made in England and so demonstrate another facet of seventeenth century English typographic skill. The original types actually may have been of foreign origin, though. This short work also reviews the career of Joseph Moxon and provides a census of copies of the second volume of his important work on English printing practices, *Mechanick Exercises.*

Bowers, Fredson. "Notes on Standing Type in Elizabethan Printing." *The Papers of the Bibliographical Society of America* 40 (1946): 205-224.
Usually type was distributed as soon as it had been used, but Bowers notes that title pages might be left standing. Also, type from uncommon fonts might not be distributed, even when the more common type in the form was. Not only did printers need to distribute type for other printing projects, but also the Stationers' Company restricted the number of copies of any edition. Since this rule sought to guarantee employment for typesetters, they would not have tolerated leaving entire volumes in standing type. Printers could get permission to keep standing type, and some printers connived with employees to skirt the restrictions of the Stationers' Company. In the course of his discussion, Bowers takes the reader inside the early seventeenth century print shop to see how books were made.

Carlson, David. "Formats in English Printing to 1557." *Analytical and Enumerative Bibliography* 2 (1988): 50-57.
As printing developed in England, books tended to get smaller. In the incunabula period, most books printed in England were folios. Between 1550 and 1557 most were octavos. Before 1500, 22.8 percent of the books from Wynkyn de Worde's press were folios; after 1500, the figure drops to 5.5 percent. This smaller format saved paper and so reduced printers' costs. Most of this article consists of tables illustrating the shift in book size that Carlson notes.

Chrisman, Miriam Usher. *Lay Culture, Learned Culture: Books and Social Change in Strasbourg, 1480-1599.* New Haven, Conn.: Yale University Press, 1982.
Looks at how the presses in Strasbourg catered to the Latinate humanistic culture or to the popular vernacular culture. Chrisman explores the book trade, where she finds clerical dominance before 1520, a period of transition between 1515 and 1549, and lay ascendancy afterwards, though the clergy and the academics continued to struggle for supremacy until the end of the century. She concludes that printing did not alter socioeconomic divisions in the city, but rather reflected

them. Michael Hackenberg wrote in *Library Quarterly* 54 (1984): 119,
"Despite the blatant bibliographical weaknesses [Chrisman's study
will] provide additional historical insight into the social role of the
book during the Reformation era and will have to be taken into
consideration by historians of the book." In conjunction with this work,
Chrisman prepared a *Bibliography of Strasbourg Imprints, 1480-1599*
(New Haven, Conn.: Yale University Press, 1982), giving full bibliographic information for 5,677 imprints.

Clair, Colin. *Christopher Plantin*. London: Cassell, 1960.
In his introduction, Leon Voet, Curator of the Plantin-Moretus Museum
(Antwerp), himself a biographer of Christophe Plantin, calls Plantin
"indubitably the greatest printer of his time[, ranking] in the history of
printing among the few giant figures who have stamped the craft with
the mark of their genius." Clair's biography, the first major account in
English, offers detailed exploration of Plantin's career, and the epilogue briefly traces the history of the business over the following three
centuries until it was sold as a museum to the city of Antwerp. Clair
notes that Plantin was not a scholar, but he was an intellectual who
published important humanist works. Clair also provides detailed
analysis of the printing of the Polyglot Bible, the epitome of Plantin's
achievement and among his greatest financial miscalculations.

Clark, Peter. "The Ownership of Books in England, 1560-1640: The
Example of Some Kentish Townfolk." In *Schooling and Society*, edited
by Lawrence Stone. Baltimore: Johns Hopkins University Press, 1976,
95-111.
Looks at book ownership in the towns of Canterbury, Faversham, and
Maidstone. In these places, church and public libraries did not exist
before 1640, so Clark argues that ownership was necessary for reading.
He ignores the possibility of borrowing. A number of Kentish citizens
in fact did own fairly extensive collections of books. By 1562 Thomas
Rolfe, a lawyer, had his own librarian. In 1623 alone Sir Edward Dering
bought some 200 volumes. Among the lower classes, book ownership
rose dramatically during this period. In the 1560s, in Canterbury only
eight percent of inventories of male inhabitants listed books, but by the
1630s nearly half do so. For Faversham the figures are fifteen percent
and forty-nine percent, respectively. The Bible was the most popular
title. Increasingly books were kept in the private bedroom rather than
in the public hall. Greater book ownership reflects increased literacy
and prosperity. Clark also associates the change with the growth of
religious dissent in the early Stuart era.

Cressy, David. *Literacy and the Social Order: Reading and Writing in Tudor and Stuart England.* Cambridge, England: Cambridge University Press, 1980.

Cressy looks at the signatures on seventeenth century petitions, wills, marriage license records, and ecclesiastical court depositions to determine literacy rates. Because writing was taught after reading, the ability to sign one's name probably indicates literacy. On the basis of the percentages of signatures versus marks on legal documents, Cressy concludes that in mid-seventeenth century England more than two-thirds of the men "lacked the capacity for basic active literacy" even though Protestant divines emphasized the importance of reading. By 1714, about half the men and a quarter of the women could write their names, though this ability was not spread uniformly among the social classes. Among the gentry, literacy was almost universal in this period, whereas farmers, servants, and women were far less likely to be able to sign their names. Literacy rates thus correspond to the social hierarchy and can serve as socioeconomic markers. David Traister wrote in the *American Book Collector* 2 (November/December, 1981): 545-546, "For anyone whose interests encompass earlier books and manuscripts, and who must therefore also worry about the people who read them, Cressy's wonderfully stimulating book is highly recommended."

Davies, David W. *The World of the Elseviers, 1570-1712.* The Hague: Martinus Nijhoff, 1954.

Davies describes his book as "an attempt . . . to give the essential facts of the history of the Elsevier family, and to show the relations of the printers to the world around them." He is especially concerned with economic and social history. The account begins with Louis Elsevier, born at Louvain in 1546 or 1547, who worked for the Plantins at Antwerp. Religious conflicts drove him to Leyden, where he established a press. He fathered nine children, who carried on the business in various Dutch cities—the Hague, Utrecht, and Amsterdam—for more than a century. Davies emphasizes the role of the Elseviers in promoting small, affordable books, though fewer than half of the Elseviers' books were in duodecimo format.

DeVinne, Theodore Low. *Christopher Plantin and the Plantin-Moretus Museum at Antwerp.* New York: Grolier Club, 1888.

This handsomely produced book begins with a brief account of Christophe Plantin, who enjoyed great prosperity in his adopted Antwerp but also endured severe financial reverses. The business recovered in the seventeenth century, then declined in the eighteenth and nineteenth

until it ceased to function in 1867. Leopold de Wael, burgomaster of
Antwerp, persuaded the city to buy the operation in 1876. It is not
purely a sixteenth century printing office, since it changed over time,
but it does show how presses operated centuries ago. DeVinne describes the museum as it was in the latter half of the 1800s, and includes
illustrations. In the course of the discussion, DeVinne explains how
books were produced in the sixteenth and seventeenth centuries.

Friedman, Jerome. *The Battle of the Frogs and Fairford's Flies: Miracles
and the Pulp Press During the English Revolution.* New York: St.
Martin's Press, 1993.
Looks at several hundred newsbooks and pulp publications to understand the mentality of ordinary English people during the period
1640-1660. Friedman offers a fascinating discussion of the content of
this material, which is filled with the miraculous, the xenophobic, the
monstrous, and the sexual. Determining the readership of this material
is difficult, as is ascertaining how it was understood. Did people believe
these fantastic tales, or did pulp pamphlets constitute the escapist
literature of the age?

Goldschmidt, Ernest Philip. *The First Cambridge Press in Its European
Setting.* Cambridge, England: Cambridge University Press, 1955.
Presents Goldschmidt's Sandars Lectures in Bibliography for 1953.
The first lecture discusses John Siberch and the ten books he printed
at Cambridge in 1521-1522. Goldschmidt uses Siberch as a jumping-
off point for exploring early sixteenth century printing and book history
throughout Western Europe. The second lecture considers the importance of Greek for the humanist movement; Siberch boasted that he
was the first English printer to print in both Latin and Greek, and
Goldschmidt explains why Cambridge in 1521 desired such work. The
final lecture examines the output of other printers in university towns.
A number of them produced humanist works and prospered, especially
Jodocus Badius van Assche in Paris, Thierry Martens in Louvain, and
John Froben in Basel. Siberch, despite his humanist sympathies, could
not succeed in Cambridge. Informative and entertaining.

_____. *The Printed Book in the Renaissance.* 2d ed. Amsterdam:
Van Heusden, 1966.
Three lectures that deal with type, illustration, and ornaments.
Goldschmidt notes that printers made and used type to suit what they
were printing. Gutenberg's Gothic was ideal for a Bible, just as Adolph
Rusch in Strasbourg, Konrad Sweynheym and Arnold Pannartz in Italy

chose roman type for Cicero. The Venetian printers used roman type for their classics of humanism. The market for such texts was glutted by the early 1470s, compelling printers to return to law books and other works that used Gothic type. The sixteenth century book generally used roman type, and it also differed from the medieval book in its illustrations and ornamentation. Instead of the illustrated book, the Renaissance favored "the picture book, the book of plates accompanied by explanatory letter-press." Alternatively, the humanists produced books with no illustrations at all. Instead of pictures the humanists adopted decorative borders and initials. The Roman arch on the title page implied that the book was a gateway to the ancient world, and architectural motifs were especially popular.

Gray, George John. *The Earlier Cambridge Stationers and Bookbinders, and the First Printer of Cambridge.* Oxford, England: Printed for the Bibliographical Society at the Oxford University Press, 1904.
As early as 1276, the Bishop of Ely declared that scribes, illuminators, and booksellers enjoyed the same protection of the university extended to scholars, and in the next century this privilege was extended to binders. Gray looks at early documents dealing with books at Cambridge, and in Part 1 he presents the information available concerning those involved with books before 1500. He provides a useful list of prices for repairing, binding, and chaining books in the late 1400s. He also notes that books could be used as pledges, and reprints a price list of those sold after they were forfeited. Part 2 treats the sixteenth century and reproduces a 1583 decree governing booksellers, binders, and stationers of the university. With illustrations of Cambridge bindings and stamps, including work by the binder John Siberch, who was also Cambridge's first printer.

_____. *John Siberch: The First Cambridge Printer, 1521-1522.* Cambridge, England: Bowes & Bowes, 1921.
Issued to celebrate the 400th anniversary of printing at Cambridge, this pamphlet first surveys the available bibliographical information about Siberch and then offers a summary view of the man and his printing. Gray briefly discusses each of Siberch's books. Gray concludes that Siberch came to Cambridge by 1520 and died or left in 1523. After Siberch's death or departure, no further printing was undertaken in Cambridge until 1584.

Harrison, G. B. "Books and Their Readers, 1591-1594." *The Library* 8 (1927): 273-302.

Harrison begins by showing that the Stationers' Register is not an infallible guide to works published. Some published works were never entered in the register, and some books were entered before they were even written. Among books published in the four years covered by this study, popular works generally appeared in black letter, while scholarly texts and those meant for cultured readers (for example, poetry) used roman typefaces. Harrison notes the wide variety of topics treated, with current events making up more than twenty percent of the approximately 550 items listed. The article is useful both for its observations about late sixteenth century English printing and for its methodology.

Hartz, S. L. *The Elseviers and Their Contemporaries: An Illustrated Commentary.* Amsterdam: Elsevier, 1955.
Louis de Louvain, a bookbinder who worked for the Plantins, changed his name, moved north from Antwerp, and founded the family of Elsevier. Elsevier borrowed money from Christophe Plantin to establish his bookselling operation in Leyden; later the firm began publishing works, and after 1616 the Elseviers became printers as well. Hartz maintains that the Elseviers bought their type from the same sources used by other Dutch printers, and the Elsevier books therefore are not typographically distinguished from those of their contemporaries. As publishers and booksellers the Elseviers excelled, and this success led to their books' being so highly esteemed among collectors. Hartz's text is enriched with numerous facsimiles of the Elseviers work, and Hartz evaluates the layout and presswork.

Johnson, Alfred Forbes. "Books Printed at Lyons in the Sixteenth Century." *The Library* 3 (1922): 145-174.
Drawing on the collection of the British Library, Johnson estimates that presses in Lyons issued some 13,000 imprints in the 1500s. Johnson considers the work of some of the major printers, such as Sebastien Gryphius (with 1,400 books to his credit), Benoit Rigaud (with 1,100), Guillaume Rouille (800), and others who were less prolific. As was true elsewhere in France, book production at Lyons peaked about 1560 and then declined, probably because of the outbreak of religious wars in 1562. Not only did the quantity of books produced declined, but also the quality deteriorated. Removed from the central authority of Paris, Claude Senneton of Lyons was able to publish Calvin's *Institution de la religion chrétienne* as late as 1565. Protestant printers began fleeing to Geneva in 1568, though they sometimes continued to put Lyons on the title page as supposed place of publication. The economic consequences of war hurt the book trade. Johnson also examines the shift in

book illustration from woodcuts to engravings during the century. The nature of Lyons' imprints confirms the revival of interest in Greek and Latin writers. As Johnson writes, "Out of the 2,380 books [in the British Library] published at Lyons, there are 313 editions of ancient Latin authors, and a further 23 editions of the Latin Fathers." Cicero is best represented (59 editions), followed by Ovid (26), Terence (22), and Virgil (21). Lyons was also an important center for medical and legal books.

_____. *French Sixteenth Century Printing.* London: Ernest Benn, 1928.

The first half of the sixteenth century in France witnessed the flowering of many fine printers—Jean Petit, Simon de Colines, Geoffrey Tory, the Estiennes, Claude Garamond. Though they drew on Italian models, their work was decidedly French, and it reflects the shift from the medieval world to the Renaissance. Johnson surveys this exciting period in French bookmaking and presents fifty illustrations that depict the beautiful products of the age.

_____. "Geoffrey Tory." *The Fleuron* 6 (1928): 37-66.

Johnson seeks to understand Tory's contributions to the sixteenth century French book. Tory has been regarded as a prime mover in the development of new type and new modes of illustration. Johnson examines Tory's woodcuts and reproduces a number of these. He also discusses the famous *Champ Fleury* with its analysis of the roman letter and the French language. Johnson concludes that Tory helped create a new style in book illustration, but there is no evidence that Tory created any new types. The ideas in the *Champ Fleury* did influence Garamond, so at least indirectly Tory affected the look of the printed page.

_____. *The Italian Sixteenth Century.* London: Ernest Benn, 1926.

Paris and Lyons produced the most beautiful books of the sixteenth century, but Italian presses produced more books, many of them of artistic as well as intellectual significance. Johnson concentrates on four printers: Antonio Blado of Rome, Francesco Marcolini and Gabriel Giolito de' Ferrari of Venice, and Lorenzo Torrentino of Florence. Following the thirty pages of text are fifty plates presenting fine examples of the typography and layout of sixteenth century Italian books.

_____. "The Supply of Types in the Sixteenth Century." *The Library* 24 (1843): 47-65.

In the early days of printing, each printer made his own types. Type-founding was, after all, Gutenberg's great achievement. By the sixteenth century, though, typefounding had become a separate industry, and all printers of a region were likely to buy their type from the same source. By the mid-1500s the trade in type had become international; Johnson notes that Robert Granjon's Double Pica Roman appears first in Lyons in 1548 and shortly afterwards in Basel and Florence. Johnson's study demonstrates that despite superficial variations, the number of different typefaces in the sixteenth century was more limited than had been previously believed.

Johnson, John de Morris, and Strickland Gibson. *Print and Privilege at Oxford to the Year 1700*. Oxford, England: Clarendon Press, 1946.
Privilege preceded print at Oxford, England: In the Middle Ages all involved with books at Oxford were regulated by the University Chancellor. Print arrived in 1478, about two years after Caxton established the first English press at Westminster. By 1486, some seventeen books had been printed at Oxford, but printing then ceased until 1517. Johnson and Gibson examine the university press's relationship with the government in the sixteenth and seventeenth centuries, paying particular attention to Archbishop William Laud's efforts to promote the learned press and John Fell's important contributions to better typography. The Appendix reprints seven important seventeenth century documents relating to the university press. The authors explore the economic conditions that limited the university press, particularly its competition with the Stationers' Company in London. Laurence Hanson observed that the authors' "wise comment illumines every aspect of the book trade" of the period (*Review of English Studies* 23, 1947, 366).

Judge, Cyril Bathurst. *Elizabethan Book-Pirates*. Cambridge, Mass.: Harvard University Press, 1934.
During the sixteenth century the Tudor monarchs sought to control the book trade, both to protect those engaged in the business and to regulate the flow of ideas. At the same time, some printers sought to circumvent these restrictions for either monetary or ideological motives. Judge examines the careers of some of these renegade printers, among them John Wolfe, Roger Ward, Robert Waldegrave, and Simon Stafford. Judge includes many transcripts of contemporary documents and offers a fascinating picture of the printing underworld of the period as well as of the Stationers' Company's efforts to enforce its monopoly.

Love, Harold. *Scribal Publication in Seventeenth-Century England*. New York: Oxford University Press, 1993.

Despite the advent of printing, much literature circulated in manuscript in the seventeenth century, as did music, newsletters, and political commentary, sometimes in hundreds of copies. Thus, works were published without being printed. Scribal publication could be promoted by author, reader, or entrepreneur; Love explores the ways scribes worked to create their copies. Part 2, "Script and Society," considers how readers perceived works in manuscript. Love suggests that print triumphed only in the eighteenth century. Even Jonathan Swift, who grew up in the seventeenth century, repeatedly stressed the contradictions of print. Part 3 explores the challenges the modern editor faces in editing scribal publications.

Marks, Saul. *Christopher Plantin and the Officina Plantiniana*. Los Angeles: Plantin Press, 1972.

Though born in France, Christophe Plantin moved to Antwerp around 1549, perhaps because of the religious intolerance that was driving other printers to Geneva at the same time. Antwerp was prospering, and it was close to the market created by the University of Louvain. Plantin worked as a binder until a wound left him unable to continue in that occupation. He therefore turned to printing, producing his first book in 1555. Plantin bought beautiful type and produced handsome books. He also earned handsome profits. In 1557, Jan Moerentorf joined the press. He latinized his name to Moretus, and his descendants continued the printing operation until the mid-nineteenth century. From the carefully kept records of the firm, one can learn much about the business of books in the sixteenth century. For example, the accounts show that in the mid-1500s a press cost about sixty florins, more than half a year's wages for a pressman. Plantin's 1567 *Dialogues françois pour les jeunes enfans* discusses the operations of a printing office, and Marks includes the office rules from about 1563.

Martin, Henri-Jean. *Livre, pouvoirs et société à Paris au XVIIe siècle*. 2 vols. Geneva: Droz, 1969.

Martin examined a large sample of imprints to understand the Parisian book trade and the cultural backgrounds of those involved in it. Martin divides the century into three parts: the flourishing early decades to about 1645; a period of crisis (1645-1660s); and the final decades, when the book trade was regulated by the state and the presses declined. Because of economic pressures, books became smaller over the course of the century. Martin argues that throughout the 1600s

302 The History of the Book

culture remained the property of the few. The aristocracy of the robe bought theological and classical works, while the aristocracy of the sword supported science, poetry, and sentimental fiction. R. A. Sayce's favorable review in *The Library* 26 (1971): 275-278 observed that Martin's "is a work of prodigious industry and learning on a period in the history of the French book which has never been studied in this depth before and . . . throws light on any number of hitherto obscure problems, by no means all of them confined to French conditions." English translation by David Gerard, *Prints, Power, and People in 17th-Century France*, Metuchen: Scarecrow Press, 1993.

Meredith-Owens, G. M. *Turkish Miniatures*. London: Trustees of the British Museum, 1963.
This little book consists of thirty-two pages of text and twenty-five plates, six of them in color. Meredith-Owens observes that Turkish illuminated manuscripts are rare, but they show a wide range of subject matter. The artistic approach in these examples is realistic, unlike the romantic treatment found in Persian illumination. Persian influence is nonetheless evident, as are borrowings from Europe and the Far East. Concentrates on works of the sixteenth and seventeenth centuries.

Mergenthaler Linotype Company. *Robert Granjon: Sixteenth Century Type Founder and Printer*. Brooklyn, N.Y.: Mergenthaler Linotype Company, 1931.
Attractively printed in 21-point Linotype Granjon, this brief account traces the career of a major French typefounder. Granjon supplied Christophe Plantin with a variety of fonts, including Hebrew, Greek, and italic, but he is most famous for his *caractères de civilité*, also known as "lettres françaises." In the preface to *Dialogues de la vie et de la mort* (1557) Granjon remarked that various designers had created national typefaces, and he wanted to do the same for France by imitating the manuscripts of the period. The style derives its name of *civilité* from two books printed with these new letters, *La Civilité puerile* (Antwerp, 1559) and *Civilité honeste pour les enfants* (Paris, 1560). Though Granjon intended this type for France, it proved more popular in the Netherlands. In the 1580s, Granjon moved to Italy, where he cut Arabic type. He died in Paris about 1590. This publication concludes with four pages showing the full range of Linotype Granjon.

Norton, F. J. *Italian Printers, 1501-1520*. London: Bowes and Bowes, 1958.
In the introduction, Norton discusses changes in the distribution of printing centers in the first two decades of the sixteenth century in Italy.

He also treats the book trade, printing patents, privileges, and licenses. The text itself offers a geographical listing and discussion of Italian printers for the period covered. Between 1501 and 1520, forty-nine Italian locales had active presses, though some of these were ephemeral. Authorities granted monopolies for particular works, but Norton argues that such privileges were not a form of censorship.

_____. *Printing in Spain, 1501-1520*. Cambridge, England: Cambridge University Press, 1966.

Norton here does for Spanish printing what the previous item does for Italy, offering much valuable information on early sixteenth century Spanish printers and printing. A. Rodriguez-Monimo commented in *Renaissance Quarterly* 23 (1973): 180 that this study "is distinguished by solid documentation, by a wealth of new bibliographical descriptions, and by an admirable clarity of exposition. . . . With this book, technical studies in the Hispanic field rise to heights never before attained."

Pattison, Mark. "Classical Learning in France: The Great Printers Stephens." *Quarterly Review* 117 (1865): 323-364.

A pleasant essay on the lives of Robert Estienne and his son Henri II. Pattison comments on the religious conflicts that drove Robert to Geneva and notes the importance of the Greek Testaments that aroused the anger of the Catholic Church. Robert Estienne established the verse division of the Bible, just as his son Henri II created the standard edition of Plato. Pattison admires Henri's ability to edit texts but challenges the printer's skills as a critic. The essay concludes with a discussion of Henri's contribution to the debate about the French language: Henri favored Greek rather than Italian borrowings. Pattison argues that Henri did not write the anonymous *Discours merveilleux de la vie de Catherine de Médicis*, an attack on the Queen Mother for assuming the Regency after the death of Charles IX.

Pettas, William A. *The Giunti of Florence: Merchant Publishers of the Sixteenth Century*. San Francisco: Bernard M. Rosenthal, 1980.

Shunning the family textile business in Florence, Lucantonio Giunta set off for Venice, attracted by its burgeoning book trade. He became both printer and publisher, and, through relatives, made himself into a multinational corporation, with branches in Rome, Lyons, and Spain. Filippo Giunta operated in Florence as a publisher of humanist works, relying on editors to provide the learning he lacked. Pettas examines the imprints of the Florentine Giuntas, their editors, and the economic and political conditions that affected the business. By 1600 the press, unable to compete with rivals in Basel, Geneva, and Antwerp, virtually disappeared from Florence. Pettas includes a checklist of books produced by the Giunta family of Florence from 1497 to 1570 and also a collection of twenty-nine relevant documents dating from 1427 to November 28, 1622. These documents are not translated into English. With a nine-page bibliography of secondary sources.

Plomer, Henry R. *Wynkyn de Worde and His Contemporaries from the Death of Caxton to 1535: A Chapter in English Printing*. London: Grafton, 1925.
Still the best biography of Wynkyn de Worde and an important history of early English printing. Discusses Wynkyn de Worde, Richard Pynson, John Lettou, William de Machlinia, Julian Notary, and a number of other English and Scottish printers active before 1535, the year of Wynkyn de Worde's death. Plomer regards Wynkyn de Worde as a good businessman, but lacking in aesthetic or literary taste. Plomer considers Pynson the better printer. Includes a good survey of the books that came from the early sixteenth century English presses.

Rostenberg, Leona. *Literary, Scientific, Religious, and Legal Publishing, Printing, and Bookselling in England, 1551-1700: Twelve Studies*. 2 vols. New York: Burt Franklin, 1965.
Brings together ten previously published essays together with two new ones, linked by an introduction and conclusion. These learned articles examine twelve members of the Stationers' Company, "their careers, the milieu in which they lived and worked, their influence upon the period and the period's influence upon them." Rostenberg ranges widely, dealing with such figures as Thomas Wight, publisher of law books; Thomas Thorpe, best known for publishing the 1609 edition of Shakespeare's *Sonnets*; the Puritan Michael Sparke; the Catholic Nathaniel Thompson; and Richard and Anne Baldwin, supporters of the Glorious Revolution. Their careers reveal the often troubled relationship between the press and the government as well as the continued importance of patronage in the seventeenth century. One also sees how publishers responded to, but also shaped, the reading tastes and intellectual outlook of their customers. Lawrence S. Thompson called the essays "a basic contribution to the bibliography of English culture of the Stuarts, the Civil War, and the Restoration, . . . a bibliographical vade mecum to seventeenth-century England" (*Papers of the Bibliographical Society of America* 59, 1965, 347).

Schreiber, Fred. "The Estiennes." *American Book Collector* 3 (May/June, 1982): 2-10.

Seeks to remove confusion caused by the existence of a dozen printers of the Estienne family, who were active in two countries over five generations spanning 162 years. Schreiber traces the family history from Henri I, who was working in Paris by May, 1502. Henri died in 1520. In 1526 Robert I succeeded him and became what Schreiber calls "the most outstanding figure in the Renaissance book-trade in France." When Robert I moved to Geneva in 1550, his brother Charles took over the Paris establishment, so that from 1551 on the Estiennes were publishing in both Paris and Geneva. Schreiber regards Robert's son Henri II as "in many ways the greatest member of the Estienne dynasty." Henri II briefly operated his own press in Geneva before succeeding to his father's business in 1559. Henri II produced the great three-volume Plato in 1578, which established the standard pagination of all subsequent editions. Similarly, his *Thesaurus Graecae Linguae* (1572) remains the fundamental reference for Greek. The expense of its production impoverished Henri, and he died destitute. Schreiber explains the famous olive tree device of the Estiennes, tracing it to Romans ix, 20, but also to a pun on the Greek "stephanos," a crown of olive branches awarded as a sign of excellence.

Spufford, Margaret. *Small Books and Pleasant Histories: Popular Fiction and Its Readership in Seventeenth Century England.* Athens: University of Georgia Press, 1981.

Spufford examines the chapbook collection assembled by Samuel Pepys and now housed at Magdalene College, Cambridge. These works were aimed at those who could not afford other forms of literature but whose taste in reading had been stimulated by increased literacy. Spufford assumes a higher degree of literacy than does David Cressy's *Literacy and the Social Order* (cited herein); she argues that chapbooks were so popular that there must have been a substantial number of readers to buy them. Spufford finds differences in outlook between the chapbooks and orthodox Protestant writings. She also notes the importance of fantasy as a motif in cheap literature, especially stories of poor people becoming suddenly rich.

Thomas, Henry. *Spanish Sixteenth-Century Printing.* London: Ernest Benn, 1926.

Unlike Italy and France, Spain retained the Gothic typeface well into the sixteenth century. Spanish books also are distinguished by their elaborate decorations, as exemplified by the title page of *Aureum opus*

(Valencia, 1515), with its ornate helmet topped with a griffin. Thomas also shows a fine Greek font used in the Complutensian Bible of Cardinal Ximenes. With fifty facsimiles.

Vervliet, H. D. L. *Sixteenth-Century Printing Types* of the Low Countries. Amsterdam: Menno Hertzberger, 1968.

For many years, Vervliet served as assistant curator of the Plantin-Moretus Museum in Antwerp, with its vast supply of old type. In this work he reproduces many sixteenth century typefaces used in the Netherlands. Vervliet devotes a section to each punchcutter and examines Gothic, roman, italic, and music types. The volume will interest not only students of typography but also those concerned with the transmission of texts because the study will help date questionable printings. Because the Dutch exported typefaces, especially to England, all students of sixteenth century European printing will find the book valuable.

Voet, Leon. *The Golden Compasses.* 2 vols. London: Routledge & Kegan Paul, 1968-1972.

The standard biography of Christophe Plantin. The title derives from Plantin's third printer's mark. Plantin became a printer after he was wounded in a brawl and so could no longer bind books. Voet emphasizes the importance of the Family of Love, a religious sect, in Plantin's career. Members supplied him with capital to set up his printing business and also bought the books he published. In 1571, Plantin was granted a monopoly for the sale of Catholic prayerbooks in Spain and its territories; by 1574, he was operating sixteen presses. Religious warfare later hurt the business, and Plantin moved from Antwerp to Leyden from 1583 to 1585. Plantin's son-in-law, Jan Moretus, continued the press at Antwerp; his other son-in-law, Frans Raphelengius, carried on the Leyden enterprise. Voet traces the subsequent history of the Plantin-Moretus press until its demise in the mid-nineteenth century. Along the way he sheds light on the printing industry of the period, and he uses the extensive documentation at the Plantin-Moretus Museum to demonstrate, in the words of the subtitle to Volume 2 of this work, "The Management of a Printing and Publishing House in Renaissance and Baroque" Europe. The account books show that paper was the most expensive component of a book; wages were second. In one day, one of Plantin's presses could produce 1,250 sheets of a standard book.

Watt, Tessa. *Cheap Print and Popular Piety, 1550-1640.* New York: Cambridge University Press, 1991.

Examines ballads, broadsides, prints, chapbooks, penny religious tracts, even printed cloth that brought the printed word to England's lower classes. These items reveal that the populace was not troubled by Protestant doctrinal questions such as the depiction of the Holy Family or deathbed repentances, subjects of woodcuts and ballads despite Protestant objections to both. Old stories from the Middle Ages retained their appeal, again suggesting the conservative nature of popular culture. As the seventeenth century progressed, ballads became more secular, though religious subjects also remained popular. The decline of ballads and woodcuts and the rise in the number of chapbooks indicates increasing literacy among the lower classes.

Chapter 14
THE EIGHTEENTH CENTURY

Ball, Johnson. *William Caslon 1693-1766: The Ancestry, Life, and Connections of England's Foremost Letter-Engraver and Type-Founder*. Kineton, England: The Roundwood Press, 1973.
Lawrence S. Thompson called this "the definitive monograph" on the subject (*Papers of the Bibliographical Society of America* 69, 1975, 145). Ball offers a detailed biography of England's first great typecaster. The book's primary concern is to trace Caslon's ancestry, and the first 300 pages deal with genealogy and Caslon's early years. Ball nonetheless also places Caslon within the context of industrialization, the book trade, journalism, and other activities that impinge on printing and typecasting. Ball presents a good nontechnical discussion of Caslon's typefounding work, and traces the history of Caslon's business and his fonts. Ball admires Caslon's types; the book is appropriately printed in monotype Caslon.

Bennett, William. *John Baskerville, the Birmingham Printer: His Press, Relations, and Friends*. 2 vols. Birmingham, England: Birmingham School of Printing, 1937-1939.
Baskerville was a leading English printer and has been credited with creating the first modern typeface. Drawing on manuscript material ignored by or unknown to previous researchers, Bennett here presents much new information about this Birmingham printer. The work also sets Baskerville within the context of his times. A standard life.

_____. *William Caslon, 1692-1766: Ornamental Engraver, Typefounder, and Music Lover*. Birmingham, England: Birmingham School of Printing, 1935.
This brief account, appropriately printed in linotype Caslon Old Face, conceded "the paucity of material, especially in regard to the childhood, youth, and early manhood" of one of England's leading typefounders. Though barely a biographical sketch, the pamphlet contains some useful anecdotes, especially concerning Caslon's musical interests. A pleasant introduction with some helpful bibliographical references. For a fuller treatment see Johnson Ball's *William Caslon, 1693-1766* cited above.

Benton, Josiah Henry. *John Baskerville, Typefounder and Printer, 1706-1775*. New York: Typophiles, 1944.

An updated version of Benton's monograph, first published in 1914. Benton shows how Baskerville was concerned with all facets of bookmaking. The printer's earlier experience with Japanware prompted his hot-pressing of the paper to create a glossy surface. He experimented with inks, and he used heavy brass plates in his presswork. Baskerville introduced greater variation between the thick and thin strokes in his typefaces and so created a modern font, though Philippe Grandjean had tried a similar design as early as 1702. The volume is nicely illustrated and handsomely printed. Its publication coincided with a Bruce Rogers-inspired revival of interest in Baskerville types.

Birn, Raymond, ed. "The Printed Word in the Eighteenth Century." *Eighteenth-Century Studies* 17 (1984): 401-514.

Birn writes in his introduction to this special issue of *Eighteenth-Century Studies*, "The five essays that follow share a common theoretical base: how the history of the printed word intersects with social, economic, cultural, and political history while at the same time illustrating the centrality of printing and publishing in the formation of modern culture." John Feather examines the eighteenth century book trade, especially in England, to reveal patterns of thought. Martha Wood Mansee looks at the emergence of the concept of authorship in eighteenth century Germany. Through a study of Henry Fielding's *Works*, Hugh Amory reveals the nature of piracy and copyright in late eighteenth century England. Robert Darnton studies book sales in the generation before the French Revolution, and Nina R. Gelbart shows how French journalists of the 1770s fused aesthetic criticism with radical politics.

Bollème, Genevieve, et al. *Livre et société dans la France du XVIIIe siècle*. 2 vols. Paris: Mouton, 1965-1970.

These two volumes, Numbers 1 and 16 in the series *Civilisations et sociétés*, offer twelve essays that explore various facets of the relationship between books and eighteenth century French culture. In Volume 1 François Furet looks at what was published and what was licensed. Jean Ehrard and Jacques Roger survey the contents of two eighteenth century journals, *Le Journal de savants* and *Les Memoirs de Trevoux*, that indicate what people were reading. Genevieve Bolléme examines the nature of popular culture of the period and finds some influence of the philosophes. Daniel Roche also considers the influence of the philosophes in provincial academies, and Alphonse Dupront concludes the volume with an assessment of the significance of book history in understanding an age. Volume 2 opens with an examination of the provincial book trade in late eighteenth century France. Jean-Louis and Maria Flandrin consider the circulation of books. Daniel Roche returns to the question of the impact of the ideas of the encyclopédistes on academies in Paris and the provinces. The remaining contributions apply linguistic theory to the study of book history. An important collection for the student of the book in eighteenth century France.

Bowyer, William. *The Bowyer Ledgers: The Printing Accounts of William Bowyer Father and Son*. New York: Oxford University Press, 1991.
Reproduces on microfiche the ledgers the Bowyers, among England's leading printers and publishers, kept between 1710 and 1777. Lists over 5,000 works and traces their progress through the printing process. Records paper and type used, format, corrections, and press runs. Indexes allow access by author, title, equipment, materials, and processes. A treasury of information about eighteenth century printing and publishing practices.

Bronson, Bertrand H. *Printing as an Index of Taste in Eighteenth-Century England*. New York: New York Public Library, 1963.
Examines conventions of printing in the period. For example, Bronson notes that until the very end of the century, black letter was not used, even by Horace Walpole's Strawberry Hill Press that operated out of a pseudo-Gothic villa. The novel's lowly status is reflected in its being published in 12mo, while poetry, more highly regarded, generally first appeared in more stately quarto. Bronson reflects on changes in style of illustration as well as typography. The William Kent illustrations that accompany James Thomson's 1730 edition of the *Seasons* suggest Claude Lorraine, whereas the 1797 version is filled with Romantic scenes. Before mid-century, title pages often are bounded by a double line. John Baskerville leapt this fence, creating a greater sense of space by omitting the border; Bronson compares this change to a similar trend in landscape gardening. Accompanying this essay are twenty-one facsimiles that provide visual support to Bronson's attractively and sympathetically printed text.

Chapman, R. W. "Notes on Eighteenth Century Book-Building." *The Library* 4 (1923/1924): 165-180.
Chapman observes that in the 1700s, as in earlier centuries, the gathering was the sheet, even for folios, though this practice could demand extra sewing in the binding of books. Signature notations were used

less frequently than before. Cancels were common. Chapman examines paper sizes and watermarks in his survey of how the eighteenth century book was made.

Cochrane, J. A. *Dr. Johnson's Printer: The Life of William Strahan.* Cambridge, Mass.: Harvard University Press, 1964.
Strahan engaged in and influenced all facets of the book trade. He was the King's Printer, he published some of the most noted writers of the age; he sold books wholesale; and he exported books to the American colonies. He was also the friend and publisher of Adam Smith, David Hume, Edward Gibbon, and Samuel Johnson (whose *Dictionary* was Strahan's most valuable literary property). This account of Strahan's life thus illuminates the many aspects of the eighteenth century world of books, from creation to distribution. Includes a generous selection of Strahan's letters. J. D. Feldman wrote that Cochrane "has thrown much light on one of the foremost printers of the eighteenth century and by emphasizing Strahan's close association with the writers of his day has illuminated the importance of the connection between literature and trade" (*Review of English Studies*, n.s. 16, 1965, 434).

Collins, Arthur Simmons. *Authorship in Days of Johnson: Being a Study of the Relation Between Author, Patron, Publisher, and Public, 1726-1780.* London: Robert Holden, 1927.
In the first quarter of the eighteenth century, writers abounded, but the reading public was not sufficiently large to support them. Even the 1709 Copyright Act did little to help authors; booksellers, on the other hand, benefited from legal protection of printed works, as they profited from the proliferation of would-be writers who kept wages low. Publishers' cooperation discouraged competition, but also allowed for the publication of expensive or risky works. As the century progressed, literacy increased, giving writers greater autonomy and more money. Alexander Pope emerges as an important figure here because of his reliance on the book-buying public rather than on publishers.

_____. *The Proliferation of Letters: A Study of the Relation of Author to Patron, Publisher, and Public, 1780-1832.* New York: E. P. Dutton, 1929.
Picks up the story of Collins' *Authorship in the Days of Johnson* (above). The reading public continued to expand, especially in London. Improved roads and the growth of towns also fostered the circulation of literature. George Gordon, Lord Byron and Sir Walter Scott benefited from these developments but also contributed to the increasing

demand for books, even for literacy. The French Revolution and religious dissent also fostered a desire for reading matter. Paine's *Rights of Man*, 1791, for example, sold 150,000 in its first year. Publishers became more generous as books proved more profitable. Periodicals, too, provided outlets for authorship, so that by the 1830s writing could yield a living wage. Collins explores the influence of the Industrial Revolution, education, and political reform on the writers and publishers of the period. Alan Pryce-Jones observed in *The London Mercury* 19 (1929): 553, "Altogether, this is an illuminating book, agreeably written, and well enough put together to give a clear collection of facts not, indeed, unknown, but hitherto forgotten."

Darnton, Robert. *The Business of Enlightenment: A Publishing History of the Encyclopédie, 1775-1800*. Cambridge, Mass.: Harvard University Press, 1979.
In 1772, Denis Diderot completed the *Encyclopédie*, issuing the final volume of plates. The first four editions of this work appeared in expensive folio format and so were unlikely to reach a mass audience. Quarto and octavo editions were more popular. By 1789, nearly 25,000 copies were in circulation, making the work a best-seller in France. Drawing on the extensive archives of the Societé Typographique de Neuchâtel, Darnton examines in detail the social and economic factors involved in producing the various editions and also their distribution. He finds that the upper and middle classes bought the encyclopedia more readily than did the lower classes. The *Encyclopédie* spread enlightenment culture beyond France also. By tracing the publication history of the work, Darnton demonstrates the transformation in commerce and in thought from the Old Regime to the Revolutionary era. *The Book Collector* 29 (1980): 162-178 concludes that "it is hard to overpraise Darnton's work. . . . It is a truly great work, much more than a great documentary history of the book trade. . . , much more than a major contribution to knowledge of one of the great intellectual movements of the century. . . . It is a book which a whole range of scholars will turn to, again and again."

_____. *Édition et sédition: L'Univers de la littérature clandestine au XVIIIe siècle*. Paris: Gallimard, 1991.
Drawing again on the archives of the Societé Typographique de Neuchâtel as well as other primary and secondary sources, Darnton argues that clandestine books were widely read in late eighteenth century France and helped undermine the monarchy. In 1775 alone, the Societé Typographique sold 110 illegal titles. In addition to exam-

ining the intellectual impact of such works, Darnton explains the workings of the underground book trade.

_____. *The Literary Underground of the Old Regime*. Cambridge, Mass.: Harvard University Press, 1982.
In the opening chapter, Darnton notes that the Revolutionary ideas of the Enlightenment were spread by literature less elevated than the works of Voltaire and Rousseau, by popularized versions of their ideas and by libelous pamphlets. Chapter 2 examines the career of Jacques-Pierre Brissot to demonstrate the byzantine relationships between the French government and the underground press. Brissot, a pamphleteer, spied for the police but also warned the Societé Typographique de Neuchâtel of government efforts to confiscate some of that publisher's imprints. Darnton next discusses the career of Abbe Le Senne, a pamphleteer who popularized Enlightenment ideas. Darnton argues that "without middlemen like Le Senne, the Enlightenment might have been contained within the salons, and its great voices could have called for the crushing of *l'infâme* . . . without raising an echo." Chapter 4 treats the provincial clandestine bookseller Bruzard de Mauvelain. In Chapter 5, Darnton looks at the operation of the Societé Typographique de Neuchâtel to understand how books were produced in the latter half of the eighteenth century, and the last chapter looks at what Frenchmen read before the Revolution. Nicolas Barker observed, "These essays make a wonderfully vivid contribution to the history of the book-trade and its relations with the society in which it existed" (*The Book Collector* 33, 1984, 102).

_____. "Reading, Writing, and Publishing in Eighteenth Century France: A Case Study in the Sociology of Literature." *Daedalus* 100 (1971): 214-256.
Emphasizes the necessity of examining what Frenchmen read, not just the literary high spots of the age, to understand the cultural milieu of the *ancien régime*. Darnton suggests that censorship in eighteenth century France encouraged underground literature to become more hostile to the government, since all involved in the production and distribution of such works were outside the pale of legitimacy—indeed, often outside France. Underground literature, while not overtly philosophical, served to undermine the government through an emphasis on scandal and immorality in high places.

Darnton, Robert, and Daniel Roche, eds. *Revolution in Print: The Press in France, 1775-1800*. Berkeley: University of California Press in

collaboration with the New York Public Library, 1989.
Produced to accompany an exhibition at The New York Public Library.
Both this volume and the exhibition examine the role of printing in the
French Revolution. The first part considers publishing before the
Revolution and notes how legal restrictions fostered an underground
press that challenged the legitimacy of the monarchy. Part 2 focuses
on the effects of the Revolution on the presses of Paris. Carla Hesse
writes, "French commercial book publishing . . . floundered as a
consequence of the dramatic deregulation of their commerce," but she
also finds that the number of publishers in Paris tripled between 1789
and 1793. Michel Vernus adds "A Provincial Perspective" to this
discussion. Vernus notes, for example, that in Franche-Comté the
Revolution brought increased availability of printed matter, especially
pamphlets, tracts, and newspapers. Part 3 looks at the products of the
liberated press to see how the many varieties of print, including
almanacs, songs, and broadsides, spread the Revolutionary ideology.
With copious illustrations.

Dodsley, Robert. *The Correspondence of Robert Dodsley, 1733-1764*.
Edited by James E. Tierney. Cambridge, England: Cambridge University Press, 1988.
Tierney writes in his preface, "As a literate and literary bookseller, who
recognized, advised, and patronized genius, Dodsley was not outdone
in his century." During his twenty-five years at Tully's Head, Pall Mall,
he published some 500 titles, including works by Edmund Burke,
Thomas Gray, Samuel Johnson, and Laurence Sterne. His correspondence, which Tierney ably annotates, reveals the inner workings of the
eighteenth century book trade. Appendices include abstracts of publishing agreements and receipts, a list of his copyright registrations and
purchases at trade sales, and a catalog of publishing agreements and
receipts of his brother, James, who succeeded Robert in the business.

Eisenstein, Elizabeth L. *Grub Street Abroad: Aspects of the French
Cosmopolitan Press from the Age of Louis XIV to the French Revolution*. Oxford, England: Clarendon Press, 1992.
Eisenstein argues that "foreign firms contributed rather more than did
domestic ones to sustaining the literary culture of the French Enlightenment." Eisenstein examines the importance of French-language
journals in conveying news about books as well as events. She looks
particularly at Prosper Marchand, largely responsible for the *Journal
historique de la république des lettres* (1732-1733). This study notes
the pan-European nature of French culture, which was spread by the

press; indeed, much of French publishing operated outside of France. This diffusion of French culture encouraged revolutionaries to believe that Austrians, Prussians, and Spaniards would rally to their cause and fostered the revolutionaries' faith in the power of the free press.

_____. *Print Culture and Enlightenment Thought*. Chapel Hill: Rare Book Collection, University Library, University of North Carolina, 1986.

Eisenstein examines a number of factors that contributed to the triumph and then collapse of the Enlightenment. Journals fostered new ideas; printed sources permitted easy reference and guaranteed uniformity of detail. Engravings and mathematical formulae "spoke" to readers across Europe and so created a pan-European community of intellectuals. This essay then briefly considers the role of printers in spreading liberal ideas. After the French Revolution, the presses that had operated on the borders of France fell under French control and so lost their freedom to present heretical ideas. Eisenstein may exaggerate the uniqueness of print in creating an international interpretive community, but she is correct in arguing for the press's ability to reproduce and disseminate information more rapidly than could the medieval scriptorium.

Feather, John. "British Publishing in the Eighteenth Century: A Preliminary Subject Analysis." *The Library* 8 (1986): 32-46.

Drawing on *Eighteenth Century British Books* (1979), Feather finds that religion remains the most popular subject, while science, technology, and the arts lag far behind. Also, "in the age of reason, the speculations of the philosophers seem to have had little attraction for English publishers," perhaps because booksellers could import such works from foreign sources. The numerous tables analyze the content of British imprints and so offer a portrait of the English political and cultural landscape. For example, Feather finds little interest in modern European languages other than French, though, again, imports supplemented native productions.

Foxon, David. *Pope and the Early Eighteenth-Century Book Trade*. Revised and edited by James McLaverty. Oxford, England: Clarendon Press, 1991.

The Lyell Lectures presented at Oxford in March, 1976. The first three chapters look at Alexander Pope's literary career, and the last two deal with problems in the editing of Pope's texts, which Pope revised not only for content but also for appearance. Pope sought to adapt typography to readership, and in general he favored a classical form that rejected extensive use of capitals and italic. Pope's literary career reflects a desire to control all aspects of book production, including profits. Among Pope's innovations was the use of the quarto rather than the folio for luxury editions. The pictorial headpiece was also his idea for the *Iliad* and became popular thereafter. An important study of the business and aesthetics of bookmaking in early eighteenth century England.

Gaskell, Philip. *A Bibliography of the Foulis Press*. 2d ed. Winchester, England: St. Paul's Bibliographies, 1986.
Robert Foulis began his career as a university bookseller in Glasgow; then, in partnership with his brother, Andrew, he became a printer and publisher. In the introduction, Gaskell discusses the operation of the press, one of the finest in the eighteenth century. The press was especially successful in the areas of design and typography, securing virtually all its fonts from the Wilson Foundry. The bibliography indicates the range of books printed, which totaled some 700 titles. For further information about the Foulis Press in the 1740s, see Gaskell's "The Early Works of the Foulis Press and the Wilson Foundry" in *The Library* 7 (1952): 77-110.

_____. *John Baskerville: A Bibliography*. Cambridge, England: Cambridge University Press, 1959.
Valuable for showing what was published by England's premier private press in the eighteenth century. Also illustrates the operation of Baskerville's printing office, which was a small affair: In 1775 his wife offered for sale "Four accurate improved printing presses, several large founts of type, different sizes, with cases, frames, screwed chases, and every other useful apparatus in the branch of trade." Baskerville's type tended to be larger than that used by his contemporaries, though his presswork was not extraordinary. He used a wide variety of papers, and he often worked for commercial publishers. Those books he printed for himself tended to be expensive. Gaskell includes a number of facsimiles as well as a nicely reproduced type specimen sheet.

Geduld, Harry M. *Prince of Publishers: A Study of the Work and Career of Jacob Tonson*. Bloomington: Indiana University Press, 1969.
More limited in its focus than Kathleen M. Lynch's *Jacob Tonson: Kit-Cat Publisher* (cited in this chapter). Geduld's study concentrates on Tonson as publisher. Though a keen businessman, Tonson also showed concern for the appearance of his works. For example, his 1697 *Virgil*, translated by John Dryden, is a most attractive book. Tonson

supported Dryden's posthumous reputation, and his editions of *Paradise Lost* made John Milton a best-seller. Tonson published the first illustrated edition of that work as well as the first commentary on Milton's text. Tonson's 1709 edition of Shakespeare was the first not in folio and the first to carry a life of the playwright. Tonson was responsible in large measure for establishing the canon of English literature in the early eighteenth century. As a member of the Whig Kit-Cat Club, Tonson also promoted contemporary authors who shared his political views. Geduld sometimes relied on old or inaccurate sources of information, but his book remains valuable.

Habermas, Jürgen. *The Structural Transformation of the Public Sphere: An Inquiry into a Category of Bourgeois Society.* Translated by Thomas Burger. Cambridge, Mass.: MIT Press, 1989.
Relates the rise of journalism and print to economic and political transformations in early modern France, Germany, and England. As John Durham comments in the *Quarterly Journal of Speech* 77 (1991): 249, "This book casts an extremely wide-ranging theoretical and historical light on the evolution of public communication in Western Europe over the past three centuries." Habermas argues that in the late seventeenth and early eighteenth centuries a new group arose in society, constituting a bourgeois public sphere that was not the state itself but yet was involved with political issues. This group arose in part because of expanded literacy and the increased production of print media, with a corresponding development of lending libraries and reading societies. Habermas observes that almost from the first appearance of this sphere, rulers sought to use the media to control the public, a process accelerated in the twentieth century. The expansion of the public sphere in the nineteenth and twentieth centuries from its elitist origins marks the growth of democracy, but that expansion has also led to a debasing of public discourse. Habermas warns of the "refeudalization of the public sphere" as public relations replaces public opinion as the basis of legitimacy. For a lengthy review, see Anthony J. La Vopa's "Concerning a Public," *Journal of Modern History* 64 (1992): 79-116.

Hesse, Carla. *Publishing and Cultural Politics in Revolutionary Paris, 1789-1810.* Berkeley: University of California Press, 1991.
In 1789, the French Revolution liberated the press from the restrictions imposed by the *ancien régime*. The aim was to propagate Enlightenment philosophy and science, but the unregulated press turned out less lofty products, "tales of private passion rather than reasoned discourses

on public virtue." Also, publishers struggled to remain in business in an unregulated environment. Government intervention in the market economy of publishing in the 1790s proved ineffectual. Not until 1810 did legislation restore order to publishing by giving property rights to editions rather than texts. At the Bourbon restoration, prepublication censorship of longer works was rejected, while shorter, more popular writings were severely restricted, thus creating what Hesse calls "a two-tiered cultural regime." In the course of her study, Hesse considers the way government regulation defined the nature of authorship.

Kernan, Alvin. *Printing Technology, Letters, and Samuel Johnson.* Princeton, N.J.: Princeton University Press, 1987.
Kernan argues that "Samuel Johnson . . . lived out, in an intense and dramatic manner, the social mutation of writers from an earlier role as gentlemen-amateurs to a new authorial self based on the realities of print and its conditions of mechanical reproduction." In this new world, authors had to find a place for themselves. Kernan argues that Johnson found in print culture a fixity lacking in his psyche and so turned to literature as a stay against disorder. This study sheds light of Johnson and also on the print culture of the eighteenth century. Kernan argues that the Age of Johnson witnessed the triumph of print and the market place over orality and patronage, and that Johnson's career both reflected and encouraged these transformations.

Korshin, Paul J., ed. *The Widening Circle: Essays on the Circulation of Literature in Eighteenth-Century Europe.* Philadelphia: University of Pennsylvania Press, 1976.
Includes three essays. Robert Darnton looks at the activities of Bruzard de Mauvelain, a clandestine bookseller who sought to circumvent the literary restrictions of the *ancien régime.* Darnton explores the problems Mauvelain confronted and also the types of books he ordered, these sales indicating what Frenchmen wanted to read. Enlightenment philosophy constituted a significant percentage of the orders, but was by no means the major category. Pornography made up another substantial portion of the books ordered. Because news was tightly censored in pre-Revolutionary France, readers were eager for information, and Mauvelain obliged them. This study reveals the French literary milieu of the 1780s and the workings of the clandestine book trade just before the revolution. Roy McKeen Wiles studies the provincial newspapers in England to understand reading tastes. Wiles argues that literacy was widespread. In the third essay, Bernhard Fabian considers the popularity of English literature in eighteenth century Germany, not

just in translation but also in the original. He finds that English reading habits migrated to Germany along with the works themselves, encouraging wider, less intense perusal.

Lynch, Kathleen M. *Jacob Tonson: Kit-Cat Publisher*. Knoxville: University of Tennessee Press, 1971.

During his career that began in 1678 and ended in 1720, Tonson published most of the leading authors of the period, including John Dryden, William Congreve, and Joseph Addison. His output has been estimated at 750 to 800 titles. Lynch's biography places Tonson within his era and reveals the conditions of publishing, writing, and reading in the late seventeenth and early eighteenth centuries. According to James T. Boulton, Lynch's study "is highly informative and thoroughly documented; it contains material of interest to the bibliophile as well as the literary historian" (*The Library* 27, 1972, 153-154).

Nichols, John. *Biographical and Literary Anecdotes of William Bowyer*. London: Author, 1782.

Nichols regards Bowyer as "the most learned printer" of the eighteenth century. Bowyer attended Cambridge University before joining his father's printing business in 1722. Nichols traces Bowyer's career, incorporating many contemporary documents and providing copious notes along with the text. Though often little more than a selective bibliography of Bowyer's imprints, Nichols' work sheds light on both an important printer and eighteenth century bookmaking.

Papali, G. F. *Jacob Tonson, Publisher: His Life and Work (1656-1736)*. Auckland, New Zealand: Tonson Publishing House, 1968.

In effect Papali's 1933 dissertation, the volume contains little evidence of research beyond that date. Though less up-to-date than Kathleen Lynch's study of Tonson, this work contains information not found in either her book or Geduld's. Papali has mined the primary printed sources and manuscripts, from which he quotes extensively. He also writes about Jacob Tonson's nephew, Jacob Tonson II, and the firm's activities after the first Tonson's retirement. Especially useful for the list of Tonson imprints, which span nearly a century, and of the authors the Tonsons published.

Pottle, Frederick A. "Printer's Copy in the Eighteenth Century." *The Papers of the Bibliographical Society of America* 27 (1933): 65-73.

The recovery of much of the printer's copy of James Boswell's *Journal of a Tour to the Hebrides* and a long continuous fragment of the *Life of Samuel Johnson* allowed Pottle to draw some conclusions about the process involved in turning a manuscript into a printed book in the eighteenth century. Most of Boswell's *Journal* is written on both sides of the leaf. Editing occurred as the printer set type. For the *Life*, Boswell wrote on only one side of the sheet, and he provided other documents, such as letters, separately, referring to them in the manuscript. He handled quotations from printed sources in the same way. Pottle writes that eighteenth century printer's copy could appear "very untidy and complicated"; but since printers worked with a small part of the text at a time, they could decipher manuscripts that would be unacceptable in modern times.

Raven, James. *Judging New Wealth: Popular Publishing and Responses to Commerce in England, 1750-1800*. Oxford, England: Clarendon Press, 1992.
The second half of this book looks at the portrayal of business in the fiction in the latter part of the eighteenth century. Of more interest to students of bibliography is the first half of the work, which examines the transformation of publishing during this period. As in other areas of business, entrepreneurs entered and revolutionized the industry, and these changes in turn affected writers. In Letter 51 of *The Citizen of the World*, Oliver Goldsmith has the bookseller Mr. Fudge observe, "Others may pretend to direct the vulgar, but that is not my way: I always let the vulgar direct me." Raven notes the increase in the number of novels published, in advertising, and in attacks on popular fiction as literacy increased and as publishers catered (or pandered) to new audiences.

Rivers, Isabel, ed. *Books and Their Readers in Eighteenth-Century England*. New York: St. Martin's Press, 1982.
Terry Belanger opens this collection of essays with a survey of the business of publishing and authorship. Pat Rogers explores the ways classics were transformed into popular literature. W. A. Speck looks at the books politicians subscribed to. The next five pieces consider various genres—classical poetry, religious works, philosophy, and science—to see what they reveal about readership. Speck finds that the peerage made up the bulk of the audience for books published by subscription; she thus questions the extent to which middle-class readership expanded in the early 1700s. Penelope Wilson finds that the Greco-Roman classics increasingly became familiar in translation rather than in their original languages, and criticism became less technical, more "sentimental." John V. Price notes the popularity of

philosophical works, and ascribes this interest at least in part to readers' desire to understand themselves. Scientific works also enjoyed popular readership, and virtually every library included some. Religious works, however, were probably the most popular, and many seventeenth century works in this field retained their readership throughout the 1700s. Jan Fergus called the book "indispensable" (*Papers of the Bibliographical Society of America* 79, 1985, 121).

Straus, Ralph, and Robert Dent. *John Baskerville: A Memoir.* Cambridge, England: Cambridge University Press for Chatto & Windus, 1907.
An important and attractively produced biography of this famous English printer and typographer. Focuses on the last twenty-five years of Baskerville's life. Straus and Dent include a bibliography of Baskerville's work and present various primary documents such as letters, agreements with Cambridge University for printing the Bible and Book of Common Prayer, and Baskerville's will. Among the appendices is a discussion of Baskerville's widow's sale of Baskerville's types to the Societé Litteraire-Typographique and the subsequent fate of these fonts.

Tyson, Gerald P. *Joseph Johnson: A Liberal Publisher.* Iowa City: University of Iowa Press, 1979.
The authors Johnson published or befriended constitute the leading radicals of the late 1700s—Mary Wollstonecraft, William Godwin, Thomas Holcroft, Joseph Priestley, and William Blake. Johnson's dissemination of unpopular ideas led to his imprisonment in 1799 for publishing what the British government regarded as a seditious pamphlet. Tyson traces Johnson's life and discusses the publisher's significance as an intellectual who fostered liberal ideas and also played an important role in the late eighteenth century book world.

Ward, Albert. *Book Production, Fiction, and the German Reading Public, 1740-1800.* Oxford, England: Clarendon Press, 1974.
Ward examines the rise of popular fiction during the Golden Age of German literature that produced Wieland, Goethe, and Jean Paul. After considering the state of German literature in the seventeenth and early eighteenth centuries (Chapter 1), Ward examines the catalogs of the Leipzig Book Fairs, which show shifts from an emphasis on scholarly and theological works in Latin to vernacular narratives (Chapter 2). In 1740, theology and scholarly works made up eighty-seven percent of the offerings. By 1800, this figure had declined to fifty-five percent, while prose narratives had tripled from ten percent to thirty percent of

the total. This change coincided with an increase in reading and in writing. In 1771, Germany had 3,000 writers; by 1800, the figure had more than tripled to 10,648. These changes, documented in Chapter 3, in turn affected the German book trade (Chapter 4). Publishing and bookselling became distinct activities, and piracy, unprofitable for scholarly tomes but remunerative for fiction, arose. Authors' earnings declined, as did the price of books. Reading societies and subscription libraries helped make books more readily available to the reading public. The final chapter discusses readers, who did not flock to secure the latest work by Goethe or Schiller. Karoline von Wobeser's sentimental, conventional *Elisa* (1795) was much more successful than those works that now form the canon of eighteenth century German literature. Ward writes that such books as *Elisa* "are in fact more representative of the age and its general atmosphere than are the works of the great writers, and clearly our picture of eighteenth-century Germany is incomplete without them." This popular literature would influence the prominent Romantic writers of the next era. Tieck, Heine, Kleist, and E. T. A. Hoffmann grew up reading escapist fiction. P. M. Mitchell wrote in *JEGP* 74 (1975): 281, "Dr. Ward has produced a superior and useful scholarly work that is well written and convincing."

Wheatley, H. B. "The Strawberry Hill Press." *Bibliographica* 3 (1897): 83-98.
For forty years (1757-1797), Horace Walpole's press operated at his Twickenham villa. Wheatley examines Walpole's early problems with finding a printer until in 1765 Thomas Kirgate came to work for him. Walpole sometimes printed large editions—1,000 copies of Gray's *Odes* (1757), for example—which he sold through the booksellers. Often, though, the press was an entertainment used to run off a few copies of a poem for visitors. The article provides a charming glimpse into an eighteenth century private press, and Wheatley includes a short list of Strawberry Hill publications. For a complete list one should consult Allen Tracy Hazen's *A Bibliography of Strawberry Hill Press* (New Haven, Conn.: Yale University Press, 1942).

Chapter 15
THE NINETEENTH AND TWENTIETH CENTURIES

Allen, James Smith. *In the Public Eye: A History of Reading in Modern France.* Princeton, N.J.: Princeton University Press, 1991.

What did people read in nineteenth and early twentieth century France? Who read? When, where, how and why did they read? These are the questions that Allen tackles in his study. Chapter 1 considers the proliferation of printed material to supply the increasingly literate populace; Chapter 2 documents this spread of literacy. How politics, education, religion, and culture influenced reading is the subject of Chapters 3 and 4. Allen looks at how artists and writers depicted the act of reading, and the final three chapters explore readers' responses. Allen finds that reading became increasingly personal, although class and even geography played a role in how individuals responded to a given text.

Altick, Richard D. *The English Common Reader: A Social History of the Mass Reading Public, 1800-1900.* Chicago: University of Chicago Press, 1957.

The nineteenth century witnessed an explosion of reading in England. Dickens' novels sold an average of 40,000 copies in monthly parts; the *Family Herald* and *London Journal* numbered readers in the hundreds of thousands. Altick explores the causes and consequences of this phenomenon as he considers the characteristics of the working-class readership. Among the issues he addresses is political reform, stimulated by the popular press, which in turn gained circulation by appealing to the masses. Reading also provided harmless recreation that promoted social tranquility after mid-century. Altick discusses the forces opposed to different types of reading matter and also the institutions, such as book clubs and public libraries, that encouraged popular reading. Mechanization, the repeal of taxes on knowledge, and the rise of journalism aimed at mass audiences also fostered reading. The presence of a large reading public altered the nature of English fiction, as authors sought to appeal to new readers who did not buy Thomas Babington Macaulay or John Stuart Mill. Altick concludes that by 1900, reading no longer fostered cultural improvement among the working classes. An important pioneering study.

Blunden, Edmund. *Keats's Publisher: A Memoir of John Taylor.* London: Jonathan Cape, 1936.

In the early 1800s, the imprint of Taylor and Hessey appeared on works by John Keats, Charles Lamb, Samuel Taylor Coleridge, Thomas Carlyle, and Thomas De Quincey, as well as on the *London Magazine.* After the dissolution of the partnership between Taylor and James Augustus Hessey, Taylor sank into respectability and obscurity, publishing textbooks for the University of London. Blunden presents a readable biography of Taylor, in the course of which Blunden discusses Taylor's publishing enterprises in the context of the book trade in the first half of the nineteenth century.

Chilcott, Tim. *A Publisher and His Circle: The Life and Work of John Taylor, Keats's Publisher.* London: Routledge & Kegan Paul, 1972.

Chilcott writes that by the nineteenth century publishers "had begun in many various ways to influence the writing of literature, proposing some of its themes, justifying its novelty to critics and reviewers, and helping to promote its reception in the reading world." The rise of readership affected all facets of book production, and many authors resented what Samuel Taylor Coleridge called "The multitudinous 'public.'" As publisher, Taylor understood the economic risks of ignoring this mass readership, and his list of publications includes popular titles. Yet he did not shun authors not likely to sell widely, and the authors he published between 1816 and 1825 have insured him a place in literary history. Chilcott shows that Taylor acted as censor, refusing to publish a scene of physical passion in Keats's "The Eve of St. Agnes," and exercising an even stronger restraining hand on the works of John Clare. Taylor's attitude reflected personal taste, not commercial timidity, for Taylor refused to publish the works of Byron, which were popular and which could have saved the firm. In 1825, the partnership between Taylor and James Hessey dissolved, and Taylor ceased to publish important literary works. A good complement to Edmund Blunden's *Keats's Publisher* (cited earlier).

Cruse, Amy. *The Englishman and His Books in the Early Nineteenth Century.* London: George G. Harrap, 1930.

Drawing on all forms of records—fiction, art, autobiography, letters, and biographies—Cruse's classic study seeks to recreate the British reading public of the early 1800s and to assess its influence on what kinds of writing were produced. Cruse notes, for instance, that the widespread practice of reading aloud encouraged authors to write for the entire family and so exclude anything that might be deemed improper. Cruse also observes that the period contained diverse reading publics. The young men at university in the 1820s were fonder of Shelley than were most of their countrymen. The proliferation of periodicals again reflects the variety of readerships, though in 1820 *Blackwood's*, the *Edinburgh Review*, and *The Gentleman's Magazine* still dominated the field. Drawing room books were created to appeal to women of fashion, while working-class readers sought edifying literature.

_____. *The Victorians and Their Reading.* Boston: Houghton Mifflin, 1935.
Continuing Cruse's *The Englishman and His Books* (see above), this volume draws on a wide variety of primary sources to trace the tides of literary taste from 1837 to the 1890s. As in the earlier work, Cruse notes the diversity of reading publics, yet certain authors, especially Charles Dickens and Alfred, Lord Tennyson, could appeal to different publics. Cruse devotes a chapter to Edward Mudie's subscription library, which catered to middle-class readers who could not afford to buy all the books they wanted to read but could readily subscribe to his lending library for a guinea a year.

Dooley, Allan C. *Author and Printer in Victorian England.* Charlottes-ville: University Press of Virginia, 1992.
Explores how the technology of printing affected nineteenth century texts. As Dooley writes in his introduction, the nineteenth century witnessed many changes in the way books were produced, "from initial typesetting through reprinted editions, and the technological changes were powerful enough to affect both the writing of Victorian literature and our reading of it." The book focuses on the period 1840-1890, and traces the publication of a book, beginning with the setting of type and moving through proofreading to printing and reprinting a text. Chapter 5 examines the reprinting of works by Robert Browning, Matthew Arnold, Alfred, Lord Tennyson, and George Eliot. Dooley also treats the wealth of documentation available to the student of Victorian literature—manuscripts, proofs, variant first editions, and revised later printings. He observes that unknown writers had less control over their works than famous ones, and some authors were more careful in supervising publication and more interested in revising than others were. The book concludes with a discussion of textual criticism. Dooley rejects both the "original intent" approach of W. W. Greg and Fredson Bowers and also the "final intent." He argues instead for a more complex examination of various stages of a work. Dooley does

not, however, despair of recovering an ideal text, a notion that is itself controversial.

Ede, Charles, ed. _The Art of the Book: Some Record of Work Carried out in Europe and the U.S.A., 1939-1950._ London: Studio Publications, 1951.
Presents examples and analysis of five facets of fine book production: type design and lettering, printing, illustration and graphic production, commercial binding, and hand-binding. Under each of these five categories, arrangement is alphabetical by country, with Europe being defined as Western Europe. Most of the contributors to the volume noted a decline in the quality of book production, and they attributed this falling-off only partly to World War II. Yet they also saw some encouraging trends. Useful for its portrait of book production in a bygone era.

Escarpit, Robert. _The Book Revolution._ London: George G. Harrap, 1966.
Sponsored by UNESCO, this book looks at the state of book production and distribution in the early 1960s. Escarpit comments on various trends, such as the increasing popularity of the paperback. The statistical tables are especially revealing. They show, for example, per capita book production in different countries. In 1952 and 1962 Israel led in this category; the United States in 1962 ranked 26th, behind Romania, Poland, Turkey, and Argentina. The tables also demonstrate the economic insignificance of books in international trade. Escarpit notes the reluctance of publishers to take risks, such as publishing new authors; and he also records the limited profits most books yield.

Flint, Kate. _The Woman Reader, 1837-1914._ Oxford, England: Clarendon Press, 1993.
Flint examines both prevailing nineteenth century theories of women readers and their practices. Medical texts, advice manuals, schools, and periodicals all addressed the questions of what women should read and the effects of reading, both in general and in terms of particular genres, such as fiction. For example, Flint quotes _Maternal Counsels to a Daughter_ (1855), which likens the appetite for fiction to that for sweets (both of which should be restrained). This "gastronomy of reading" informs many comments of the time. Yet in practice, women's tastes ranged widely, as Flint discovers in diaries, letters, and autobiographies. Books could forge a reading community, but Flint emphasizes, too, the individual nature of an encounter with a text. She examines the treatment of reading within fiction, and she looks at paintings dealing

with this subject. Eschewing generalizations, this work offers insights into the reading habits and attitudes of Victorians and Edwardians.

Howe, Ellic, ed. *The London Compositor: Documents Relating to Wages, Working Conditions, and Customs of the London Printing Trade, 1785-1900.* London: Bibliographical Society, 1947.
In 1785, forty master printers agreed with their workmen to establish a scale of prices; the pact varied from previous practice, in which the Stationers' Company regulated all aspects of the printing trade. By the eighteenth century, this guild system had become weak, but employers and employees had never before negotiated a bilateral agreement. In the introduction Howe presents a number of documents dating from the sixteenth, seventeenth, and eighteenth centuries to illustrate working conditions in the trade, and he briefly surveys printing in the nineteenth century. The remainder of the volume offers primary documents and annotations that reveal the nature of printing and publishing in the 1800s. A fascinating and informative collection of documents.

Howsam, Leslie. *Cheap Bibles: Nineteenth Century Publishing and the British and Foreign Bible Society.* Cambridge, England: Cambridge University Press, 1991.
The British and Foreign Bible Society hoped that the propagation of the Gospel would benefit the English poor as well as those living in foreign lands beyond the reach of the Church. Because the poor had to pay for the Society's Bibles, they would learn to save money. While the Society probably did not affect the lives of the poor, it did alter book production, promoting the combination of the printing and binding industries, for example, and seeking new materials from which to make paper. This volume contains much information on book production in early nineteenth century England.

Keynes, Geoffrey. *William Pickering, Publisher: A Memoir and a Hand-List of His Editions.* London: The Fleuron, 1924.
In 1828, having been a publisher for eight years, Pickering adopted the Aldine device of dolphin and anchor for his own. Like the Renaissance printer/publisher Aldus Manutius of Venice, Pickering sought to produce good books at reasonable prices. Fine printing per se was not his aim. In 1828, Pickering also met Charles Whittingham, Jr., and in 1830 Whittingham became Pickering's printer. Among the works that Pickering issued during his career were the "Diamond Classics" (miniature editions of great English works), the "Aldine Poets" in fifty-three volumes, and the "Italian Classic Poetry" series. He also issued original

work, including books by Samuel Taylor Coleridge, Thomas Love Beddoes, and Coventry Patmore. After Pickering's death in 1854, his son revived the business (1858), which continued until 1878, and the name endured through the firm of Pickering and Chatto. Keynes traces William Pickering's career and provides a bibliography of his output, together with numerous attractive facsimiles.

Kiel, Hanna. "Tendencies in German Book-Printing Since 1914." *The Fleuron* 4 (1925): 71-97.
Kiel argues that before World War I the commercial presses in Germany were producing better work than the private presses, which preferred innovation to excellence. The war led to a scarcity of good materials, and in the immediate postwar years design was subordinated to luxury. After 1920, German printing began to improve, though a number of the fine presses that Kiel cites, such as the Officina Serpentis, the Ernst-Ludwig Press, and the Janus Press, all began before the war. Kiel praises the "tendency to classicism" that she regards as characteristic of German books in the early 1920s. Includes nine facsimiles that illustrate the range of German fine printing.

Klancher, Jon P. *The Making of English Reading Audiences, 1770-1832.* Madison: University of Wisconsin Press, 1987.
Examining the periodical literature of the Romantic era, Klancher focuses on four groups of readers: the middle class, a mass audience, "a polemical radical readership," and intellectuals. Klancher devotes a chapter to each. He notes that *Blackwood's Magazine* and the *Edinburgh Review*, for example, sought to create an audience by intimating that their readers belonged to a select group. Writers for the *Hive*, the *Penny Magazine*, and other such publications appealed to the urban masses, while radical authors sought to change society. The writings of William Wordsworth and Samuel Taylor Coleridge represent yet another attempt to reshape readers and reinterpret the nature of literature. A final chapter considers the implications of this study for modern critical theories. Klancher concludes that "it is no longer possible to read the texts of the past as though they had always been written for the modern interpreter. Even the foundational texts of British Romanticism acknowledged in the intense friction of their language the presence of contrary readings and resistant texts."

Lewis, John. *The Twentieth Century Book: Its Illustration and Design.* 2d ed. New York: Van Nostrand Reinhold, 1984.

Filled with facsimiles, this volume presents Lewis' views on the well-made book, which unites craftsmanship and art. The account begins with the 1890s and the conflict between art nouveau and historicism—a conflict that, Lewis argues, persisted well into the twentieth century. The volume notes how various art movements such as German expressionism and surrealism have influenced book design. The *Times Literary Supplement* for December 21, 1967 called the first edition "scholarly and intelligent as well as beautifully illustrated."

McAleer, Joseph. *Popular Reading and Publishing in Britain, 1914-1950.* London: Oxford University Press, 1992.
McAleer examines in detail three firms catering to mass audiences: D. C. Thomson, a leader in comic books; Mills and Boon, purveyors of women's romances; and the Religious Tract Society. He also draws on Tom Harrisson's Mass Observation Project, which monitored the reading habits of Londoners between 1937 and 1946. McAleer finds that publishers responded to the demands of readers, and the attempt by the Religious Tract Society to shape readers' tastes led to the Society's decline. McAleer notes that readers of mass fiction do not generally "graduate" to more highbrow material. John Sutherland in *The London Review of Books* called this study "a model of what publishing history should be—sober, broadly comparative, solidly researched, illuminating" (May 13, 1993, 24).

McGann, Jerome. *Black Riders: The Visible Language of Modernism.* Princeton, N.J.: Princeton University Press, 1993.
Argues that "what the circulating library and the three-decker format did for nineteenth-century fiction, the Renaissance of Printing accomplished for twentieth-century writing, especially poetry." McGann explores the relationship between the texts of modern literature and the printing of these works. William Morris was concerned with the appearance of even his earliest publications. His unique copy of *A Book of Verse* (1870) fuses "the words and the verse forms, the calligraphy, the decorative work, coloring, and page design." This same concern for integration informs Morris' imprints at his Kelmscott Press. William Butler Yeats, Ezra Pound, and Wallace Stevens were other modernists concerned with the appearance of their poetry on the page, who regarded bibliographical context as inseparable from the text. Many late twentieth century poets remain involved with the publication of their works. McGann cites as an example Jack Spicer, for whom "the 'thingness' of the book [expresses] his ideal of poetic disclosure." Thus, modernist poetry should be approached in the form it was given by the writer.

Emily Dickinson, for instance, should be read in manuscript. McGann includes thirty-five facsimiles to illustrate his argument.

McLean, Ruari. *Modern Book Design from William Morris to the Present Day*. London: Faber & Faber, 1958.
Like other historians of the book, McLean traces the revival of printing to William Morris, who rebelled against the drabness of late Victorian books. In America, Theodore Low DeVinne and Daniel Berkeley Updike were effecting a similar resurrection of the book arts. McLean's account traces the development of book design into the 1950s. The volume discusses important figures in the field, and stresses the need to design books that will serve both author and readers.

_____. *Victorian Book Design and Color Printing*. 2d ed. Berkeley: University of California Press, 1972.
Argues that "more exciting things happened in book design between 1837 and 1890 than in any other comparable period in the history of the world's printing." Though color printing, for example, had existed since the fifteenth century, the Victorians were the first to print extensively in color. McLean pays particular attention to the work of such figures as George Baxter, Henry Shaw, Owen Jones, and Henry Noel Humphreys. Bindings as well as illustrations became more colorful and ornate. An attractive production itself, well-illustrated with numerous black-and-white and sixteen color plates. A standard work on the subject.

McMurtrie, Douglas C. *Modern Typography and Layout*. Chicago: Eyncourt Press, 1929.
Printed in Stellar Bold typeface and with headings in Ultra Modern (designed by McMurtrie), this book argues for new approaches to book design. McMurtrie here rejects serifs and presents a case for layouts more eye-catching than the traditional block of print. McMurtrie examines publications like *Vogue* and *Vanity Fair* that adopted modern design, and also notes that some magazines, like *American Mercury*, did not. Includes specimens of forty-eight modern types and examples of new designs. *American Mercury* called the book "valuable to everyone who has to do with printing" (19, 1930, 253).

Merriam, Harold G. *Edward Moxon: Publisher of Poets*. New York: Columbia University Press, 1939.
When Moxon, himself a poet, began publishing in 1830, he fostered poets. His first significant publication was *Italy*, by his friend Samuel Rogers. Rogers paid for the elaborate illustrations and so underwrote

the expensive book, which lent prestige to the new firm. Moxon went on to publish works by better-known authors, including William Wordsworth, Elizabeth Barrett Browning, and Tennyson. Merriam examines Moxon's thoughts on publishing, his business practices, and his relationship with the poets that he published.

Morison, Stanley. *Modern Fine Printing.* London: Benn, 1925.
Arranged geographically, this work presents many examples of twentieth century printing and design from Europe and the United States. Morison champions the commercial publishers, though many of the finest examples included here come from private presses. Morison regards Germany in the early twentieth century as the leading producer of attractive books, and he notes the French propensity for subordinating typography to illustration. In his discussion of the various examples, Morison provides his own views on the aesthetics of printing and book design.

Newdigate, B. H. *The Art of the Book.* London: Studio Publications, 1938.
Filled with examples of beautiful type, illustration, and binding produced in Europe and America in the early decades of the twentieth century, this volume examines the trends and practices in fine printing. Newdigate also discusses typographers and others in the book industry who contributed to the book arts of the period. While many of the items here were issued in expensive, limited editions, the Everyman Library edition of Edward Gibbon's *Autobiography* also receives attention for its dust jacket, designed by Eric Ravilious. A good historical survey.

Shillingsburg, Peter L. *Pegasus in Harness: Victorian Publishing and W. M. Thackeray.* Charlottesville: University Press of Virginia, 1992.
Looks at the profession of author in Victorian England by examining Thackeray's relations with his publishers. In the process, the book explores how the book trade "impinged on the writer" and, more generally, how the business of publishing operated and how books were assembled. Especially useful are Chapters 4 and 5: The former discusses the market for books and the issue of copyright; the latter examines how books were produced in the mid-nineteenth century. Includes Thackeray's contracts, to illustrate the financial side of authorship.

Smiles, Samuel. *Memoir and Correspondence of the Late John Murray, with an Account of the Origin and Progress of the House, 1768-1843.* 2 vols. London: John Murray, 1891.

In 1768 John MacMurray, a retired marine lieutenant, purchased the
bookselling establishment of William Sandby at 32 Fleet Street, London. Ten years later MacMurray's son, John Murray, the subject of
Smiles's book, was born, and in 1795 the young man began working
in his father's business. John Murray would emerge as a leading figure
in early nineteenth century publishing despite his tendency to support
authors he liked, regardless of their popularity. Yet his taste coincided
sufficiently with that of readers to make the firm successful with such
authors as Byron and Sir Walter Scott. The many letters included here
offer glimpses into publisher-author relations as well as into the business of publishing in the early 1800s.

Srebrnik, Patricia Thomas. *Alexander Strahan: Victorian Publisher*. Ann
Arbor: University of Michigan Press, 1986.
Though not as famous as John Murray or Constable, Strahan played a
significant role in Victorian letters, publishing many best-sellers of the
era and periodicals that included among their contributors Prime
Minister William Gladstone, art historian John Ruskin, and poet/essay-
ist Matthew Arnold. Seeking a wide audience for good literature,
Strahan hoped to improve society as well as circulation. His efforts to
make literature popular included commissioning illustrations from
artists like William Holman Hunt, Edward Burne-Jones, and J. E.
Millais. Strahan's business skills lagged behind his literary enthusiasm,
and financial exigencies forced him to appeal for money from conservative Congregationalists, who altered the tone of his magazines. Yet
he played an important part in the creation of mass readership in
Victorian England. Srebrnik is especially good in the discussion of
periodical publication, Strahan's major activity in the mid-1800s. John
Sutherland called Srebrnik's book "a model of what publishing history
should be. . . . It is both rigorously historical and sound in its literary
judgments. . . . Altogether this is a book to be grateful for" (*Nineteenth-
Century Literature* 42, 1987, 122).

Symonds, Emily Morse. *At John Murray's: Records of a Literary Circle,
1843-1892*. London: John Murray, 1932.
Writing under the pseudonym George Paston, Symonds continues the
story of Samuel Smiles (cited earlier), looking at the firm of Murray
under John Murray III. The third John Murray avoided modern poetry
and fiction, but among his publications was Charles Darwin's *Origin
of Species* (1859). Symonds examines the effects of political, social,
and legal developments (such as the 1842 copyright bill) on publishing

as she traces the fortunes of the firm. She shows that Murray was less imaginative than his father, but demonstrated keen business acumen.

Twyman, Michael. *Printing, 1770-1970: An Illustrated History of Its Development and Uses in England.* London: Eyre and Spottiswoode, 1970.

Twyman writes in his introduction, "This book is primarily intended for the layman interested in printing and social history and for the student of typography and graphic design who might want to have an introduction to the history of the field in which he intends to practice." The focus is on non-book materials, though the factors that affected non-book printing also changed the printing of the book. In the first part of the volume, Twyman discusses these influences: the information explosion (Chapter 1), new technology (Chapter 2), and color printing (Chapter 3). Other chapters treat the shift from printing as craft to printing as industry (Chapter 4), the introduction of new letterforms, and changes in illustration and design. Part 2, consisting largely of illustrations, shows how printing reflected the period, as in the depiction of rural life, transportation, or war. An attractive and informative volume that Ruari McLean called "one of the most interesting and original books on this subject to appear for many years" (*Connoisseur* 177, May, 1971, 63). Andrew Horn similarly praised it as "an enlightening exposition and very useful reference work" (*Library Quarterly* 43, 1973, 421).

Chapter 16
THE BOOK IN AMERICA

Berthold, Arthur B. *American Colonial Printing as Determined by Contemporary Cultural Forces 1639-1763*. New York: New York Public Library, 1934.
Three factors influenced the development of printing in British North America: population, education, and the attitude of the authorities. Berthold looks at the introduction of printing into each of the thirteen colonies and then considers publications under twelve categories: theology, philosophy, science, education, social sciences, economics, political science, law, applied science and arts, literature, history, and bibliography. In New England, theological works predominated, in the Middle Colonies literature, and in the South law. Berthold also examines the growth of the colonial press. The first twenty-five years (1639-1663) account for only one percent of its output, whereas fifty-four percent was produced in the last twenty-five years (1739-1763). The largest relative growth came, however, between 1664 and 1688, when output increased nearly fivefold, and presses were established in Boston and Philadelphia.

Blumenthal, Joseph. *The Printed Book in America*. Boston: David R. Godine, 1977.
In his preface, Blumenthal writes, "The purpose of this volume is to trace the main currents in the development of the printed book in America and to present its leading practitioners." In fact, Blumenthal focuses largely on the twentieth century; the period 1638-1900 occupies only one-third of the text and emphasizes individual printers or publishing houses. The latter two-thirds of the volume continues to emphasize individuals but also notes more general developments, especially in the area of fine printing. Blumenthal knew many of the people he discusses, making the book especially valuable for students of this subject. Includes seventy plates, mostly drawn from twentieth century examples, that illustrate changes in the art of the book.

Boynton, Henry Wolcott. *Annals of American Bookselling 1638-1850*. New York: John Wiley & Sons, 1932.
Issued to celebrate the 125th anniversary of John Wiley & Sons, this volume focuses on the printers, publishers, and booksellers in the British

colonies of North America and the early republic. Boynton deals primarily with activity in Boston, Philadelphia, and New York from the establishment of the Cambridge Press to the eve of the Civil War. The book offers glimpses into the fascinating characters who dominated the book culture of the country—people such as Benjamin Franklin, the printer/publisher Isaiah Thomas, the book-peddling parson Mason Locke Weems, and the Philadelphia publisher Matthew Carey. Despite the occasional error of fact, the study is a treasury of information and anecdote. In 1991, Oak Knoll Press reissued the book with an introduction, a short list of corrections, and a bibliography for further study.

Brodhead, Richard C. *Cultures of Letters: Scenes of Reading and Writing in Nineteenth Century America*. Chicago: University of Chicago Press, 1993.

Brodhead argues that writing responds to its cultural and social milieu. To understand literature, one must also understand the conditions that created it. The antebellum novel, for example, was read and produced by the middle-class, and it expressed and promoted middle class values, particularly the rejection of bodily correction in favor of what Brodhead calls "disciplinary intimacy." Nathaniel Hawthorne's "veiled lady," Priscilla, in *The Blithedale Romance* reflects the expanding role of women in mass entertainment, including fiction. The cult of domesticity of the nineteenth century fostered writing specifically aimed at children. Louisa May Alcott found her niche in this market, but she thus abandoned other literary outlets such as the *Atlantic*, with emphasized highbrow culture. Yet even Alcott's novels mirror social distinctions. Regionalism in late nineteenth century fiction responded to increased homogeneity and urbanization. Local color writing often portrays an oral culture, but its readership was divorced from the subject matter. Published in magazines like the *Atlantic*, this type of writing appealed to a social elite who enjoyed "the primitive . . . as [a] leisure outlet," and who embraced nativism at a time of extensive immigration. Brodhead devotes a chapter to Sarah Orne Jewett as a pioneer in redefining women writers' relationship to art, and the final chapter looks at Charles W. Chestnutt's peculiar rendition of regionalism as fiction dealing with race. Throughout, Brodhead demonstrates that "writers can only ever emerge into authorship by working from within some peculiar situation, with the specific obstructions and advantages that situation contains."

Davidson, Cathy N., ed. *Reading in America: Literature and Social History*. Baltimore: Johns Hopkins University Press, 1989.

The first two essays—an introduction by Davidson and the opening chapter by Robert Darnton—address the general issue of the history of the book. The other eleven contributions consider aspects of reading and literacy in America from colonial times to the twentieth century. These pieces, chronologically arranged, show how the history of the book interacts with concerns such as gender ("Literary Instruction and Gender in Colonial New England"; "Sense and Sensibility: A Case Study of Women's Reading in Late-Victorian America"), race ("The Word in Black and White: Ideologies of Race and Literacy in Antebellum America"; "Reflections on the Changing Publishing Objectives of Secular Black Book Publishers, 1900-1986"), and popular culture ("Chapbooks in America"; "A Republican Literature"). James R. Kelly called this important collection "consistently remarkable, informative, and challenging" (*Papers of the Bibliographical Society of America*, 84, 1990, 193).

Davis, Richard Beale. *A Colonial Southern Bookshelf*. Athens: University of Georgia Press, 1979.
Davis examines the contents of Southern libraries in three areas: history, politics, and law; religion; and belles lettres. From this examination of books, Davis speculates on the nature of eighteenth century Southern thought. He finds widespread ownership of books; law books were popular for their utilitarian value. The histories owned tended to support Whig/libertarian politics, as reflected in Thomas Jefferson's *A Summary View of the Rights of North America*. Davis argues that religion did not play as important a role in Southern thought as it did in Puritan New England, and that conversely fiction, drama, and humor were more important in the South.

Gilmore, William J. *Reading Becomes a Necessity of Life: Material and Cultural Life in Rural New England, 1780-1835*. Knoxville: University of Tennessee Press, 1989.
James R. Kelly called this work "a well-conceived, substantial, and remarkable piece of historical exegesis" (*Papers of the Bibliographical Society of America* 83, 1983, 558). Drawing on nearly 400 estate inventories, Gilmore looks at reading habits in the rural upper Connecticut River Valley between 1760 and 1830; by the latter date, Gilmore argues, "Knowledge increasingly derived from printed matter had become as much a part of daily life in rural New England as food, shelter, and clothing." Throughout the period, religious writing remained by far the most popular form of publication. Newer forms of literature such as novels were more likely to be found in towns and

villages and among the rural upper class. This study places literacy and reading within the larger issues of material culture and intellectual history as it describes daily life and thoughts of the people of Vermont in the early republic.

Hackenberg, Michael, ed. *Getting the Books Out: Papers of the Chicago Conference on the Book in Nineteenth-Century America.* Washington, D.C.: Center for the Book, Library of Congress, 1987.
Nine essays explore "the production, marketing, distribution, and use" of printed matter in nineteenth century America. Michael Winship's opening essay looks at a trade sale in 1856 as an example of a popular mid-nineteenth century means of transferring property among publishers and raising money for firms with excess stock. James N. Green looks at Matthew Carey's efforts to secure Southern and Western markets around 1800, and Hackenberg considers the use of subscription publishing. Book distribution in the Midwest and West is the subject of Madeleine B. Stern's essay, and Michael H. Harris examines the role of circuit-riding ministers in distributing religious works in the Ohio Valley before 1850. Alice D. Schreyer's essay considers author-publisher relations. Robert D. Harlan discusses the rise of publishing in San Francisco between 1850 and 1869, and Bruce L. Johnson writes of the role chromolithography played in promoting California. The concluding contribution, by Terry Belanger, looks at libraries of the Old Northwest and their enduring legacy.

Hall, David D., and John B. Hench, eds. *Needs and Opportunities in the History of the Book: America, 1639-1876.* Worcester: American Antiquarian Society, 1987.
This collection of conference papers examines the history of the book from diverse perspectives. William S. Pretzer deals with labor history and technology in the publishing and printing industries. Michael Winship looks at publishing from the perspective of capital rather than labor. James Gilreath considers issues of distribution, and suggests that demand rather than supply hampered the dissemination of literature. David Grimsted surveys studies of popular culture. G. Thomas Tanselle's essay concludes the volume with a plea for more careful examination of the book as a physical object. The essays provide useful bibliographical surveys and suggest areas for further investigation.

Heininger, Mary Lynn Stevens. *At Home with a Book: Reading in America, 1840-1940.* Rochester, N.Y.: Strong Museum, 1986.
By 1840, literacy was widespread and the demand for prose fiction

extensive. Books provided not only recreation, but also a source of prestige. P. F. Collier and Sons' Harvard Classics (1909) and the Book-of-the-Month Club (est. 1926) capitalized on the desire to read the "right" books without missing anything important. The first part of Heininger's essay surveys the popularity of fiction in the period. Parts 2 and 3 examine the book as a symbol as depicted in art and architecture. She relates developments such as the "reading chair" and "library rocker" to the culture of books and notes that the size of a book reflected content and audience: "'Fat' books implied masculinity and serious work or study." A brief but informative overview.

Hornung, Clarence P., and Fridolf Johnson. *Two Hundred Years of American Graphic Art: A Retrospective Survey of the Printing Arts and Advertising Since the Colonial Period.* New York; George Braziller, 1976.
Through 351 illustrations and brief commentary, this volume traces major developments in American printing and illustration from the colonial period to the mid-twentieth century. It notes changes in typography, increasing artistic sophistication, and technological developments. Advertising always served as an impetus to typographical innovations, and many of the illustrations depict ads. Development in the fine arts also have influenced printing and graphic art, and these factors are reflected in this book.

Hudak, Leona M. Early American Women Printers and Publishers, 1639-1820. Metuchen, N.J.: Scarecrow Press, 1978.
Arranged chronologically, this volume highlights twenty-five women who operated presses or owned printing establishments in the colonial period and early republic. Hudak provides biographical sketches, followed by a bibliography of works produced by the printer or publisher. Bibliographic notes offer suggestions for further reading, and a lengthy bibliography appears after the ten appendices. These appendices supplement the text with such information as a list of other early American women printers, firsts by American women printer/publishers, and American women who served as official colonial or state printers.

Joyce, William L., et al., eds. *Printing and Society in Early America.* Worcester, Mass.: American Antiquarian Society, 1983.
Ten papers covering the book trade and the effects of the book and printing in the colonies and antebellum America. David Hall discusses "The Uses of Literacy in New England, 1600-1850," tracing the growth of secular literature and a "civil religion" to replace Puritanism. The next three essays explore aspects of bookselling, and the following

five consider cultural aspects of the book. Richard D. Brown's afterword brings together the findings of the other studies and argues for the importance of such bibliographical studies for understanding the nation's culture and history.

Kaestle, Carl F., et al. *Literacy in the United States: Readers and Reading Since 1880*. New Haven, Conn.: Yale University Press, 1991.
The book's first two chapters present "the major issues and findings in the field" of literacy, considering both texts and readers. Chapters 3 and 4 then look at literacy rates. Chapters 5-7 consider American reading habits, addressing the questions of how much Americans spend on books and how much they actually read. The final three chapters examine how literacy and print have affected people's lives. The authors find that Americans were more homogeneous as readers in 1980 than they were in 1890, when the working class rarely bought books. At the same time, "the average expenditure by book buyers and the average portion of disposable income devoted to books have declined." The authors see literacy as "a tool of assimilation to mainstream culture," but it can also preserve differences, as with gender-specific magazines. Throughout, the authors consider policy implications, and they provide an extensive bibliography for further study.

Lehmann-Haupt, Hellmut, Lawrence C. Wroth, and Rollo G. Silver. *The Book in America: A History of the Making and Selling of Books in the United States*. 2d ed. New York: R. R. Bowker, 1952.
An updated version of the first (1937) edition, though to accommodate new information (most of which deals with publishing and bookselling after 1890) the book sacrificed an eighty-six page section on book collecting and libraries. Lawrence C. Wroth provided the sections dealing with the book to 1860; for the early nineteenth century he received help from Silver. These first two sections examine details of printing and bookmaking, then look at the book trade. About three-fourths of the volume deals with the post-Civil War era, and here Lehmann-Haupt concentrates on publishing and bookselling, though he also explores industrialization and other factors that have affected the design and manufacture of the book. This shift in emphasis in the text from printer to publisher reflects the increased importance of the latter in the post-1860 book world. A standard history.

Littlefield, George Emery. *The Early Massachusetts Press, 1638-1711*. 2 vols. Boston: Club of Odd Volumes, 1907.
The Cambridge Press began operation in 1638. In 1711, a fire de-

stroyed all but one of Boston's bookshops. Littlefield devotes a chapter to each of the early Massachusetts printers. Also includes chapters on the founding of Harvard College (which housed British North America's first printing press), the first, second, and third printing houses in the colony, and John Eliot, whose writings, especially his translation of the Bible into Algonquin, occupied the Cambridge Press for many years. The text includes a number of facsimiles, and reprints important contemporary documents relating to the presses and printers of colonial Massachusetts. Much of the second volume consists of reproductions of two rare books, *A Monumental Memorial of Marine Mercy* (Boston: Richard Pierce for James Couse, 1684) and *The Daniel Ratcher* (1713) by Richard Steere. Littlefield argues that the latter was printed by John Allen of Boston.

McMurtrie, Douglas C. *A History of Printing in the United States.* Vol. 2, *Middle and South Atlantic States.* New York: R. R. Bowker, 1936.
The only volume published in a projected four-volume set, this book looks at printing in Pennsylvania, Maryland, New York, New Jersey, Delaware, the District of Columbia, Virginia, South Carolina, North Carolina, and Georgia to 1800. Arrangement is geographical. Includes many facsimiles and a good, though dated, bibliography. The index was to have appeared in the final volume of the series, so this volume lacks this useful feature. Still an important contribution to the history of printing in early America.

Madison, Charles Allan. *Book Publishing in America.* New York: McGraw-Hill, 1966.
Examines important and some minor publishers from colonial times to 1965. Madison writes, "I have ... tried to indicate the specific character and scope of major book firms by sampling their publications, discussing the specific nature of their enterprise, and delineating the men controlling them." Emphasis is on the cultural rather than the economic aspects of publishing, although finances are not totally ignored. Arrangement is chronological, with four major divisions (to 1865, 1865-1900, 1900-1945, 1945-1965); the same company may therefore appear in more than one section. Madison regards the period 1865-1900 as the golden age of publishing, when firms exhibited courtesy and harmony. He sees increasing decline from these ideals, especially after 1945, although some firms, such as Braziller and Atheneum, retained their independence and integrity. Concludes with a chronology of publishing events and a bibliography. A fact-filled volume, especially useful as a source of information for particular firms.

Oswald, John Clyde. *Printing in the Americas*. New York: Gregg, 1937. Arranged geographically with some thematic interludes, this work offers a survey of printing and printers throughout the Western Hemisphere. Given the scope of the volume, even its 565 pages of text can offer little more than a summary of key events and figures. Thomas Short, Connecticut's first printer, receives one paragraph, and the state itself six pages, which is five more than many Latin American countries get. Though no topic receives thorough attention, the book is filled with facts, and topical chapters address in some detail such subjects as "Equipment of the Colonial Printshop" (Chapter 5), "Women in Early American Printing" (Chapter 17), and "Machines and Methods" (Chapter 68). Well- illustrated. Still a useful reference.

Reynolds, David S. *Beneath the American Renaissance: The Subversive Imagination in the Age of Emerson and Melville*. New York: Alfred A. Knopf, 1988.
Studies seven major nineteenth century American writers—Ralph Waldo Emerson, Henry David Thoreau, Walt Whitman, Edgar Allan Poe, Nathaniel Hawthorne, Herman Melville, and Emily Dickinson—in the context of their age. These literary figures reflect popular culture of their period. Reynolds shares Melville's view, expressed in "Hawthorne and His Mosses" (1850): "Great geniuses are parts of the times; they themselves are the times, and possess a corresponding coloring." *Moby Dick*, for instance, draws on Shakespeare but also on sermons, sensational novels of the day, temperance tracts, native humor, and mysteries. Beyond specific sources, Reynolds explores the socioliterary spirit of the age embodied in the works of the writers of the American Renaissance.

Silver, Rollo G. *The American Printer, 1787-1825*. Charlottesville: University Press of Virginia, 1967.
What were the living and working conditions for printers in the early republic? What equipment did they use? How did they conduct their business? Silver offers " a picture of the craft of printing between the colonial period and the arrival of mechanization." The first chapter looks at the apprentice system and the attempts by printers to organize and regulate the trade. The second chapter examines the equipment of a printing office, the third the business of printing, which Silver portrays as precarious. The relationship between authors and printers and the shift of printer to publisher are the subjects of Chapter 4. Chapter 5 considers the spread of printing. The final chapter looks at typography and illustration, which improved during the period studied,

although no truly beautiful American books emerged from the presses of the early republic. Focus is on the Northeast, where most of the printing was done, though Chapter 5 ranges as far as Texas and Illinois. With bibliographic footnotes. Roy Stokes commented in *The Library* 24 (1969): 353-354, "The whole of this book has a refreshing aspect partly due to the liveliness of . . . Silver's writing and partly to the considerable amount of contemporary material on which he has drawn and much of which he has embodied in his text. . . . His achievement is considerable: an eminently readable text with a plenitude of references to all-too-little-known works." A good supplement to Lawrence C. Wroth's *The Colonial Printer* (cited in this chapter).

_____. *Typefounding in America, 1787-1825*. Charlottesville: University Press of Virginia, 1965.
Silver writes in his preface, "The purpose of this volume is twofold: to extend the history of American typefounding beyond the colonial period and to present a selection from the specimens of the founders, thereby providing a useful tool for those who wish to know more about the letter forms cast in America." The story begins with the Scotsman John Baine, though before the Revolution there had been efforts at typefounding in the British colonies. The most successful of the firms in the early republic was established by two other Scotsmen, Archibald Binny and James Ronaldson (who bought Baine's tools in 1799, and in 1806 acquired Benjamin Franklin's tools also). The Monticello type developed by these two men has endured (and was used for Silver's book), and the firm continued until it was acquired by the American Type Founders in 1892. Silver also discusses minor typefounders (Chapter 2), the expansion of the industry (Chapter 3), changes in technology (Chapter 4), and the importation of type (Chapter 5); throughout the period, American printers imported type from Europe, though a twenty percent tariff imposed after the War of 1812 helped the American industry become "firmly and permanently established." Silver's account ends in 1825, when American typefounding became mechanized. Well- illustrated with numerous type specimens.

Stern, Madeleine B. *Books and Book People in Nineteenth-Century America*. New York: R. R. Bowker, 1978.
In telling the fascinating stories of various publishers and booksellers, Stern places their lives and work within the larger context of American culture of the 1800s. Elizabeth Palmer Peabody's Foreign Circulating Library in Boston contributed to the dissemination of European literature in America. The Mormon booksellers Charles R. Savage and

George M. Ottinger of Salt Lake City brought literature to the West, and through the art of photography fostered an appreciation of Western landscape. In the 1860s Henry Frank established a Hebrew publishing house in San Francisco. Though most of the chapters here appeared as articles first, the collection makes them more accessible, and taken together they provide a portrait gallery that supplements John Tebbel's more comprehensive history.

Tebbel, John. *A History of Book Publishing in the United States.* 4 vols. New York: R. R. Bowker, 1972-1981.
The most comprehensive study available on the subject, drawing heavily on the extensive holdings of R. R. Bowker Company's library. The first volume extends from the first colonial press in Cambridge, Massachusetts to 1865. Volume 2 covers the period 1865-1910; Volume 3 the interwar years; and Volume 4 1940-1980. Though arrangement is chronological, many of the units focus on particular topics, such as eighteenth century best-sellers or censorship in the 1940s. Together these volumes trace the rise of publishing from a cottage industry to the business of giant corporations. Especially useful as a reference for particular companies or individuals.

Thomas, Isaiah. *The History of Printing in America, with a Biography of Printers.* 2d ed. 2 vols. Albany, N.Y.: J. Munsell, 1874.
As Marcus A. McCorison observed in his preface to the 1970 Weathervane reprint, Thomas' book "is still the beginning point for most investigations into the history of American printing, for he provides the tantalizing clues from which his successors have built their own studies." Though this is partly a secondary source, much of the information Thomas included derived from personal knowledge. Thomas began his printing career as an apprentice to Zechariah Fowle in 1756, and though he published his history in 1810, he continued to make manuscript revisions until his death in 1831. These were incorporated, together with additional information, in the 1874 edition. Arrangement is geographical, and the book concentrates on the printers and publishers who shaped American book culture in the seventeenth and eighteenth centuries.

Warner, Michael. *The Letters of the Republic: Publication and the Public Sphere in Eighteenth Century America.* Cambridge, Mass.: Harvard University Press, 1990.
Following Jürgen Habermas' *The Structural Transformation of the Public Sphere* (1962), Warner argues that the ideology of republican-

ism affected the uses of print. He rejects the theory of Elizabeth Eisenstein and others that print affected ideology: Print technology, he argues, lacks "an ontological status prior to culture." Controversies over tobacco regulation (Maryland), currency (Massachusetts), and libel (New York) fostered the development of a public sphere that used print to redefine the relationship between governors and governed, and linked citizenship to literacy. By the 1760s, newspapers, pamphlets, and broadsides constituted an important element of printing, making print "coextensive with the public sphere." Print can create a public; a printed constitution creates a nation, the people for whom the constitution exists. As Warner writes, "The Constitution's printedness allows it to emanate from no one in particular and thus from the people." Illiteracy would prevent people from participating in the republic based on letters, and "polite" literature could break down the union of the people by fostering individualism. Warner's concluding chapter shows how Charles Brockden Brown's *Arthur Mervyn* seeks to avoid the problem of polite literature by placing itself within the republican ideology of virtue. The villain, Welbeck, seeks to use literature for selfish, not public, ends. Opponents of the novel worried, as Brown did, that "the environment of fictitious identification might no longer entail public knowledge or civic activity." Warner's prose is denser than necessary, but the argument is elegant and persuasive.

Wentz, Roby. *Eleven Western Presses: An Account of How the First Printing Press Came to Each of the Eleven Western States.* Los Angeles: Los Angeles Club of Printing House Craftsmen, 1956.
　　Wentz writes in his foreword, "This book . . . attempts to bring together in one place what is known, or surmised, on the how, when, and where of the advent of the first printing press in each of the eleven western states," that is, New Mexico, California, Oregon, Idaho, Utah, Washington, Nevada, Arizona, Colorado, Montana, and Wyoming. Wentz discusses the early imprints of each state and the problems pioneer printers confronted, such as the lack of paper. Includes a helpful bibliography.

Winship, George Parker. *The Cambridge Press 1638-1692: A Re-examination of the Evidence Concerning the Bay Psalm Book and the Eliot Indian Bible.* Philadelphia: University of Pennsylvania Press, 1945.
　　An important history of the first press in British North America, this study offers detailed discussions of the various Cambridge imprints. It reprints important documents revealing the press's activities and relates its products to the history of the period. For example, Winship

notes that as population in Massachusetts increased, so did the demand for books. By 1665, Cambridge had three presses and two printers (who did not always cooperate). The debate over the Half-Way Covenant inspired a number of imprints. Allyn B. Forbes called this an important contribution "to the social and intellectual history of seventeenth-century New England. . . . No one . . . has surpassed Mr. Winship in demonstrating how all the various currents in the life of the community pass through the printer's office in their course" (*New England Quarterly* 19, 1946, 250).

Winterich, John Tracy. *Early American Books and Printing*. Boston: Houghton Mifflin, 1935.

After an opening chapter dealing with the bibliography of early American imprints, Winterich presents a pleasant and informative survey of American printing beginning with New England (Chapter 2), and proceeding through the other colonies (Chapters 3-4). Chapter 5 deals with newspapers, Chapter 6 with magazines. The seventh chapter gives a brief overview of the "tools of the trade," noting the scarcity of type in the colonial period and the problems of transporting equipment. Chapter 8 examines belles lettres. Chapters 9 and 11 deal with the westward movement of printing, Chapter 10 with the rise of the professional author in America. The volume concludes with suggestions for collectors. Some subjects, such as Benjamin Franklin, receive extensive treatment; others, like printing in Virginia, get a page. Despite this unevenness, Winterich's book provides a sound survey of printing in America before the Civil War and discusses many of the important works that appeared during this period. Milton Ellis observed that "not only connoisseurs in the field but scholars and bibliophiles of all kinds will read it with both enjoyment and profit" (*American Literature* 9, 1937, 98).

_____. *Three Lantern Slides: Books, the Book Trade, and Some Related Phenomena in America: 1876, 1901, and 1926*. Urbana: University of Illinois Press, 1949.

Drawing on *Publishers Weekly*, Winterich describes the state of the book world in America over a fifty year period. Some issues, such as pricing, remain constant concerns for the trade. Others rise and vanish. The years that Winterich chooses all witnessed important developments, such as the founding of the American Library Association in 1876, the creation of the Nobel Prize for Literature in 1901 (though no American won it until 1930), and the establishment of the Book-of-the-Month Club in 1926.

Woodbridge, Hensley Charles, and Lawrence S. Thompson. *Printing in Colonial Spanish America*. Troy, N.Y.: Whitson, 1976.
Printing began in Mexico a century before the establishment of the Cambridge Press in British North America. By 1538, Juan Cromberger of Seville had provided a press, and Juan Pablos, the first known Mexican printer, also was sent by Cromberger, who paid for the equipment and transportation in return for most of the profits. Woodbridge and Thompson trace the history of printing in Mexico to 1600. In Chapter 2 they turn to Peru, which received a press in the early 1580s; the first Peruvian imprint is dated 1584. Subsequent chapters deal with early printing in Old Paraguay (which included parts of Brazil, Uruguay, and Argentina), in the region of the Rio de la Plata, Central America, New Granada, Chile, and the Spanish Antilles. Throughout Spanish America, printing was largely for religious or legal purposes. With forty facsimiles illustrating the early presswork of Latin America. Includes an extensive bibliography.

Wroth, Lawrence C. *The Colonial Printer*. 2d ed. Portland, Maine: Southworth-Anthoensen Press, 1938.
A standard history, frequently reprinted, covering all facets of book production in the colonies, including information about the presses, typefounding, ink, paper, conditions of labor and trade, and bookbinding. Despite the title, the second edition extends its discussion to 1800 and so includes Florida, Maine, Kentucky, Tennessee, Ohio, and Mississippi, as well as the original thirteen colonies. Wroth concludes that while much of American printing was mediocre or worse, at its best it mirrored the architecture and landscaping of the period to express "that cool, balanced serenity which characterizes the mind and manners of the eighteenth century." Kenneth R. Murdock in the *New England Quarterly* 12 (1939): 179, described Wroth's study as "by all odds the best book on its subject[;] it is more than a history of printing, and is replete with information and suggestions for the intellectual and literary historian."

_____. *Some Reflections on the Book Arts in Early Mexico*. Cambridge, Mass.: Department of Printing and the Graphic Arts, Harvard College Library, 1945.
Although Aztec and Mayan cultures had produced books, the colonial Mexican imprints were purely European in design. By 1540, Juan Pablos, a representative of Juan Cromberger of Seville, was operating a press in Mexico City. The paper, press, and type all came from Spain, and the printing has what Wroth calls a "primitive and uncompromis-

ing" quality. In the 1550s, Pablos brought over from Spain the type-founder Antonio de Espinosa, who produced roman and italic letters to supplement the imported supply of rounded Gothic. Espinosa may also have produced woodcuts for Pablos. After 1559, Espinosa established his own imprint. Wroth argues that throughout the sixteenth century, Mexican printing offices produced their own type, just as early European printers had done. The first commercial type foundry in the New World was established in Mexico City in 1770. Wroth discusses woodcut illustrations, binding, and book design, as well as printing. Wroth admires Mexican imprints for their "vigor, strength, and individuality." With fifteen plates reproducing early Mexican printing and illustrations. A handsome and informative thin folio.

Zboray, Ronald J. *A Fictive People: Antebellum Economic Development and the American Reading Public.* New York: Oxford University Press, 1993.

By 1850, fiction had created a cohesive culture from the disparate elements that made up America in 1800. For fiction to operate on a national level, it had to be mass-produced and widely distributed. Technological innovations in printing and transportation coincided to allow for these conditions to obtain. Schools, meanwhile, fostered a demand for books by promoting literacy. Socioeconomic conditions also encouraged those seeking upward mobility to write and read. In Chapters 10 and 11, Zboray examines the inventory of a New York City bookstore and the loan patterns of the New York Society Library as case studies illustrating these cultural forces treated in Chapters 1-9. The final chapter summarizes the influence of print from colonial times to 1850. While literature created interpretive communities that replaced earlier, local groupings, not everyone participated in the community of print. The South, with its isolated farms and low literacy rate, was largely excluded from this print culture. Appendices look at literacy rates and describe the classification systems used by the New York Society Library. With a thirty-five-page bibliography that attests to the scholarship that underlies the book's perceptive analysis.

PART IV

MISCELLANEOUS SUBJECTS

Chapter 17
BOOK COLLECTING

Manuals

Ahearn, Allen. *Book Collecting: A Comprehensive Guide.* New York: G. P. Putnam's Sons, 1989.
Most of the work is devoted to a list of collectible books (about 3,500) with prices one can expect to pay. Preceding this list are chapters advising the novice about what to collect, where to collect, how to learn more about books, what makes books valuable, and how to build, care for, and dispose of a collection. Ahearn's advice is always sound. He notes, for example, the importance of condition and warns that the absence of a dust jacket can greatly diminish the value of an item. Appendices explain how to identify first editions; provide a glossary; and list pseudonyms, book dealers, and auction houses. Includes a selected bibliography.

Allan, R. B. M. *The Book Hunter at Home.* 2d ed. London: Philip Allan, 1922.
The nine chapters comprising this handsome volume explore Allan's adventures among books, his library and some of his favorite volumes, the care of books, and the need for specialization. He tells of the book not bought and the subsequent regret, of the catalog item desired but already sold, and of the joy of securing the long-sought rarity. He stresses the importance of original condition, includes instructions on building inexpensive but handsome and sturdy bookshelves, and explains the significance of bibliographies. The book's last chapter provides a list of fifty-four possible areas in which to collect, and Allan genially concludes, "May your 'finds' be frequent, cheap, clean, tall, perfect, and broad of margins, and may you never suffer from borrowers, book-worms, acid-tanned leathers, clumsy letterers, and insecure shelf-fastenings."

Brook, G. L. *Books and Book-Collecting.* London: Andre Deutsch, 1980.
An entertaining and informative volume. Chapters cover collecting areas; the making of books; the care of books; trends in book collecting; some great collectors, booksellers, and forgers; and the disposal of a collection. Brook observes that "to be collectible a book needs to be

complete, clean, and undisturbed," and that the last of these qualities is the hardest to find. He also notes that what constitutes collectible condition varies. One would expect higher standards of a Kelmscott Press *Chaucer* than of a Victorian children's book, and a missing leaf from a fifteenth century work would be more acceptable than a similar defect in a modern first. Brook advises that one need not wait until death knocks to dispose of a collection or at least sell off some books, especially if one's interests change or space becomes limited.

Dunbar, Maurice. *Books and Collectors.* Los Altos, Calif.: Book Nest, 1980.
In his preface, Dunbar writes, "This book was written for the intellectually curious, the reader of books, the literate, the educated (formally or otherwise) amateur to whom the idea of book collecting is appealing. . . . Both the plutocrat and the proletarian are necessarily excluded." The twenty-one short chapters cover a variety of subjects, including limited and book- club editions, the care of books, dealing with booksellers, and sources of books, among them garage sales and flea markets. With useful explanations of standard catalog abbreviations and a glossary of common Latin phrases. Includes a helpful bibliography for further study.

Farmer, Bernard J. *The Gentle Art of Book-Collecting.* London: Thorson's, 1950.
In ten short chapters, Farmer presents his views and advice on assembling a library. He begins by addressing the question "Why collect books?" and then considers why certain authors are collectible (literary value, monetary value, curiosity, association with other authors, and importance to a specialist). Other chapters explain terms used in the antiquarian book world, the way to identify a first edition and to acquire a desired book, and the nature of bibliographic "points" that distinguish certain works. Farmer also discusses caring for books. In the final chapter, he offers his guesses as to which authors will prove collectible. A pleasant volume.

Iacone, Salvatore J. *The Pleasures of Book Collecting.* New York: Harper & Row, 1976.
Part 1 of this guide for the novice explores "The Nature of Book Collecting." The ten chapters in this unit include "The Pleasures of Book Collecting," "The History of Book Collecting," "What Makes a Book Worth Collecting?" "First Editions," "Impression, Issue and State," and five desirable categories of books for collectors—early printed books, private press books, fine bindings, signed copies, and

association copies. In Part 2 Iacone deals with the mechanics of book collecting, with advice on such matters as where to find collectible books, how to identify first editions, and how to care for rare books. Part 3 reprints four classic essays on collecting: Reginald Brewer's "Buying and Selling," Barton Currie's "Dealers and Dealer Psychology," Vincent Starrett's "Have You a *Tamerlane* in Your Attic," and A. S. W. Rosenbach's "Mighty Women Book Collectors." Also provides a glossary of terms used in the antiquarian book trade, a selective bibliography, and a list of antiquarian booksellers. Readable and informative, with many illustrations of collectible books.

Matthews, Jack. *Collecting Rare Books for Pleasure and Profit*. New York: G. P. Putnam's Sons, 1977.
Matthews first defines "rare book," a term he acknowledges is elusive. He next discusses rare books as an investment and stresses the importance of having the "right" edition ("The Point of Points"). Most of the volume deals with collecting areas: early printing, Americana, modern firsts, illustrated and private press books, children's literature, and detective and science fiction. Matthews also discusses how to acquire, care for, and sell old books. With a glossary of bibliophilic terms and a selected bibliography. Matthews writes well, but the emphasis on the profit rather than the pleasure of collecting can be annoying.

Muir, Percy H. *Book-Collecting as a Hobby in a Series of Letters to Everyman*. 2d ed. London: Gramol, 1945.
A classic since its first appearance, because it is filled with sound advice. The first letter, "How To Begin," urges the fledgling collector to adopt a plan and to start slowly. Letter II offers suggestions about what to collect. In Letter III, Muir explores the question of first editions—what are they and why are they desirable. Letter IV explores collating to determine whether a book is complete; here Muir offers some details on how a book is made. Letter V considers "How To Judge Values," and notes that condition is crucial. Letter VI, "How To Transform Mountains into Molehills," lists references that will enlighten the perplexed collector, and Letter VII gives a capsule history of book production. The second edition added a supplementary letter demystifying the bookseller's catalog. A second volume, published by Cassell (London), appeared in 1949 as *Book-Collecting: More Letters to Everyman*, with chapters on "The Joys and Woes of a Book-Collector," "How To Proceed," "How To Use a Bibliography," "What To Do about Auction Sales," "Is Book-Collecting an Investment?" "Is There Money in Old Bibles?" and "The Antiquarian Booksellers' Association."

Peters, Jean, ed. *Book Collecting: A Modern Guide*. New York: R. R. Bowker, 1977.
A useful gathering of twelve essays. William Matheson opens the volume with a definition of book collecting. Robin G. Halwas and Robert A. Wilson write respectively on buying from dealers and at auction. The antiquarian book market is the subject of Robert Rosenthal's contribution. Lola L. Szladits writes about collecting manuscripts. Terry Belanger surveys descriptive bibliography. Joan M. Friedman writes about forgeries. Caring for a collection is William Spawn's topic; organizing it is Jean Peters' concern. Katharine and Daniel Leab deal with appraisal. Susan O. Thompson relates collecting to the world of learning, and G. Thomas Tanselle adds an excellent and extensive bibliographic essay that covers all areas of interest to the collector. Especially helpful for the beginner, but more advanced collectors will take comfort from Thompson's essay and may take warning from Peters and the Leabs.

Rees-Mogg, William. *How to Buy Rare Books: A Practical Guide to the Antiquarian Book Market*. Oxford, England: Phaidon, 1985.
Intended for the would-be collector. Part 1 deals with the fundamentals of collecting: reasons for collecting, the nature of the antiquarian book trade, how to read a catalog, where to buy and how to sell, and what to avoid. Rees-Mogg rightly emphasizes the importance of condition. Part 2 examines collecting areas: early printers, English literature, scientific and medical books, books about America and Australia, travel and natural history, the history of ideas, and fine bindings. In Part 3, Rees-Mogg tells the reader how a book is assembled, and Part 4 explains caring for rarities. With a glossary and list of common catalog abbreviations, addresses of dealers and auction houses, and a bibliography. Attractively printed and illustrated.

Storm, Colton, and Howard Peckham. *Invitation to Book Collecting: Its Pleasures and Practices, with Kindred Discussions of Manuscripts, Maps, and Prints*. New York: R. R. Bowker, 1947.
Intended for the novice, who "will find here an examination of the motives for collecting, a survey of important collectors of the past, descriptions of collectible items in several fields; an explanation of the buying, selling, and pricing of rarities; some cautions to be observed; and suggestions for some new paths in collecting." The authors discuss both what and how to collect, and provide much sound advice. For example, they note that one need not pursue what others

already are seeking, that age and price are not necessarily directly related, and that one need not be rich to collect (though a heavy purse helps).

Wilson, Robert A. *Modern Book Collecting.* New York: Alfred A. Knopf, 1980.

Wilson focuses on collecting modern first editions. Himself a collector of Gertrude Stein, Ezra Pound, W. H. Auden, and Edward Albee, Wilson also published modern firsts (under his Phoenix Bookshop imprint) by such writers as Marianne Moore, Richard Wilbur, Allen Ginsberg, Elizabeth Bishop, and Louis Zukofsky. Wilson explores sources for collectors, caring for books, and selling them. While the focus is on books published since the late nineteenth century, many of the pointers here apply to any form of collecting.

Winterich, John T. *A Primer of Book Collecting.* New York: Greenberg, 1926.

In Part 1, "The Quarry," Winterich talks about collectible books and explains what makes them desirable. Part 2, "The Chase," shows the novice how to acquire the items treated earlier. Winterich explains that book collecting is not exclusively an avocation (or vocation) of the rich; there are many types of book collecting that can prove spiritually and even financially rewarding. A charmingly informative work with advice that is still applicable despite the book's age.

Biographical Directories

Cannon, Carl L. *American Book Collectors and Collecting from Colonial Times to the Present.* New York: H. W. Wilson, 1941.

This monumental study remains the only full-fledged history of the subject. Cannon traces book collecting in America from Thomas Prince (1687-1758), whom Cannon calls "the father of American bibliography," to Henry E. Huntington (1850-1927) and Henry Clay Folger (1857-1930). The volume is especially strong for the nine-teenth century, when many of America's greatest private libraries were assembled. In addition to discussions of important bibliophiles, Cannon devotes chapters to specific areas of collecting, such as Americana, English literature, modern literature, local history, and Shakespeare. Despite its occasional omissions and its age, the work remains indispensable.

De Ricci, Seymour. *English Collectors of Books and Manuscripts (1530-1930) and Their Marks of Ownership.* Cambridge, England: Cambridge University Press, 1930.
The text of the four Sandars Lectures De Ricci gave at Cambridge in 1929. As the compound title indicates, De Ricci had two concerns. One was to provide a brief history of English book collecting over four centuries, the other to indicate how one could determine provenance. In the course of his discussion, he traces the fortunes of various collections, a subject about which he had encyclopedic knowledge. He notes, for example, that the Bridgewater Library, begun about 1600 by Sir Thomas Egerton, passed to the Huntington Library in San Marino, California, en bloc, in 1917. Famous collectors such a Sir Thomas Phillips (1792-1872) and the Fourth Earl of Ashburnham (1797-1878) receive individual chapters; lesser figures are grouped together. A standard reference.

Dickinson, Donald C. *Dictionary of American Book Collectors.* New York: Greenwood Press, 1986.
Presents biographical sketches of 359 major collectors who had died by 1985. Dickinson discusses the collector's interests and his or her significance in the development of American book culture. The work notes the fate of the library, whether dispersed at auction or institutionalized; and Dickinson also lists primary and secondary bibliographical references. Provides a wealth of information gathered by one of the leading authorities on the history of the book in America. An excellent place to begin research on any collector included.

Elton, Charles, and Mary Elton. *The Great Book-Collectors.* London: Kegan Paul, Trench, Trubner, 1893.
Traces the collecting of books from antiquity to the nineteenth century. Some of the figures here, like Sir Thomas Bodley and Petrarch, are familiar, though the Eltons' discussion even in these cases in valuable. Other figures are likely to be less familiar to the general reader. Niccolò de' Niccoli of Florence, for example, an important figure in Renaissance humanism, assembled one of the finest libraries in Italy and allowed the general public to use it. Gian-Vincenzio Pinelli of Padua also built a library open to scholars. Well-written and attractively illustrated.

Fletcher, William Younger. *English Book Collectors.* London: Kegan Paul, Trench, Trubner, 1902.

Fletcher offers biographical sketches of one hundred English book collectors. The first chapter deals with royal collectors from Edward IV to William IV. Fletcher then returns to the fifteenth century and John Fisher, Bishop of Rochester (1469-1535), who was executed with Thomas More for opposing Henry VIII's break with the Papacy. The last entry concerns the poet, decorator, and fine printer William Morris (1834-1896), who assembled a fine library of manuscripts and early printed books. Fletcher notes highlights of the collections and gives a sense of the men—there are no women in this century of collectors—who created them. Useful and readable.

Quaritch, Bernard, ed. *Contributions Towards a Dictionary of English Book-Collectors and also of Some Foreign Collectors Whose Libraries Were Incorporated in English Collections or Whose Books Are Chiefly Met with in England.* London: Bernard Quaritch, 1892-1921.

An alphabetical list of seventy-eight collectors. Each entry includes a biographical sketch and a catalog of principal books. The sketches also discuss the disposition of the collection. Some entries are brief, such as that for Stanesby Alchorne (d. 1800), whose library contained only about 200 volumes—but nine of them had come from the press of William Caxton, the first English printer. The Alchorne library was purchased en bloc by Lord Spencer, who kept some of the books and sold the rest. Major collectors receive more attention. Thus, the Fourth Earl of Ashburnham receives fourteen pages; his library included nearly 4,000 manuscripts, as well as a wealth of printed material. With selected portraits and occasional facsimiles.

Memoirs and Histories

Arnold, William Harris. *First Report of a Book-Collector.* New York: Dodd, Mead, 1898.

Bookseller, writer, collector, and bibliographer, Arnold assembled two libraries of books and manuscripts devoted primarily to nineteenth century British and American authors. His *Ventures in Book Collecting* (New York: Charles Scribner's Sons, 1923) presents his bibliographic autobiography from the vantage point of the end of his life—he died on January 2, 1923. *First Report* looks at his collecting from the other end of his bibliophilic career, when he had been collecting for less than a decade. His delight in his books is clear, and his advice on such matters as original condition and the danger of an unlimited bid at auction remain sound.

Browne, Irving. *In the Track of the Book-Worm*. East Aurora, N.Y.:
Roycroft Printing Shop, 1897.

A collection of delightful essays and poems by a collector of extra-
illustrated books. Throughout, Browne conveys his understanding of
the follies of bibliomania and his joy in being thus afflicted. For
example, he concludes "My Friends the Books" with the lines, "My
memory is full of graves/ Of friends in days gone by:/ But Time these
sweet companions saves,—/ These friends who never die." In "Poverty
as a Means of Enjoyment in Collecting," he portrays an experience
known to most collectors: "To haunt the book-stores, there to see a
long-desired work in luxurious and tempting style, reluctantly to abandon it for the present on account of the price; to go home and dream
about it, to wonder . . . whether it will ever again greet your eyes; to
conjecture what act of desperation you might in heat of passion commit
toward some more affluent man in whose possession you should
thereafter find it; to see it turn up again in another book-shop, its charms
slightly faded, but yet mellowed by age . . . ; to ask with assumed
indifference the price, and learn with ill-dissembled joy that it is now
within your means, to say you'll take it; . . . to go forth from that room
with feelings akin to Ulysses when he brought away the Palladium
from Troy . . .—this is indeed pleasure denied to the affluent, . . . and
only marred by the palling which always follows possession and the
presentation of your book-seller's account three months afterwards."
Browne's *Ballads of a Book-Worm* (East Aurora, N.Y.: Roycrofters,
1899) presents fifty-three charming short poems on book collecting.

Burton, John Hill. *The Book Hunter*. Edinburgh: W. Blackwood & Sons,
1862.

A pleasant exploration of the nature of book collecting. Part 1, "His
Nature," considers the character of the bibliophile. Here Burton presents such characters as "Inch-rule Brewer," who "is guiltless of all
intermeddling with the contents of books, but in their external attributes his learning is marvelous." Another figure is Magnus Lucullus,
Esq.: "He must have the best and most complete editions, whether
common or rare; and . . . they must be in perfect condition." Part 2
examines the functions of the bibliophile, Part 3 his clubs. Many of
these, such as the Roxburghe (England) and the Camden, initiated
publishing programs, and these publications are the subject of the final
unit. Combines information with entertainment.

Carter, John. *Books and Book-Collectors*. Cleveland: World, 1957.

A gathering of eighteen essays. The first section presents seven book collectors: Thomas James Wise, Rowland Burdon-Muller, James T. Babb, Carroll A. Wilson, Michael Sadleir, Wilmarth Sheldon Lewis, and Lord Rothschild. In the next unit, Carter discusses the work of the typographers D. B. Updike and Stanley Morison. Section 3 offers five essays on areas of collecting: detective fiction, "off-subject books," (books by authors who wrote on topics other than what they are generally known for, such as H. G. Wells's *Text-Book of Biology*), A. E. Housman, three-decker Victorian novels, and fashions in collecting. In 1934, Carter and Graham Pollard exposed the forgeries of T. J. Wise (*An Enquiry into the Nature of Certain Nineteenth Century Pamphlets*). Section 4 adds two essays to this discussion. These are followed by reflections on the need for accurate bibliographical descriptions of nineteenth century books, and the work concludes with two "Frivolities," one describing the rediscovery of a lost Gutenberg Bible and its sale to Charles Scribner, the other reprinting Carter's review of his own *ABC for Book Collectors*. Here he comments, "The author of this book must be either a fool or a knave," and he opines that collectors will buy the work chiefly to locate errors for which to chide the author. A charming book.

_____. *Taste and Technique in Book Collecting.* 3d impression. London: Private Libraries Association, 1970.
The text of Carter's 1947 Sandars Lectures at Cambridge. The third impression adds his 1969 presidential address to the Bibliographical Society (England). Examines roughly a century of collecting in America and Britain, beginning with the great sale of the library of John Ker, third Duke of Roxburghe, in 1812. Notes how interests have changed, and how collectors have increasingly tended to specialize. In Part 2, Carter explores methods of collecting, addressing such issues as tools and terminology (Chapter 9), bookshop and auction room (Chapter 10), and questions of rarity and condition. The 1969 presidential address, which forms the epilogue, examines the condition of collecting twenty years after the Sandars lectures. In 1969, Carter found more institutional collecting and an increased importance of auction houses.

Currie, Barton. *Fishers of Books.* Boston: Little, Brown, 1931.
In this classic work, Currie, a collector of the first water, discusses the joys and tribulations of the bibliophile. In the course of the work, he surveys the book-collecting world of the late 1920s and early 1930s, offers portraits of great collectors and booksellers of the period, including A. Edward Newton and A. S. W. Rosenbach, and provides some useful advice for the novice. Like other counsellors, he advocates

specialization, but in "The Seductions of Happy-Go-Lucky Collecting" he confesses to the joy of buying a 1529 antiphonal well outside his collecting interests. He also notes the folly of spending $5,000 on a first edition of Thomas Gray's "Elegy Wrote in a Country Churchyard," a folly he does not regret. While most of the volume treats Currie's own book- hunting (or, as he prefers to say, book fishing), it includes useful advice for the novice, such as how to identify a first edition and how to deal with dealers. Richly illustrated and highly readable.

De Bury, Richard. *The Philobiblon*. Durham, England, 1345.
The first work devoted entirely to the love of books. Richard de Bury was a noted bibliophile; in the volume's twenty short chapters he defends his passion. He argues that "all things decay and waste away in time, and those whom Saturn begets he ceaseth not to devour. Oblivion would overwhelm all the glory of the world, had not God provided for mortals the remedies of books." At the end of his treatise, he acknowledges that his passion may have led him into the occasional venial sin, a confession that will be as recognizable to the present-day collector as the love of books that pervades the rest of the text.

Dibdin, Thomas Frognall. *The Bibliomania: Or, Book-Madness; Containing Some Account of the History, Symptoms, and Cure of This Fatal Disease. In an Epistle Addressed to Richard Heber, Esq.* London: Longman, Hurst, Rees, and Orme, 1809.
A response to Dr. Ferrier's 1809 publication of similar title, this initial 87-page text (including index) grew by 1842 to 618 pages. In this first edition, Dibdin surveys some notable victims of bibliomania, among them Roger Ascham and his pupil, Queen Elizabeth I. Richard Heber, to whom the work is addressed, was a noted early nineteenth century collector who before his death had filled six houses with books. Dibdin discusses the symptoms of bibliomania, such as a desire for books printed on vellum and for early printed works. He concludes by suggesting that reprints, public libraries, and good bibliographies may allay the disease. In 1811, Dibdin expanded his volume and turned it into dialogue, elaborating on the subject. Despite his precious prose, Dibdin captures the spirit of aristocratic book collecting in the Regency.

Egan, Maurice Francis. *Confessions of a Book-Lover*. Garden City, N.Y.: Doubleday, Page, 1922.
The five chapters here treat Egan's early reading, his favorite poets (among them Dante), novelists, letter-writers, biographers, writers of

memoirs and miscellaneous subjects. Egan's tastes are sometimes idiosyncratic, but his enthusiasm and knowledge illuminate the book and demonstrate that he merits the epithet he accords himself in his title.

Field, Eugene. *The Love Affairs of a Bibliomaniac.* New York: Charles Scribner's Sons, 1896.
Written as Field was dying, this volume records his passion for books, beginning with his first encounter with the *New England Primer* he found in his grandmother's collection. At his Uncle Cephas' house he came upon *Robinson Crusoe*, another enduring love. Many other works subsequently shared his affection. All collectors will recognize themselves in Field (with his love of reading in bed, his fondness for the smell of books, his delight in the perusal of catalogs), and will agree with his invocation, "How far-reaching is thy grace, O bibliomania! How good and sweet it is that no distance, no environment, no poverty, no distress can appall or stay thee. Like that grim spectre we call death, thou knockest impartially at the palace and at the cottage door. And it seemeth thy especial delight to bring unto the lonely in desert places the companionship that exalteth humanity."

Hazlitt, William Carew. *The Book Collector.* London: John Grant, 1904.
A discursive history of book collecting, combined with advice to fledgling bibliophiles. Well before John Carter's *Taste and Technique in Book Collecting* (cited earlier) Hazlitt observed that certain categories of books enjoy a vogue and then decline in popularity. He talks about the great English collectors and their libraries, and he provides much information about the then-standard bibliographies. He also explains how books are made, and what makes a book desirable. Especially useful for its portrait of the book- collecting world at the beginning of the twentieth century.

Jackson, Holbrook. *The Anatomy of Bibliomania.* 2 vols. London: Soncino Press, 1930-1931.
Modeled on Robert Burton's *Anatomy of Melancholy* in style, Jackson's work in thirty-two chapters examines all facets of collecting. Part 21, for example, deals with book-hunting: "No sport so seductive, so rich in temptations, falls, repentances, so fraught with achievements and disappointments." He defends collecting "when its object is not ostentation of possession, but use." He concedes that the love of books can become corrupt. Like his mentor, Burton, Jackson has filled his pages with quotations, some of them in Latin; but, unlike Burton,

Jackson provides translations. A classic in the field. Richard Le Gal-
lienne praised the work in his review in *The New York Times* for
July 26, 1931 as "at once a masterly synthesis of all that has ever been
felt and written about books by the book lovers of the past and the
amalgam of an original creation" (p. 2).

Joline, Adrian A. *The Diversions of a Book-Lover*. New York: Harper &
Brothers, 1903.
In sharing his enthusiasm for books, Joline discusses his own library
and offers advice and observations to the would-be collector. He notes,
for example, that auction prices are always low for books one has and
high for books one wants. He suggests areas of collecting, such as
county histories, and he warns against rebinding old books. Joline also
notes changes in fashion. One fashion that he does not condemn is
extra-illustration (adding prints to a book), though he warns against
excess. An entertaining account.

Jordan-Smith, Paul. *For the Love of Books: The Adventures of an Impecunious Collector*. New York: Oxford University Press, 1934.
"What I have really tried to do in this little book of mine is not so much
to indicate my methods of collecting—though I have not always
refrained from boasting gossip—as to reveal my reasons for loving and
collecting the books I have about me." Jordan-Smith explores his
collecting interests—Americana, late nineteenth and early twentieth
century British literature, Robert Burton, Norman Davey, Caradoc
Evans, and others. He conveys his delight in acquiring and owning his
books, and in the course of the volume offers useful pointers to those
who share his delight in ink, paper, cloth, and leather—in short, in the
book as a physical object.

Lewis, Wilmarth Sheldon. *Collector's Progress*. New York: Alfred A.
Knopf, 1951.
Lewis was the leading twentieth century collector of Horace Walpole
material, reassembling a large portion of Walpole's library (dispersed
in 1842) and of the letters Walpole wrote and received by the thousands. Lewis explains here how he progressed from collecting house-
flies to Walpole, and the course of his book- collecting career, which,
like that of true love, did not always run smooth. He tells of his
encounter with a bookseller he calls "X," who sold him a set of chairs
purportedly once the property of Samuel Johnson, Charles Lamb's tea
caddy, Gainsborough's easel, and a pillow made by Mrs. William Blake
for her husband. Lewis returned all but the tea caddy, doubting the

authenticity of his other purchases. Yet this same suspect X produced the architect's drawings for Walpole's Twickenham villa, Strawberry Hill. Lewis demonstrates his skill and luck as he writes engagingly about his pursuit of Walpole.

Merryweather, Frederick Somner. *Bibliomania in the Middle Ages*. London: Merryweather,1849.
Merryweather focuses on the role of the monasteries, especially in England, in preserving texts from the seventh to the fifteenth century. Benedict Biscop, for example, undertook five trips to Rome in the seventh century to buy books for his monastery at Wearmouth, where The Venerable Bede later wrote his important history, which drew on Benedict's acquisitions. Merryweather notes that William Britone of Glastonbury Abbey listed 400 volumes in the monastic library in 1248. In addition to Bibles and works of the Church Fathers, the collection held books by Livy, Sallust, Virgil, Cicero, Boethius, Horace, and Juvenal. The Franciscans and Dominicans assembled admirable libraries. In the fifteenth century, the Greyfriars Library in London profited from a four-hundred-pound donation from the Lord Mayor Dick Whittington. An authoritative study.

Munby, A. N. L. *Phillipps Studies*. 5 vols. Cambridge, England: Cambridge University Press, 1951-1960.
Sir Thomas Phillipps, a bibliomaniac of the highest order, sought to collect a copy of every book ever made. In the course of his eighty years, he accumulated an unequaled collection of manuscripts and a wealth of printed works. Munby's five volumes trace the history of Phillipps' book buying and its aftermath. Volume 1 deals with the catalogs of Phillipps' acquisitions. The second volume treats Phillipps' troubled family affairs. The third and fourth volumes explore the formation of the library, and the final volume its dispersal. Nicolas Barker prepared a one-volume distillation of this work, *Portrait of an Obsession* (New York: G. P. Putnam's Sons, 1967). In 1971 Sotheby Publications reissued the complete five-volume set in two volumes with some additions and corrections.

Newton, A. Edward. *The Amenities of Book Collecting and Kindred Affections*. Boston: Atlantic Monthly Press, 1918.
Newton taught a generation of bibliophiles what and how to collect, and he continues to influence the susceptible with his charming essays. In the introduction to this, his first, book, composed of articles that had appeared earlier in the *Atlantic Monthly Magazine*, he said that he

wanted "to write a little story about my books—when and where I had
bought them, the prices I had paid, and the men I had bought them
from." The little story extended over nine volumes, among them *A
Magnificent Farce and Other Diversions of a Book-Collector* (1921),
The Greatest Book in the World and Other Papers (1925), *This Book
Collecting Game* (1928), and *End Papers: Literary Recreations*
(1933). On the final page of the proofs of *The Greatest Book in the
World*, Newton wrote, "The end of all scribblement is to amuse."
Newton admirably achieved this end, as the many editions of his works
and their collectibility attest. Were these works published in the 1990s,
the Surgeon General would require a warning label stating that reading
them might prove hazardous to one's pocketbook, for Newton's enthusiasm for collecting is presented in such a way that it must prove
contagious.

Rees, John Rogers. *The Pleasures of a Book-Worm.* London: Elliot Stock,
1886.
Rees shares his delight in the books he collected; in the process, he
reveals the psyche of the bibliophile. Thus he remarks, "If the Tenth
Commandment really does include books, we freely confess to having
often broken it." Similarly, he recognizes that "the reader's song is of
the drawn curtain and the fire-flicker, the subdued light of the lamp and
the wild rush of the wind without. At such a time his books are doubly
friends; they partake of his security from the raging inclemency, and
share the hospitality which friend proffers friend in storm-time and in
need." One of the best sections is "Glimpses of Earthly Paradise," with
its list of ideal association copies, such as Charles Lamb's Beaumont
and Fletcher's plays (1679) and William Wordsworth's copy of James
Thomson's *Castle of Indolence.* Equally charming is Rees's *The Diversions of a Bookworm* (London: Elliot Stock, 1886).

Roberts, William. *The Book Hunter in London: Historical and Other
Studies of Collectors and Collecting.* London: Elliot Stock, 1895.
Essentially a history of London book collecting from the Middle Ages
to the end of the nineteenth century, with some delightful diversions,
such as a chapter on the humors of book catalogs and another on good
places for "bookstalling" around 1895. Among the medieval book
collectors that Roberts discusses is the Earl of Warwick, who owned
fifty manuscripts—then a substantial private library. By the fifteenth
century London had several important collections, such as that owned
by the Franciscans. Roberts notes many collectors during the Renaissance, among them Thomas More and Henry VIII. The dissolution of

the monasteries was a boon to private collectors. The golden age of English book collecting, according to Roberts, was the eighteenth century, when many great libraries were begun. The volume concludes with sketches of some collectors contemporary with Roberts. Reliable and readable.

Savage, Ernest Albert. *The Story of Libraries and Book-Collecting*. London: G. Routledge & Sons, 1909.
For much of history, the story of libraries has been that of individual book collectors. In Egypt and Mesopotamia, collections of books were associated with temples, and in the Greco-Roman world, public libraries such as that in Alexandria existed, but even this was assembled by the royal collectors Ptolemy I and his successors. Similarly, the public library of Pergamon was largely the creation of Eumenes II. Many of the Renaissance humanists also opened their personal libraries to the public, thus contributing to the spread of learning, and even the Boston and New York Public Libraries have been enriched by donations of such collectors as George Ticknor and James Lenox. Savage offers a good survey of individual collectors and of the formation of public libraries from antiquity through the nineteenth century.

Starrett, Vincent. *Penny Wise and Book Foolish*. New York: Covici Friede, 1929.
A volume of reminiscences and advice by a noted bookman. The opening chapter, "Have You a *Tamerlane* in Your Attic," inspired a successful search for this rarest of nineteenth century titles in American literature. In "The Diamond in the Dust Heap," Starrett urges the collector to "frequent all the shops, the greater as well as the lesser. . . . Somewhere in the heaps and tons of old books that line the walls of bookshops or gather dust in the outside bins, there are choice and desirable items of charm and of value." Although Starrett was writing in 1929, at the height of bibliomaniacal prices, he stressed in "The Rationale of Book Collecting" that the hobby is at base sentimental, and he argues that one should read the books one buys. Like all other true collectors, Starrett cautions against rebinding, and he writes feelingly of the joys of catalogs and personal bookplates.

Targ, William, ed. *Bouillabaisse for Bibliophiles*. Cleveland: World, 1955.
Like his earlier *Carrousel for Bibliophiles* (see following), this volume brings together a charming collection of reading on the joys of book collecting. The anthology opens with John Carter's "Definition of a Book Collector." Carter concludes that members of the species have

"a reverence for, and a desire to possess, the original or some other specifically admirable, curious, or interesting edition of a book he loves or respects or which has a special place among his intellectual interests." Lawrence C. Blochman's tale of "The Aldine Folio Murders" appears here, as does Carolyn Wells's account of her great Walt Whitman collection, along with many other delightful pieces.

_____. *Carrousel for Bibliophiles*. New York: Philip C. Duschnes, 1947.
An enjoyable gathering of poems, essays, and stories on the subjects of books and collecting. Among the selections are Christopher Morley's short piece "In a Second-Hand Bookshop," a bit of Thomas Frognall Dibdin's description of bibliomania, and Ben Abramson's advice on smuggling books into the house when one's wife objects to collecting. The piece observes that only men need this advice: "Any woman who met with opposition in this matter or any other, would probably resort to the swift and simple expedient of divorce." Other entries include part of Richard de Bury's *Philobiblon*, essays by A. Edward Newton, Holbrook Jackson, and William Hazlitt, and an ingenious mock rare book catalog by Francis P. Farquhar.

Uzanne, Octave. *The Book-Hunter in Paris: Studies Among the Bookstalls and the Quays*. London: Elliot Stock, 1893.
Uzanne concentrates on the booksellers who operate along the Seine and those who have patronized this source of bargains. Booksellers began gathering at the Pont Neuf in the seventeenth century. They were temporarily banished but soon returned. Laurence Sterne, in his *Sentimental Journey* (1768), tells of visiting the Quai Conti in search of a copy of Shakespeare. In Uzanne's day, the Seine in Paris was lined with bookstalls. Uzanne discusses the operation of these outdoor shops and notes some of the leading sellers of the time. He also devotes a chapter to the frequenters of this bibliophilic paradise. An appendix describes a banquet held on November 20, 1892 for the stall-keepers of the quay. Xavier Marmier left a thousand francs to pay for the meal; Uzanne includes the menu and records the events of the night. Filled with fascinating anecdotes of the booksellers and book hunters of the Paris quays.

Chapter 18
BOOKSELLING

Barnes, James J. *Free Trade in Books: A Study of the London Book Trade Since 1800.* Oxford, England: Clarendon Press, 1964.
In 1829, London booksellers met to regulate the price of books in order to limit discounting. The rules were not rigorously enforced, and in 1850 booksellers met again to emphasize their opposition to reducing retail prices. Most of this volume deals with an attack mounted against these restrictions. Charles Dickens, John Stuart Mill, and Thomas Carlyle were among the authors who joined discontented book dealers in their effort to abolish all trade restrictions on books. Free trade triumphed, but in 1899 the Net Book Agreement codified the fixed prices most booksellers had sought for much of the nineteenth century. Barnes's last chapter examines the establishment and consequences of the agreement. K. W. Humphreys wrote, "This is an excellent book, well produced and carefully documented. . . . The subject is an important one and especially valuable for the literary history of the nineteenth century" (*Modern Language Review* 60, 1965, 259).

Blayney, Peter W. M. *The Bookshops in Paul's Cross Churchyard.* London: Bibliographical Society, 1990.
In the period 1550-1600, Paul's Cross Churchyard was "the unrivalled centre of retail bookselling in London, and consequently in England." Indeed, Blayney writes that by 1641, "every frontage in the Cross Yard either was, or had been, a bookshop." Because of the survey undertaken after the 1666 Fire of London, Blayney was able to identify with great precision the locations of many of these stores. Blayney's maps show where each shop was, and he provides a brief history of each. He identifies twenty-eight of these establishments and observes that other shops were located in the bays between the cathedral buttresses. Blayney identifies eleven of these. Appendix I discusses shops that were established in the New Jewry, where at least eighteen operated by the early 1650s. Appendix II criticizes the map of London of around 1520 that appeared in Volume III of *The City of London from Prehistoric Times to c. 1520* (Oxford, 1989), and Appendix III provides an index to Blayney's work by stationer and sign. An excellent guide to the London book trade during the reign of Elizabeth I, and a valuable contribution to the city's history.

"Bookselling in the Thirteenth Century." *Cornhill Magazine* 9 (1864):
475-479.
This anonymous article recreates the restrictive bookselling conditions
of the 1200s, when universities controlled the stationarii, who sold
books on commission and also lent books. Prices were controlled, and
the university had to approve the sale of any volume. The article argues
that the primary factor limiting bookselling was public indifference
rather than price or official regulation. In the next century, when
demand increased, so did supply.

Brotherhead, William. *Forty Years Among the Old Booksellers of Philadelphia, with Biographical and Bibliographical Remarks.* Philadelphia: A. P. Brotherhead, 1891.
Brotherhead began selling books at the corner of Sixth and Market
Streets, Philadelphia, in 1849, with a stock worth about $60. He sold
primarily British works because only three of his customers wanted
Americana. In 1850, Brotherhead writes, Philadelphia's population of
300,000 supported fifteen antiquarian booksellers. In 1891, with a
population of about a million, the city had only a dozen sellers of old
books. In addition to surveying the state of bookselling, Brotherhead
provides fascinating portraits of collectors and dealers. For example,
he talks of Moses Polock, uncle of the great bibliopole A. S. W.
Rosenbach. Polock hated to part with his books, and this reluctance
was heightened by his sale of the *Laws* of New York (New York:
William Bradford, 1694) to George Brinley, Jr. for $16; at the Brinley
auction the volume fetched $1,600. Brotherhead writes engagingly,
and his book serves as an important source of information on American
bookselling in the latter half of the 1800s.

Christianson, C. Paul. *Memorials of the Book Trade in Medieval London:
The Archives of Old London Bridge.* Cambridge, England: D. S.
Brewer, 1987.
In the Middle Ages, the Bridge House was responsible for preventing
London Bridge from falling down. Christianson looks at the records
from the Bridge House for the fifteenth and sixteenth centuries for
information about the book trade. The archives show that the price of
parchment did not vary between 1390 and 1520, but paper became
increasingly popular. The book trade remained centered near St. Paul's
Cathedral throughout the period. Christianson examines not just the
contents but also the composition of the Bridge records to identify
individual scribes and to learn more about late medieval bindings,
paper, parchment, and scribal techniques.

Duff, E. Gordon. *A Century of the English Book Trade: Short Notices of All Printers, Stationers, Book-Binders, and Others Connected with It from the Issue of the First Dated Book in 1457 to the Incorporation of the Company of Stationers in 1557*. London: Bibliographical Society, 1905.

In his introduction, Duff surveys the book trade between the invention of printing to 1557. Printing came relatively late to England. In 1485, Peter Actors was appointed King's Stationer, but no King's Printer was named. The book trade grew slowly, and foreigners dominated bookselling in the late fifteenth and early sixteenth centuries. In 1554, Parliament limited the rights of foreigners engaged in the book trade, and England tried to restrict the importation of foreign books as well. The volume presents biographies of those engaged in the trade and cites references for further study. Appendix II lists the signs of London booksellers; these include the Bishop's Head in St. Paul's Churchyard, the Mermaid in Lombard Street, and the Saracen's Head at Holborn. An important study.

Dunton, John. *The Life and Errors of John Dunton*. London: S. Malthus, 1705.

At the age of fourteen, Dunton was apprenticed to the London bookseller Thomas Parkhurst. The economic dislocations following the Duke of Monmouth's rebellion in 1685 encouraged Dunton to go to New England, where he remained for much of 1686. After avoiding England for another two years because of his debts, he returned in 1688 and for a time prospered as a publisher and bookseller, occupations generally joined in that period. Dunton's 1705 autobiography reveals much about literary conditions of the late seventeenth century, and includes character sketches of figures involved in the trade. Shortly after 1705, Dunton turned to authorship and journalism; he died in obscurity in 1733.

Ettinghausen, Maurice L. *Rare Books and Royal Collectors: Memoirs of an Antiquarian Bookseller*. New York: Simon & Schuster, 1966.

Ettinghausen began his career in 1901, when he went to work for C. G. Luzac, publisher and purveyor of Oriental books. This autobiography records Ettinghausen's adventures during half a century in the rare book trade. From 1905 to 1914, he worked for Ludwig and Jacques Rosenthal of Munich. After World War I, Ettinghausen joined Maggs Brothers (London) as manager of the foreign department. The Second World War ended that phase of his career, and he became associated with Albi Rosenthal (Oxford, England), great-nephew of Ludwig Rosenthal. The book barely touches on this final phase of Ettinghausen's career, devoting most of its attention to his years with Maggs. An appendix reprints some of the letters King Manuel of Portugal wrote to him; the correspondence indicates the type of client Ettinghausen served. Other customers were King Farouk of Egypt, Baron Maurice de Rothschild, J. P. Morgan, and Henry Huntington. The books and manuscripts that Ettinghausen dealt with were as glorious as his customers, including the Codex Sinaiticus Petropolitanus, the oldest known manuscript of the Old and New Testaments (early fourth century), which Etting-hausen secured for the British Museum for 100,000 pounds. *The Papers of the Bibliographical Society of America* 61 (1967): 154, commented, "Written with tact, wisdom, a not-too-solemn sense of humor, and infinite bibliographical learning, these memoirs will have an enduring place in the active collection of all bookmen."

Everitt, Charles P. *Adventures of a Treasure Hunter*. Boston: Little, Brown, 1951.

Everitt spent sixty years as an antiquarian bookseller specializing in Americana and American literature; he completed these memoirs shortly before his death in 1951. He writes engagingly about his successes: He once paid a quarter for three pamphlets, one of them *Miles Overland Expedition to California* (1851), which he sold to Henry R. Wagner, bibliographer of the American West, for $1,000; another anecdote tells how he acquired a lot of pamphlets at Stan V. Henkels' auction rooms in Philadelphia for $45 and sold one of them to Henry Huntington for $1,010. He also tells of books he did not acquire but should have. Much here on leading dealers and collectors of the first half of the twentieth century, and Everitt shares his deep bibliographic knowledge.

Fabes, Gilbert H. *The Romance of a Bookshop, 1904-1938*. S.l.: Privately printed, 1938.

William and Gilbert Foyle began their bookselling career by disposing of their old textbooks. Their first place of business was their kitchen. At the age of seventeen, Gilbert was running the brothers' shop in Peckham, a London suburb, while William, age eighteen, worked as a clerk during the day and helped with the books in the evenings. From Peckham the Foyles moved into the heart of the city and expanded their stock, which previously had consisted largely of school and examina-tion texts. By 1938, the company was selling some 40,000 books a week and employed 300 people. Fabes traces the rise of the firm, and his chronicle is enhanced by a selection of photographs.

Feather, John. *The Provincial Book Trade in Eighteenth-Century England.* Cambridge, England: Cambridge University Press, 1985.

When the Licensing Act lapsed in 1695, London lost its monopoly on printing. Over the next century, the provincial book market expanded, but it continued to be supplied largely by London publishers. As Feather writes, "The Londoners were the producers; the country booksellers were the retailers." Country newspapers provided the advertising the London publishers needed to reach the nonmetropolitan market, and newspaper proprietors served as middlemen in handling orders. While publishing remained centered in London, the number of provincial bookshops rose from two hundred located in fifty towns in 1700 to 1,100 in more than three hundred towns by 1800. Feather examines the markets, distribution system, and the country bookshops themselves. He also devotes a chapter to the provincial printing office. Appendices include documentary evidence, such as the inventory of Ellen Feepound's bookshop in 1776 and John Cheney's printing office in 1788. Hugh Amory expressed reservations about this study, but concluded his review in the *Papers of the Bibliographical Society of America* 81 (1987): 199-206, by observing, "Everyone interested in books will take something away from [Feather's work], and he has assembled such a tasty smorgasbord of information—including some charming engravings of country bookshops."

Goodspeed, Charles E. *Yankee Bookseller.* Boston: Houghton Mifflin, 1937.

Having lost his job as a seller of farm equipment, Goodspeed in 1898 opened a secondhand bookshop in Boston shortly before Christmas, using his $600 in savings to stock his shelves. Goodspeed later declined an offer of $20,000 from a customer who wanted to become a partner. Among the books Goodspeed handled was Edgar Allan Poe's *Tamerlane* (1827), one of the rarest works in American literature. In fact, he handled one-third of the known copies, two of six. His account of this episode shows that sometimes the only task harder than finding a rare volume is selling it. This charming and informative book is a testimony to Goodspeed's integrity. The *Times Literary Supplement* for January 8, 1938 commented, "*Yankee Bookseller* is full of good stories about collectors, bargains, varieties, disappointments and finds" (p. 29).

Greg, W. W., E. Boswell, and William Alexander Jackson, eds. *Records of the Court of the Stationers' Company, 1576-1640.* 2 vols. London: Bibliographical Society, 1930-1957.

The first volume deals with the period to 1602, the second and larger volume extends the work's coverage to the English Civil War. Much of the information here deals with internal matters relating to the Stationers' Company, but the volumes also reveal much about the workings of the book trade, which the Stationers' Company regulated. One sees here the concern with foreign competition and piracies. One of the most notable of the latter was Robert Waldegrave's piracy of Philip Sidney's *Arcadia* in 1599. One finds here questions of pricing and edition size, arguments with the Cambridge University Press, and attempts to regulate London pressmen, as well as important bibliographical information. For example, George Wither's *The Scholars Purgatory* was begun on the press of George Wood, but after he had completed two gatherings his press was seized, and the book was completed by another printer. S. C. Roberts wrote that "anyone with even a slight knowledge of seventeenth-century documents will recognize at once the massive quality of Mr. Jackson's scholarship and for everyone concerned with the history of English book-production the volume will be a standard work of reference" (*Review of English Studies* 10, 1959, 91).

Hanff, Helene. *Eighty-four, Charing Cross Road.* New York: Grossman, 1970.
On October 5, 1949, the author Helene Hanff responded to an advertisement by the London booksellers Marks & Co., located at 84 Charing Cross Road, sending a list of titles she wanted. She was not a book collector in the manner of Henry Huntington or J. P. Morgan; she wanted second-hand books in inexpensive but attractive editions, and she could not find these in New York. This letter set off a lengthy correspondence recorded here and in *The Duchess of Bloomsbury Street* (1974). These letters not only record Hanff's bookselling dealings with Marks & Co. and so illuminate the state of the business, but also show the human side of dealing in books, as Hanff comes to know the staff of the shop three thousand miles away. Also provides an excellent recipe for Yorkshire pudding.

Hunt, Richard W., I. G. Philip, and R. J. Roberts, eds. *Studies in the Book Trade in Honour of Graham Pollard.* Oxford, England: Oxford Bibliographical Society, 1975.
A collection of fifteen essays that deal with books from the fifteenth to the late twentieth century. Included here is Paul Morgan's study of eight letters, found in bindings, that concern the Oxford book trade in the first half of the seventeenth century and show the town's importance in supplying books in the western part of the country. Harry Carter looks at the early account books of the Oxford University Press, Terry

Belanger considers Jacob Tonson's Shakespeare copyright, Giles Barber examines the European book trade in the late eighteenth century, and Michael L. Turner writes of Tillotson's Fiction Bureau, supplier of fiction to provincial and colonial newspapers in the late nineteenth and early twentieth centuries. A scholarly assemblage.

Isaac, Peter, ed. *Six Centuries of the Provincial Book Trade in Britain.* Winchester, England: St. Paul's Bibliographies, 1990.
A collection of fourteen papers presented at the Eighth Seminar on the British Book Trade, held in Durham, England, in July, 1990. F. W. Ratcliffe begins the volume with "The Contribution of Book-Trade Studies to Scholarship," in which he observes that "the book trade is one of the many vehicles which offer insights into the growth of the nation. The provincial book trade is an important part of it. . . . If the full potential of the study into the provincial book trade is to be brought before scholarship, the subject needs to be focused and brought into an integrated whole." A. I. Doyle then looks at the English provincial book trade before printing. Paul Morgan considers the provincial book trade in England in the sixteenth and seventeenth centuries. Jeremy Black writes about the provincial press in the eighteenth. Other studies deal with Wales ("The Welsh Printing House from 1718 to 1818"), Ireland ("Patrick Neill and the Origins of Belfast Printing"; "Some Late Eighteenth- and Early Nineteenth-Century Dublin Printers' Account Books: The Graisberry Ledgers"), and Scotland ("Working Towards a History of Scottish Book Collecting"). Concludes with a bibliography of works on the history of the book trade in northern England published since 1965.

Kaye, Barbara. *The Company We Kept.* London: Werner Shaw, 1986.
Continues *Minding My Own Business* by Kaye's husband, Percy Muir (cited in this chapter). The Muirs had taken a house in Essex, England, in 1938; during the Second World War, this house also served as their bookshop. Kaye tells of the hardships of trying to buy and sell books in the midst of a war, and she offers much social history along the way. The account concludes with the end of the European war in 1945.

Knight, Charles. *Shadows of the Old Booksellers.* London: Bell and Daldy, 1865.
Without attempting to write complete biographies of England's leading booksellers from 1660 to the end of the eighteenth century, Knight presents these figures to create what he calls "something like a connected story of literary progress, in its commercial relations," of the

period. Because booksellers were also publishers and often operated printing offices, Knight's account surveys the entire book world of the late seventeenth and eighteenth centuries. Includes chapters on such prominent figures as Thomas Guy, Jacob Tonson, Samuel Richardson, John Newbery, Robert Dodsley, and James Lackington (whose Temple of the Muses Knight visited in 1801). In *The London Mercury* 16 (1927): 303, I. A. Williams wrote of a 1927 reprint that the book offers "a pleasant medium through which to pick up miscellaneous information about printers, booksellers, and the conditions of the book-trade."

Kraus, H. P. *A Rare Book Saga: The Autobiography of H. P. Kraus.* New York: G. P. Putnam's Sons, 1978.
   Apprenticed at the age of seventeen, Kraus opened his first shop in Vienna in 1932. The arrival of the Nazis in 1938 ended this phase of Kraus's career. In 1939, he came to America, where a sale to Lessing Rosenwald, collector of early illustrated books, salvaged Kraus's business—which grew into one of the leading antiquarian houses in the country, if not the world. The book's thirty-one illustrations suggest the range of material that Kraus handled, including the Gutenberg Bible, William Caxton's *Recuyell of the Historye of Troye* (the first book printed in English), a copy of the *Declaration of Independence*, and the first American type specimen book. Much is covered here on the vagaries of the antiquarian book trade and on collectors. Peter Ludwig collected illuminated manuscripts from Kraus, then sold some back to raise money for Pop Art, then bought back the manuscripts when he tired of the paintings. In 1953, Kraus sold to the Morgan Library a copy of the *Missal Speciale*, then dated about 1450 and considered the first book printed from movable type in Europe. The Gutenberg Bible has reclaimed that title, and Kraus's volume is now dated 1473.

Lackington, James. *Memoirs of the Forty-five First Years of the Life of James Lackington.* 7th ed. London: Printed for the author, 1794.
   Written in the guise of forty-seven letters and first published in 1791, this work recounts the life of one of England's most enterprising booksellers. He showed his mercantile talents early; at the age of ten he undertook to sell pies for a baker in financial difficulties and soon made the baker prosperous. At the age of fourteen, he was apprenticed to the shoemaker George Bowden. In 1774 he set up his own bookstall, which he combined with a shoemaking shop. Five years later, he issued his first book catalog, listing 12,000 volumes, and by 1791 he claimed to sell 100,000 books a year that earned him £4,000 annually. Among

his innovations in the book trade was the sale of remainders to the public at reduced cost; previously such books had been sold cheaply only to other dealers, who destroyed most of the copies and sold the rest at the regular price. By the end of the eighteenth century, Lackington's Temple of the Muses at Finsbury Square was England's largest bookshop. In 1804, Lackington published a sequel to his memoirs, *The Confessions of J. Lackington*, but this work lacks the interest of the earlier volume.

Landon, Richard G., ed. *Book Selling and Book Buying: Aspects of the Nineteenth Century British and North American Book Trade*. Chicago: American Library Association, 1978.
Terry Belanger leads off this collection with an essay on changes in the London book trade between 1750 and 1850. Judith St. John deals with children's books. Books sold in parts is the subject of Mihai H. Handrea's contribution. Books in parts allowed a new, poorer reading public access to fiction. Newspapers provided another source of fiction for these readers, as Michael Turner discusses in his essay, which highlights Tillotson's Fiction Bureau. Douglas Lockhart considers the activities of Toronto publisher J. Ross Robertson. Franklin Gillian examines vanished Victorian novels and four collectors who sought to preserve such material; Robert Nikirk writes about two American book collectors, William Loring Andrews and Beverly Chew, who helped found the Grolier Club.

Lawler, John. *Book Auctions in England in the Seventeenth Century (1676-1700)*. London: Elliot Stock, 1898.
In 1604, the Elseviers in Holland sold the library of George Dousa by auction. William Cooper held the first English auction in 1676. By 1700, some 350,000 titles worth a quarter of a million pounds had passed under the auctioneer's hammer in England. Drawing on catalogs of the period, Lawler discusses the auctioneers, their offerings, and their practices (which resemble those of Sotheby's in the 1990s). Auctions served to dispose of libraries assembled by collectors, but also provided a convenient method for booksellers to dispose of excess stock. Because prices often were lower than those charged by dealers, auctions allowed impecunious readers to gain access to printed matter. An excellent monograph.

Littlefield, George Emery. *Early Boston Booksellers, 1642-1711*. Boston: Club of Odd Volumes, 1900.
Offers thumbnail sketches of the thirty-four booksellers, most of whom

were also publishers, active in Boston from the establishment of the Massachusetts Bay Colony to the disastrous fire of 1711 that destroyed all but one of the city's bookshops. Littlefield notes that in the colony's first decades, bookselling could not provide a livelihood; Hezekiah Usher sold many different commodities, including fur, lumber, sugar, and cotton, along with books. Littlefield writes of John Foster, the first printer in Boston; John A. Lewis regarded him as the equal of Benjamin Franklin as a polymath. Nicholas Boone, who published the first newspaper in British North America (1704), and Henry Phillips, who fought one of the first duels in Boston, are treated here. Littlefield reveals the diversity of personalities that contributed to making Boston the literary and publishing capital of the American colonies.

Low, David. *With All Faults*. Tehran, Iran: Amate Press, 1973.
In 1926, Low went to work as a cataloguer for the London auctioneer Hodgson's. This account begins with a survey of London bookshops in the interwar period and of the dealers who operated them. Low also discusses the country bookstores in England, Scotland, and France. Later chapters deal with American collectors, female book buyers, three private collections, erotic literature, Peter Kroger (a spy who masqueraded as a bookseller), Low's encounter with Count Potochiof Montalk, who made Hodgson's the official booksellers to the (nonexistent) Court of Poland, and Guido Morris and his Latin Press. These reminiscences offer a portrait of the antiquarian book world of the 1920s through the 1960s.

Magee, David Bickersteth. *Infinite Riches: The Adventures of a Rare Book Dealer*. New York: Paul S. Eriksson, 1973.
Magee states in his preface, "I have tried here to write about the adventure of selling rare books, the unusual persons encountered, the entertainment derived from a business beyond the comprehension of the majority of mankind." Because of his fondness for Francis Bacon, Magee was hired by John Howell, the great San Francisco bookman, in 1925. Three years later, Magee set up shop on his own, and his memoirs recount the experiences of selling old books for the next forty-five years. Magee concludes that "the rare book business is a highly agreeable way of making very little money," but he declined a university post because he preferred the life of a bookseller. J. M. Edelstein commented in *The Papers of the Bibliographical Society of America* 68 (1974): 341, "David Magee's 'adventures' are not only a perceptive account of the book trade, of the eccentricities of collectors and the vagaries of book collecting, . . . but also a story full of

excitement, charm, and amusing anecdotes, done in an engaging style
which succeeds admirably in combining simplicity and elegance."

Marston, E. *Sketches of Booksellers of Other Days*. New York: Charles
Scribner's Sons, 1901.
Biographical essays dealing with eight English booksellers of the
eighteenth century: Jacob Tonson, Thomas Guy, John Dunton, Samuel
Richardson, Thomas Gent, Alice Guy, William Hutton, and James
Lackington. The accounts of the these leading figures in the trade serve
as a history of bookselling and publishing of the period. Includes
portraits of the subjects.

_____. *Sketches of Some Booksellers of the Time of Doctor
Johnson*. London: Sampson Low, Marston, 1902.
Complements Marston's *Sketches of Booksellers of Other Days* (see
above). The twelve chapters include biographies of Michael Johnson
(father of Samuel Johnson), Andrew Millar, Thomas Davies, Thomas
Osborne (whom Samuel Johnson knocked down with a folio when the
bookseller was being insolent), Bernard and Henry Lintot, Robert and
James Dodsley, Thomas Evans, John Nichols, William Bowyer, and
Edward Cave. Two chapters deal with the booksellers' organizations
The Friends of Literature (1805-1811) and the earlier Booksellers'
Literary Club. Filled with anecdotes that illuminate the literary life of
the eighteenth century and that show how the booksellers of the period
took on the role of literary patron previously held by the aristocracy.

Morris, Henry. *Trade Tokens of British and American Booksellers and
Bookmakers, with Specimens of Eleven Tokens Struck Especially for
This Book*. Newtown, Pa.: Bird & Bull Press, 1989.
Booksellers and others involved in the book arts have occasionally
issued tokens, usually in small denominations, primarily as a form of
advertisement. Morris traces the history of this quaint device and lists
all known examples from England and America. This volume includes
many illustrations, together with eleven specially-made tokens, seven
of which are from book dealers.

Muir, Percy H. *Minding My Own Business: An Autobiography*. London:
Chatto & Windus, 1956.
In 1930, Muir joined the firm of Elkin Mathews, which had been
founded in 1887. Much of the book deals with the finances of the firm,
but the account also offers portraits of leading book people of the
period. A. Edward Newton, the Philadelphia collector of eighteenth

century books, was a customer, as was the Horace Walpole devotee W. S. Lewis of Farmington, Connecticut. Muir enjoyed Lewis' annual visits but did not care for Newton. Muir was a pioneer in the selling of first editions of music. In 1933, he went to Germany to buy scores and found great pieces such as Schubert's *Winterreise* at bargain prices. This account ends with the coming of World War II. For the sequel, see Barbara Kaye's *The Company We Kept.*

Mumby, Frank A., and Ian Norrie. *Publishing and Bookselling.* 5th ed., rev. London: Jonathan Cape, 1974.
In the preface to the second edition, Mumby wrote that he sought "to tell in outline the whole story of English bookselling—tracing its origin as far as possible in the days of ancient Rome; its struggle for existence through the Dark Ages; and its subsequent organization and development through the centuries down to the present day." As the many editions of the book indicate, this work has become a classic. It is especially strong on the nineteenth and twentieth centuries. The first two hundred pages arrive at the mid-1800s, and the following century receives almost twice that space. Includes a seventy-page bibliography. Mumby's section, covering the book trade to 1870, is more readable than Norrie's, but the entire volume is an indispensable reference.

Myers, Robin, and Michael Harris, eds. *Development of the English Book Trade, 1700-1899.* Oxford, England: Oxford Polytechnic Press, 1981.
A collection of five papers. Myers deals with the bookseller and retailer of gossip about the eighteenth century literary scene, John Nichols. J. A. Downie considers freedom of the press in eighteenth century England. He argues that the 1712 Stamp Act sought only to raise revenue, not to restrict publications, and he finds growing government tolerance for the press. Michael Harris looks at how the London booksellers organized to control periodicals and so promote book sales. John Sutherland's contribution examines the organization of the book trade in the late nineteenth century, as exemplified by the Publishers' and Booksellers' Association, the Net Book Agreement, and the Society of Authors. Peter Thorogood discusses the poet Thomas Hood, whose father was a publisher—the Hood of Vernor, Hood, and Sharpe—and the poet's relationship to the trade.

——————. *Economics of the British Booktrade, 1605-1939.* Cambridge, England: Chadwyck-Healey, 1985.
Brings together eight papers presented at the sixth annual conference on book trade history held at the University of London's Extra-Mural

Department. Myers' essay on the financial records of the London Stationers' Company from 1605 to 1811 leads off the volume. John Hetet's essay follows; it examines a particular facet of these records, the Wardens' Accounts in the 1660s and 1670s, to understand the role of the company as censor. Michael Turner looks at the Stationers' Company's personnel in the period 1800-1830. Robert and Sir Francis Gosling, who united banking and bookselling, provide the subject for Frank Melton's contribution. John Hewish considers the role of the Patent Office as publisher; Mirjam Foot writes about bookbinders' prices. The career of Moses Pitt allows Michael Harris to place bookselling within a framework of general economic activity in late seventeenth century London, and James Barnes concludes the volume with a piece on innovative trade practices between 1819 and 1939.

_____. *Maps and Prints: Aspects of the English Booktrade.* Oxford, England: Oxford Polytechnic Press, 1984.
This collection of five essays begins with Sarah Tyacke's contribution, "Samuel Pepys as Map Collector." Pepys's collection of maps remains largely intact at Magdalene College, Cambridge, with 1,100 items. Tyacke observes that Pepys bought wherever he could. In the 1670s, there were ten London dealers in maps; by 1705, there were fifteen. Richard Mount, a dealer in navigational books and sea atlases, was a friend and adviser who helped Pepys with his projected *Biblioteca Nautica*, a bibliography of works on navigation. Michael Harris discusses London guidebooks in the late seventeenth and early eighteenth centuries. The earlier guidebooks were intended to be sold to foreigners, but soon the English also became targets. Iain Bain examines various ways of reproducing wood engravings in the early nineteenth century; Ralph Hyde discusses the career of the nineteenth century artist Robert Havell, Jr., who engraved the plates for Audubon's *Birds of America* and who, before moving to the United States, was a prosperous print-seller and dealer in art supplies. John Ford's concluding essay looks at the Ackermann business, begun in 1794 by Rudolph Ackermann and still in operation. The volume includes some black-and-white illustrations that supplement the text. These reproductions are adequate but unimpressive.

_____. *Sale and Distribution of Books from 1700.* Oxford, England: Oxford Polytechnic Press, 1982.
Michael Harris' lead article demonstrates that between 1670 and the 1760s, crime paid, at least for publishers and booksellers, who found a ready market for accounts of trials, executions, and criminal biogra-

phies. Ian Maxted looks at book sales in Devon. Major publications still came from London but were distributed through local publishers, especially newspaper publishers. Maxted notes increasing local publication of ephemera in the late eighteenth century. This popular literature was distributed by hawkers. Giles Barber writes about international trade in books in the eighteenth century. Gwyn Walters talks about the research value of early auction and booksellers' catalogs, and Robin Myers discusses the sale of books by auction between about 1720 and 1847. An informative, well-researched collection of essays.

Norrington, Arthur Lionel Pugh. *Blackwell's, 1879-1979: The History of a Family Firm*. Oxford, England: Blackwell, 1983.
Benjamin Henry Blackwell opened his bookshop at 50 Broad Street, Oxford, on January 1, 1879, with a stock of new and second-hand books worth 180 pounds. By the end of his second year in business he had realized a profit of 226 pounds, ten shillings. In 1913, a Publications Department became a separate entity under the supervision of the founder's son, Basil Blackwell. One of his editorial assistants was Dorothy L. Sayers. By 1946, Blackwell's truly could be termed Booksellers to the World; in 1979, the firm's business totalled over twenty-seven million pounds. Much here on the book business in general of the later nineteenth and the twentieth centuries, charmingly presented. The text is enriched with thity-two photographs and facsimiles.

Parker, Wyman W. *Henry Stevens of Vermont: An American Book Dealer in London, 1845-1886*. Amsterdam: N. Israel, 1963.
Born in Vermont in 1819, Stevens, a graduate of Yale, sailed for England in July, 1845, as a fledgling bookseller. By 1852, he had become a member of the Royal Society of Antiquaries and a prosperous dealer in antiquarian books. In addition to advising the British museum in the field of Americana, he supplied America's leading collectors of the period, among them James Lenox, John Carter Brown, George Brinley, Jr., and Edward Crowninshield. Parker traces Stevens' eminent forty-year career and provides a bibliography of Stevens' writings. Offers a good portrait of the antiquarian book trade in the Victorian era in Britain and America.

Parks, Stephen. *John Dunton and the English Book Trade: A Study of His Career with a Checklist of His Publications*. New York: Garland Publishing, 1976.
A biography and extensive bibliography of a leading late seventeenth and early eighteenth century bookseller and publisher. Parks provides

a good sense of the age and of the problems that Dunton faced in a world that was dividing into two print cultures, popular and sophisticated. This study draws heavily on Dunton's own *Life and Errors* (1705), but Parks's chapter notes reveal his extensive scholarship. Appendices examine Dunton's relations with his authors and the rest of the trade, pseudonymous publications, and the Conger system that allowed publishers to raise capital and spread the risk of a publishing venture by sharing costs and profits. The bibliography describes 479 items; Dunton claimed to have written, published, or printed 600.

Plant, Marjorie. *The English Book Trade: An Economic History of the Making and Sale of Books.* 3d ed. London: George Allen and Unwin, 1974.

A standard study, first published in 1939. Plant writes that she intends to examine "the economic development of the English book trade, the structural form which it gradually evolved, the problems of supply and demand which it encountered and overcame, the techniques which it adopted and discarded, the social and economic relationship which arose between masters and men." Plant concentrates on the trade since the introduction of printing, though she offers brief comments on the production and sale of manuscripts. The first half of the volume deals with the hand-printed book; the second half concentrates on the nineteenth and twentieth centuries. Plant shows how the book trade was affected by social and economic conditions. For example, in the sixteenth century, teachers and clergymen, who might be expected to be buyers of books, lacked the money to do so; and the working class lacked the leisure and income needed for reading. Plant is especially good in recording the transformations of publishing and bookselling over time. The eminent bibliographer Michael Sadleir, reviewing the first edition for *The Spectator* (162, June 16, 1939, 1044-1045), observed that Plant's book "is an invaluable compendium of technical and economic facts."

Pollard, Graham, and Albert Ehrmann. *The Distribution of Books by Catalogue from the Invention of Printing to A.D. 1800. Based on Material in the Broxbourne Library.* Cambridge, England: Roxburghe Club, 1965.

More than just a discussion of book catalogs, this volume traces the history of the book trade in Europe from the fifteenth to the nineteenth century. Trade quickly became international, and printers used various methods to advertise their wares. Colophons were one way to advertise, and Caxton's famous broadside represents another: "If it please any man spiritual or temporal to buy any piece of two and three commemorations of Salisbury Use imprinted after the form of this present letter which be well and truly correct, let him come to Westminster into the almonestry at the Red Pale, and he shall have them good cheap," Caxton proclaimed around 1477 in his effort to sell his *Sarum Ordinale*. By the sixteenth century, booksellers were issuing small pamphlets as well as broadsides to publicize their offerings, and the Aldus family issued larger booklets in folio or quarto. Catalogs proliferated in the seventeenth century and began to be issued regularly. Auction catalogs constitute another category and are treated separately here. A lovely volume filled with facts and facsimiles.

Pottinger, David T. *The French Book Trade in the Ancien Régime, 1500-1791*. Cambridge, Mass.: Harvard University Press, 1958.
Pottinger seeks "to survey the business of making, marketing, and distributing all kinds of books from the end of the incunabula period down to the Revolution." Part 1 looks at authors, Part 2 at the development and administration of the book trade. In Part 3, Pottinger discusses the journeymen and apprentices, and the volume concludes with treatments of papermaking, book illustration, and binding. Pottinger traces the French government's unsuccessful efforts to regulate the trade, and he explores the ways other government actions affected book production. For example, the revocation of the Edict of Nantes (which had granted religious toleration to Protestants) hurt the paper industry and caused skilled Huguenot printers to flee the country.

Randall, David A. *Dukedom Large Enough*. New York: Random House, 1960.
Randall entered the book trade in 1929 and left in 1956 to become curator of the J. K. Lilly, Jr. rare books library at Indiana University. His first assignment for E. Byrne Hackett of the Brick Row Bookshops, Inc., was to attend the Jerome Kern sales at Anderson Galleries (New York). This sale marked a high point in book collecting and long held the record for the most expensive library sold at auction in the United States. The volume is arranged by collecting interests and collectors rather than chronologically, but this pattern does not interfere with the rich portrait of the antiquarian book trade and its most prominent figures during the second quarter of the twentieth century. One of the finest of booksellers' memoirs, with valuable information about dealers and collectors.

Reichmann, Felix. "The Book Trade at the Time of the Roman Empire." *Library Quarterly* 8 (1938): 40-76.

By the latter half of the fifth century B.C., Athens had a well-developed book trade. Socrates in his *Apology* says that the works of Isocrates and Anaxagoras are readily available. Euthydemus (c. 400 B.C.) owned a complete manuscript of Homer. Caesar and Cicero both employed scribes, suggesting that copies were not readily available unless collectors made them. Under the empire, publishing developed. Quintilian speaks of his publisher, Tryphon. Reichmann argues that slaves wrote to dictation. He discusses the writing materials used—papyrus predominated during the early centuries A.D.—and the form of the book, mainly rolls for classical literature until the fourth century. Rome and Alexandria became publishing centers that exported Latin and Greek works, respectively. A trade in rare books also existed. Reichmann cites Varro's *De biblio thecis*, which gives instructions on how to choose books. Public and private libraries became increasingly common, and while some collectors relied on copyists, the trade must also have been a source of supply.

Roberts, William. *The Earlier History of English Bookselling*. London: Sampson Low, Marston, Searle, & Rivington, 1889.
In his introduction to the 1967 Gale Research Company (Detroit) reprint, Leslie Shepard described this work as "the best general history of English bookselling from its inception to the early eighteenth century." The first chapter addresses bookselling before Caxton. Little information is available about the book trade in England before the late Middle Ages. From the fifteenth century onward more is known. Roberts first offers a chronological overview (Chapters 1-4), then a geographical survey (Chapters 5-7); and in Chapters 8-12 he discusses five leading booksellers of the eighteenth century: Jacob Tonson, Bernard Lintot, Edmund Curll, John Dunton, and Thomas Guy. A readable, reliable account.

Rosenbach, A. S. W. *A Book Hunter's Holiday: Adventures with Books and Manuscripts*. Boston: Houghton Mifflin, 1936.
A sequel to *Books and Bidders* (1927), this volume deals with Rosenbach's bibliographic adventures in such fields as the love letter, mysteries, newsletters, presidential libraries, almanacs, frauds, and Christmas books. Rosenbach recounts, for example, his pursuit of *Dracole*, printed in Nuremberg about 1488. The work deals with Dracole Waida, the original Dracula. Rosenbach also tells of his quest for the rare *A Caveat or Warning for Common Cursetors* (1567), which reveals the English underworld during the reign of Elizabeth I. He writes of paying the record price for a book from George Washington's library and of

acquiring the only known copy of the first (1733) edition of Benjamin Franklin's *Poor Richard's Almanac*. Holding a Ph.D. in English from the University of Pennsylvania, Rosenbach knew his books as a scholar and collector as well as a bookseller; in his memoirs he makes them into living things, explaining not only why they are valuable but also why they are important. Witty and informative.

_____. *Books and Bidders: The Adventures of a Bibliophile*. Boston: Little, Brown, 1927.
Rosenbach begins this account of his bibliographic adventures with a reminiscence of his uncle Moses Polock, Philadelphia bookseller, who fostered Rosenbach's love of books and the trade. In the course of the memoir, Rosenbach recalls some of his greatest triumphs—and they were legion—such as his discovery of the long-lost first edition of Samuel Johnson's *Prologue Spoken at the Opening of the Theatre in Drury Lane* (1747), or his 1920 acquisition of a love letter from John Keats to Fanny Brawne. Rosenbach's purchase of the letter at the Anderson Galleries auction rooms in New York elicited a delightful sonnet (reprinted in the book) from Christopher Morley. Rosenbach was at the height of his powers in the 1920s; this book demonstrates why he was known as the Napolean of the auction rooms and one of the world's greatest booksellers. Includes portraits of many of America's greatest collectors, who repeatedly found themselves in Rosenbach's shop. Carl Rollins observed in the *Saturday Review of Literature* 4 (1928): 501, "A multitude of experiences in Europe and America—in libraries, English mansions, and auction rooms—told with gusto and a good memory make entertainment for the reader. And throughout one feels that the writer has a very real feeling for the books he talks of."

Rostenberg, Leona, and Madeleine B. Stern. *Between Boards: New Thoughts on Old Books*. Montclair, N.J.: Allanheld & Schram, 1977.
The authors, who specialize in works of the Renaissance, recount a number of their adventures in the rare book trade, whether searching for a unique presentation copy of Erasmus' *Encomium Moriae* (1511) or finding a book even its author didn't know about (Louisa May Alcott's *Will's Wonder Book*, 1870, issued by her publisher without attribution, reprinting a serialization in *Merry's Museum*). An insider's look at antiquarian bookselling, with information on such matters as how catalogs and dealers' collections are assembled. The authors display wit and charm as they anatomize such banes of a bookseller's existence as "The 'Darling' Non-Customer" or the "Friendly Librarian Who Has Just Been Passing Through."

_____. *Old and Rare: Forty Years in the Book Business.* Santa Monica, Calif.: Modoc Press, 1988.

An updated version of their 1974 book. Rostenberg begins by describing her early fascination with Renaissance imprints and her inability to persuade her dissertation director at Columbia University (which would eventually award her a Ph.D.) to share her interest. She spent five years working for the bookseller Herbert Reichner, a difficult master but one who taught her much about the trade. In 1944, she struck out on her own, and soon her friend Madeleine B. Stern joined Leona Rostenberg—Rare Books. The rest of the volume recounts the women's adventures as they search for books in England, the Continent, and America. The final chapter surveys their career since 1974. Lawrence S. Thompson observed of the first edition that *Old and Rare* "might well serve as a text for apprentices in the [antiquarian book] trade" (*Papers of the Bibliographical Society of America* 70, 1976, 288).

Shaylor, Joseph. *Sixty Years a Bookman, with Other Recollections and Reflections.* London: Selwyn & Blount, 1923.

In September, 1857, Shaylor was "sent on trial" to a bookseller at Stroud and then apprenticed to him. In 1864, Shaylor entered the employ of Simpkin, Marshall & Co., London, working twelve- and fourteen-hour days, with few vacations. He notes the effect of the Elementary Education Act, which increased the demand for schoolbooks; and he discusses other changes that he observed. Shaylor advocates cooperation among booksellers and publishers, and supports the idea of free libraries.

Snelling, O. F. *Rare Books and Rarer People: Some Personal Reminiscences of "The Trade."* London: Werner Shaw, 1982.

In January, 1950, Snelling began working at Hodgson's auction rooms. In 1967 Sotheby's absorbed the firm; Snelling continued with his new employer until 1981. This memoir is filled with anecdotes about many prominent—and marginal—figures in the antiquarian book trade, particularly John, Sidney, and Wilfrid Hodgson, and offers the general reader a pleasant tour of this often-mysterious world. Includes a portfolio of historic photographs.

Sowerby, E. Millicent. *Rare People and Rare Books.* London: Constable, 1967.

Educated at Girton College, Cambridge, Sowerby served her apprenticeship in the rare book trade with Wilfred Michael Voynich of London. World War I ended this first phase of her career some nineteen months after it began, but the war forced the firm of Sotheby, Wilkinson and Hodge to break with tradition and hire a female cataloguer. This phase of Sowerby's career ended in 1923; in 1925, she began the third stage of her bookselling life with A. S. W. Rosenbach of Philadelphia, with whom she remained until 1942. The volume is filled with anecdotes about the great book people she knew and about the world of rare books in the first half of the twentieth century.

Spencer, Walter T. *Forty Years in My Bookshop*. London: Constable, 1923.
Spencer became a London bookseller in 1883. By 1923, his shop occupied four stories. Spencer recounts his experiences as an antiquarian bookseller. He began auspiciously by attracting the custom of William Wright, a rich bookie with a love of Charles Dickens. Spencer's other customers included most of the leading English writers of the period. Americans, too, frequented the shop; Spencer tells of selling books to George Vanderbilt, Henry J. Heinz, and Robert Hoe. The account is filled with information about books and authors, and it is enriched with reproductions of nineteenth century color plates by "Phiz" (Hablot K. Browne), William Makepeace Thackeray, and George Cruikshank.

Stern, Madeleine B. *Antiquarian Bookselling in the United States: A History from the Origins to the 1940s*. Westport, Conn.: Greenwood Press, 1985.
Stern's introduction offers a summary of the volume and observes how the story of bookselling in America parallels that of the country's history. The volume itself is arranged geographically, beginning appropriately with Boston, where Hezekiah Usher operated the first bookshop in colonial America. In the eighteenth century, Philadelphia replaced Boston as the colonial book center; in turn it was supplanted by New York. Subsequent chapters treat Cincinnati, Chicago, St. Louis and Kansas City, San Francisco, and Los Angeles. The South and selected booksellers also receive individual chapters. Stern concludes with a bibliographic essay, again organized geographically. An important study that revives antiquarian booksellers and recounts "their tastes and temperaments, their trials, their struggles, and their achievements, to clothe [them] once again in flesh and blood."

Stevens, Henry. *Recollections of Mr. James Lenox of New York and the Formation of His Library*. London: Henry Stevens & Son, 1886.
"In July 1845, a young man from Vermont, at the age of twenty-six, I found myself in London, a self-appointed missionary, on an antiquarian

and historical book-hunting expedition, at my own expense and on my own responsibility, with a few Yankee notions in head and an ample fortune of nearly forty sovereigns in pocket." So Stevens describes the beginning of his bookselling career. His autobiography provides an entertaining and enlightening portrait of the nineteenth century world of books. Especially arresting is his account of buying at auction an unrecognized copy of the *Bay Psalm Book*, the first book printed in British North America. Repeatedly he speaks of great treasures available at what seem in retrospect absurdly low prices, but at the time struck collectors as ridiculously high, as when both James Lenox and John Carter Brown refused to pay $50 for a rare 1645 Cambridge (Massachusetts) imprint. In 1927, the John Carter Brown Library paid $17,500 for another copy of that work.

Taubert, Sigfred. *Bibliopola, Bilder und Texte aus der Welt des Buchandels.* 2 vols. New York: R. R. Bowker, 1966.
Taubert has selected 258 illustrations of bookselling. These are reproduced in Volume 2, together with accompanying text. The first volume shows details of these pictures and incorporates Taubert's commentary. The earliest example dates from the first century A.D. and shows a book dealer (though it may depict a librarian or collector) with parchment scrolls. The first bookshop illustration comes from twelfth century China. Taubert's text is tri-lingual (English, German, and French). Lawrence S. Thompson claimed that "Herr Taubert has provided a work of enduring value for bookmen of all persuasions, not simply historians of the book trade" (*Papers of the Bibliographical Society of America* 62, 1968, 161).

Thin, James. *Reminiscences of Booksellers and Bookselling in Edinburgh in the Time of William IV.* Edinburgh, Scotland: Printed for private circulation by Oliver & Boyd, 1905.
James Thin began his bookselling career at the age of twelve in 1836; he was the entire staff of his employer and worked from 9:00 A.M. to 9:00 P.M. six days a week, performing the duties of "clerk, bookkeeper, and general amanuensis." In 1836, Edinburgh claimed ninety-three booksellers. Thin takes the reader on a tour of these and comments on the owners. Since the book trade, especially in old books, attracts or creates eccentrics, Thin's account includes many amusing anecdotes. When a customer asked Robert Brown to see a particular volume, Brown replied, "I see it up there, but I canna be bothered going up there for it to-night." An important memoir for the study of Scottish bookselling in the nineteenth century.

Winger, Howard W. "Regulations Relating to the Book Trade in London from 1357 to 1586." *Library Quarterly* 26 (1956): 157-195.

Looks at the three sources that regulated booksellers: the Church, the Crown, and the Stationers' Company. During the period before Caxton, Church and State co-operated to suppress the writings of John Wycliffe and his followers. Printing changed the book trade; in the first forty years of printing in England, virtually all printers were foreigners. The king and Parliament initially protected the new industry and its productions. The Reformation prompted another wave of Church and State repression of works regarded as heretical. Yet certain religious books received government support. Opposition to royal policies also was censored. Thus, pamphlets condemning the burning of Edinburgh in 1544 were themselves put to the torch. Under Edward VI, Protestant books were promoted, Catholic works suppressed. His sister Mary reversed this policy. Mary's marriage to Philip II of Spain proved unpopular. In November, 1554, Parliament imposed the punishment of the loss of the right hand for writing, selling, or printing seditious works. In May, 1557, the Company of Stationers received a royal charter to regulate the book trade. The Privy Council did not stop censoring books, though. John Stubbs and William Page lost their right hands for a 1579 pamphlet opposing the marriage of Queen Elizabeth to a French duke, and in 1586 the Star Chamber attempted to limit the number of presses in London and the rest of England.

Wolf, Edwin, with John Fleming. *Rosenbach: A Biography*. Cleveland: World, 1960.

Written by two of Rosenbach's former employees, both of them eminent bookmen in their own right, this biography traces the life of the preeminent American bookseller of the first half of the twentieth century. Wolf and Fleming document Rosenbach's legendary purchases and sales, which included the manuscript of *Alice in Wonderland*, for which Rosenbach paid $75,000 and which he sold at twice that figure. The book also details Rosenbach's role in creating the great public and private collections of the period, and it includes much about Rosenbach's private life, especially his sometimes difficult relationship with his brother. Rosenbach does not always appear admirable, but he is never dull. Robert Greenwood wrote in the *San Francisco Chronicle* for December 18, 1960, "This book will undoubtedly become a classic in its genre, and will be read with consuming interest by bibliophiles, bookmen, librarians, publishers—anyone who believes in the greatness of books" (p. 22). That prediction has come true.

Chapter 19
PRIVATE PRESSES

Bibliographies

Haas, Irvin. *Bibliography of Modern American Presses*. Chicago: Black Cat Press, 1935.

Lists the publications of forty-five private presses that began printing in the late 1920s and early 1930s. Haas notes the founder of the press and provides a brief history before giving a full bibliographic description of each item. Some of the presses proved ephemeral, but others, like the Black Cat Press (established by Norman W. Forgue in Chicago in 1933) and the Ward Ritchie Press, named for its founder and begun in 1932, went on to become distinguished and their publications are sought by collectors. This work is especially useful for identifying early imprints of such presses.

Tomkinson, Geoffrey Stewart. *A Select Bibliography of the Principal Modern Presses, Public and Private, in Great Britain and Ireland*. London: First Edition Club, 1928.

Presents "information about the work of nearly a hundred modern presses, all of which are either now engaged in printing books or have been so engaged within the last half century," that is, since the 1870s. For each press, Tomkinson provides a short introduction explaining the history of the press and the aims of its founder. He then presents a bibliography of the press's imprints. In Part 1, Tomkinson treats the presses that interested collectors in the 1920s; Part 2 deals more briefly with other presses that have, since the publication of this work, become more popular. Among these are the Hogarth Press of Leonard and Virginia Woolf, and the Shakespeare Head Press, founded in 1904 by Arthur Henry Bullen.

General Studies

Bellamy, B. E. *Private Presses and Publishing in England Since 1945*. New York: K. G. Saur, 1980.

Bellamy seeks "to examine the varied nature of private publishing and printing presses in England, to describe the way in which they have developed during the last thirty years, and to discover what their relationships are with the commercial printing and publishing industries." The first part of this book provides an overview of private presses in England since the eighteenth century, though the account moves quickly to the late nineteenth and twentieth centuries. This section includes brief sketches of private printers, examines the revival of fine printing after the Depression and World War II, and explores in some detail private- press printing of poetry. In the second part, Bellamy looks at eight modern presses, devoting a chapter to each: the Cuckoo Hill Press, the Shoestring Press, the Keepsake Press, the Kit-Cat Press, Poet and Printer, the Plough Press, the Mandeville Press, and the Basilisk Press and Bookshop. The work concludes with a chapter on the marketing of private-press books. Provides a ten-page bibliography of secondary sources and a checklist of the imprints of the eight presses treated in Part 2. Includes some attractive facsimiles. Hardly a comprehensive overview but still useful, especially for students of the eight presses covered in detail.

Cave, Roderick. *The Private Press.* 2d ed., rev. and enl. New York: R. R. Bowker, 1983.

Cave accepts John Carter's definition of a private press as one whose owner "is more interested in making a good book than a fat profit. He prints what he likes, not what someone else has paid him to print." Such presses go back to the earliest years of printing, and Cave's history therefore opens with the incunabula period. Though the account proceeds chronologically, Cave also groups presses by purpose. Thus, the printing of Petrus Apianus, Tycho Brahe, and Edward Rowe Mores is grouped together as scholarly, though the printers' lives span 250 years. Similarly, the presses of Louis XV, Louis XVI, and the Marquis de Bercy of the late eighteenth century are seen as playthings with an educational purpose. Despite Cave's broad definition of the private press, more than two-thirds of the book is devoted to the period since 1890 and the revival of fine printing, the period conventionally regarded as the heyday of the private press. An engagingly written, informative, and handsome volume.

Farmer, Geoffrey. *Private Presses and Australia.* Melbourne, Australia: Hawthorn Press, 1972.

Begins with a brief survey of the English private presses between 1890 and 1940, and then discusses some of the pioneer fine presses in Australia. Hal E. Stone's publications between 1910 and 1913, for example, reveal some influence of William Morris's Kelmscott Press.

Perce Green, between the World Wars, emerged as Australia's first full-time typographer and book designer; his *Windsor Book* (1921) demonstrates his indebtedness to the Doves Press. Farmer notes that the Australian private-press movement has never been dominated by one figure, nor has it influenced commercial book production. Following Farmer's historical essay are two appendices. The first lists presses and owners, the second provides a checklist of publications of each of the presses.

Franklin, Colin. *The Private Presses.* 2d ed. Aldershot, England: Scolar Press, 1991.
More limited chronologically than Roderick Cave's similarly titled volume (see above), this work begins with the Daniel Press established in the mid-nineteenth century, and it focuses on a selection of British presses; it makes no effort to be comprehensive. The presses Daniel, Kelmscott, Ashendene, Essex House, Vale, Eragny, Doves, Gregynog, Gogmagog, Golden Cockerell, and Shakespeare Head—all are deservedly famous for the high quality of their work, and Franklin's discussion not only analyzes these presses and presents their history but also relates them to their period. Thus, the Vale and Eragny Presses are seen as part of the art nouveau movement and the revolt against technology. John Turner has provided a selected bibliography of the imprints of the presses Franklin discusses. For many of the items, he includes original cost and prices realized in the 1960s through the 1980s. James D. Hart called the first edition "a useful, lively, and perceptive study" (*College and Research Libraries* 34 (1973): 162. The same terms apply to the second edition.

Grannis, Chandler B., ed. *Heritage of the Graphic Arts: A Selection of Lectures Delivered at Gallery 303, New York City Under the Direction of Dr. Robert L. Leslie.* New York: R. R. Bowker, 1972.
Brings together twenty-two essays by leading typographers discussing other major figures in twentieth century fine printing. Hermann Zapf leads off the collection with a survey of printing history; he concludes that printers should study the past but should also express the present in their work. The next eighteen pieces explore the work of such figures as William Morris, Frederic William Goudy, Bruce Rogers, Giovanni Mardersteig, and the Grabhorns. Some of these people had their own presses; others worked for printing houses. The three concluding essays return to more general considerations. Hugh Williams addresses "Quality in Book Production"; F. Baudin deals with changes in typography, and Beatrice Warde concludes with "Typography—Art or

Exercise?" She warns against innovation for its own sake and emphasizes the artistic capabilities of type design and printing.

Jackson, Holbrook. "The Revival of Printing." In his *The Eighteen Nine-
ties: A Review of Art and Ideas at the Close of the Nineteenth Century.*
New York: Alfred A. Knopf, 1922, 255-266.
Jackson concentrates on the work of four presses that inspired a revival
in private presses and in printing generally: the Vale (Charles Ricketts),
Kelmscott (William Morris), Essex House (C. R. Ashbee), and Doves
(T. J. Cobden-Sanderson). Jackson discusses their publications, notes
the outstanding features of the work of each, and praises their efforts
to create beautiful books that take as their models the excellent typography of the fifteenth century master printers.

Johnston, Alastair. "Literary Small Presses Since World War II in Europe
and America." *American Book Collector*, n.s. 2 (May/June, 1981):
13-19.
Considers eight small presses: Untide, White Rabbit, Jargon, Auer-
hahn, Divers, Goliard, Trigram, and Fulcrum. All seek "to produce an
attractive and agreeable text in as well-made a manner as possible."
The first four are American, the latter four English and Continental.
Johnston offers a brief history of each press and provides a selected
bibliography of its publications.

Lerner, Abe. *Assault on the Book: A Critique of Fine Printing at Private
Presses in the United States Today.* North Hill, Pa.: Bird & Bull Press,
1979.
A sane and thought-provoking talk presented at the Double Crown
Club, London, on September 28, 1978. Lerner begins by decrying what
he sees as the excesses of many private presses in late twentieth century
America. Acknowledging that much fine work is still being done, he
praises, among others, the Bird & Bull Press, the Janus Press of Claire
Van Vliet, Barry Moser's Pennyroyal Press, Walter Hamady's Perish-
able Press Limited, and William Everson's Lime Kiln Press. The work
of Richard Biggs serves as an example of what Lerner dislikes—the
appeal to the viewer rather than the reader. He also objects to the
outpouring of poor poetry from private presses and calls for "higher
literary standards in the choosing of texts."

Pollard, Alfred W. "Private Presses and Their Influence on the Art of
Printing." *Ars Typographica* 1 (Autumn, 1934): 36-42.
Pollard argues that "it is in the general encouragement and raising of

ideals rather than in providing specific models that [William] Morris and those who have really caught his spirit have . . . influenced for good the craft of printing." Pollard first surveys the state of English printing over the centuries. He finds that English printing achieved a degree of excellence in the eighteenth century that it did not attain again until the end of the nineteenth. Pollard sees William Morris as the source of the revival of printing. Though D. B. Updike and Bruce Rogers were not directly influenced by Morris' typography, they succeeded because Morris had shown that the public would pay for well-made books.

Ransom, Will. *Private Presses and Their Books.* New York: R. R. Bowker, 1929.
Ransom's opening chapter, "What Is a Private Press?" defines a private press as "the typographic expression of a personal ideal, conceived in freedom and maintained in independence." Following a brief survey of early private presses such as Horace Walpole's at Strawberry Hill, Ransom turns to the 1890s, when a number of notable fine presses began. Ransom continues his account of such presses in England and America into the 1920s. A concluding chapter deals with private presses on the Continent. More than half the book consists of checklists of the publications of numerous private presses, making this an important bibliography for the period covered.

Standing, Janet. *The Private Press Today.* Wymondham, England: Kings Lynn Festival, 1967.
An exhibition catalog representing forty presses at work in the post-World War II period, almost all of them British. For each press, Standing offers brief descriptive notes regarding aims and methods. She also includes checklists of publications for most of the presses and notes articles about them. With some facsimiles. A good source of information about some lesser-known printers.

Turner, Gilbert. *The Private Press: Its Achievement and Influence.* London: Association of Assistant Librarians (Midland Division), 1954.
Turner proposes "to examine the reasons which led to [the] renaissance of fine printing, to demonstrate some of its principal achievements, and, most important of all, to attempt some assessment of its influence upon the commercial printing of books in our time." Turner sees the private-press movement of the 1890s as part of the pre-Raphaelite "revolt against that commercialism and ugliness which was the result of the whole-hearted Victorian acceptance of the artistic consequences

of the Industrial Revolution." The essay then examines the work of the Kelmscott, Doves, Essex House, Vale, Ashendene, Golden Cockerell, and Gregynog Presses. Turner argues that the commercial presses began to improve under the influence of the private-press movement, but change came slowly. Yet by 1950, commercial publishers were committed to good taste in their books.

Individual Presses

The Ashendene Press

Franklin, Colin. *The Ashendene Press*. Dallas: Bridwell Library, Southern Methodist University, 1986.
The definitive history of this private press, which Franklin calls "the greatest of them all." Presents much unpublished material (including letters and scrapbooks), dealing with the press, together with a discussion of each book printed. Much here on the activities of the press's founder, C. H. St. John Hornby. A beautiful book, with twenty-eight pages of illustrations.

Newdigate, Bernard H. "Mr. C. H. St. John Hornby's Ashendene Press." *The Fleuron* 2 (1924): 77-85.
Traces the history of the Ashendene Press from its founding in 1895 to 1923. Hornby began printing in his father's house at Ashendene in Hertfordshire, and this location gave the press its name. In 1899, the Ashendene Press moved to Chelsea. Newdigate discusses the influence of William Morris and Emery Walker on Hornby. Walker, who had been Morris' mentor, helped cut the Subiaco type, modeled after that of the first printers in Italy, who established their press at the monastery at Subiaco. Hornby secured his paper from the mill that had supplied Morris, and his ink came from the same source that Morris had used. Unlike Morris' books, though, Hornby's are not decorated, except for typographic ornaments. The only exception is the 1902 *Song of Solomon* on vellum. Newdigate provides a list of Ashendene imprints to 1923 and includes a facsimile.

The Catnach Press

Hindley, Charles. *The History of the Catnach Press*. London: C. Hindley (the Younger), 1886.

Born in 1769, John Catnach served his printing apprenticeship with his uncle, Sandy Robinson, in Edinburgh. Catnach established his first press at Berwick-upon-Tweed, then moved to Alnwick, where he began printing fine editions with the wood-engraved illustrations of Thomas Bewick and Luke Clenwell. In 1808, the press moved to Newcastle-upon-Tyne, where the business failed, and the Catnach family moved again, this time to London. John's son James took over the failed press and began producing broadsides and popular literature that made him prosperous. When he died in 1841, he left an estate worth many thousands of pounds. Hindley's book traces the history of this press and includes many facsimiles.

The Curwen Press

Harley, Basil. *The Curwen Press: A Short History*. London: Curwen Press, 1970.
Divides the history of the press into three periods. The first Harley calls the Tonic-Sol-Fa phase after the system of musical education championed by the press's founder, John Curwen, who began printing his own instruction manuals in 1863. By the end of the nineteenth century, the Curwen Press was a major publisher of music. In 1916 Harold Curwen, who had studied calligraphy under Edward Johnson and had learned about printing at Leipzig, assumed control of the press and began emphasizing typography and design. His presence inaugurated the press's second phase. He attracted Claud Lovat Fraser, artist and designer, and Oliver Simon, who oversaw the printing. For Harley, the second period of the Curwen Press ends in 1956 with Simon's death. The third phase witnessed an increased emphasis on lithography; and while letterpress was not neglected, job printing for industry expanded. Filled with facsimiles of Curwen Press productions, the text occupying one side of the page, facsimiles the other.

Simon, Herbert. *Song and Words: A History of the Curwen Press*. Boston: David R. Godine, 1973.
The Reverend John Curwen started the Curwen Press in 1863 as part of his Tonic-Sol-Fa School, which used an unconventional musical notation system to teach singing. In the last quarter of the nineteenth century the press's publications revolutionized the teaching of music. Under the influence of William Morris and the Arts and Crafts movement, Harold Curwen, John's grandson, made the press a force in the world of fine printing. Simon presents the personalities behind the

press and discusses its operations in terms of business and art. Simon ends his account in 1933, when the author joined the press's board of directors. An appendix lists imprints for the period 1920-1935.

The Daniel Press

Madan, Falconer. *The Daniel Press: Memorials of C. H. O. Daniel, with a Bibliography of the Press*. Oxford, England: Oxford University Press, 1921.
Born in 1836, Charles Henry Olive Daniel began printing at the age of nine, inking type with his thumb. In 1863 he became a Fellow of Worcester College, Oxford, and in 1874 he brought his press from Frome to Oxford, where he returned to printing. In 1877, Daniel began using the Dutch types that John Fell had secured for Oxford University Press in the seventeenth century and which had lain neglected for 150 years. In 1882, Daniel secured a proper press to replace his smaller one, and the press remained in operation until 1919. In fact, this volume, though issued by Oxford University Press, was printed on Daniel's press. Daniel has long been recognized as a pioneer in the revival of fine printing in England. The book opens with several tributes to Daniel. Madan then presents a brief sketch of the man and his press, followed by a detailed annotated bibliography of the Daniel Press imprints. Of value to historians and collectors.

The Doves Press

Cobden-Sanderson, Thomas James. *The Journals of Thomas James Cobden-Sanderson, 1879-1922*. 2 vols. New York: Macmillan, 1926.
These journals, edited by Cobden-Sanderson's son, Richard, open when Cobden-Sanderson is thirty-nine and conclude with an entry dated September 2, 1922, five days before his death. Of particular interest to historians of the private-press movement are those entries that allow one to trace Cobden-Sanderson's growing interest in the book arts, to which he came late, after giving up his law practice at the urging of his wife. On June 24, 1882, he reports being urged by the wife of William Morris to take up bookbinding. On January 16, 1884, he is reading Joseph Cundall on the subject and imagines "beautiful books and beautiful bindings, all produced in our own pure, still workshop." On January 12, 1900, he resolves to add printing, calligraphy, and illumination to his bindery, and on April 29 of that year he reports renting 1 Hammersmith

Terrace and engaging a compositor, J. H. Mason. The entry for August 31, 1916 reports, "The Doves Press type was designed after that of Jensen (sic); this evening I began its destruction. I threw three pages into the Thames from Hammersmith Bridge." The journals also record Cobden-Sanderson's great love for his wife, his fondness for solitude, and his social interactions, and his responses to events of the day, as when he writes on October 19, 1916, "The daily massacre of young and middle-aged, but especially the young men, is appalling, and there seems no end to it." Includes a checklist of Doves Press imprints.

Dreyfus, John. "New Light on the Design of Types for the Kelmscott and Doves Press." *The Library* 29 (1974): 36-41.
In 1888, after seeing Emery Walker's lantern slide enlargements of early typography, William Morris suggested that the two men design a new type face. Dreyfus explains how Morris studied enlargements, especially the reproductions of the work of the fifteenth century Venetian printers Nicolas Jenson and Jacobus Rubens, and then modified these types for the Kelmscott Press. T. J. Cobden-Sanderson could not design his own type, but he shared Morris' admiration for Jenson's fonts. Cobden-Sanderson engaged Edward Prince to cut type for him (1899-1901).

Franklin, Colin, ed. *Doves Press: The Start of a Worry*. Dallas: Bridwell Library, Southern Methodist University, 1983.
Presents a number of newly discovered letters dealing with the quarrels between the partners of the Doves Press. The collection opens with T. J. Cobden-Sanderson's letter to Emery Walker, dated January 20, 1906, asking to dissolve their partnership to allow Richard Cobden-Sanderson to take over the press. Emery Walker would be allowed the use of the types. Later, T. J. Cobden-Sanderson rejected this idea, and the type ended up in the Thames. These letters shed additional light on the controversy that led to this unfortunate conclusion.

_____. *Emery Walker: Some Light on His Theories of Printing and on His Relations with William Morris and Cobden-Sanderson*. Cambridge, England: Privately printed, 1973.
Franklin notes that Walker's rules were "Honour Jenson, set solid, look to type, and discipline ornament." These rules underlie the work of the Doves Press but also that of the Cuala Press and the Janus Press (Germany). Walker's 1888 address to the Arts and Crafts Exhibition inspired Morris' Kelmscott experiment, and Walker remained a mentor to Morris, Stanley Morison, and others. The first two chapters explore

Walker's contributions generally; the third deals with his relationship with Morris, and the fourth treats his more troubled involvement with T. J. Cobden-Sanderson.

Nash, John R. "Mr. Cobden-Sanderson's Two-Handed Engine." *The Book Collector* 25 (1976): 491-506.
Reconsiders the role of Thomas James Cobden-Sanderson in the establishment and success of the Doves Press. Nash argues that Emery Walker deserves more credit than he has received. Walker designed the type; and while Cobden-Sanderson had the time to supervise the daily operations of the press, the principles that informed the Doves Press books had been established by Walker. Cobden-Sanderson's violations of those ideas could produce unfortunate results, as with Tennyson's *Seven Poems and Two Translations* (1902), which Walker called "a failure," though the much-admired large red initial "I" that begins the Doves Bible was also Cobden-Sanderson's innovation and had been opposed by Walker. Nash traces the controversy between Walker and Cobden-Sanderson, recounts the destruction of the Doves types (which legally belonged in part to Walker), and reflects on the failure of historians of the book to give Walker his due.

Strouse, Norman H., and John Dreyfus. *C-S the Master Craftsman: An Account of the Work of T. J. Cobden-Sanderson.* Harper Woods, Mich.: Adagio Press, 1969.
This attractive leaf book, with two leaves from Doves Press imprints, includes two essays. Strouse discusses Cobden-Sanderson's work generally, and Dreyfus explores his relationship with Emery Walker. Strouse notes that Cobden-Sanderson came late to the book arts, taking up binding in 1882 at the suggestion of William Morris' wife. In 1893, he established the Doves Bindery, which remained in operation until 1921. Strouse devotes less attention to the Doves Press, but touches on Cobden-Sanderson's controversy with Walker. Drawing on letters, Dreyfus discusses Cobden-Sanderson's resentment of Walker's involvement with day-to-day operations of the press, and how that resentment culminated in the demise of the Doves Press and destruction of its beautiful fonts.

The Eragny Press

Genz, Marcella D. "A History of the Eragny Press, 1894-1914." Ph.D. thesis, University of California at Berkeley, 1990.

The son of the French impressionist painter Camille Pissarro, Lucien Pissarro came to England in 1890. Under the influence of the Kelmscott Press and Charles Ricketts, Lucien Pissarro and his wife, Esther Bensusan Pissarro, founded the Eragny Press in 1894. Drawing on family archives at the Ashmolean Museum, Oxford (England), and the Eragny Press imprints themselves, Genz offers a history of this private printing venture. Genz first discusses Lucien Pissarro's life in France, then considers the establishment of the press. Chapter 2 deals with the operation of the press, Chapter 3 with the marketing of the books. In the final chapter, Genz places the works of the press within the context of the Arts and Crafts movement and presents the theories that underlie the Pissarros' work. Includes a bibliography of the press's thirty-two imprints and a transcription of the account books. Argues that the Eragny Press deserves more recognition than it has received.

Meadmore, William Sutton. *Lucien Pissarro: Un Cœur Simple*. New York: Alfred A. Knopf, 1963.

This biography begins with a chapter on Lucien Pissarro's father, Camille (né Jacob), the first of three generations of artists. Lucien was born on February 20, 1863. In 1884, Camille moved to Eragny, France, which would give its name to Lucien Pissarro's private press. Meadmore notes Lucien's early fascination with bookmaking, and his friendship with Charles Ricketts (founder of the Vale Press) and Charles Shannon stimulated that interest. In 1894, Lucien Pissarro produced his first book, *The Queen of the Fishes*, on handmade Japanese paper, with a handwritten text and sixteen woodcuts. Meadmore writes, "Nothing produced by private presses has ever surpassed the delicate colourings of the wood blocks Lucien made for the Eragny Press. . . . He was a pioneer in using colour in wood engraving." Pissarro's wife, Esther, helped with the books. This chronological account draws heavily on family papers and includes reproductions of Lucien Pissarro's work, as well as historic photographs. Though the Eragny Press is but one aspect of Lucien Pissarro's career, the book is useful for anyone interested in that subject.

The Gogmagog Press

Chambers, David, Colin Franklin, and Alan Tucker. *Gogmagog: Morris Cox and the Gogmagog Press*. Pinner, England: Private Libraries Association, 1991.

Morris Cox started the Gogmagog Press to publish his own poetry. He included illustrations in color—some of the later books consist entirely of pictures—and bound his books well. Hence his publications appeared in limited numbers, never more than a hundred copies of the thirty-five titles issued under the Gogmagog imprint. This volume of essays was issued to celebrate Cox's ninetieth birthday. Chambers discusses Cox's printing techniques; Tucker argues that Cox was a talented poet, and Franklin, Cox's editor at Routledge, offers a survey of the author/printer's career. The volume also includes an exchange of letters between Cox and Corrie Guyt (a South African collector of Cox's work), a selection of Cox's poetry, prefaces, and colophons, and a bibliography of the Gogmagog Press. Sebastian Carter called the volume "an absorbing study of one of printing's swash characters" (*Times Literary Supplement*, June 12, 1992, 26).

The Golden Cockerell Press

Dreyfus, John. *A Typographical Masterpiece*. San Francisco: Book Club of California, 1990.
Dreyfus presents much new information about the production of the 1931 Golden Cockerell edition of the *Four Gospels*, designed by Eric Gill and Robert Gibbings. Dreyfus found Gill's drawings for the engravings and also drawings for the type and the patterns and punches used to make that type. Includes forty-one illustrations.

Mosley, James. "Eric Gill and the Golden Cockerell Type." *Matrix* 2 (1982): 17-22.
Between 1925 and 1933, Gill contributed illustrations or decorations to a dozen books of the Golden Cockerell Press. He also designed the type for the 1931 *Four Gospels*. Mosley traces the stages of this project, as Gill gained confidence as a typographer. Mosley regards Gill's Joanna type as more attractive, but the Golden Cockerell type suited the book and the press's owner, Robert Gibbings.

The Grabhorn Press

Anderson, Greg. "The Grabhorn Press." *Print* 3 (Summer, 1942): 54-67.
Anderson begins his account with the arrival of the Grabhorns in San Francisco; he thus ignores the Indiana phase of the press. Edwin and Robert Grabhorn initially gave away their work as a way of advertising

their printing skills. Anderson traces the changing taste of Edwin Grabhorn, who first published books dealing with fine printing, then shifted to literature and later still to Californiana. This last category continued to sell well during the Depression. The article discusses the different types used by the press, its illustrators, binding, and paper, and Anderson examines some of the most noteworthy productions of the press. Anderson concludes that the Grabhorns were most successful with books of fewer than two hundred pages, but he concedes that the larger volumes also have their appeal.

The Gregynog Press

Haberly, Loyd. *An American Bookbuilder in England and Wales: Reminiscences of the Seven Acres and Gregynog Presses*. London: Bertram Rota, 1979.

Haberly supervised the Seven Acres Press and, for a time near the end of its life, the Gregynog Press. He recounts his experiences with both. Shortly after he became associated with Gregynog, he was forced to supply poetry for the press's annual Christmas book. He oversaw the production of *Eros and Psyche* (1935), and he discusses his involvement with other Gregynog imprints. Haberly writes that some condemned his conservative designs but claims that these put Gregynog "in the five-star class, along with the Kelmscott, Doves, and the Ashendene." A pleasant, anecdote-laden account filled with personalities, though short on details.

Harrop, Dorothy A. *A History of the Gregynog Press*. Pinner, England: Private Libraries Association, 1980.

Gwendoline and Margaret Davies, the owners of the Gregynog Press, knew nothing about printing. The press sprang from the Davies' philanthropic efforts to support Welsh artists and craftsmen who had suffered in World War I. Over the course of eighteen years (1922-1940), the press issued forty-five books and hundreds of pieces of ephemera. Harrop discusses the history of the press and provides a bibliography of its imprints. She is especially helpful in dealing with the people involved and their sometimes stormy relationships. Paul Morgan wrote in *The Book Collector* 30 (1981): 264, "Miss Harrop is to be congratulated on having written the definitive account of this press in a readable and scholarly way, and the Private Libraries Association for publishing it in such a pleasant way."

Johnson, B. S. "The Gregynog Press and the Gregynog Fellowship."
   Private Library 6 (Spring, 1973): 4-15.
   Johnson enjoyed a six-month fellowship sponsored by the University
   of Gregynog, and in this article he discusses his adventures in printing
   on the Albion Press that had produced the first Gregynog imprints. He
   offers some glimpses into the problems that printers would have faced
   at Gregynog, includes some informative photographs, and gives a
   sense of place of this Welsh private press.

The Hours Press

Cunard, Nancy. *These Were the Hours: Memories of My Hours Press.*
   Carbondale: Southern Illinois University Press, 1969.
   Nancy Cunard, a "golden girl" of the 1920s, established the Hours
   Press in 1928, and over the next three years, using an old Belgian
   handpress, she produced twenty-four books. Among these were works
   of literary importance such as the first one-volume edition of Ezra
   Pound's *XXX Cantos* and the first appearance of Samuel Beckett in
   print. This memoir, prepared shortly before Cunard's death in 1965,
   discusses in detail her activities as a printer and book designer, and it
   provides glimpses into Parisian life of the 1920s and 1930s. With a
   good introduction by Hugh Ford, who edited the text.

The Kelmscott Press

Dunlap, Joseph R. *The Book That Never Was*. New York: Oriole Editions,
   1971.
   In 1865, William Morris imagined a volume of poetry, with hundreds
   of woodcut illustrations by Edward Burne-Jones. The book would
   contain twenty-four narrative poems and would appear as a sumptuous
   folio. Morris and Burne-Jones worked on this project for several years;
   Dunlap reproduces a number of the woodcuts that were to accompany
   the text, and he presents some hypothetical pages of the book that never
   was. *Love Is Enough* was another project that never saw the light of
   day. Morris did publish his *Earthly Paradise*, and Burne-Jones used
   some of his designs for other purposes, including a frieze for the Earl
   of Carlisle's London house. The real legacy of the book that never was
   appeared in the Kelmscott Chaucer. A fascinating chapter in Morris'
   bookmaking career.

Forman, Harry Buxton. *The Books of William Morris: Described with Some Account of His Doings in Literature and in the Allied Arts.* Chicago: Way and Williams, 1897.

In the opening chapter, Forman presents a capsule biography of Morris. Most of the volume consists of an annotated bibliography of Morris' writings, including those printed at the Kelmscott Press. Forman notes the connection between *The Roots of the Mountains* (1890), printed at the Chiswick Press, and Morris' own work at the Kelmscott. Useful for its discussion of Morris' lifelong concerns with art, literature, socialism, and the saga.

Franklin, Colin. *Printing and the Mind of Morris: Three Paths to the Kelmscott Press.* Cambridge, England: Rampant Lions Press, 1986.

One path that led Morris to the Kelmscott Press was, according to Franklin, his elaborate prose style, which Franklin regards as "decorative experiments." The second path proceeds from Morris' books that were nicely produced, especially *The House of the Wolfings* (1889), *The Roots of the Mountains* (1890), and *Gunnlaug the Worm-Tongue* (1890). But even *The Oxford and Cambridge Magazine*, Morris' first literary effort, shows concern for printing. Morris' propaganda, published in broadsides and pamphlets, tended to appear in unattractive formats that provided another impetus for founding the Kelmscott press as a reaction to this ugliness.

Morris, William. *The Ideal Book: Essays and Lectures on the Arts of the Book.* Edited by William S. Peterson. Berkeley: University of California Press, 1982.

Includes eight pieces by Morris together with Sydney Cockerell's brief account of the Kelmscott Press and the text of four interviews with Morris originally published in the 1890s. The collection opens with an essay Morris never published, "Some Thoughts on the Ornamented Manuscripts of the Middle Ages," in which Morris argues that next to a beautiful house, a beautiful book is the most important object that art can create. He adds, "To enjoy good houses and good books in self-respect and decent comfort, seems to me to be the pleasurable end toward which all societies of human beings ought now to struggle." These essays repeatedly reflect Morris' sense that medieval books provide the finest examples of beauty, and among printed works those that appeared in Venice before the arrival of the Renaissance were superior to anything that followed. Five of the pieces here focus on illustration. The sixth, "Printing," shows how well Morris and Emery Walker agreed on the virtues of early printing. The seventh essay sets forth Morris' thoughts on the ideal book, and the final selection presents his aims in founding the Kelmscott Press. Peterson's introduction notes Morris' unique contribution but places it within the context of the late Victorian love of the Middle Ages and the revolt against technological ugliness. Enriched with Kelmscott facsimiles and other illustrations. Titles are printed in Morris' Golden Type, the text is set in Bembo (based on Aldus Manutius' 1495 roman type), and initials are taken from the Kelmscott Chaucer.

_____. *A Note by William Morris on His Aims in Founding the Kelmscott Press*. Hammersmith, England: Kelmscott Press, 1898.
The last item printed by the Kelmscott Press, this brief document summarizes Morris' ideas about the Book Beautiful. Morris wanted handmade paper from linen fibers, type that did not exhibit a sharp contrast between thick and thin lines, and tight arrangement of words, letters, and lines. Although he wanted the page to be beautiful "by force of mere typography," his career as a decorator and his admiration of medieval illustrations and woodcuts prompted embellishment, but this was always to harmonize with the typography.

Needham, Paul, Joseph Dunlap, and John Dreyfus. *William Morris and the Art of the Book*. New York: Pierpont Morgan Library and Oxford University Press, 1976.
An exhibition catalog of 101 items, most of them donated by John M. Crawford, Jr. to the Pierpont Morgan Library. Needham writes on Morris as book collector, Dunlap on Morris as calligrapher, and Dreyfus on Morris' typography. With 114 plates, some in color. A sound survey of the man and his books.

Peterson, William S. *A Bibliography of the Kelmscott Press*. Oxford, England: Clarendon Press, 1984.
Although the Kelmscott Press printed for only seven years (1891-1898), it was, Peterson writes, "probably the most influential and certainly the most famous of all the private presses." In his introduction Peterson offers a useful bibliographic essay dealing with secondary sources and includes short discussions of Morris' types, paper, copy-texts, ink, illustrations, ornaments, cancels, bindings, presses, staff, bindings, publishers, and finances. The bibliography itself is divided into five sections: published works (fifty-three), unfinished books (of which there were over twenty), advertising circulars (fifty-one), ephemera, and contracts and memoranda relating to the books. Peterson goes beyond mere bibliographic description to provide informative sidelights on the genesis and progress of various projects, and also gives references for

further investigation. With twenty-three illustrations, most of them facsimiles, showing the artistry of the press. Joseph R. Dunlap wrote in the *American Book Collector* 7 (February, 1986): 40, "The present volume is a repository of a vast amount of information pertaining to all aspects of the Kelmscott Press, its history, and its publications, and is a tribute to the compiler's powers of seeking and organizing it."

_____. *The Kelmscott Press: A History of William Morris's Typographical Adventure*. Berkeley: University of California Press, 1991.
The standard history of the press. Peterson first discusses Victorian printing generally, which was not uniformly bad and which increasingly reflected an interest in early typography. The second chapter explores Morris' early efforts to design beautiful books. Peterson then treats the founding of the press (Chapter 3), Morris' designs for the Kelmscott Press (Chapter 4), and the decorations that are the best-known feature of Kelmscott books (Chapter 5). The business of the press is the subject of Chapter 6; the press earned money, though copies of *The History of Godefrey of Boloyne* had to be given away. Chapters 7 and 8 look at the creation of four Kelmscott titles: *Poems by the Way* (1891), *The Love-Lyrics and Songs of Proteus* (1892), *The Golden Legend* (1892), and the Chaucer (1896). The text concludes with an account of the closing of the press and of Morris' printing legacy. Appendix A provides a checklist of the press's books; Appendix B reprints the notes of Emery Walker's 1888 lecture that inspired Morris to create the Kelmscott Press; and Appendix C lists some early expenses of the press. With many facsimiles and illustrations. The volume is itself an attractive example of bookmaking.

Robinson, Duncan. *William Morris, Edward Burne-Jones and the Kelmscott Chaucer*. Rev. ed. Mt. Kisco, N.Y.: Moyer Bell, 1982.
The Kelmscott Chaucer is not only the masterpiece of the Kelmscott Press but also one of the landmarks in printing history. Robinson traces the evolution of this volume from a modest book to its final form. He shows designs planned but not used, and reproduces the original drawings from which the woodblocks were engraved, together with many of the engravings themselves. An informative biography of a beautiful book.

Sparling, H. Halliday. *The Kelmscott Press and William Morris, Master Craftsman*. London: Macmillan, 1924.
Sparling was for a brief time Morris' son-in-law. Shortly before Spar-

ling's death he provided an important history of the Kelmscott Press. Sydney Cockerell supplied a description of the press, together with an annotated bibliography of the books and ephemera (included in the volume). Sparling observes that Morris did not choose fifteenth century type and the handpress merely for the sake of antiquarianism. Morris wanted excellence, and he selected paper, type, and presses that produced the beautiful books he wanted. With a portrait of Morris and sixteen other plates.

Thompson, Susan Otis. *American Book Design and William Morris.* New York: R. R. Bowker, 1977.
Even before Morris began the Kelmscott Press, some American book-makers wanted to produce fine books. Morris' typographical adventure served as a catalyst to impel these printers and others to reject the ugly, cheap books that were flooding the market. Thompson examines Morris' impact on such figures as Bruce Rogers, Daniel Berkeley Updike, Elbert Hubbard, and other leaders of early twentieth century fine printing. Boston and Chicago proved fertile soil for Morris' ideas; New York was less receptive. Thompson also considers the Arts and Crafts movement, art nouveau, and what she calls the aesthetic move-ment, all of which influenced book design at the turn of the century. With over a hundred facsimiles and a lengthy bibliography. James Wells praised the volume: "Those new to the subject will find it a comprehensive and valuable introduction; those who already know the field will discover much that is new to them and will be challenged to reexamine many of their previous judgments" (*Papers of the Bibliographical Society of America* 73, 1979, 137). Alan Fern agreed, writing that "this study will remain a basic source book for years to come for anyone working in the recent history of the American book" (*Library Quarterly* 49, 1979, 232).

John Henry Nash

Harlan, Robert D. *Chapter Nine: The Vulgate Bible and Other Unfinished Projects of John Henry Nash.* New York: Typophiles, 1982.
An addendum to Harlan's biography of Nash (cited below). Harlan first discusses a number of projects that Nash was forced to abandon. These include a monumental edition of Virgil, the *Areopagitica* of Milton, *Two Years Before the Mast,* and some volumes of California interest, among them *Old San Francisco,* his first lapsed endeavor. His great ambition was to produce a Bible. As early as 1921, he was thinking

about this enterprise, and by 1930 he had chosen his text—the Latin Vulgate—and typeface. Unable to find patrons or secure subscriptions, Nash eventually was forced to abandon his plan. Harlan presents in some detail Nash's unsuccessful negotiations to get funding and includes Nash's designs for what would have been his magnum opus.

_____. *John Henry Nash: The Biography of a Career*. Berkeley: University of California Press, 1970.
H. Richard Archer wrote in *Library Quarterly* 41 (1971): 267, "Mr. Harlan has provided readers, collectors, and librarians with a scholarly and readable account of the man who was acclaimed as 'the Aldus of San Francisco.'" Harlan begins his account with Nash's arrival in San Francisco in 1895 as a skilled typesetter. Nash quickly found employment despite the hard economic times resulting from the 1893 Panic. In 1916, Nash set up his own press, and in the 1920s, he was San Francisco's preeminent printer. Harlan explores Nash's relationship with rich patrons, major publishers like Scribner's, and the Book Club of California. The 1930s witnessed the decline of the press, though Nash continued to print into the 1940s. Harlan concludes that Nash was a better technician than he was an artist, and that he was an effective educator in the area of fine printing. An appendix briefly describes the library and museum that Nash assembled and that now resides at the University of California at Berkeley.

The Nonesuch Press

Dreyfus, John. *A History of the Nonesuch Press*. London: Nonesuch Press, 1981.
Dreyfus divides the history of the Nonesuch Press into four periods: 1923-1929, 1929-1936, 1936-1952, and 1953-1975, and he traces the press's varying fortunes. Francis Meynell and his wife Vera Mendel (who supplied the three hundred pounds to start the enterprise) receive much attention. Dreyfus also includes chapters on design and production and the press's publishing accomplishments. Much of the volume is devoted to a descriptive catalog of Nonesuch imprints, and appendices present the printers' devices used, an analysis of the accounts between 1928 and 1936, and a list of Francis Meynell's printers, keyed to the books they produced. Dreyfus concludes that Nonesuch showed that attractive and well-made books could be created "with materials and mechanical methods . . . available to any publisher," and that these books could even earn a profit.

Meynell, Francis. *My Lives*. New York: Random House, 1971.
The autobiography of the founder of the Nonesuch Press. The plural "lives" reflects Meynell's diverse experiences. Son of the poet Alice Meynell, he was himself a minor poet, as well as journalist, rationing advisor during World War II, sportsman, and advisor to the Cement Workers' Federation. Meynell's greatest achievement was establishing the Nonesuch Press in 1923. The press never had much money, and in 1937 Meynell was forced to sell it to George Macy. In 1953 Meynell revived the press along modest lines. *The New York Times Book Review* for September 12, 1971, commented succinctly, "Likable man and book" (p. 64). The text is set appropriately in Nonesuch Plantin.

The Officina Bodoni

Barr, John. *The Officina Bodoni*. London: British Library, 1978.
In 1922, Giovanni Mardersteig (also called Hans) began printing in Montagnola di Lugano, Switzerland, using types cast from the original matrices that had been created by Giambattista Bodoni in the late eighteenth century. In 1927, Mardersteig moved the press to Verona, where it remained for the rest of Mardersteig's life. He died in 1977. This volume was prepared in association with an exhibit of Mardersteig's work at the British Library. Though not a comprehensive bibliography, the volume describes many of Mardersteig's works and offers useful annotations. It includes numerous facsimiles, and reprints Mardersteig's 1929 description of how he produced his books.

Ewald, Friedrich. "The Officina Bodoni." *The Fleuron* 7 (1930): 121-131.
Written when the press was still young, this essay treats the origins of the press and its first products. Ewald admires Mardersteig's work, but he recognizes that the early imprints were imperfect. With Dante's *Vita Nuova*, Mardersteig achieved that high standard that subsequently characterized all his productions. Though using the name and type of the eighteenth century Italian typographer, Mardersteig remained independent and modern, as his layout and title pages demonstrate. Useful for those seeking information on the early days of the press.

Mardersteig, Giovanni. *The Officina Bodoni: An Account of the Work of a Hand Press, 1923-1977*. Hans Schmoller, ed. and trans. Verona: Edizioni Valdonega, 1980.
The book begins with a historical account of the press and its founder.

This section is followed by a brief bibliography of secondary sources and a short explanation of how the Officina Bodoni made its books. Mardersteig provides an annotated bibliography of all works issued by the press to 1977. With many facsimiles that illustrate the high quality of the work. The *American Book Collector* called the book a readable and essential "reference for the study of what must surely be the pre-eminent fine printer of our time" (1, May/June, 1980, 59).

Schmoller, Hans. "A Gentleman of Verona." *Penrose Annual* 52 (1958): 29-34.
Recounts the history of Hans Mardersteig's press, largely through a survey of twelve facsimiles attractively reproduced. The first of these is Goethe's *Das Roemische Carneval*, printed in Bodoni type, which Mardersteig used with permission from the Italian government. When that government commissioned Mardersteig to produce an edition of the works of Gabriele d'Annunzio, the printer moved from Switzerland to Verona. Here he began designing type, cut by Charles Malin of Paris; Schmoller includes examples of these fonts, which he briefly analyzes. Also included are reproductions of illustrations that Mardersteig used. Though Mardersteig is most famous for his work with the handpress, in 1948 he established the Stamperia Valdonega, which used modern equipment while maintaining the highest standards of book production.

_____. *Two Titans, Mardersteig and Tschichold: A Study in Contrasts*. New York: Typophiles, 1990.
Schmoller explores the contrasting techniques of two great twentieth century bookmen. Mardersteig used handpresses, handmade paper, and had his books bound by hand. Jan Tschichold used machine-set fonts, power presses, commercial papers, and edition binding. Yet both produced beautiful books, however different their products are. A pleasant and sound introduction to the work of both men. Embellished with thirty-one illustrations.

Author Index

Note: Index lists all authors and editors whose works appear in this bibliography.

411

SUBJECT INDEX

ABOUT THE AUTHOR

Joseph Rosenblum received his master's degree in library science from the University of North Carolina at Chapel Hill and his Ph.D. in English from Duke University. He has taught at Duke, the University of Mississippi, Guilford College, Guilford Technical Community College, High Point University, and the University of North Carolina at Greensboro. His articles have appeared in a variety of journals and reference works, and in 1990 he won second prize in the Oxford University Press English Detective Fiction contest. His other books include *Shakespeare: An Annotated Bibliography* and *American Book Collectors and Bibliographers* (editor). Rosenblum lives in Greensboro, North Carolina, with his wife, Suzanne, his daughter, Ida, and his three Himalayan cats: Hodge, Lily, and Wilmarth.